Praise for

ıntegral city 3.7.
Reframing complex
challenges for gaia's
Human Hives

For those who make the city, and—especially—cities, their life/work place par excellence, this is probably the most comprehensive, inclusive and balanced framing of their field—broadly, and integrally, defined—that they are ever likely to encounter. It focuses on reframing complex challenges, but the main—almost pre-requisite—challenge involves a fundamental reframing of their own, whole, selves, in a wholeness-privileging project like no other.

This is not for the faint of heart, or the weak of will; it actually calls for an extraordinary generosity of spirit, and an embrace of the fundamental spirituality of it all. Practitioners will be called to account, and especially to care, to an unprecedented degree. Professionals will be challenged to address not simply what they profess, but how and—especially why—they profess, in ways that will shake them to their professional core. Purpose will become the object of exquisite discernment—ongoingly, always—with reflection-in-action as default mode.

In bald terms the call is to deepen care, raise context and widen capacity: to go on an outer and inner journey—to take caring to new levels, and new levels of mastery; to scale up and out—and down and in, addressing evolution and involution; and to aim for a capacity of overview that is also an integration, an integration-in-action that is as much spirituality-in-action. The explicatory framing is applied Integral theory, leavened by Spiral Dynamics, with a guide who is first and foremost a practitioner, who very much walks her talk—with the sensibility of a grandmother caring deeply for the world being bequeathed to her granddaughter. The author models 'integral' as a reframe of 'professional', and we wonder—who might be inclined to follow her example?

Drawing on the metaphor of the city as human hive, and inspired by the incredibly productive life of bees, you will be challenged to identify 'the 20 kilos of honey' that defines your purpose, and your modus operandi. It will engage not only your 'minding' (your normal 'thinking') but will take you very much into the realms of your hearting and souling. The understanding on offer is as much an over-standing (and an inner-standing, and an outer-standing). It takes 'all-round' and 'as-a-whole' to mind-boggling new interpretations; and your caring will never be the same, nor as nuanced, again; 'care-taking' takes on a whole new visceral meaning.

Being proficient, or professional—or simply being a human being rather than a human doing—is further reframed as 'beeing for Gaia'. The provenance is as delicious as life-sustaining honey.

— **Ian Wight** PhD FCIP GTB, Senior Scholar, City Planning, University of Manitoba

Where do we begin to heal our world in crisis? Marilyn Hamilton has chosen one key entry point—the city—the unit of human culture she calls "the human hive". And she has explored, in many diverse ways, how cities can make wise choices to address their challenges and create more healthy futures.

Dr. Hamilton helps her reader understand cities and how to foster civic regeneration by looking through a rich suite of powerful integrative lenses. Each reveals something unique about the life of a city, and they reveal the patterns that connect the peculiar challenges and opportunities of thousands of cities.

In the three Integral City volumes she synthesizes and applies an encyclopedic range of powerful integrative frames to help cities dialogue skillfully, plan consciously and evolve cooperatively. She is one of the most creative social architects applying integral and evolutionary tools to practical real-world challenges. If you care to understand a city, the Integral City books are a crash course in bringing a birds-eye meta-systemic intelligence to the task.

The third volume may be the most ambitious and elegant of them all. It reframes the means with which we can bring our best intelligence to the hyper-complex challenges of the 21st Century in terms of care, context and capacity, a useful original system for understanding different crucial dimensions of what must be necessary for successful collaboration among a city's stakeholders. Her writings renew hope by uncovering and highlighting many hidden opportunities for cities to lead the way toward a regeneration of human culture amidst our crises of fragmentation.

— **Terry Patten**, Author A *New Republic of the Heart:An Ethos for Revolutionaries*, Co-Author *Integral Spiritual Practise*, Founder Integral Heart

No longer are cities defined by a single slowly evolving Worldview as they have tended to be up until the erosion of both modern and post-modern Worldviews failed to provide fair, equitable and resilient cities for all. Current trends in sustainable or smart cities have proved insufficient to encompass and include the degree of complex thinking needed. A complexity that defies individual or expert group planning. A complexity that needs to involve us all in the development of self-organising evolving cities which allow us to define who we are and what we want from our co-created urban environment. A city capable of holding various cultures and Worldviews that can be technically resilient and can be socially relevant and culturally inclusive for all it's citizens. Marilyn's *Integral City* 3.7 and the other two earlier volumes are part of the evolving process that defines the actions we all need to be involved in if our cities are to be places we love to be a part of.

— **Paul van Schaik**, Founder IntegralMENTORS, Creator and publisher of the *Integral UrbanHub series—Thriveable Cities* and Executive Director Integral Without Borders

Imagine human hives who know how to connect. They can map their existing connections, align people to purpose and priorities. They can amplify what works, let go of what doesn't and continuously improve the value they contribute to Gaia" [Appendix Fl: Imagine the City as a Human Hive"]. From the breadth and depth of her work, Hamilton's third book in the Integral City series appears to be a scientific and philosophical exploration of the challenges facing a burgeoning humanity increasingly nested in urban environments. But it is much more than that. It is also a handbook for stewards of the growth and structure of living cities as well as for curators of complex evolutionary learning communities. Her work explores the scientific bases for the emergence of collective wellbeing in hypercomplex human communities and their potential for expressing intelligence through networked connections between and among them. In an age of increasingly volatile, uncertain, complex and ambiguous environments, Hamilton's work is an essential guide for understanding the evolution of a city as a learning system and how to fulfill it's potential as a true expression of Gaia.

— **Alexander Laszlo**, PhD,

- 57th President of the International Society for the Systems Sciences (ISSS) and Chair of the Board of Trustees
- President of the Bertalanffy Center for the Study of Systems Science (BCSSS)
- President of the Honorary Board of Advisors of the World Complexity Science Academy (WCSA)
- Director of the Doctoral Program in Leadership and Systemic Innovation at the Buenos Aires Institute of Technology (ITBA)

What is truly amazing about the book and its author is that they serve as guides for the real-world heroes dealing with the real-world issues, while offering a direct connection to the timeless dimension of ever-present Wisdom and Wholeness.

Integral City 3.7 is an indispensable aide for anyone reaching beyond the obvious and mundane in a beautiful journey to holistic living in the cities we could consciously co-create.

Marilyn's work inspired us to set a high goal of integrally developing 1000 cities to transform our country and the future of Earth.

— **Lev Gordon**, CoFounder of Living Cities Movement, Russia

In this Book 3 [of the Integral City series], Marilyn Hamilton brings out very clearly the essential dimensions, notably the spiritual one, that will allow integral cities to be at the leading edge of planetary renewal. By emphasizing the depth and interconnectedness of caring, contexting, and capacity building at multiple scales—from the individual to the ecoregion—and with a long-term perspective, she guides us wisely in the systemic exploration of the most complex challenges of social/economic/environmental sustainability and resiliency. What an inspiring, thoughtful and coherent invitation to evolve cities into conscious, inclusive, learning, and self-evolving meta-organisms!

— **Alain Gauthier**—Executive Director, Core Leadership Development—Co-founder of the Society for Organizational Learning—Member of Bay Area Integral—Author: *Actualizing Evolutionary Co-Leadership—To Evolve a Creative and Responsible Society*

This book is committed to unravelling the paradox of the city as intractable global problem and inescapable solution for continuing and thriving human life on Earth. Marilyn Hamilton coins new terms for the new ideas in the emerging paradigm of the city as living developmental system. The contemporary city is an unsustainable collage without composition or conscience. In wisdom looking deeply forward many generations, the emerging Integral City articulated here gives hope for the wholeness of people and planet. Read it, let your brain recover, then get to work.

— **Mark DeKay**, Professor of Architecture, University of Tennessee, author, *Integral Sustainable Design: Transformative Perspectives*

Marilyn Hamilton continues to amaze with her hundred year plus vision for the human hive. Marilyn's ongoing application of meta-theory with prime focus on self, other, place and planet is inspiration for us all. Her work shapes and informs Integral Councils and Integrated Development. This book and the series is a must read for all those voices; the Citizens, Civil society, Civic Managers and Business.

— **Chris Woodhouse**, Founder of the Integrated Development Framework, Integral Councils and Inaugural chair of Integral Institute Australia.

One of the brightest lights in my universe, Marilyn Hamilton keeps deepening her exploration of the capacities needed to make cities thrive. She is among the few who dare to engage in energetic enquiries and explicitly address the role of other life forms in shaping the life conditions for those of us who inhabit what she calls 'human hives'. Having been part of several of her constellations, I can testify to the impactful insights that come out of tapping into the knowing field under her attuned guidance. I applaud her for offering clear language, models and practices for the emerging intelligence we need to keep our cities livable for its citizens and a force for good in their local ecology. May those we appoint to administer and govern our human hives benefit from the theoretical and practical frameworks that I know the author is happy to come and share even more of than she has done in this groundbreaking book.

— **Lisette Schuitemaker**, Chair of Trustees of the Findhorn Foundation, Scotland. Author *The Eldest Daughter Effect*; *Alight*; *The Childhood Conclusions Fix*. City dweller of Amsterdam, The Netherlands

More integral thinking and strategies for the future of our cities from one of the planet's best systems thinkers, Marilyn Hamilton.

— **Hazel Henderson**, CEO, Ethical Markets Certified B. Corporation, author *Mapping the Global Transition to the Solar Age* and other books.

integral city 3.7

Reframing Complex Challenges
for Gaia's Human Hives

MARILYN HAMILTON

AMARANTH
PRESS

AMARANTH
PRESS

Amaranth Press, LLC
5123 W 98th St #1081
Minneapolis, MN 55437
amaranthpress.net
contact@amaranthpress.net

ISBNs:
Print: 978-0-9980317-0-5
eBook: 978-0-9980317-1-2

Cover and Interior Design by Kathryn Lloyd

First edition

10 9 8 7 6 5 4 3 2 1

This book is dedicated to the evolution of a planet of integral cities, Gaia's reflective organ system.

Like the other books in the Integral City series, it is dedicated to creating thriving human hive habitats for the 7th generation from now.

TABLE OF CONTENTS

1, PART 1: *Deepening Care*

LIST OF FIGURES

LIST OF TABLES

INTRODUCTION

WHOLING THE HUMAN HIVE

How can we design a city for the wellbeing of our granddaughters and future generations in a way that adds value to all Life on Earth?

That is the question that jet-propels me from my verdant city-in-the-country existence in the central Fraser Valley of British Columbia to the farthest reaches of the universe and has made me take notice of how the discoveries of space pioneers such as Edgar Mitchell astronaut, the Voyageur I and II space exploration program designers, Elisabet Sahtouris evolution biologist and Elon Musk inventor, contribute to designing conditions for optimal human hives.

On this journey I have asked related questions that might reveal the mysteries of living well in cities—How do we wake up the human hive as a whole? Why should I care for her resilient souls, understand the context of people's goals, develop organizational capacity for critical roles, amplify sustaining energy flows or heal the traumatic impact of warring blows?

This is the third book in the Integral City series that are the virtual logs of my voyage on a mission to redesign the city as a whole. In the tradition of an Action Research Sequence **What, So What, Now What**, this is the **Now What** book.

In the first book I proposed **What is an Integral City?** *Integral City: Evolutionary Intelligences for the Human Hive* examined the evidence for a new paradigm of the city that is a living human system, complex in its dynamics and evolutionary in its nature. I considered in each chapter an intelligence that applied to the city, presaging James Lovelock's conjecture that humans are the reflective organ of the living Earth or Gaia. In Book One I intended to offer a developmental point of view, integrating perspectives that recognize the fractal patterns in human systems that repeat and resonate from the smallest individual scale, up through increasing levels of complexity—families, teams, organizations, sectors, communities and cities.

In the second book I explored **So what are the ways we can know, act, relate and create in an Integral City?** *Integral City Inquiry and Action: Designing Impact for the Human Hive* described the processes that Integral City practitioners have developed to apply the intelligences to developing the quality of life in the city. From a developmental point of view, in Book Two I differentiated two aspects of the whole that makes up the city; namely, the Placecaring left hand quadrants of the Integral model (consciousness and culture) and the Placemaking right hand quadrants (behaviors and systems/infrastructure). In each chapter I described the processes that the Integral City Team has discovered for engaging people through integrally designed inquiry and action to achieve impact that resonated for self, others, place and planet. At the time of writing Book Two I was really struck with the Pope's encyclical "Laudato Si" (Francis, 2015) especially the chapter on Integral Ecology as it explored how to embrace human systems in a way that values all the developmental expressions of person, place and planet that coexist in the living city.

In this third book I turn to the question **Now what do we do as a result of our evidence, inquiry, action and impact?** *Integral City 3.7* expands my perspective of change in the human system from the individual city to a planet of cities. As I trace out the implications of an Integral City operating system at a higher, more complex level, I attempt to integrate them from a developmental point of view that even moves beyond the planetary view to the Kosmic view.

The Kosmic view I offer in the first chapter shares the **overview effect** that has inspired me to see the city as a living system in the context of the planet. Looking for a way to connect with my granddaughter's more colloquial point of view, I paradoxically venture into outer space and borrow the descriptor "overview effect" from the observations of astronauts. They first noticed that the view of Earth from space, changed their mindsets, worldviews and relationship to Earth. Some space explorers like Edgar Mitchell (Mitchell & Williams, 2001) were so impacted by their unexpected spiritual experience of Oneness on their space journey, that they turned their scientific gaze onto the relationship between science and spirituality. By the time I met Mitchell in 2002 he had become the founder of the Institute of Noetic Sciences (IONS) and influenced the thinking of a whole generation of advanced researchers, who in turn became my mentors either directly or indirectly. People like social anthropologist Marilyn Schlitz, philosopher Ken Wilber, biologist Rupert Sheldrake, organizational leader Margaret Wheatley and inspirator Willis Harman inspired me to explore the invisible worlds of energy, fields and spirit that co-exist and in-form the visible worlds of matter, life and ecology.

Under the influence of such advanced thinkers, you might say that I enjoyed a blinding flash of the obvious (BFO), when I noticed that the city, as the most complex human system yet created, is visible from space. That overview of Gaia and the visibility of cities gave me the key to experiencing an **integrating effect**, re-minding me that human systems impact the Earth systems that have evolved us. With the intention of connecting to wellbeing in a way that my granddaughter can relate to, in this book I privilege the whole system view of the city as the "human hive". Just as she and her mother's catering business uses the organic produce from their own gardens, pollinated by the beehives they now keep, I pursue the implications of the "hive mind" and "hive intelligence" that I explored in Books One and Two. Now I want to deepen the proposition that humans are Gaia's Reflective Organs (Lovelock, 2009), by proposing that individual humans are cells and our organizations are organelles in Gaia's living system. While cities—with all their fractal functions (mirroring the functions of individual humans (Hamilton, 2008a; Miller, 1978)) act as human hives or organs of Gaia's living system. As I continue to observe cities in action, I think these human hives really do act like the energy nodes of Gaia's reflective organs. And taken as a whole, I see that

Earth's cities really do have the potential to evolve not just one Reflective Organ, but (like pollinating bees) can become a whole Reflective Organ System for Gaia. Thus, I naturally surmise that for my granddaughter's great grandchildren (and their great grandchildren, unto the 7th generation from now—as the First Nations consider in their decision making), our collection of human hives may one day be recognizable as a veritable Planet of Integral Cities.

HOLOGRAPHIC DIMENSIONS

So, in Book Three as I consider the implications of evolving a Planet of Integral Cities I take journeys into three holographic dimensions: Care, Context and Capacity. I allege that the dimensions are holographic because I find it virtually impossible to separate caring from the context of the life conditions in which care is expressed. Moreover, how I (and my granddaughter) care is determined by my/her capacity for care, and that capacity is developed within the context of life conditions that can only be appreciated through expanding levels of capacity. (See Figure 1.)

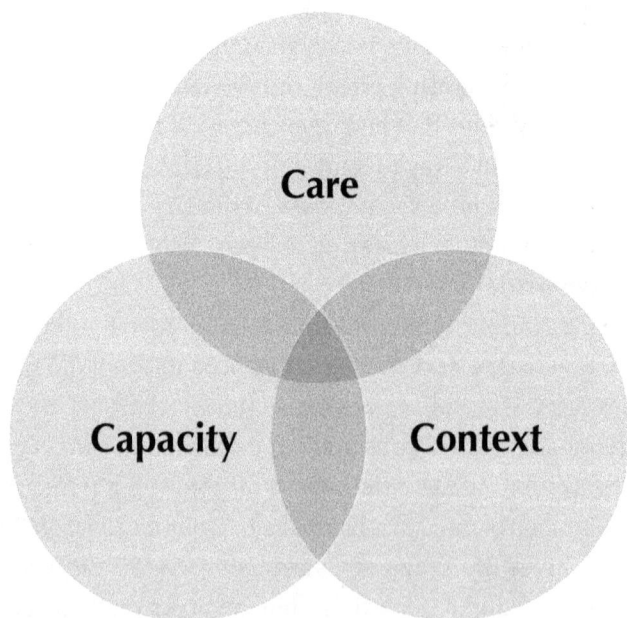

Figure 1: Interlocking Holographies of Care, Context, Capacity

In the process of contemplating the magic and mystery that the holography of the city provides I have discovered an almost infinite kaleidoscope of lenses to consider these three dimensions. Like the bees pollinating herbs in my granddaughter's garden, I invite you to play with me as if we had aggregate eyes with capacities to reveal aspects of the whole human hive—eyes that show us how to open hearts that care, enter habitats that can change our interpretation of context and expose capacities we didn't realize we possessed.

Because I consider that this holography is fractal in nature, I frame this trio of dimensions as the qualities that my granddaughter and all living human systems at all scales possess (Capra, 1996) as they **survive, adapt** and **regenerate**. As I turn the kaleidoscope of the whole system, thinking of my granddaughter's life, I notice: Caring may influence her Context and/or Capacity; Context may amplify her Capacity and/or Caring; Capacity Building may embrace both her Caring and Contexting.

As I have also explored how the triad shows up in my own leadership, my granddaughter's development and those of my university students, I have noticed morality, space and time intersect in ways that seem to grow the nest of fractals as a whole (Hamilton, 2015). I have glimpsed privileged expressions of moral influence in Care—for example, when a health care worker breaks the rules to look after a whole neighborhood (as Frederic Laloux (2014) documents about the "Teal" Netherlands' health care system of Buurtzorg). I have seen the impact of expanding spatial influence in Contexting when an activist has recognized that water quality can be a matter of life and death for a whole city (Walkerton, Ontario, 2000). And I have witnessed the dynamic time influence in Capacity Building when an elder touches the life of a teenager with tough love that transforms them from a gang member to an entrepreneur (Food for Thought (Hamilton, 2010)). When I contemplate the combination of Care, Contexting and Capacity Building as a continuum in the very real lives of my own family, then I appreciate that cities are extensions of these qualities. Cities—human hives—are habitats where my granddaughter and all the people she interacts with are constantly transacting, recalibrating and even transforming their practices of leadership within the dimensions of morality, space and time.

Deepening Care Expands Inner Journey

Caring in my granddaughter is an expression of moral influence. Caring may be considered her **inner journey**. It gives her an **inner view** of her reality. She experiences it as four perspectival stances: herself as I; others as You/We; habitat as It; and planet as Its.

Deepening care unfolds her patterns of expanding the circles of care. Children, like my granddaughter, first learn how to survive and gain the basic behaviors for living. As an infant human "self" she started out by being completely dependent on "others" for traversing this stage of existence. In her case, the others were parents and immediate family members. (In other cases, they may be family surrogates.)

As my granddaughter progressed through this stage she became increasingly more capable of caring not just for her own survival but contributing to the care of others within the family unit. This natural progression (also mirrored by young bees in the beehive (Gould, et al, 1988) opened her up to a sense of belonging—which germinated care for progressively larger scales of influence in the family, friends, school, neighbors, workers, groups, community, city, nation and planet. (Until now, she operates a business taken over from her mother; enjoys the challenges of being a mother and spouse herself; and serves clients from around the world in a movie catering business.) In basic terms, in a healthy environment, we can see that care expands from ego/self, to ethno/others, to place/city, to all life/planet.

As the study of capacity building has shown (discussed below) when the object of care moves from the inner subjective (self) and intersubjective (others) to the outer objective (habitat) and interobjective (city) dimensions, the circles of care become stabilized at more complex levels (Cooke-Greuter ,1999, 2002; Fowler, 1981; Gilligan,1982; Graves, 1971, 1974, 1981, 2003, 2005; O'Fallon, 2010; Kegan, 1994; Torbert, 2004; Wilber, 1995,1996, 2000). Healthy caring becomes imbued with belonging and attachment that is experienced as deep love and spiritual connection to self, others, city and planet as inextricably interlinked. This array of deep care may be the source of the experience of Oneness that is shared by all faith systems (Weaver,2017). I summarize this depth of care in the Master Code: caring for self, others, place, planet (Hamilton, 2008, 2017). For the first time in history humans (like my granddaughter) have the opportunity to practice this kind of care simultaneously at all levels, which in itself is reflexive and reflective as one level of care mirrors the other levels of care. Furthermore, this kind of care reveals the Goodness, Truth and Beauty of spiritual depth and blossoms into a creativity that permeates all the co-existing realities of the city.

Raising Context Expands Outer Journey

Contexting as an expression of spatial influence is my granddaughter's **outer journey**. It gives her an **overview**. She generally experiences context in terms of progressively expanding boundaries: home, street, school, neighborhood, city, eco-region, nation, continent, hemisphere, planet.

Context expands as her care deepens—and vice versa. It is as though the expansion of her inner dimension of care enables the expansion of her outer dimension of space. As a developing human, she literally expands her views of the outer world—thus expanding the boundaries to which she belongs and is attached. My granddaughter has moved from her parents' home, to her own home, with spouse and child and all the expanded opportunities that work, recreation and travel offer her.

In spatial terms, we usually think of these boundaries as horizons that contain our caring mindsets, worldviews and behaviors. As we mature these boundaries also contain organizations that become progressively more complex (as described in **Widening Capacity** below).

My granddaughter probably senses these contexts in terms of material objective artefacts—like resources, materials and buildings—as well as systems, infrastructures and the environment—like roads, water systems, communication devices, topographies, geographies and ecologies. In fact, my granddaughter faced all these realities as she moved from a rented house to building her own house on acreage where she and her husband had to build the systems and structures to support the rudiments (and luxuries) of daily living.

Many whose lives and interests become context driven (e.g. builders, engineers, architects, farmers, cooks, manufacturers, biologists, physicists, chemists) ignore or overlook that our outer contexts determine and limit our inner caring and integrating capacity dimensions. As we are coming to see however, perceptions and expansions of context are as much driven by caring and capacity building as the other way around. For instance, as my granddaughter has discovered, it was impossible for her architect to imagine and design a house for her without reference to what they as designers cared about, what she and her husband valued and what the expertise of the design/build team had the capacity to manifest.

At the same time, raising context meant my granddaughter was progressively improving her apprehension and understanding of the life conditions in which she operates. In evolutionary terms, when humans were an early species on Earth, the environmental life conditions—from which the species emerged—had the overwhelming influence over human life—restricting behaviors through all the elements of geography, ecology and climate that provided both sustenance and threat. For tens of thousands of years (or possibly hundreds of thousands of years) humans were contained in local contexts that became the objects of care that sustained and taught people what and how it was possible to live. As both caring and capacity dimensions expanded within local contexts, those boundaries expanded and the boundaries of the local were traversed into the watersheds, the regional, the continental, the oceanic, the global and as we have now explored, into the Earth-orbital and solar systems—with the ambassadors of our satellites pushing out into galactic and intergalactic spheres.

My granddaughter is beginning to see that the boundaries that provide supportive containment for her new house (public roads, wild forests, natural streams) also limit the systems she can develop within those given contexts, as well as her access to the resources that expand possibilities for family care and wellbeing (through belonging, attachment and capacity building). When we quip that, "the grass is always greener on the other side of the fence", we are recognizing that more potential always seems to lie outside the systems we set out to develop—in a seemingly infinite array of systems, outside systems, outside systems of context, etcetera.

Recognizing this array of nested systems, researcher of complex human development, Clare Graves (Graves, 1971, 2005) proposed, that life conditions create an overview of ever-evolving human contexts, where humans are inextricably intertwined into a double helix of inner caring (values) systems and outer contexting life conditions. Together these constantly influence and change each other resulting in the emergence of ever more complex capacities as shown in Figure 2.

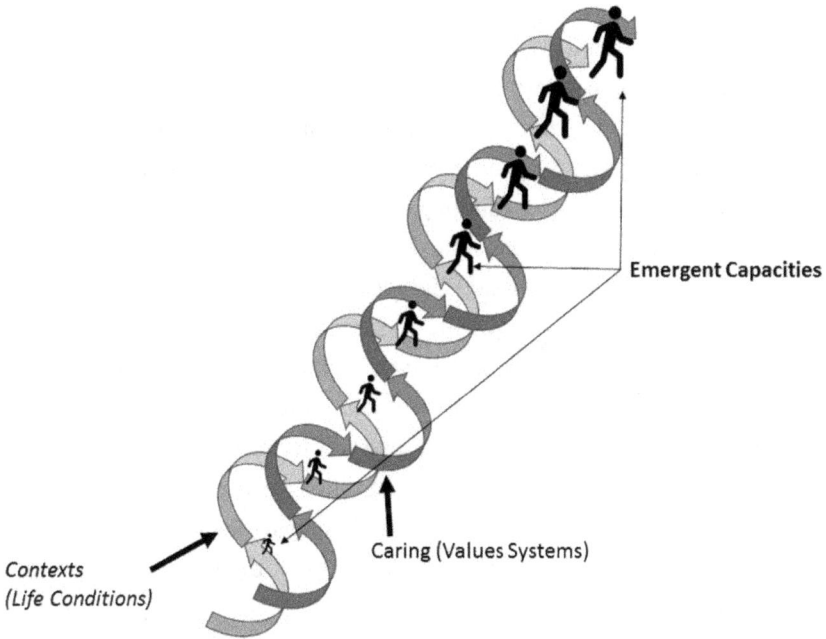

Emergent Capacities

Caring (Values Systems)

Contexts
(Life Conditions)

Figure 2: Graves Double Helix of Contexts, Caring, Capacities

Widening Capacity Integrates Inner Care & Outer Context

Measuring capacity reveals my granddaughter's capability, competence and performance. Capacity reflects the dimensions that enable her to grow care and contexting over her lifetime. It energetically integrates her inner dimensions with her outer dimensions and vice versa. As such, capacity is an expression of dynamic time influence on the energetic and evolutionary journey of her life. Capacity reveals my granddaughter's response systems for dynamic change. Her capacity progressively complexifies as she (as nexus of the whole trajectory of human history) organizes her (human) expressions of leadership, organizational roles, systemic structures/infrastructures, human settlements (including house, street, community, city) and ultimately a whole planetary system of cities.

If we think of caring as the dimension of moral influence and contexting as the dimension of spatial influence, we can consider capacity building as the dimension of change, that is the dimension of time influence. Because my granddaughter lives in both the inner dimension of caring and the outer dimension of contexting, as a living system she necessarily also lives on and in an evolutionary time dimension.

When I look at my granddaughter, I see that caring provides her fundamental life force for surviving (as child, youth, adult), and contexting provides her fundamental life force for adapting to her environment(s) (at home, school, work, business, house location), while her capacity provides her fundamental life force for regenerating (as supplier, designer, employer, mother).

In terms of her individual life cycle, capacity building tracks the stages of maturity through fetus, infant, child, youth, parent, adult, grandparent and elder. The building of capacity is represented by her inner growth of caring and her outer response-ability to life conditions. Thus, regeneration not only is represented by her bodily birth-death cycle but the "never-ending quest" (1974, 2005) of psychological, emotional, intellectual (and even epigenetic (Lipton, 2005) development from her generation to the next.

As she traverses the stages of development, (like all humans) her earlier capacities are transcended and included in later stages of development (Cooke-Greuter ,1999, 2002; Fowler, 1981; Gilligan,1982; Graves, 1971, 1974, 1981, 2003, 2005; O'Fallon, 2010; Kegan, 1994; Torbert, 2004; Wilber, 1995,1996, 2000). However, although her bodily cycle is designed to respond to contexting conditions, so she can progress through the different life cycle stages, there is no guarantee that her inner stages of potential development will be commensurately achieved (however much I as a grandmother might wish it so).

Graves (1971, 1974, 1981, 2003, 2005) identified the six conditions necessary for capacity building to happen at any given stage of development. His research identified seven distinct stages of development along the double helix—with an eighth one showing promise of emerging at the conclusion of his research (in 1987). Graves was one of the first psychologists who recognized that the stages of capacity building in humans produced a natural hierarchy of complexity, where each stage in the sequence of development provides the foundation for the subsequent stage of development.

As other studies of social sciences have come on stream, this developmental sequence has become widely recognized as global and transcultural—with great variations in surface expression dependent on contexting life conditions. And although different researchers have expressed the levels of complexity in multiple ways (Wilber, 2000), the capacity building sequence itself has become as affirmed for humans as the comparable unfolding for bees in the beehive (anon, 2017).

One of the simplest algorithms for the trajectory of complexifications is offered by Robert Kegan (Kegan & Lahey, 2001) who points out that when my granddaughter can make object that which was previously subject, she will be able to reveal what was her inner subjective focus as an outer objective target of observation (which we would see as "care" and "contexting"). For example, when she gradually took over the catering business that her mother started, she moved from responsive receptive employee to responsible activating employer who is now managing other employees and a multiplicity of resources and decisions.

Thus, she is discovering, the widening of capacity has another more complex aspect to it—capacity expands to include how she organizes herself to regenerate in the world. As she expands her contexts and expands those she includes in her caring circles, she needs progressively more complex organizational patterns and processes to achieve the balance between her inner lives and outer lives. These organizational patterns emerge in her own life time—just as they have emerged over historical time of the human species—and include family hearths, kinship clans, friendship kingdoms, bureaucracies, entrepreneurial endeavors, social enterprises, ecological networks and global stewardships.

Collaborating Across Holarchies of Care, Context, Capacity

As we consider the implications of Care, Contexting and Capacity we can see that each of them is built on a set of nested holarchies (for definition see Glossary).

Holarchies of care emerge from the deepening of care from ego, to ethno, to place and planet.

Holarchies of context emerge from the raising of our horizon lines to include greater and greater spatial boundaries, thus expanding our overview of life conditions from local, to regional, to continental to planetary.

Holarchies of capacity mature the organization of our living systems from time horizons where our actions are measured with immediate effect to ever-lengthening horizons where the consequences of our actions can be measured in days, weeks, months, years, decades, centuries and even millennia (Dutrisac et al, nd).

Thus, the impacts of capacity building sprout in my granddaughter's simple family-based home and evolve to the very complex movie catering business (using environmentally sensitive ingredients, materials and waste management systems) and maybe someday could even expand to serving the International Space Stations or satellites now roaming the galaxies.

These nested holarchies all offer opportunities for cross-connection and collaboration that can exponentially expand their power and potential for evolving our human systems to a more complex level. They give us interdependent access points for engaging with the city as an indivisible wholeness—a veritable form of "divine" activism, that Patten (2018, Chapter 3) describes as "radical". Patten suggests the paradox of considering wholeness in the face of the multi-faceted nature of reality in the city is essential for "sacred activism" that can synthesize both fragmentation and a profound sense of belonging to a whole that embraces us as both individuals and collectives.

INTEGRAL CITY INTELLIGENCES

When I look at the three thrusts of caring, contexting and capacity building, that distinguish humans living at the city scale, I can see the 12 Intelligences of an Integral City that I explored in Book 1 (see Appendix C1: Definitions of 12 Intelligences), how they are tracked on the Global Positioning Compass (GPS) described in Book 2 (see Appendix C3: Integral City GPS Locator), and why we explore them in Chapter 2 through Sahtouris' evolutionary living system principles.

Caring Intelligences

Using the GPS as a locator for the whole set of intelligences, I situate the Individual and Collective intelligences of caring in the inner circle of quadrants: Inner, Outer, Cultural and Social. These intelligences represent the relationships between the self, others, place and planet that are embedded in the Master Code. I explored them in Book 1 in Chapters 5 to 8.

Contexting Intelligences

I locate the intelligences of contexting on the GPS in the outer ring where they remind us of the overview we gain from the intelligences derived from the Ecosphere, Emergence, Integral Knowing and Living. These intelligences represent the boundaries that frame our contexts. I explored them in Book 1 in Chapters 1 to 4.

Capacity Intelligences

The intelligences of capacity building I locate in the middle ring of the GPS where they offer strategies to negotiate our contextual boundaries and deepen our circles of care through the intelligences of Inquiry, Navigating and Meshworking. I explored them in Book 1 in Chapters 9–11.

Growing Impulse

Finally, the intelligence that energizes all the others as the Evolutionary impulse lies at the center of the GPS. I explored this in Book 1 in Chapter 12. It is the intelligence that enables the living systems of the city to change, adapt and evolve. Evolutionary intelligence enables the developmental unfolding of caring, contexting and capacity.

DEVELOPMENTAL CYCLE

As noted above, this is the third book in the Integral City book series. As such it mirrors the developmental cycle that seems to operate in human systems—just like the story of my granddaughter—at each level of complexity and across all levels of complexity. Looking at my granddaughter as our exemplar, at the individual scale, within the Integral Movement (B. Brown, 2011, 2013), these stages are often referred to as: Waking Up (gaining her sense of self), Growing Up (discovering her capacity to change and create), Opening Up (moving from self-centeredness to caring for friends, family and all her clients) and Tuning Up (gaining the awareness of a higher power, spiritual life and universal truths).

Furthermore, another process cycle—Cleaning Up—represents the incomplete, blocked or dissociated elements of her stage progression. These manifest in the form of shadows that block the flow of her positive capacities or "dignities" at all stages, with negative forces or "disasters".

Like the human systems of my granddaughter's individual life cycle, I propose that the human system at the scale of the city moves through all these stages as it matures and in fact have derived the Integral City book cycle from it. The sequence of Integral City books that has emerged has focused on Scaling Up (Book 1), Acting Out (Book 2), Goaling Up (Book 3) and a fourth book is anticipated to look at Wholing Out (as we anticipate exploring the Eras of Cities).

Paradoxically the Cleaning Up process parallels each of these city stages because it arises from the seeds of dissonance when caring and capacity are misaligned with context. These dissonances arise as we outgrow one system and start to move with resistance into the next system. The dissonances provoke the current system (and sub-systems) to change to respond more effectively to the threats to life that disturb the fundamentals of surviving, adapting and regenerating. Cleaning Up is foundational to sustainability (in other words to the continuance or survival of systems) and resilience (the responsiveness of systems to their environment). The seemingly intractable problems that cities face can only be solved by discovering how to transcend and include the dilemmas and solutions of less complex stages into more complex expressions of care, context and capacity (especially at time of writing in 2017 when a stream of never-ending conflicts in Barcelona, Manchester, Paris, Brussels, Nice, Lahore, San Bernardino, Orlando, Dallas, Fort McMurray, London, Munich, Rio de Janeiro resound on every newscast).

An Integral City approach not only calls forth the requisite resources to do Clean Up by re-aligning care, context and capacity, but recognizes that Integral City "activators" (like grandmothers who defend, guide, coach and support their granddaughter's wellbeing), are called to stand as witnesses to the pain and discomfort of the breakdown and reallocation of resources that naturally occur during both the cleansing and growth processes as the city emerges into its next natural stage.

In this way of growing through stages, each book of the Integral City series builds on the prior book(s) and hopefully expands our understanding of the Integral City paradigm that goes beyond mindsets and overviews to provide the elements for a whole new operating system for the city.

Scaling Up

Book 1 explored the basics of the 12 Integral City Intelligences. It described in terms of those intelligences how we live as families, clans, human habitats and city systems. It offered a new paradigm of the city through the quadrants, levels and lines of the city.

Acting Out

Book 2 explored the functions within the city, offering a methodology to develop the city applying the 12 Intelligences, 4 Roles, 4 Voices, 8 Values Sets and Vital Signs Monitors. It provided strategies for Placecaring and Placemaking.

Goaling Up

Book 3 now sets out to explore at a more advanced level how to grow up through setting and realizing the goals to address intractable problems that arise from the misalignment of caring, contexting and capacity building that underlie city economies, collaborations, and interactions as a growing planet of cities (with all the growing pains of each stage).

Wholing Out

Book 4 is intended to examine the evolutionary patterns of power, authority and influence that flow through cities, enabling connections, alignment and integration of whole systems of individual cities and the impact these systems appear to have on a whole planet of cities.

CORE PATTERNS USED FOR ANALYZING WHOLENESS IN THE CITY

As the most complex system yet created by humans, the city can only really be appreciated as a whole. However, the city is not only a living system, but it is both complex and adaptive. Therefore, it is always seething with dynamic change at multiple scales that influence and impact one another, a condition that makes it very challenging to keep a focus on the whole.

Patten (2018, Chapter 3) writes that cultivating wholeness is an evolutionary imperative and must become not only a project but a practice.

Throughout this book we have woven together 3 frames of wholeness that help explain the city as a whole. The first frame is the evolutionary history of the world, including the anthropocentric era from which humans and our cities have emerged. The second frame is the story of the honey bee, the species that sits on the tree of life at the apex of the invertebrates, as the complementary branch to homo sapiens sapiens who sits at the apex of the vertebrates. The third frame is the set of five maps that shapeshift the metaviews of wholeness in the Integral City.

We have elected to explain them fully either at their first mention in the book and/or in an Appendix that provides a full explanation for subsequent references in the book. Here is a concordance for the three frames of wholeness and where they will be primarily referenced in the book.

Frame 1: Evolution of the World

The basis for Frame 1 is a graphical representation of the evolution of the world, based on the research of Dr. Brian Eddy (2003, 2005, 2006). This compact view of evolutionary time, space and moral evolution provides the core knowledge to understand the ABC waves of evolution—the Cosmic, the Biologic and the Anthropocentric. This pattern is first explained in Chapter 6 (Human Security) and concisely referenced in Chapter 15 (International Development). Appendix D offers the reader a full description for reference at any time.

Frame 2: Honey Bee Living System

The basis for Frame 2 derives from the story of the honey bee—a species that is 100 million years old (that demonstrates a purpose and a language) as told by Howard Bloom (2000) in the *Global Brain*. There he identifies the operational functions within the honey beehive as: conformity enforcers, diversity generators, resource allocators, inner judges and intergroup competitors. Bloom—a paleoentomologist and keen observer of the human condition posited that humans conducted themselves in a self-similar way as the bees. I have translated the 5 functions of the beehive into the 4+1 Voices and Roles of the human hive. I borrowed the metaphor of the beehive to coin the term "human hive". I have further taken the performance of the purpose of the hive (to produce 20 kilos of honey per year and thereby pollinate the ecoregion) and the communication capacities of the honey bee to indicate desirable life-serving parallels in the evolution of sustainability and resilience in the human hive.

This frame is used in these chapters: Chapter 2 (Creativity); Chapter 8 (Diversity); Chapter 10 (Organizational Wellbeing); Chapter 15 (International Development); and Chapter 16 (Conclusion). It is also explained fully in Appendix E.

Frame 3: 5 Maps that Shapeshift Metaviews of the Whole City

The basis for Frame 3 commenced in the first book in this Integral City series. From the beginning of the series, we have attempted to navigate the city as a whole, by offering a collection of maps that act like a set of blueprints showing the city from multiple integrally-informed perspectives. Map 1 is a plan view of intelligences. Map 2 is a holarchic view of nested city systems. Map 3 is a fractal view of co-existing developmental scales. Map 4 is a structural view of organizations. Map 5 is a spiritual view.

Each map conveys the wholeness of the city from different perspectives that shapeshift from one to the other—like a Rubik's cube of rotations. Each map conveys an aspect that contributes to defining the city as a whole and yet each map needs its "cousin" maps to flesh out and add greater depth, richness and definition.

In this book we have clustered the maps together in Appendix B so that the reader can access the images and the explanations at any time. Certain chapters reference these maps more than others. In those chapters we give brief summaries of the value of the maps to the topic under discussion (e.g. Chapter 5, Security; Chapter 8, Diversity Generation; and Chapter 15, International Development) but also refer the reader to the fuller discussions in Appendix B.

REFRAMING COMPLEX CHALLENGES IN 3 PARTS

This Book 3 is not just a book on more advanced theory—but rather it reframes challenges and issues in the human hive and on the planet, that are so complex, they call forth an Integral design intelligence. Book 3 could reference Christensen's (2015a, 2015b) 2 volumes as launching platforms that explore *Innovative Development* and *Developmental Innovation* from the perspectives of integrally informed global practitioners of Gravesian and Spiral Dynamics integral processes. Springboarding from that trajectory, this Book 3 explores implications about the competing pluralities (of worldviews, cultures and strategies) from the perspective of how the Integral City could recalibrate care, contexting and capacity building. Some chapters might be considered practical applications; others may tend towards thought experiments related to intractable problems; but each of them offers a reframe to a core challenge all our cities face. Many of the chapters are based on peer reviewed and/ or commissioned articles previously published by a variety of journals in a variety of sectors (chosen in order to "test" the acceptance of an Integral City paradigm from different disciplines).

Part 1: Deepening Care—explores Spirituality, Creativity and the Master Code.

Part 2: Raising Contexts—explores Cities as Trigger Points and Tipping Points, the Invisible City and Security in the Human Hive.

Part 3: Widening Capacity—explores 4 scales of Capacity Building in human systems: Leadership, Organizations, Systems and the City.

Glossary—provides key definitions used throughout the book.

Note on Spelling: Several words are capitalized throughout the book:

- **Integral** is capitalized when referring to the Integral philosophy including multiple lineages from Wilber, Graves/Beck, Laszlo and others; as well as Integral City.
- **Voices** refers to the 4+1 Voices of the Integral City (citizens, civic managers, civil society, business/developers, other cities).

By exploring real issues and challenges on the voyage to generating value for all Life, this book is by no means an exhaustive examination of intractable challenges in the human hive. Rather it has selected representative wicked problems to show how an Integral City would approach them. It is intended to add to the frameworks, constructs, principles and ecology of understanding, enabling and manifesting an Integral City as a next stage in the evolution of co-creating a Planet of Integral Cities. It is a book by a grandmother for the daughters, sons, grandchildren and great grandchildren unto the seventh generation who are growing cities into Gaia's Reflective Organs and all Earth cities into her planetary Reflective Organ System.

REFERENCES

anon. Walkerton E. coli outbreak. *Wikipedia*. Retrieved from https://en.wikipedia.org/wiki/Walkerton_E._coli_outbreak

anon. (2017). The Life Cycle of the Honey Bee Family. Chatsworth, California: The Valley Hive.

Bloom, H. (2000). *The Global Brain: The Evolution of Mass Mind from the Big Bang to the 21st Century*. New York: John Wiley & Son Inc.

Cook-Greuter, S. (1999). *Postautonomous ego development: its nature and measurement* (Doctoral dissertation), UMI Dissertation Information Services UMI #9933122, Harvard Graduate School of Education, Cambridge, MA. Available from UMI Dissertation Information Services UMI #9933122 UMI Dissertation Information Services UMI #9933122 database.

Cook-Greuter, S. (2002). The development of action logics in detail. Retrieved from www.cook-greuter.com

Dutrisac, M., Fowke, D., Koplowitz, H., & Shepard, K. (nd). *Global Organization Design: a dependable path to exceptional business results based on Requisite Organization principles*. Retrieved from Toronto.

Eddy, B. (2003). *Sustainable Development, Spiral Dynamics, and Spatial Data: A '3i' Approach to SD*. Paper presented at the Spiral Dynamics integral, Level II, Ottawa, 2003, Ottawa, ON.

Eddy, B. (2005). Place, Space and Perspective. *World Futures*, 61, 151–163.

Eddy, B. (2006). *The Use of Maps and Map Metaphors for Integration in Geography: A Case Study of Mapping Indicators of Sustainability and Wellbeing*. (PhD), Dept. of Geography and Environmental Studies, Carleton University, Ottawa.

Fowler, J. W. (1981). *Stages of Faith: The Psychology of Human Development and the Quest for Meaning*. San Francisco: HarperSanFrancisco.

Francis, P. (2015). *Encyclical Letter Laudato Si: On Care for Our Common Home.* Rome: The Holy See.

Gilligan, C. (1982). *In a Different Voice: Psychological Theory and Women's Development.* Cambridge, MA: Harvard University Press.

Gould, J. L., & Gould, C. G. (1988). *The Honey Bee.* New York: Scientific American Library.

Graves, C. (1971). *A systems conception of personality: Levels of existence theory* Paper presented at the Washington School of Psychiatry, Washington, DC.

Graves, C. (1974). Human Nature Prepares for a Momentous Leap *The Futurist,* 8(2), 72–78.

Graves, C. (1981). Summary statement, The emergent, cyclical, double helix model of the adult human biopsychosocial systems (Publication no. http://www.clarewgraves.com/articles_content/1981_handout/1981_summary.pdf). Retrieved July 3, 2002.

Graves, C. (2003). *Levels of Human Existence: Transcription of a Seminar at Washington School of Psychiatry, Oct. 16, 1971.* Santa Barbara: Eclet Publishing.

Graves, C. (2005). *The Never Ending Quest: A Treatise on an Emergent Cyclical Conception of Adult Behavioral Systems and Their Development.* Santa Barbara, CA: ECLET Publishing.

Hamilton, M. (2008). *Integral City: Evolutionary Intelligences for the Human Hive.* Gabriola Island BC: New Society Publishers.

Hamilton, M. (2010). *Mapping the Values of Abbotsford and Developing a Prototype for an Integral Vital Signs Monitor of City Wellbeing* Retrieved from Victoria, BC, Canada.

Hamilton, M. (2015). SDi in the Integral City. In T. Christensen (Ed.), *Innovative Development: Emerging Worldviews and Systems Change.* Tucson, Arizona: Integral Publishers.

Hamilton, M. (2017). *Integral City Inquiry and Action: Designing Impact for the Human Hive.* Tucson, Arizona: Integral Publishers.

Kegan, R. (1994). *In Over Our Heads: The Mental Demands of Modern Life.* Cambridge, MA: Harvard University Press.

Kegan, R., & Lahey, L. L. (2001). *How the Way We Talk Can Change the Way We Work: Seven Languages for Transformation.* San Francisco: Jossey-Bass.

Laloux, F. (2014). *Reinventing Organizations.* Retrieved from http://www.reinventingorganizations.com/purchase.html

Lipton, B. (2005). *The Biology of Belief: Unleashing the Power of Consciousness, Matter and Miracles*. Santa Rosa, CA: Mountain of Love/Elite Books.

Lovelock, J. (2009). *The Vanishing Face of Gaia*. New York: Harmony Books.

O'Fallon, T. (2010). *The Collapse of the Wilber Combs Matrix: The Interpenetration of the State and Structure Stages*. Paper presented at the Enacting an Integral Future Conference, John F. Kennedy University.

Patten, T. (2018). *A New Republic of the Heart: An Ethos for Revolutionaries (Sacred Activism)*: North Atlantic Books.

Torbert, W., & Associates (Eds.). (2004). *Action Inquiry: The Secret of Timely and Transforming Leadership*. San Francisco: Berrett-Koehler Publishes Inc.

Weaver, L. (2017). Turf, Trust, Co-Creation, and Collective Impact. Retrieved December 10, 2017, from Tamarack Institute http://www.tamarackcommunity.ca/library/turf-trust-co-creation-collective-impact

Wilber, K. (1995). *Sex, Ecology and Spirituality: the spirit of evolution*. Boston: Shambhala Publications Inc.

Wilber, K. (1996). *A Brief History of Everything*. Boston: Shambhala Publications Inc.

Wilber, K. (2000). *Integral Psychology*. Boston: Shambhala Publications Inc.

PART 1

Deepening Care

This first Part explores Care through three gateways: Spirituality, Creativity, and the Master Code.

Chapter 1 opens the gateway of **spirituality**. In terms of intelligences, spirituality is intimately enmeshed (if not causal to) the evolutionary impulse that lies at the center of our GPS (see Appendix C3). It was a spiritual impulse that lead me to write Books 1 and 2. As the prime author, Spirit was a guiding energy that revealed the 12 Integral City Intelligences, 4 Voices, Master Code and made the astonishing connections between the living systems of the species homo sapiens sapiens with the species apis mellifera that suggested the reality of the "human hive". Spirit was behind every idea, each word and all the chapters of Books 1 and 2. Yet, as many readers pointed out, although Spirit was a major actor in Book 2's first chapters describing the "Knowing Field", Spirit was not explicitly honored with its own chapter So, in this third book I share my thoughts on how Spirit is waking up the human hive through the involutionary and evolutionary cycle that manifests care in our cities through beauty, goodness and truth.

Chapter 2 opens the gateway of **creativity**. Waking up to creativity in the human hive brings us into the realms of individual intention and expression and how that influences collective attention and realization of our shared intentions for care. While spirituality is our impulse, I suggest that creativity is the pulse that measures our aliveness and underlies our capacity for care in the city. Like spirituality, creativity is ever-present in individuals but not always attended with intention. When we are aware of this sacred connection, we declare that we are inspired! But creativity's manifestation at the collective and city scale is greatly linked to human development. Creativity emerges through stages of development, often precipitated by the urges of diversity generation (see Chapter 8) at the early phase of new discovery and then birthed into acceptance as more people in the human hive wake up to the greater care for life that new creations can enable.

Chapter 3 re-opens the gateway of the **Master Code**. This is the gateway first opened in the exploration of Integral City Intelligences in Book 1, Chapter 12, and in the exploration of Inquiry Action and Impact in Book 2, Chapters 3 and 4. The Master Code codifies the relationship of the core holons in the human hive through their caring for self, others, place and planet. The Master Code both symbolizes and energizes the life-giving nature of spirituality and creativity that are embedded in the concept and reality of expanding our circles of care. By growing this sacred space progressively greater, we not only make the human hive resilient, we develop as individuals and collectives and evolve as a species.

1

SPIRITUALITY IN THE HUMAN HIVE: INVOLUTIONARY & EVOLUTIONARY CYCLE OF LOVE

An earlier version of this chapter was first published as: Hamilton, M. (2011). Integral Spirituality in the Human Hive: A Primer *in Trialog.*

This chapter on Spirituality may be considered the missing chapter from Book 1 (Hamilton, 2008). That book felt like it was written **by** Spirit, but this chapter is the exploration and explication of how that spiritual source, resource and field emerged what has become paradigm, operating system and inspiration for the Integral City.

> *Humans are Gaia's reflective organ.*
>
> — James Lovelock

CHAPTER SUMMARY

This chapter explores spirituality in the human hive using the Integral City framework and exploring the roots of the Master Code. It proposes that spirituality contributes to the quality of reflective capacity in the city with influences on design, planning and building. As an involutionary/evolutionary impulse, spirituality underlies the emergence of all life forms, including the most complex human system of all, the city. Multiple states and stages of spirituality influence place, space and grace in the city. Changing worldviews at the ego-ethno-world-Kosmic-centric stages of development recapitulate the meaning of spirituality to individuals and cultures and impact structures in church/synagogue/temple/sanctuary that contribute capacities to the city as well as create conflicts within and across the silos of education, health and governance domains. Spirituality in the human hive is source, field and resource to the city's Goodness (Caring), Truth (Contexting) and Beauty (Capacity).

Keywords: spirituality, grace, space, place, caring, contexting, capacity building, involutionary, evolutionary

INTRODUCTION

Take Care of Yourself.
Take Care of Each Other.
Take Care of this Place
Take Care of this Planet.

Such is the Master Code for living well in the human hive (Hamilton 2008, 2017) as explored in Chapter 3. Essentially, this is an injunction for spiritual wellbeing in the human hive.

WHAT IS THE HUMAN HIVE?

The human hive—the equivalent habitat for our species of the honeybee's hive—represents man's most complex system yet created. In all its qualities—both dignities and disasters—it is an expression of the deepest essence of man's creative capacities. James Lovelock (2009) recently recognized homo sapiens as Gaia's most reflective organ. If that is the case, then we might ask what are the qualities of a reflective organ and why would evolution call forth such a capacity? In 1901, Nobel laureate and author of the "Life of the Bee" (a classical reference still consulted for its incisive observations) Maurice Maeterlinck (1954) observed in comparing humans to the honeybee, that the purpose of all evolutionary beings is "read in the distinguishing organs, whereto the others are all subordinate". In the human, the "duty . . . flame . . . and spirit is "evident in the production of "cerebral substance" that spreads over the universe as an "incomprehensible flame".

It would appear that, the concentration of our beings in the collective habitat of the city has the potential to add "purity, power, disinterestedness, and freedom to the ardor" (Maeterlinck, 1954) with which we create all manner of thoughts, actions, relationships and artefacts. The city, thus, is a natural habitat for spirit and spirituality because it is an inborn quality of who we are.

4 Maps that Reveal Spirituality in the City

If the city is an evolutionary system, then it must be understood as a living system that has qualities that are complex, adaptive, fractal, holographic and morphic in nature. As a complex adaptive living system, city dynamics can be appreciated by examining the four essential maps developed in Book 1 (Hamilton, 2008a)) and through this exploration add a fifth (as seen in Appendix B: Integral City Maps (1–5)). The first four maps included:

1. Map 1: the four-quadrant perspectival map of holonic reality
2. Map 2: the nested holarchy of city systems
3. Map 3: the scalar-fractal relationship of micro, meso and macro social holonic human systems
4. Map 4: the complex, adaptive, dynamic structures of change

Each map gives us a different view of the whole city and helps us to understand the interrelationship of individuals, groups, sectors and sections and the city as a whole. However, each map represents only a partial view of the system. But they can be conceptually (and technologically) hyperlinked with each other to give us a more comprehensive, complete picture of the interconnected human hive. A brief description follows (in the shaded text) of the contribution each map reveals about spirituality in the human hive (with illustrations shown in Appendix B: Integral City Maps (1–5)).

Map 1: The City as Holon— The Four Quadrant, Eight Level Map

This map shows that reality in the city arises from both an individual/collective and an interior/exterior expression (Wilber, 1995). The intersection of these two polarities creates four quadrants that reveal four realities we can label as:

1. Upper Left (UL): individual—interior/ internal/ subjective/intangible
2. Lower Left (LL): collective—interior/ internal/ intersubjective/intangible
3. Upper Right (UR): individual—exterior/ external/ objective/tangible
4. Lower Right (LR): collective—exterior/ external/ interobjective/tangible

Each of the four quadrants reveals a perspective that has produced a domain of knowledge about the city. The Upper Left (UL) holds the knowledge bases of the aesthetics and fine arts. The Lower Left (LL) holds the knowledge bases of the humanities. The Upper Right (UR) holds the knowledge bases of the life sciences. The Lower Right (LR) holds the knowledge bases of the hard sciences. In this way our institutions of higher learning organized the knowledge about the transcendent patterns of universal information and gave academic voice to the four perspectives common to all languages (expressed as I, We, It and Its) as summarized in Table 1.

Table 1: 4 Perspectives and Academic Faculties
1. Upper Left (UL) (I)—aesthetics and fine arts
2. Lower Left (LL) (We)—humanities
3. Upper Right (UR) (It)—life sciences
4. Lower Right (LR) (Its)—hard sciences

The value of Map 1 to seeing spirituality in the city is that it situates not only perspectives but methodologies of seeing the city as a whole living system (as was explored in Book 2 (Hamilton, 2017)). It locates the parts, partial views and fragments of the city so that they can inform one another and be viewed as an integrated system where what happens for instance in the LL cultural beliefs of the city can be linked to the LR systems of safety, family law and recreational facilities, as well as individual UL beliefs and UR actions. (This map is analogous view to a "plan view" of the human hive.)

Map 2: The Nested Holarchy of City Systems

The city as a human system is a nest of systems made up of centers (Alexander, 2004), holons (Koestler, 1976) or nested holons (Sahtouris, 1999). The systems have orders of complexity, so that the holons, wholes and centers are nested into holarchies (Wilber, 1996c) or panarchies (Gunderson & Holling, 2002) where levels of complexity emerge over time.

The value of Map 2 to the spiritual life of the city is that it reveals that every individual is a member of multiple city sub-systems or sectors (family, workplace, education system(s), healthcare system(s), place(s) of spiritual practice, neighborhood, city hall, and environment). Spiritual energy travels both from and to individuals and sub-systems creating spheres of influence, networks, communities of practice and meshworks as they become densified and aligned.

Map 3: The Scalar Fractal Relationship of Micro, Meso and Macro Social Holons

Map 3 of the city arises from the insights of non-linear mathematics. Fractal geometry reveals the algorithms of natural systems — the beautiful, repeated patterns that result from the application of simple rules of relationship that apply at multiple levels of scale. Map 3 conveys how capacity development in individuals contributes to capacity in families, organizations and communities, while also revealing the reality of capacity dilution and amplification in social holons. A social holon is any group of people. Its quali-

ties are not summative but dynamic capacities that come from the unique contributions of each individual holon in the social grouping.

At every level of scale, repeating fractal patterns of human systems reveal that the health (vibrant or dis-eased) of the city is deeply embedded in the patterns or principles that contribute to the health of the individual holons and the social holons they belong to — families, teams, organizations, the neighborhood, city hall, nation and the world.

The value of Map 3 to viewing spirituality in the city is revealed in considering the nature of wholeness that the individual expresses cannot be fully manifested or stabilized (for example to deepen spiritual practise) until a critical mass of the individuals' membership in social groups takes on a supportive expression (for example, a minimum critical number joining the practise so that it is socially accepted or even economically established). Usually one group or cohort will find it difficult to be successful until a critical mass of groups also enlists in developing capacity (for example, reaching out across faith systems to some kind of transorganizational ministerial council). The saving grace that the new sciences reveal is that only about 10 to 15 percent of a population need change in order that the whole system shifts towards that change.

Map 4: The Complex Adaptive Structures of Change

Map 4 conveys the stages of structural organizational change in the city. As a living system, the human systems in the city are constantly in the flux of adapting to life conditions that arise from its external situation in a climatic-geological context. Adaptations also arise from the internal situation where citizens develop consciousness capacities to adapt to bio-psycho-cultural-social needs. In fact, both external and internal adaptiveness co-arise (as we saw from Map 1).

The dynamics of change are best pictured as vectors (or developmental lines) that expand the four quadrants of the whole city outward from the seminal center as it adapts to the provocations in its life conditions. These vectors are the outward pointing arrows on Map 1. Map 4 makes visible the city's UR complexifying neural networks and LR complexifying organizational structures over time. These structures emerge as responses to challenges that face the city as it evolves. One can think of the eight structures illustrated in Map 4 as being clustered into four major "change centers": Levels 1–2 are ego-centric; Levels 3–4 are ethno-centric; Levels 5–6 are world-centric; and levels 7–8 are Kosmic-centric. The dynamics of

the city's long-term stages of change are reflected initially in temporary states of change. These states reflect its resilience under duress: how well does it survive in turbulent or chaotic conditions (like Cairo and Tripoli in the 2011 Arab Spring, or Paris under terrorist attack in 2015) or in breakthrough and stabilizing conditions (like Beijing or Rio de Janeiro in the 2008 and 2016 Olympics or Bangalore in the booming 2000's)?

When each stage of change stabilizes city organizational structures, the dilemmas caused by over-use of key performance initiatives eventually lead organizations in the city to develop more complex structures that transcend and include the prior structures. By contrast, in times of instability and uncertainty, organizations in the city may risk down-spiraling into less complex structures in order to find older more stable "comfort zones". (This is particularly visible after natural or revolutionary disasters such as those affecting New Orleans, Sendai Japan, Sarajevo, Baghdad or Aleppo.)

Map 4 gives us an ideal trajectory of structural change, but also has embedded in its assumptions, no guarantees of an ever-upward shift—the direction of change to more or less complex systems depends on the capacities of the individuals and groups (reflected in Map 3) to adapt to the challenge.

The value of Map 4 is that it provides a map of structural complexity for a multiplicity of spiritual practices. Spirituality can be expressed at all eight levels of complexity identified in this evolution-ary map (with more coming on line as developmentalists predict). Each LR structure is related to a LL spiritual value system that enables the city's spiritual life to be expressed so it transcends and includes all the spiritual ego-ethno-world centricities simultaneously alive in the 21st century city.

Combining the Maps into a GIS System

When the four maps of the city are combined, they offer multiple lenses to view the human hive. One can conceive of them as different views from a Google Earth© kind of perspective—and organize them into a Global Spiritual Information System (GSIS). By shifting from one map view to another, it is possible to see the tetra-arising, holarchical, evolutionary, developmental, adaptive dynamics of spiritual relationships in the whole city.

WHAT IS SPIRITUALITY?

Now that we have a way of appreciating the dynamics of the human hive and how to access spiritual realities through an integrated mapping system, our next question has to be, what is spirituality? How might unpacking the meaning of the 'reflective organ' that manifests 'cerebral substance' reveal spirituality?

On a never-ending quest within an ecology of Integral influences, I consider **spirituality to be a universal life force that cycles through existence as an involutionary and evolutionary impulse. The first stage of the cycle, called involution, originates at the non-dual "source" that lies at the center of existence where it descends from the invisible to the visible; from the immanent to that which is presenced; from the unmanifest to the manifest. The second stage of the cycle, called evolution, attracts all creation back to source so that it ascends from the manifest to the source; from the visible to the invisible; from gross physical bodies to**

subtle energetic bodies to causal energetic bodies to non-dual source. Spirituality is not outside of city creation but embedded in it as the source, field and resource of its core.

How this cycle started is now the preoccupation of much scientific and cosmological speculation, nicely summed up by the question (Beck & Cowan, 1996, p. 285), ". . . If the Universe began with a big bang, perhaps there was a consciousness that guided the pushing of the plunger that set it off?"

Ken Wilber (2001) has despaired for much of his career that empirical science has reduced spirituality to simple explanations grounded in the Integral Model's right hand quadrants of objective/interobjective existence. But Wilber (2001, 2006) points out that it is a methodological fallacy to use the right hand epistemologies of poiesis (both auto and social), empiricism and systems to know reality in either of the left hand quadrants of consciousness and culture. Instead he conjectures (Wilber, 2007, p. 155) that spirit has many faces. ". . . 'spirituality' can be used, and has been used, to refer to quadrants, levels/stages, lines, states, and types. . . . Each of these usages is valid, but we must state which aspect of spirituality we are referring to, because otherwise our conclusions are all diametrically opposed to each other and end up deeply contradictory."

Our reflective organs may know spirituality (or God) in all four quadrants of our Integral reality: as spiritual experience (UL); action flow state (UR); collective ecstasy (LL); and collective creation (LR). Spirituality is also known as an UL and LL intelligence (or line) that is capable of growing from ego to ethno to world to Kosmic levels of development for individuals and cultures. It is also the impulse that drives all city manifestation. So, referring back to the four maps that reveal the many faces of the Integral City, we can appreciate why Wilber cautions that we must use appropriate methodologies to know each reality.

HOW DOES THE HUMAN HIVE SOURCE SPIRITUALITY?

To appreciate how spirituality creates the human hive, we can consider the paradox that spirituality (experienced as spiritual energy) reveals an evolutionary scaffold of quality and cultures and emerges as an energizing container (or field).

Spiritual Levels as Qualities and Cultures of the City

Combs (2002) traces the evolution of qualities that relate to spirituality. He explains that individuals experience reality differently depending on their levels of consciousness development. Using both Cook-Greuter's and Wilber's coordinates to determine levels of development Combs posits that at the higher levels (7 through 10) a person may feel the "gravity of the Absolute pulling him or her forward, toward greater identity with the ultimate nondual condition" (p. 149). He suggests that the Level 7 equates to experience at the subtle realm, Level 9 relates to the causal realm and Level 10 with the non-dual realm. (It should be noted that antecedents to all of these frameworks came in the research of (amongst others) Fowler (1981) on "Stages of Faith" and Armstrong (1993) in exploring the "History of God".)

As consciousness has developed, eight levels of bio-psycho-social worldviews have emerged (with more coming on line) (Beck & Cowan, 1996, p. 302) that reframe spiritual referents into a multi-levelled scaffolding that can inquire into multiple spiritual concerns. Level 8 asks what are the spiritual needs of all life on earth and in the city? Level 7 asks what level of the evolutionary spiral is active in any situation and what are its spiritual needs? Level 6 considers how the greater community can express spiritual caring for all members? Level 5 explores how spiritual spheres of influence impact individual success? Level 4 inquires how to follow the One Right Way of spiritual authority? Level 3 demands to know how spiritual "Power Gods" favor positions of (city/earthly) power? Level 2 asks how the spiritual places and ancestors are honored? Level 1 senses the spirits of the city's land, sea, air and life forms.

Each of these levels, or Kosmic addresses, has **dignities**—core values that add value to healthy spiritual expression—and **disasters**—core shadows that detract from healthy spiritual expression (Wilber, 2001) . In order for the city to develop with alignment for purpose, values and plans, the spiritual dignity of each level must be transcended and included as the next stage of complexity emerges in the hierarchy (while the disaster must be recognized and released). When this is done at any given level, the meaning of spirituality is essentially recalibrated and takes on the expanded mission of the next level of complexity in the city.

It is the challenge for the spiritual health of any city to find a way that reconciles these different levels and views of spirituality expressed in religious LR structures and UR practices in the 21st century. This is particularly true in cities where the cross-roads of ego-centric Power Gods and ethno-centric One Right Way spiritual traditions are at odds with one another and all other views of spiritual expressions—such as we are seeing in Jerusalem (the clash of all three Abrahamic religions), in Baghdad and Tehran (Shia versus Sunni), Calcutta (Hinduism versus Islam) and Jakarta (with clashes of Islam, Buddhism, Animism and Christianity).

What Wilber, Combs and Beck and Cowan frame is that different individuals and cultures are at different levels of development (that will only mature at the pace determined by their life conditions). As a result, cities will always have a developmental spectrum of spiritual practices that address the spiral of spiritual concerns.

The developmental maturity level of individual spirituality will depend greatly on the culture of the social holon(s) to which the individual belongs. In general, the city's variety of cultural expressions, will depend as much on its governance system (and its national immigration and refugee policies) as on its geographical location in the world today. For example, Scandinavian cities tend still to have relatively homogenous cultures and therefore stable spiritual expression; whereas many European cities, such as Paris, Copenhagen, Brussels and Amsterdam, have toxic mixes of indigenous national cultures and colonial immigration cultures (intermingled with humanistic and spiritual-but-not-religious views). Such wide chasms of spiritual expressions too often threaten peaceful bridge building.

The relevance of spiritual development to city wellbeing is especially influential on how the city develops its purpose, identity, vision, values, cultural relationships and even its infrastructures. When a city can be aligned around core spiritual expressions in an explicit way, it can more easily make healthy change to the quality of life of all citizens. This is evident in the criteria used today to judge sustainable cities and the cities who are selected as exemplars. Cities like Curitiba, Vancouver and Songpa are recognized for an alignment of their sustainability plans as evidenced by measurable indicators (many of which are set out in Book 2, Appendix G (Hamilton, 2017). But it is the vibrancy of the visionary leadership of mayors (like former mayor and architect Jaime Lerner in Curitiba) and city management (like sustainability expert, Sadhu Johnson in Vancouver) that allows for spiritually inspired leaders to translate resiliency principles into sustainability practices.

A few cities like Singapore have created governance systems that embrace multiple ethnic groupings, by defining "spiritual divides" that celebrate different spiritual expressions while enforcing common denominators of respectful behaviors, national service and strict rules of law and order (Beck & Cowan, 1996, p. 306; Banyan, June 2017).

Spiritual Energy as a Container

The spiritual qualities and cultures that are revealed in quadrants and levels become integrated when we see the city is a container for spirituality (and therefore a boundary that contains the panoply of gods, goddesses and God that have emerged from various spiritual traditions). The difference between a container and a quality, is that the container is a holonic structure that holds qualities, elements, configurations and other wholes.

Spiritual containers in the city can be considered in three key scales (Esbjörn-Hargens & Zimmerman ,2009; DeKay, 2011):

- Self
- Culture
- Nature

The **Self** as a spiritual container is governed by the Kosmic address of the person and is governed by their UL attention and intention and UR actions. As such these spiritual containers are personal and subjective expressions, evidenced by individual belief and behavior boundaries. Wilber (2007, p. 199) proposes that Self represents the first person/face of God—the UL "I" in Map 1 of the city.

A multiplicity of Selves makes up the spiritual container of **Cultures** in the city. In this respect we can think of city Culture(s) as the Kosmic address(es) of shared spiritual values and visions of the social holon(s) that hold(s) them. They tend to represent a center of gravity of multiple addresses, extending across approximately four developmental levels (Ego–Ethno–World–Kosmic). As such the Cultures are intersubjective agreements whose spiritual expression weaves a nest of belief systems. Their boundary is invisible but is understood by all who belong to it and (often easily) inferred by all who don't belong. These LL spiritual cultures are fundamental to the structural containers which are their LR analogues as spiritual institutions. LR spiritual structures include the temples, churches, mosques and places of worship where all the LL beliefs, dogmas and religions that represent the spiral of spiritual worldviews are practised. (Interestingly architect Christopher Alexander refers to the neighborhood containers in the city as "hulls", borrowing the term from ship building. I would propose we could think of LR structural spiritual containers as hulls floating on a LL sea of culture.) Wilber calls spirit as Culture the "Great Thou" or "We" and the 2nd person/face of God (2007, p. 199)–the LL "We" in Map 1 of the city (see Appendix B).

The third spiritual scale of the city is **Nature.** Nature embraces the living system that the city is both a part of in the biosphere and physiosphere and represents an expression of the natural human system. Nature is fundamental to natural law which governs all life. It is the spirit of Life itself in all its evolutionary and involutionary magnificence. Nature contains both Culture and Self and together the three scales embrace the life-giving values of Beauty, Truth and Goodness (McIntosh, 2007). Wilber calls Nature the "Great Web of Life" and the 3rd person/face of God (2007, p. 199)–the UR and LR "It" and "Its" quadrants in Map 1 of the city.

Perhaps **when we admit all three faces of God as aspects of the spirituality of the city, we approach a definition of the "spirit of a city"?**

The city as spiritual container holds not only the spiritual lives of its citizens, but also the artefacts that emerge as spiritual expression. These artefacts include all the systems, structures and infrastructures associated within the LR built city. And although we tend to point at the cathedrals, mosques and synagogues as centers of spiritual life, in fact the "soul" of the city is expressed in all its built form. DeKay (2011) writes of the linkage between the UL developmental capacities of designers and their LR expression through design, of structures of all kinds. Alexander (1977, 2002, 2004a, 2004b, 2004c) has developed a philosophy and methodology that explains how the city's aliveness (and therefore its spiritual manifestation) can be heightened by careful attention to the design and relationship of centers. Interestingly a common practise across all spiritual practice is some kind of centering prayer, meditation, chant, or mantra—so it appears that centering is recognized as intrinsic to spiritual connection (and even an involutionary one that attracts spirit downward and inward from Source, as explained below).

In the busy-ness of the city, one of the greatest challenges for individuals and groups to connect to their spirituality may be to find places of spiritual refuge away from the city's sheer propensity for over-stimulating the senses. The cacophony of city living too often drowns out the calmness of centers, centering and spiritual focus. Therefore, it is becoming increasingly important to reclaim traditional aspects of city design where the connection with quiet centers is made available to all citizens for spiritual practise. Such focal points offer opportunities for Self-Centering (e.g. meditation rooms in the airport); Culture-Centering (e.g. chapels or recreational centers in the neighborhood square) and Nature-Centering (e.g. community gardens, public parks, pocket parks and nature trails).

HOW DOES SPIRITUALITY RESOURCE THE HUMAN HIVE?

Spirituality may not only serve the city—but in fact *make* the city—by resourcing it in three primary ways that emerge three in-spired zones: through the way of service emerges the zone of Grace; through the way of practise emerges the zone of Space; and through the way of cultural expression emerges the zone of Place.

Spiritual Service @ Grace Making

The human hive has millions of stories of spiritual service—in many cities representing all the world's religions. Once these diverse religious practices were described as spiritual paths, but with today's richness of cultural plurality, we recognize a spiritual ecology (Patten, 2010). The city container is a wonderful convergence vessel where spiritual practices differ, conflict, align and/or grow from one another. The Integral City is becoming a vessel where new kinds of spiritual acceptance bridge, integrate and evolve spiritual practise into something that is becoming Integral or even universal. Patten (2010, p.4) says that, "The new integral evolutionary spirituality both accommodates and resolves the apparent contradictions among the diverse forms of wisdom it integrates. It embraces the paradoxes of theistic and non-theistic spirituality, of 1st-person, 2nd-person, and 3rd-person mysticism."

Graceful Voices

Represented in the ecology of voices are pastors, rabbis, imams and abbots speaking for their spiritual traditions and civil society. Other informal citizen activists speak for the rights of diverse spiritual practices.

Yet other actors are institutionalized in City Hall as managers of UR city systems and LR infrastructures that enable citizens to attend places of congregation, both public and private. Still other actors are developers and evolutionaries, creating new forms of spiritual expression, education and wellbeing systems.

A lifelong activist for human and civil rights, Patten (2010) points out that the modern, postmodern and Integral ages have created a whole new spectrum of helpers in the city. While the traditional spiritual leaders held the power of positional office (e.g., the Pope at the head of church institutions or the local pastor in the city church), modern helpers apply spiritual practices in the psychotherapy room or coach business organizations; postmodern helpers may include relationship counsellors, doctors, personal trainers, yoga instructors, martial artists, dance teachers and all manner of media from books to recordings; Integral helpers are now appearing as spiritual directors, life coaches and reaching out through the internet into mind/heart/spirit space (the noosphere proposed by Teilhard de Chardin, 1966, 1972) where individuals and groups have not previously been able to be accessed.

Moreover integrally informed spiritual activists can be touching the spiritual lives of stakeholders in all quadrants, levels, lines, states and types because they are informed by Integral frameworks that allow them to be effective "meshworkers" (D. Beck, 2010; Hamilton, 2008a, p. 221). Meshworkers and meshweavers use the Integral framework to design spiritual habitats aligning actors, practices and resources to enable practitioners to evolve to their next natural step of spiritual development. They apply precepts identified (Beck & Cowan, 1996) at the Turquoise 8th level of development, where the Kosmic-centric "AQtivist and AQtivators" (terms coined by me to describe activists and activators using AQAL— all quadrants, lines, levels, types in their activism) enjoy "wonder, awe, reverence, humility, unity and a refreshed value for simplicity . . . [monitoring] both self and situation as a participant-observer . . . [where] life is the most important thing there is; but my life is unimportant." (p.291)

Core Spiritual Values

The richness of such frames hints at an elegance of integration in the 7,000-year-old human hive that starts to mimic that of the hundred-million-year-old beehive. Core values that have been identified across the perennial spiritual wisdoms of virtually all human hives (McIntosh, 2007) are giving meshworkers and meshweavers the vision of Beauty, Goodness and Truth that imbue spiritual life at all expressions of Self, Culture and Nature.

McIntosh (2007, p. 141) explores the inner and outer qualities of these core values as anchors that enable a holographic view of spiritual manifestation in the human hive.[1] He suggests that Beauty is manifested through the interiors as appreciation and through the exteriors as expression. He proposes that Goodness is manifested through the interiors as stillness and through the exteriors as service. He sees Truth is manifested through the interiors as learning and through the exteriors as teaching.

SPIRITUAL PRACTISE @ SPACE MAKING

Research into Spiritual Intelligence

Spirituality in the city is dynamically manifested through all city actors. The actors and their capacities are present in all of the quadrants, levels, lines, relationships, and structures of the Maps 1,2,3 and 4 (and in all types of horizontal preferences expressed by individuals that appear to have biological roots and stay with a person throughout their lifetime, such as those identified by Myers-Briggs, Enneagram, etc.). Thus, implicit and explicit spiritual practitioners generate spiritual space or capacities in many ways.

Framing the knowledge, skills and abilities of spiritual intelligence, Wigglesworth (2002, 2004, 2006, 2014) has defined it as "the ability to behave with Compassion and Wisdom while maintaining inner and outer peace (equanimity) regardless of the circumstances." (2004, p. 4)

1, I note that McIntosh references quadrants differently for these values. He relates Beauty to UR/LR; Truth to UL and Goodness to LL. My exploration of spirituality references Beauty to UL and Truth to UR/LR. Goodness is LL. If you see the holographic nature of the quadrants this may be a moot point. My argument is intended to make my offering of Map 5 coherent.

With research deriving from Goleman's Emotional Intelligence and Zohar's Spiritual Intelligence, Wigglesworth has parsed spiritual intelligence into four quadrants with the broad themes of UL Higher Self Awareness, UR Higher Self Mastery, LL Universal Awareness and LR Social Mastery/ Spiritual Presence. Her assessment technology measures each of the spiritual skills on a scale of 1 (basic understanding) to 5 (advanced mastery).

Other research (Hamer, 2004, p. 23) demonstrates the UR genetic basis of spirituality, in aspects of self-forgetfulness, transpersonal identification and mysticism. Likewise it appears that UR/LR altruism is not only UR hard wired, it fires a pleasure center in the brain, thus reinforcing the practice every time it is repeated—"being selfless is ultimately the most self-serving option because it feels so good to give"(McTaggart, 2011, p. 107).

Even, recent developments in city happiness research has shifted into inquiry about the influence that spirituality has on wellbeing, social relationships, social class and cultural values (Wills, Hamilton, & Islam, 2007a, 2007b; Hamilton, 2017).

Field Making

Evidence about spiritual behaviors, attitudes, shared practices and practise systems, suggest that a field effect is emerging in the city (McTaggart, 2001; Sheldrake, 1988). The field probably arises because the city as container causes the multiplicity of exchanges within and across holons and social holons to converge the chaos into patterns that sustain. Florida (2005, 2008) and Landry (2007) have pointed out how the alignment of creativity value sets produce creative and artful cities that attract more people who value similar qualities in the city. A kind of "spiritual groove" becomes carved in the energetic field, that through repetition reinforces itself and creates a field of attraction.

Sheldrake describes the co-emergent influences of UL mental activity, UR human behavior, LL cultural and LR social systems as morphic fields which contain an inherent memory (p. 113).[2] Book 2 (Hamilton, 2017) describes our explorations in Integral City with a version of the morphic

---

2, I admit, it is especially tempting for the advocate of the human hive, to borrow Sheldrake's insights because of his study of animal and insect life, including bees that reveals trans-holonic/ social holonic memories that he proposes are accessible by specific members of a species from their species morphic field.

field known as the Knowing Field accessed through systemic constellation work (Chapters 1 and 2). Within the framework of spirituality in the human hive, it may be that the morphic/Knowing Fields are the cumulative subtle and causal energetic fields exhibited by individuals. They may become accessible as transpersonal spiritual "stores" by those who are especially bonded through common experience, practise, cultures and systems in the convergent space-making container of the city (McTaggart, 2011; Douglas, D., Hamilton, M., 2013).

SPIRITUAL CULTURAL STRUCTURES @ PLACEMAKING

Through the yin and yang (interior and exterior) polarities of Beauty, Truth and Goodness core values, proposed by McIntosh, we gain an appreciation of the Integral City as a kind of hologram. (In fact Wilber (Wilber, 2006) offers an Integral "calculus" exploring a similar proposition in *Integral Spirituality* that opens up a hall of Integral mirrors that might overwhelm the novice spiritual seeker of the human hive, but may satisfy the spiritual adept.)

Bruce Sanguin (2007) recognizes Beauty as a strong principle of the evolutionary impulse, calling it the "aesthetic principle". As former minister of an Integral church with strong roots in traditional Christian practices, he guided his congregation to share spiritual inspiration found in his book, *Darwin, Divinity and the Dance of the Cosmos.* He uses both positional leadership within his place of worship, but also implicit leadership within the city as a whole.

Sanguin (2007, p. 121) served his congregation with deep UL insights into the immanent process of spiritual involution and evolution, recognizing "the hidden wholeness, the non-coercive intelligence . . . nudging . . . formations of increasing elegance, beauty and diversity." He recognized the sacred LL practices of ritual and the differing Integral contributions many churches can bring to spiritual place making in the city. He (Sanguin, 2008, pp. 94–97) dared to ask *What Colour is Your Christ?* and explored the whole spiral of spiritual life in the city that arises from serving the Tribal Christ, the Warrior Christ, The Traditional Divine Scapegoat Christ, Christ as CEO, the Egalitarian Christ, the Integral Christ and the Mystical Christ. (What city spirit might be released, if similar appreciative inquiries could be made through all of the city's spiritual leaders, whether they be priest-esses, rabbis, imams, shamans, witches or atheists?)

As a meshworker, Sanguin stretches well beyond the LL beliefs of an Integral spirituality and articulates the LR structures that enable one church and many places of worship in the human hive to align their ser-vice of Goodness so that all quadrants and all levels of complexity are spiritually embraced.

Such explorations of practical spiritual place making also point to the immanence of spirituality in all key sectors of the city. Using the sectors of Map 2 (Appendix B), spirituality runs like rivers through all of them connecting them all in the spiritual ocean of the city. These different tributaries undoubtedly impact the design of the human hive from grand-est structural expression like streetscapes and cathedrals, to the most sensitive reflective capacities of collective intelligence, to the smallest daily impulse of personal kindness (Alexander, 2002, 2004a, 2004b, 2004c; Hamilton, 2008a; Wills et al., 2007a).

Essentially from a sustainability perspective, all the sectors and voices of the city must serve its wellbeing, like different organs serving the body of the whole. The spiritual DNA of city wellbeing (as Beauty, Truth and Goodness) aligns the quadrants where:

- Education serves UL;
- Healthcare serves UR;
- Civil Society serves LL;
- Private Sector Production/Manufacture serves LR.

It used to be that the role of the voice of City Hall's Civic Managers would align key sectors in service to the wellbeing of the whole human hive. But as we proposed in Book 2 (Hamilton, 2017), it has become apparent that the role of the voice of Civil Society (containing all expressions of the faith community) has a special role to play as Integrator of the Voices of the human hive. Whether it be the voice of Civic Managers or Civil Society acting as Integrator, it is apparent that an absence of spiritual aliveness in any of the city's voices, stakeholders or sectors undermines the wellbeing of the city. On the other hand, an embrace of active spiritual aliveness in any of them (and as is becoming obvious from enacting the Master Code, in all of them simultaneously) can catalyze the entire wellbeing of the city.

MAP 5: SPIRITUALITY IN THE CITY

In reviewing our constructs, we come to a final question. Is there a spirituality map of the city that reveals Grace, Space and Place? Is there a way to see that Goodness, Truth and Beauty are core spiritual values of the Integral City with both vertical and horizontal locations (or Kosmic addresses)? Spirituality itself responds in this holographic way (and is summarized in Table 2):

At the **Source** level of city spirituality exists the Absolute, ever-present (caring) life force of spirituality that is Love and the non-dual ground of Being. This is anchored by the core value of Goodness and the spiritual zone of Grace. It is presenced as the infinite ground of spiritual abundance. It is accessed by Stillness and enacted by Service.

At the **Field** level of city, spirituality emerges the (contexting) qualities of personal and transpersonal energy that arise from subtle and causal memory patterns of evolutionary spiritual intelligence. This is anchored by the core value of Truth and the spiritual zone of Space. It is presenced by dynamic learning spiritual memory. It is accessed by Learning and enacted by Teaching.

Table 2: Spirituality in the Human Hive

Source/Field/ Resource Level	Core Spiritual Value Anchor	Resource Quadrant	Spirituality Zone	Mode of Access	Mode of Enactment
Caring Source/ Ground of spiritual abundance	Goodness	LL	Grace	Stillness	Service
Contexting Field of spiritual memory	Truth	UR/LR	Space	Learning	Teaching
Capacity Resource Container of living human hive	Beauty	UL	Place	Appreciation	Expression

At the **Resource** level of city, spirituality emerges the manifest (capacity) qualities of the "big three" (Beauty, Truth and Goodness). This is anchored by the core value of Beauty and the spiritual zone of Place. It is presenced through the container of the living human hive. It is accessed by Appreciation and enacted by Expression.

From this analysis we can then offer Map 5 as Spirituality in the human hive (as shown in Figure 3).

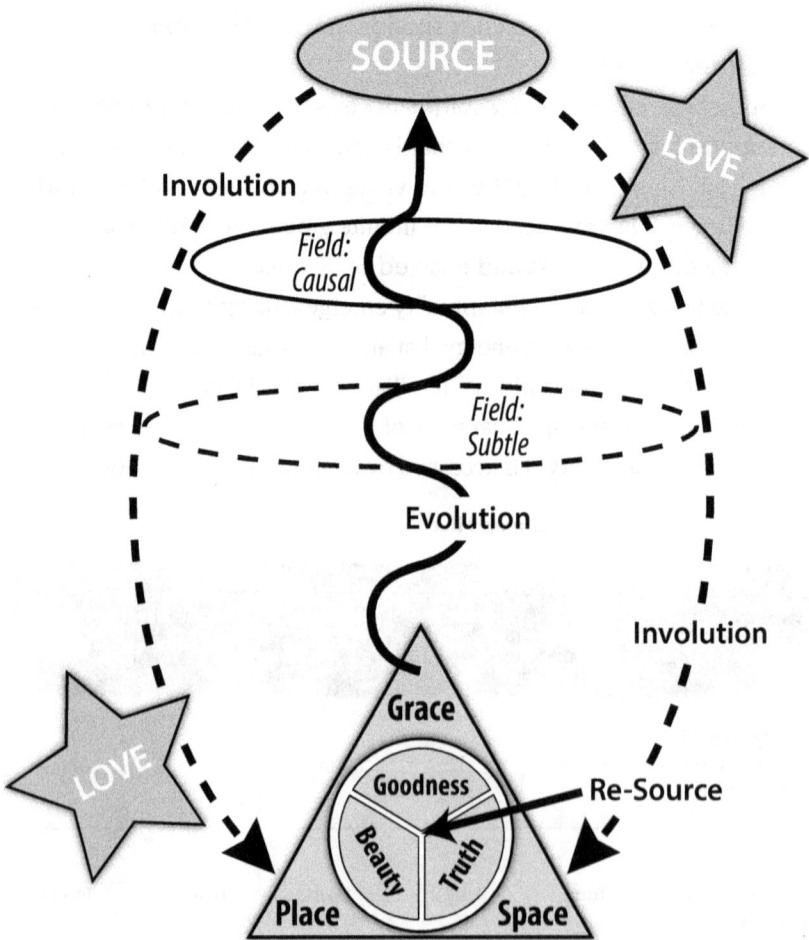

Figure 3: Map 5—Spirituality in the Human Hive

CONCLUSION

This chapter has acknowledged that spirituality in the human hive is driven by an evolutionary/involutionary impulse; that it reveals itself in individual and collective lives as qualities, cultures and containers that can be situated in five Integral maps of the city. Our exploration of spirituality in the human hive integrates Caring source, Contexting field(s) and Capacity Building resources for Goodness, Truth and Beauty (which when we work with city energies, become translated into purpose, identity, vision, values, creativity, relationships and systems). As such, spirituality is an Integral reality of the human hive and the author of the Master Code which reflects the three faces of God and the three zones of spirituality:

Take Care of Self (I @ Source/Resource).

Take Care of Others/Culture (We/You @ Field).

Take Care of this Place/Planet/Nature (It/Its @ Resource/Source).

REFERENCES

Alexander, C. (1977). A Pattern Language. USA: Oxford University Press.

Alexander, C. (2002). The Phenomenon of Life. (September 1, 2004 ed. Vol. 1). Berkeley, CA: Center for Environmental Structure.

Alexander, C. (2004a). The Luminous Ground. (September 1, 2004 ed. Vol. 4). Berkeley, CA: Center for Environmental Structure.

Alexander, C. (2004b). The Process of Creating Life. (September 1, 2004 ed. Vol. 2). Berkeley, CA: Center for Environmental Structure.

Alexander, C. (2004c). A Vision of a Living World. (September 1, 2004 ed. Vol. 3). Berkeley, CA: Center for Environmental Structure.

Armstrong, K. (1993). A History of God: The 4,000-Year Quest of Judaism, Christianity and Islam. New York: Ballantine Book.

Banyan. (2017, June 1). How foreigners misunderstand Singapore. The Economist.

Beck, D. (2010). Natural Designs for Meshworking. Retrieved from Gaiaspace, Meshworking, Private.

Beck, D., & Cowan, C. (1996). Spiral Dynamics: Mastering Values, Leadership and Change. Malden, MA: Blackwell Publishers.

Combs, A. (2002). The Radiance of Being: Understanding the Grand Integral Vision Living the Integral Life. St. Paul, Minnesota: Paragon House.

DeKay, M. (2011). *Integral Sustainable Design*. London, UK: Earthscan.

Douglas, D. C., & Hamilton, M. (2013). Knowing Cities: The Knowing Field and the Emergence of Integral City Intelligence. *The Knowing Field* (22), 25–32.

Esbjörn-Hargens, S., & Zimmerman, M. (2009). *Integral Ecology: Uniting Multiple Perspectives on the Natural World*. Boston: Shambhala Publications Inc.

Florida, R. (2005). *Cities and the Creative Class*. New York: Routledge.

Florida, R. (2008). *Who's Your City: How the Creative Economy is Making Where to Live the Most Important Decision of Your Life*. Toronto: Random House Canada.

Florida, R. (2017). *The New Urban Crisis: How Our Cities Are Increasing Inequality, Deepening Segregation, and Failing the Middle Class—and What We Can Do About It*. New York: Basic Books.

Fowler, J. W. (1981). *Stages of Faith: The Psychology of Human Development and the Quest for Meaning*. San Francisco,: HarperSanFrancisco,.

Gunderson, L. C., & Holling, C. S. (Eds.). (2002). *Panarchy: Understanding Transformations in Human and Natural Systems*. Washington, DC: Island Press.

Hamer, D. (2004). *The God Gene: How Faith is Hardwired Into Our Genes*. New York: Doubleday.

Hamilton, M. (2008). *Integral City: Evolutionary Intelligences for the Human Hive*. Gabriola Island BC: New Society Publishers.

Hamilton, M. (2017). *Integral City Inquiry and Action: Designing Impact for the Human Hive*. Tucson, Arizona: Integral Publishers.

Landry, C. (2007). *The Art of City Making*. London, UK: Earthscan Comedia.

Lovelock, J. (2009). *The Vanishing Face of Gaia*. New York: Harmony Books.

Maeterlinck, M. (1954). *The Life of the Bee*. New York: Mentor.

McIntosh, S. (2007). *Integral Consciousness and the Future of Evolution: How the Integral Worldview is Transforming Politics, Culture and Spirituality*. St. Paul, Minnesota: Paragon House.

McTaggart, L. (2001). *The Field: The Quest for the Secret Force of the Universe*. New York: Harper Perennial.

McTaggart, L. (2011). *The Bond: Connecting Through the Space Between Us*. New York: Free Press.

Patten, T. (2010). *Toward the Emergence of Integral Evolutionary Spiritual Culture*. Paper presented at the Enacting an Integral Future Conference.

Sanguin, B. (2007). *Darwin, Divinity and the Dance of the Cosmos: An Ecological Christianity*. Kelowna, BC, Canada: Wood Lake Publishing Inc.

Sanguin, B. (2008). *Emerging Church: A Model for Change and A Map for Renewal*. Kelowna, BC, Canada: Wood Lake Publishing Inc.

Sheldrake, R. (1988). *The Presence of the Past: Morphic Resonance and the Habits of Nature* (1995 ed.). Rochester, Vermont: Park Street Press.

Teilhard de Chardin, P. (1966). *Man's Place in Nature* (B. Wall, Trans.). New York: Harper & Row, Publishers.

Teilhard de Chardin, P. (1972). *The Phenomenon of Man* (B. Wall, Trans.). New York: Fontana Books.

Wigglesworth, C. (Producer). (2002, May 6, 2011) Spiritual Intelligence and Leadership. retrieved from http://www.consciouspursuits.com/Articles/Articles.aspx

Wigglesworth, C. (Producer). (2004, May 6, 2011) Spiritual Intelligence and Why It Matters. retrieved from http://www.consciouspursuits.com/Articles/Articles.aspx

Wigglesworth, C. (2006). Conscious Evolution: Where the Universe is Going and How to Join the Journey. Houston, TX: Spiralling Conscious, LLC.

Wigglesworth, C. (2014). SQ21: *The Twenty-One Skills of Spiritual Intelligence*. New York: SelectBooks

Wilber, K. (1995). *Sex, Ecology and Spirituality: the spirit of evolution*. Boston: Shambhala Publications Inc.

Wilber, K. (2001). *Marriage of Sense and Soul*. New York: Random House.

Wilber, K. (2006). *Integral Spirituality*. Boston: Shambhala Publications Inc.

Wilber, K. (2007). *The Integral Vision*. Boston: Shambhala Publications Inc.

Wills, E. H., Hamilton, M., & Islam, G. (2007a). Subjective Well-being in Cities: Individual or Collective? A Cross Cultural Analysis. Paper presented at the Wellbeing in International Development Conference.

Wills, E. H., Hamilton, M., & Islam, G. (2007b). Subjective Wellbeing in Bogotá (B), Belo Horizonte (BH) and Toronto (T): A Subjective Indicator of Quality of Life for Cities. Bogotá: World Bank.

CREATIVITY AND CARE IN GAIA'S REFLECTIVE ORGAN

CHAPTER SUMMARY

This chapter proposes that creativity is the natural result of the meshworking of living human systems. Creativity in human systems occurs at all scales represented by the Integral City model. A meshwork emerges within multiple scales of human systems from cycles of self-organizing adaptations and innovations to life conditions and the formation of learned habits or intelligences that translate principles and codes into a perpetual stream of creativity. The symbiotic relationship of organelles/organizations emerges an organ-like capacity of creativity for the human hive that is on the evolutionary verge of becoming Gaia's Reflective Organ. The human hive emerging as Gaia's Reflective Organ is by nature caring in creative ways that are both self-organizing and ordered. We can design to amplify creativity and therefore aliveness as the city evolves.

Key Words: creativity, Integral, meshwork, human hive, organelle, organization, Gaia's reflective organ, aliveness

> For every one thousand gardens that we create without . . .
> may we create ten thousand gardens within.
>
> —Rumi

Humans are Gaia's reflective organ.
—James Lovelock

We get order for free (Kauffman, 1993). It is built into the natural evolution of things. In the process, we also get creativity for free. In fact, the two properties are inextricably linked, and we can't have one without the other.

WHAT IS CREATIVITY?

A very simple definition of creativity is that it is the process from which something new emerges or arises when you combine two or more elements (particles, waves, ideas, materials, people, roles, organizations, cultures, structures etc.). When inspired by the unending possibilities of creativity for the "creative class" and its leverage on city economies Richard Florida noted, humans are infinitely creative—everyone is capable of being creative and frequently demonstrates this capability throughout their daily lives (Florida, 2005, 2008). Likewise, Charles Landry (2007, 2008, 2017) has explored the impacts of interculturalism, the art of city making and the psychology of the city on creativity, recognizing that creativity is endemic to the city.

This chapter proposes that creativity in the city is the natural result of the process of meshworking in living human systems. A meshwork (described below) emerges from cycles of self-organizing and learned habits. The cycles produce organelle-like structures and processes which enable the city to provide water, food distribution, waste management, power, transportation, and communication—in other words all the functions that manage energy, matter and information. The symbiotic relationship of the organelles (aka functioning systems) emerges an organ-like capacity that we call the city or human hive. This most complex of human systems is on the evolutionary verge of becoming a reflective organ of Gaia herself (and even evolving a global meta-city system of reflective organs). A surprising consequence of the meshworking processes that are creating Gaia's reflective organs is that by nature they are both creative and ordered.

If creativity is a process by which new connections are made, making new connections lies at the heart of who we are as human beings—homo sapiens sapiens—the human conscious of our consciousness. Creating connections is the process by which our brains and minds have made themselves and the process by which our caring relationships to self, others, the world and the Kosmos co-creates the habitats where we live.

We take it as given that human systems at the individual and collective level are developmental and evolutionary (Hamilton, 2008). It would appear from both biological and cosmological science that the history of the universe has bequeathed us with evolutionary capacities that manifest both externally crystallizing creations (Capra, 1996; Maturana & Varela, 1987, 1992; Mitchell & Williams, 2001; Elizabeth Sahtouris, 1999, 2017) and internally conscious creations (Abrams & Primack, 2006; Laszlo, 2004; Wilber, 1995, 1996a).

INTEGRAL FRAMEWORK

Enabling the understanding of the proposition that creativity is evolutionary and developmental, is an Integral framework that integrates the external and internal creative capacities and outcomes through four lenses (referenced in brackets by the pronouns we use to describe them):

- external individual creativity—(it) objective creative acts create behavioral expression and habits. This emerges objective Truth.
- external collective creativity –(its) inter-objective creative systems create structures, and infrastructures. This emerges interobjective systemic Truths.
- internal individual creativity—(I) subjective creative reflections create imagination and inspiration. This emerges subjective Beauty.
- internal collective creativity—(We) intersubjective creative beliefs create values and relationships. This emerges intersubjective Goodness.

The Integral framework (developed by Wilber (Wilber, 1995, 2000, 2006, 2007) and applied to cities by Hamilton (2008, 2017a)) offers a way of situating a multiplicity of views about creativity (that are inextricably tied to our exploration of Spirituality and its relationship to the "big 3" of Truth, Beauty and Goodness discussed in Chapter 1). An Integral view of these creative capacities can be modeled in a variation of Map 1 in Figure 4, showing the Integral quadrants that we discussed in Chapter 1 (also see Appendix A).

Figure 4: Integral City Framework for Creativity Lenses

INTERNAL INDIVIDUAL CREATIVITY—(I) subjective creative reflections, create imagination, inspiration; Beauty	**EXTERNAL INDIVIDUAL CREATIVITY—(IT)** objective creative acts, create behavioral expression, habits; Truth
INTERNAL COLLECTIVE CREATIVITY—(WE) intersubjective creative beliefs create values, relationships; Goodness	**EXTERNAL COLLECTIVE CREATIVITY—(ITS)** interobjective creative systems, structures, infrastructures; Truths

This model has the interesting quality of being fractal at every holonic scale of human systems: individual, family, organization, community, city, society. These scales can be nested within one another as a holarchy, as shown in in Appendix B Map 2.

Connections and thus creativity can occur within or amongst any of the quadrants of reality in Map 1 or within or amongst any of the scales shown in Map 2.

CREATIVITY ARISES FROM PRINCIPLES OF LIVING SYSTEMS

While the Integral model looks like a theoretical flat depiction of the city and its creativity, it is a conceptual map of a very dynamic living human system. Elisabet Sahtouris (1999, 2010, 2017), evolution biologist brings the Integral framework to life by describing the living cell using the metaphor of a city. In true fractal fashion, her set of Principles for Living Systems reflect the patterns of life at the microscopic level of the cell, while at the same time applying powerfully at the macroscopic level to the scale of human life in the city.

When we consider the Principles of Living Systems and how they contribute aliveness, creativity and innovation to the Integral model of the human hive, we gain some understanding of the principles that underlie creativity at all scales in the city. Sahtouris' 15 Principles of Living Systems can be applied to the city as follows.

Principle 1: Self-creation (autopoiesis) means that a city would need to create a habitat for people that respected the wisdom and resources of its people in relationship to the ecological, geological and biological life conditions of its location and climate.

Principle 2: Complexity (diversity of parts) means that a city would optimize the functioning of its parts by appreciating and supporting the diversity of its 4 Voices—so that **citizens** (Producers), **business/inventors** (Diversity Generators), **civic managers** (Resource Allocators) and **civil society** (Integrators) can work differently together to achieve a shared vision.

Principle 3: Embeddedness in larger holons and dependence on them (holarchy) means that a city would be a model of sustainability and resilience as it recognized that it was part of the larger system of human and other living systems contained in the eco-region, nation, continent and planet.

Principle 4: Self-reflexivity (autognosis, self-knowledge) requires the city as a system of systems, along with its collective groups (organizations, associations, neighborhoods, teams, families) and individuals are enabled and encouraged to be lifelong learners. This attitude to learning starts with the practise of mutual trust and respect. It depends on regular reflective dialogue, feedback and working towards life-giving projects for all.

Principle 5: Self-regulation/maintenance (autonomics) balancing efficiency and resilience is the city-wide practise of managing resources, goals, plans and decisions so the economy is healthy, and everyone experiences wellbeing. Self-regulation is a form of practical governance that engages all 4 Voices of the city.

Principle 6: Response-ability to internal and external stress or change requires the 4 Voices of the city to share information openly and take decisions related to resolving their internal tensions and also to pay attention to the 5th Voice of the City represented by other cities in the eco-region (as friendly or unfriendly neighbors). Responding to stresses in a healthy and creative way enables resilience and response-able change.

Principle 7: Input/output of matter, energy and information with other holons means that the city creates an innovation eco-system that recognizes all 4 Voices (and cities in other eco-regions) and their institutions (especially infrastructures, manufacturers, food producers, schools/ universities, business, innovation labs and health systems) are aligned into a circular economy that supports equitable access to matter, energy and information for all.

Principle 8: Transformation of matter, energy and information; no non-recyclable waste means sharing and tracking the matter, energy and information flows (governed by Principle 7) so that all output from one holon or function is input for another holon or function and no waste results. This is tracked by an integrated sustainability plan that tracks the vital signs of life for all holons/functions.

Principle 9: Communications among all parts requires that cities create information systems that connect all Voices/Stakeholders with technology to optimize and inform decisions for/with/as the 4 Voices of the city (and state, region, nation, world).

Principle 10: Empowerment, full employment of all component parts tasks the city with creating education and training from k-U to create the conditions for full employment, that coordinates students, interns, business and government and supports the economy's innovation ecosystem.

Principle 11: Coordination of parts and functions calls for cities to design and practise governance that is fair, transparent, accountable and accessible so people feel safe, caring and can relate to each other easily and often in the coordination of their creativity as they live, work, play and learn.

Principle 12: Balance of interests negotiated among parts, whole and embedding holarchy requires that the city and its organizations (serving all 4 Voices) balance efficient management of all functions so they are mutually supportive and resourced for resilience to change (meaning parts serve whole, and whole serves parts and together they serve the holarchy of human systems in the city).

Principle 13: Reciprocity of parts in mutual contribution and assistance asks the city to design and align its sub-systems and functions so that they are mutually supportive and able to assist each other when stressed and/or celebrate with one another when goals are achieved.

Principle 14: Conservation of what works well is a basic survival strategy for all human systems in the city—to retain and support that which is life-giving as foundational for adapting to changing life conditions, sustainability, resilience and creative regeneration.

Principle 15: Innovation and creative change of what does not work well is a corollary to Principle 14—it is important for cities as innovation ecosystems to identify what is not working, to cease or change the practise and design improvements that work better and/or optimally.

CONNECTING PRINCIPLES OF LIVING SYSTEMS TO INTEGRAL CITY INTELLIGENCES

In this exploration of creativity in the human hive, the 12 Intelligences of the Integral City naturally emerge from the Principles of Living Systems. While we could propose that the Principles of Living Systems represent the dynamic, ever-present self-organizing aspects of the living system of the city, the 12 Intelligences, reflect the evolution of its habits or learned behaviors.

An Integral view of the city's operation recognizes that as a living system it develops intelligences that are contributing to the emergence of Gaia's reflective organ (Hamilton, 2008a). These include intelligences that:

- Build capacity in the Individual (Inner and Outer)
- Build capacity in the Collective (Culture and Structures)
- Develop Inquiry intelligences for generative exchanges
- Catalyze Meshworking strategies to bridge sectors, silos, stovepipes & solitudes
- Design feedback and feed forward loops for Navigational direction
- Respond to critical Contexts: Ecospherical, Emergent, Integral, Living
- Express Evolutionary Intelligence

These intelligent habits have formed in the city and represent its qualities of aliveness (capacities for surviving, connecting to its environment and regenerating (Capra, 1996). Together the Principles and Intelligences underpin the city's potential for evolving into a reflective organ for Gaia. Because the Intelligences arise from the Principles of Living Systems, not surprisingly, we find that the taxonomies of the Intelligences and the Principles reflect one another.

In fact, Integral City Intelligences represent its core creative capacities derived from the Principles of Living Systems.

Below, I link the Intelligences to Sahtouris' Principles of Living Systems, so we can reveal their qualities of aliveness. In many cases one of the Principles manifests in multiple Integral City Intelligences because of their holographic, interconnected and even non-local nature. (Appendix C sets out concise definitions of the Integral City Intelligences. We have given full definitions of the Integral City Intelligences in Book 1 (*Integral City: Evolutionary Intelligences for the Human Hive* (Hamilton, 2008) and on the website www.integralcity.com.)

Principle 1: Self-creation (autopoiesis) is reflected in the Eco, Emergent and Living Intelligences.

Principle 2: Complexity (diversity of parts) is reflected in Eco and Emergent Intelligences.

Principle 3: Embeddedness in larger holons and dependence on them (holarchy) is reflected in Integral and Living Intelligences.

Principle 4: Self-reflexivity (autognosis, self-knowledge) is reflected in Integral, Inner and Storytelling/Culture Intelligences.

Principle 5: Self-regulation/maintenance (autonomics) balancing efficiency and resilience is reflected in Integral and Living Intelligences.

Principle 6: Response-ability to internal and external stress or change is reflected in Individual (Integral, Inner, Outer), and Collective (Building/Structure and Storytelling/Culture) Intelligences.

Principle 7: Input/output of matter, energy and information with other holons is reflected in Living, Inner and Building/Structure Intelligences.

Principle 8: Transformation of matter, energy and information; no non-recyclable waste is reflected in Living, Inner and Building/Structure Intelligences.

Principle 9: Communications among all parts is reflected in Integral, Inquiry, Meshworking and Navigating Intelligences.

Principle 10: Empowerment, full employment of all component parts is reflected in Eco, Emergent, Living and Meshworking Intelligences.

Principle 11: Coordination of parts and functions is reflected in Eco, Emergent, Living, Meshworking and Navigating Intelligences.

Principle 12: Balance of interests negotiated among parts, whole and embedding holarchy is reflected in Eco, Emergent, Living and Inquiry Intelligences.

Principle 13: Reciprocity of parts in mutual contribution and assistance is reflected in Eco, Emergent, Living and Meshworking Intelligences.

Principle 14: Conservation of what works well is reflected in Eco, Emergent, Living and Meshworking Intelligences.

Principle 15: Innovation, creative change of what does not work well is reflected in Eco, Emergent, Living and Evolutionary Intelligences.

The human hive meshworks all of these Intelligences (defined in Appendix C1) to think about, act in, relate to and work towards creating the optimal conditions for human emergence at all levels of scale.

MESHWORKS, CREATIVITY AND EVOLUTION

At the smallest scale of the city's human systems in the individual mind/brain/body system, a natural process of ongoing connecting generates a meshwork. A meshwork emerges from patterns in the brain/nervous system, resulting from the neuro-chemical connections of synapses and nerve endings that produce a hairnet-like mesh of axons (Bleys, Cowen, Groen, Hillen, & Ibrahim, 1996). A meshwork is characterized by major primary connective pathways that produce and intersect secondary, tertiary and many further levels of connectedness. It appears that a meshwork **self-organizes** connections and when a certain density and/or repeated use of pathways arises, a **hierarchy of complexity** emerges that enables the brain/body to replicate the patterns (and the capacities that arise from them) allowing retention of learning and efficiencies of energy use. This **cycle of self-organizing and hierarchical patterning** continues throughout a lifetime, allowing the brain/body to build up a repertoire of learned behavior while continuing its capacity for self-organizing adaptiveness to dynamic environments and never-ending stimuli (Hamilton, 2010).

The meshworking process lies at the heart of creativity that happens with unceasing regularity on the micro-scale as life conditions shift and change, but meshworking also manifests in creativity on a macro-scale that produces new structures, processes and patterns. These get locked into living systems (including our cities) like habits or intelligences and enable them to evolve over time. When we look at the history of cities we can see the emergence of distinctive eras that are marked by creative discoveries that produce structural changes (in other words Structural Intelligence) such as those emerging from harnessing a progression of denser energies like those from the wheel, the horse, the combustion engine and now the electric (driverless) car.

On an individual human level, we can map these embodied structures through fMRI scanning of our brains. On a city scale level, we can view them as the result of living the Principles and forming the Intelligences. We can also assess the co-related structures of consciousness that we manifest in the city as external artefacts through Traditional, Modern, Post-Modern or Integral levels of complexity (D. Beck, 2010; D. Beck, 2010; Dekay, 2011, Hamilton, 2010; Wilber, 2006).

The study of the psychology and sociology of human systems in cities reveals these meshworks as interconnected patterns of concepts, constructs, contexts and cultural systems (Cook-Greuter, 1999, 2002; Dawson-Tunik, 2005; De Landa, 1995, 2006; Esbjörn-Hargens & Zimmerman, 2009; O`Fallon, 2010). The evolutionary human capacity to make meaning (Bateson, 1972; Beck, 2000, 2001; Kegan, 1994; Kegan & Lahey, 2001) creates an ecology of mind that reveals, startling webs of meaningful relationships that have been discovered and rediscovered through a variety of processes: mind mapping (Buzan, 1988, 1989, 2001), thought clustering (Rico, 1983) archetypal patterning (Alexander, 1977; Cameron, 1992), meme mapping (Aunger, 2002; Beck & Cowan, 1996; Blackmore, 1999; Dawkins, 1976) and cultural coding (Rapaille, 2006). Landry (Landry & Murray, 2017) contends that creativity is multiperspectival, and suggests that the acts of observation, design and action (reminiscent of an action research cycle) are impacted by the very psychology of the actors involved in creating the city (proposed also by DeKay (2011)). Thus, evidence has emerged that shows that the creative connections that have emerged in our external bio-physical brain and material systems and structures, was precipitated by the creative con-nections that have arisen in our inner psychological mind (consciousness) and values-based relationships (cultures).

In other words—a meshwork is Integral and whole-centric. It manifests in realities that can be defined as objective, interobjective, subjective and intersubjective (as in Figure 4 and Appendix 2, Map 1). A meshwork is also fractal and its fractalness resonates at different scales in human systems: individuals, workplaces, healthcare systems, education institutions, communities, faith/recreation organizations and city hall (as shown in Map 4 in Appendix B).

Evolution's Creative Trajectory

Creativity that rests on the tendency of the universe to be connective is by definition both evolutionary and developmental. Creativity has a 13.7-billion-year trajectory, that enables us to look back and see the emergence of progressively more complex forms of creative consciousness and manifestation over the evolution of the universe and humankind. Cities, as outcomes of human creation can be situated along that line of development, unfolding progressively more complex city systems, cultures, characters and forms across history, geography, mythos, logos, ecologies and sustainability strategies (Hamilton, 2008).

In fact, the most complex systems that humans have created are our cities—living systems that embrace us and reflect us. And yet not all cities are created equal. With the proposition that creativity is "the great leveler", Florida (2005, p. 5) differentiated thriving cities from those that are merely surviving, proposing that certain human types, actions and organizational sectors contributed to city creativity in ways that set certain cities apart. However, more recently, Florida's research has revealed that creativity is not a mere mono-culture that cities can capture and exploit, but that creativity is a quality of city resilience and is transpersonal and cross-sectoral (Florida, 2005, 2008, 2017). This quality of transferable creativity enables cities to respond to change at any scale, arising from multiple causes including, unforeseen disasters or new political relationships. Ironically the "New Urban Crisis" that Florida (2017) identified recently can only be resolved by creating the conditions for creativity to flourish in all endeavors of the human hive as a continuous background (self-organizing) condition of the natural process of evolutionary meshworking.

It is becoming apparent that creativity is not a "nice-to-have" quality of the city, but a necessary one for a city to realize its highest potential. Creativity is a self-perpetuating pattern that can be amplified or thwarted by the life conditions we enable that encourage or block its continuous flow through the city.

Evolving Human Creativity into Gaia's Reflective Organ

Author of the Gaia hypothesis, James Lovelock (2009) proposes that humans are Gaia's most "reflective organ". This aligns with the distinctiveness of our species as homo sapiens sapiens—the human able to reflect on our own awareness. The study of the developmental, evolutionary capacity of human consciousness suggests that as consciousness matures, it grows from being ego-centric, to socio/other-centric to world-centric and finally Kosmo-centric (Beck & Cowan, 1996; Cook-Greuter, 1999, 2002; Dawson-Tunik, 2005; Kegan, 1994; O`Fallon, 2010; Torbert, Livne-Tarandach, Herdman-Barker, Nicolaides, & McCallum, 2008; Wilber, 1995, 2006). Thus, reflective capacity is not an absolute capacity but one that develops over a lifetime and evolves over a species' existence.

While each person has reflective capacity with potential for development along an ever-complexifying path, individuals have different centers of developmental gravity that reflect their emergent capacity (as do any collectives, or social holons that are comprised of multiple individuals).

In considering Lovelock's proposition that humans are reflective organs, we can consider that individuals are more like single cells within such a reflective organ. As such they are not likely to contribute their full potential until they have connected into a multi-purposed collective that functions like an organelle (or organelle system) in service to a greater city organ (Elizabeth Sahtouris, 1999, 2010, 2017) and eventually, as multiple cities, become a meta-system of interconnected organs in service to Gaia.

At today's stage of evolution of the city, Gaia's reflective organ is in a formative phase. It has not yet emerged a full operational ecology of symbiotic support that can serve both individual and collective survival as well as habitat renewal and thus Gaia's wellbeing (Taylor, 2008). But at the current stage of the city's emergence, individual cities are showing potential to become functioning organs of Gaia and are struggling to realize the inherent value of emerging a fully functioning organ capacity (that could eventually emerge into a trans-global organ system). For example, New York is the organ of trade and London is the organ of finance.

It is becoming possible to glimpse, in certain regions with advanced governance systems (like the Netherlands and the European Union) clusters of cities which might become the first (world-centric) "reflective organ" system (as was noted by Miller and his research team in the 1960's and 1970's (Miller, 1978)). Furthermore, the reality of this "reflectiveness" as visible light, is being mapped by Gulden from space (Florida, 2005, p. 22).

Creating Gaia's Organs and Processes of Innovation

Cities that thrive optimize creativity at all scales within the city. They operate as living systems designed not just as ecosystems for innovation as an end in themselves but in the context of creating wellbeing for all of Gaia's life. Book 2 (Hamilton, 2017) in our Integral City series outlined processes to impact innovation and wellbeing through placecaring and placemaking in the ecosystem of the city.

Those processes are grounded in Elisabet Sahtouris' Principles of Living Systems (as set out above). They give us a checklist to review the design guide that aligns how we "retrofit" our cities so that they operate with these Living Principles. The Principles enable placecaring and placemaking to emerge—but usually in a different sequence than the principles are set out above, because cities with a history and culture require a sequence of steps to align to those Principles and make change possible to the existing systems.

We suggest a natural sequence for the creative renewal of the city involves the key steps of: Discovery, Strategic Planning, Contexting Sustainability & Resilience, Connecting & Communicating and Governing. We can review a city's approaches to creative placecaring and placemaking with the steps set out in Table 3 below (with parenthetic links to the numbered sequence of the Principles of Living Systems from above).

Table 3: Steps for Creative Renewal of the City

DISCOVERY
1. Value history, traditions culture that works well for all (14)
2. Enable creative change to replace what does not work with what works better (15)
3. Create valued and valuable city vision with wisdom and resources for all (1)
4. Appreciate great diversity of the 4+1 Voices (producers, inventors/artists, resource allocators and integrators—citizens, business, civic managers, civil society) (2)

STRATEGIC PLAN
5. Create an innovation eco-system for a thriving economy that engages manufacturers, universities, business, innovation labs (7)
6. Create conditions for full employment through training from k-U, coordinating youth, interns, business, government (10)
7. Learn in school and practise day to day: mutual trust and respect; dialogue; feedback; teamwork; life-long learning and life-giving projects/processes for all (4)
8. Balance interests for healthy economy and wellbeing for all by engaging 4+1 Voices of the city in setting goals, planning, deciding (5)
CONTEXT SUSTAINABILITY & RESILIENCE
9. Create an integrated sustainability plan to measure sustainability climate, energy, water, food and finance for city and eco-region and create a circular economy (8)
10. Add value to economy and eco-region, nation, planet for resilience (6)
11. Create information systems that inform decisions for/with/as 4+1 Voices of the city and state, region, nation (9)
12. Be a model of sustainability & resilience for other cities in eco-region, nation, continent and planet (3)
13. Respond to stresses at all scales to create resilient city where stakeholders work together to create wellbeing conditions for all (13)
CONNECT & COMMUNICATE
14. Connect all Voices/Stakeholders with communication technology to optimize communication internally and the rest of world (9)
GOVERN
15. Design and practise governance that is fair, transparent, accountable, and accessible, so people feel safe, caring and relate to each other easily and often (11)
16. Balance efficient management of all city functions with extra resources so city is resilient to change (12)

VALUE AND ROLE OF CARE IN CREATIVITY

As explained in Chapter 1, the ground of being is characterized as Love and accessed by Goodness and is expressed as Beauty and Truth (see

Appendix B Map 5). Thus, creative connections are intrinsically emerging from the involutionary influence of Source as Love and the evolutionary expression of Goodness, Beauty and Truth through the emergence of Resources in the circles of care in human systems. In other words, creativity is inextricably inspired by Love of which we become more conscious as our conscious development wakes us up to expand the circles of care from self to others to city to planet to Kosmos. The profound implications of this relationship of Love to care and creativity have been deeply explored by Mark DeKay (2011) in *Integral Sustainable Design*, where he describes the impact of expanding care on the designer, the creative process and the design outcome (as quoted by Hamilton, 2017, p.373).

In the city, we have not only the effects of creative designers, but the impacts of the acts of the 4 Voices as creative citizens, civic managers, civil society and businesses. Moreover, the city contains this ever-evolving meshwork of creativity through the self-organizing and ordering actions of multiple scales of humanity simultaneously. The infinite potential for creativity could be the source of an infinite potential for chaos. But the cycles of meshworking are governed by the power of caring that manifest in the order that care can bring (as seen in the energetic flow through Source, Field and Resource as described in Chapter 1, Figure 3).

For creative acts or creative outcomes are only likely to sustain their existence if they are of service to the alignment of care at all levels of scale. For example, driverless cars must bring rewards not only to individuals, but families, businesses/organizations, neighborhoods, communities and the city as a whole.

In other words, it appears that the cells and organelles in Gaia's reflective organ are rescued from chaos and brought into order by the power and alignment of care.

Align Caring and Creativity with Aliveness

One of the more confounding differences between the human hive and the beehive (see Appendix E) is the existence for the bees of an energy-based goal that informs and motivates the cycle of conformity enforcement and diversity generation (for more on diversity generation see Chapter 8). While the beehive works toward the survival objective of producing 20 kilos of honey per year, the human hive for the most part has disconnected from (or not yet formulated) any such unifying objective.

Despite the fact that the human capacity for reflection enables infinite creativity, ironically the disconnection from a purpose-driven feedback loop sets up the conditions for creativity without care or context. Without purpose, care or context for the endless contributions of creativity, the human hive wastes not only its inner reflective resources but its outer energy resources as well. In order to find our way back to the alignment of caring and creativity (and the expression of Beauty), architect Christopher Alexander (2002) suggested that we examine the qualities of aliveness (that are outlined in Table 4) as we create artefacts for the city. He notes (as we have proposed above) that we get creativity for free—it is built into the natural order of things. Furthermore, Alexander (2002, p. 239) in his designs, deeply anchors aliveness and creativity to strong centers, which I propose arise from the alignment of circles of care, context and capacity building.

Table 4: Alexander's Qualities of Aliveness (Alexander, 2002, p.239)

• Levels of scale
• Strong centers
• Boundaries
• Alternating repetition
• Positive space
• Good shape
• Local symmetries
• Deep interlock and ambiguity
• Contrast
• Gradients
• Roughness
• Echoes
• The void
• Simplicity and inner calm
• Not-separatedness

Creative Impulse Emerges Master Code of Care

If, aliveness drives the creative impulse at the center of our nature, it also drives and emerges the Principles of Living Systems and Integral City Intelligences. With that dynamic, the conditions are set to emerge the Master Code of Care.

The Integral City Master Code is a synthesis of all the Living System Principles into 4 key injunctions:

- **Care for your SELF (so that you can)**
- **Care for OTHERS (so that all of us can)**
- **Care for our PLACES (so that together we can)**
- **Care for our PLANET.**

Each of the Principles of Living Systems when applied at the scale of the city, appears to embrace all 4 scales of the Master Code—self, others, place, planet. We propose further, that the Integral City Master Code calls forth a 4-part practise that is essentially spiritual (explored further in Chapters 1 and 3).

Moreover, practising all 4 levels of care simultaneously has become possible to accomplish for the first time in history because of the stage of evolution human systems have emerged in the "organelles" of organizations, technology, communication and communities. That means that each level of care builds the context and capacity to enable care at the next level.

If we want to know how to practise the care that we seek to live with this Master Code, we need only pay attention to the Principles of Living Systems. They provide us both the course that creative life should naturally follow, and the directions for "course correction" of our creative activities through the discipline of care.

Practising the Principles of Living Systems with intention and attention in/with/as the Integral City reveals that they offer guidance not only for the expression of our Intelligences but also for creatively designing, strategizing and learning the lessons of sustainability and resilience.

The great reward is that by honoring the Principles of Living Systems, we create the conditions for an evolutionary emergence that not only generates but coheres Integral City Intelligences with the Master Code of

care. It creates a beautiful meshwork of human systems at the city scale—
summarized in Table 5 below.

Table 5: Meshwork Sahtouris' Principles of Healthy Living Systems, Integral City Intelligences, Master Code of Care, Innovation Ecosystem

(Elisabet Sahtouris from Planetary & Personal Health 1 July 2009 and Notes by Marilyn Hamilton relating to Integral City Intelligence (from Integral City: Evolutionary Intelligences for the Human Hive, January 2010)

Sahtouris' Living Systems Principles	Integral City Intelligences	Master Code of Care	Integral City @ Thriving Innovation Ecosystem
Self-creation (auto-poiesis)	Eco-Emergence-Living	Self/Others/ Place/Planet	Create valued and valuable city with wisdom and resources for all (3)
Complexity (diversity of parts)	Eco-Emergence	Self/Others/ Place/Planet	Appreciate great diversity of producers, inventors/artists, resource allocators and integrator—citizens, business, civic managers, civil society (4)
Embeddedness in larger holons and dependence on them (holarchy)	Integral-Living	Self/Others/ Place/Planet	Be a model of sustainability & resilience for other cities in eco-region, nation, continent, planet (12)
Self-reflexivity (autognosis, self-knowledge)	Integral-Inner-Cultural	Self/Others/ Place/Planet	Learn in school and practise day to day mutual trust and respect; dialogue; feedback; teamwork; life-long learning and life-giving projects/processes for all (7)
Self-regulation/ maintenance (auto-nomics) balancing efficiency and resil-ience	Integral-Living	Self/Others/ Place/Planet	Balance interests for healthy econ-omy and wellbeing for all by engag-ing 4 Voices of the city in setting goals, planning, deciding (8)
Response-ability to internal and external stress or change	Integral-Inner-Outer-Social–Cultural	Self/Others/ Place/Planet	Add value to economy and eco-region, nation, planet for resil-ience (10)
Input/output of matter, energy and information with other holons	Living-Inner-Outer-Social	Self/Others/ Place/Planet	Create innovation eco-system for thriving economy that engages manufacturers, universities, busi-ness, innovation labs (5)
Transformation of matter, energy and information; no non-recyclable waste	Eco-Living-Inner-Social	Self/Others/ Place/Planet	Create an integrated sustainability plan to measure sustainability cli-mate, energy, water, food, finance for city and eco-region and create circular economy (9)

Sahtouris' Living Systems Principles	Integral City Intelligences	Master Code of Care	Integral City @ Thriving Innovation Ecosystem
Communication among all parts	Integral-Inquiry-Meshworking-Navigating	Self/Others/Place/Planet	Create information systems that inform decisions for/with/as 4 Voices of the city and state, region, nation (11) Connect all Voices/Stakeholders with communication technology to optimize communication internally and rest of world (14)
Empowerment, full employment of all component parts	Eco-Emergence-Living-Meshworking	Self/Others/Place/Planet	Create conditions for full employment through training from k-U, coordinating youth, interns, business, government (6)
Coordination of parts and functions	Eco-Emergence-Living-Meshworking-Navigating	Self/Others/Place/Planet	Design and practise governance that is fair, transparent, accountable, accessible, so people feel safe, caring and relate to each other easily and often (15)
Balance of interests negotiated among parts, whole and embedding holarchy	Eco-Emergence-Living-Inquiry	Self/Others/Place/Planet	Balance efficient management of all city functions with extra resources so city is resilient to change (16)
Reciprocity of parts in mutual contribution and assistance	Eco-Emergence-Living-Meshworking	Self/Others/Place/Planet	Respond to stresses at all scales to create resilient city where stakeholders work together to create wellbeing conditions for all (13)
Conservation of what works well	Eco-Emergence-Living-Meshworking	Self/Others/Place/Planet	Value history, traditions culture that works well for all (1)
Innovation, creative change of what does not work well	Eco-Emergence-Living-Evolutionary	Self/Others/Place/Planet	Enable creative change to replace what does not work with what works better (2)

Note: Numbers in brackets in column 4 indicate cross-reference to the sequence of steps set out for developing Innovation Ecosystems above.

LESSONS FOR ALIGNING CREATIVITY WITH PRINCIPLES, INTELLIGENCES & CARE

It seems that Sahtouris, Laszlo, Graves, Bloom, Holling and Diamond have come to similar conclusions. Although, life conditions change (because of the interaction of the bio-psycho-cultural-social human systems with landscape, climate, ecology, and/or other cultures), in order to survive, both individuals and groups in the global human system must now make some conscious, caring, creative choices before our status quo traps us or kills us. As a living system, caring is in our spiritual DNA; connection-making is our built-in quality; and creativity is our birthright. Our human hives need to shift from uncaring or careless connecting and happenstance creativity to care-full connecting and collaborative co-creativity to live into our evolutionary potential as Gaia's "reflective organ".

Perhaps the lessons of the honey bee (Appendix E) can inform us of the simple rules to which we need to pay attention in order to prevent the collapse of human hive systems? For humans that must mean a re-embrace of our legacy of caring, so that the patterns of creativity and the principles of sustainability expand within our human hives through redesigning systems and structures (Alexander, 1977, 2002), reinventing organizations (Laloux,2014) and including beyond our human hives (Sahtouris, 1999, 2010, 2017; Patten, 2018) care for the eco-regions we can potentially renew. It seems imperative that a core strategy that human systems need to adopt is to move from an ego-centric internally focused form of city development to an eco-centric externally focused form of development so that cities contribute to the creative thriving of the eco-regions that supports our human hives. By expanding our circles of care, we will naturally contribute to the thriving of our cities as "reflective organs" in service to our eco-regions. And perhaps, this would be the natural evolutionary stage that would eventually enable the development of a world-centric "reflective organ" system (and eventually even a Kosmo-centric one)?

If cities are to be Gaia's "reflective organs", we must ask ourselves, how do we develop such a caring, creative, reflective organ?

An Integral view of the city sees the human hive as a living system, fully capable of operating as an organ with organelle/role structures that enable the emergence of caring, reflective intelligences (Hamilton, 2008, 2010, 2017b). As such the human hive has the potential to emerge qualities that create optimal conditions for human innovation and emergence and eco-regional resilience.

The human hive, acts as the container to magnify and focus the caring capacities of individual reflectiveness into a collective intelligence that has the potential to become Gaia's true "organ of reflection".

In order to create a path forward, here are the lessons that we need to shift our cities into creating Gaia's creative, caring "reflective organ":

1. Accept the evolutionary calling of our human hives as Gaia's "reflective organ" and create systems of conscious reflection eco-regionally at first, and then transglobally as possible. Discover the caring purpose for each city. What is the equivalent of the city's 20 kilos of honey that enables city survival and eco-regional resilience?

2. Enable connections of all kinds across all scales of human systems.

3. Encourage creativity that not only experiments and discovers new possibilities as diversity generation, but cares to serve an eco-centric level of being that understands its energy needs, eco-regional effects and powers of consciousness.

4. Recalibrate creativity to greater levels of caring and complexity in the city as emergent capacities evolve.

5. Meshwork with intention to expand the circles of care and connect leaders in and across all scales of human endeavor, with a particular focus at the scale of healthy organelles/organizations (Laloux, 2014).

6. Notice the messages of our organelles/roles. What are our 4+1 Voices saying and doing?—make their communications and actions transparent, accountable and open to discussion.

7. Invent and implement feedback systems (vital signs monitors) that report the status of care, from quadrants, levels of complexity, holons with distributed input and core commentary (interpretation).

8. See the human hive as a microcosm of the World:

   a. Ego-Centric—self caring, self surviving

   b. Socio/Ethno-Centric—homogenous neighborhoods, ghettos, local ecologies calling for "We-centric" care

   c. World-Centric—city in caring service to eco region ecologies and all living beings

   d. Kosmo-Centric—city in caring service to Earth /solar system/ galaxy/universe.

9. Each individual plus all our systems of development should develop four quadrant ego-ethno-world-Kosmo-centric practices to evolve our caring and consciousness.

10. Be ready to shift caring behaviors in worldcentric cities because our knowledge and spheres of influence with other parts of the world enable us to be models for viable care and change.

If the intelligence of bees enables the thriving of their hives, species and environment (even in the face of Colony Collapse Disorder), surely the creative intelligence of humans can enable the expansion of our circles of care and the thriving of our cities, species and environment?

REFERENCES

Abrams, N. E., & Primack, J. R. (2006). *The View from the Centre of the Universe: Discovering our Extraordinary Place in the Cosmos.* New York: Riverhead Books, Penguin Group.

Alexander, C. (1977). *A Pattern Language.* USA: Oxford University Press.

Alexander, C. (2002). *The Phenomenon of Life.* (September 1, 2004 ed. Vol. 1). Berkeley, CA: Center for Environmental Structure.

Aunger, R. (2002). *The Electric Meme: A New Theory of How We Think.* New York, NY: The Free Press

Bateson, G. (1972). *Steps to an Ecology of Mind.* New York: Chandler Publishing Company, Ballantine Books, Inc.

Beck, D. (2000). MeshWORKS™: A Second Tier Perspective & Process. The Spiral Dynamics Group.

Beck, D. (2001). Human capacities in the integral age: How value systems shape organizational productivity, national prosperity & global transformation. Paper presented at the International Productivity Conference. Retrieved from http://www.integralworld.net/beck7.html

Beck, D. (2002). Spiral Dynamics in the Integral Age. Paper presented at the Spiral Dynamics integral, Level 1.

Beck, D. (2010). Natural Designs for Meshworking. Retrieved from Gaiaspace, Meshworking, Private

Beck, D. (2010). personal email communication. In M. Hamilton (Ed.) (Meshworking ed.). Abbotsford, BC.

Beck, D., & Cowan, C. (1996). *Spiral Dynamics: Mastering Values, Leadership and Change*. Malden, MA: Blackwell Publishers.

Beck, D., & Linscott, G. (2006). *The Crucible: Forging South Africa's Future* (hardcover ed.). Columbia, MD: Cherie Beck, Coera.us, Center for Human Emergence.

Benjamin, A., & McCullum, B. (2009). *A World Without Bees*. London, UK: Guardian Books.

Blackmore, S. (1999). *The Meme Machine*. Oxford, UK: Oxford University Press.

Bleys, R. L. A. W., Cowen, T., Groen, G. J., Hillen, B., & Ibrahim, N. B. N. (1996). Perivascular Nerves of the Human Basal Cerebral Arteries I. Topographical Distribution(16), 1034–1047. Retrieved from http://journals.sagepub.com/doi/full/10.1097/00004647-199609000-00029 doi:10.1097/00004647-199609000-00029

Brackney, S. (2009). *Plan Bee: Everything You Ever Wanted to Know About the Hardestworking Creatures on the Planet*. New York, NY: Penguin Group Inc.

Brown, B. (2005a). Theory and Practice of Integral Sustainable Development—An Overview, Part 1: Quadrants and the Practitioner. AQAL Journal, 1(2).

Brown, B. (2005b). Theory and Practice of Integral Sustainable Development—An Overview, Part 2: Values, Developmental Levels and Natural Design. AQAL Journal, 1(2).

Brown, B. (2005c). Theory and Practice of Integral Sustainable Development—An Overview, Part 3: Current Initiatives and Applications. AQAL Journal, 1(2).

Buzan, T. (1988). *Make the Most of Your Mind*. London: Pan.

Buzan, T. (1989). *Use Your Head*. London: BBC Books.

Buzan, T. (2001). *Head Strong*. London: Thorsons, HarperCollins Publishers.

Cameron, J. (1992). *The Artist's Way*. New York: Jeremy P. Tarcher/Putnam Books.

Capra, F. (1996). *The Web of Life: A New Scientific Understanding of Living Systems*. New York: Anchor Books, Doubleday.

Cook-Greuter, S. (1999). *Postautonomous ego development: its nature and measurement*. Unpublished Doctoral dissertation, UMI Dissertation Information Services UMI #9933122, Harvard Graduate School of Education, Cambridge, MA.

Cook-Greuter, S. (2002). The development of action logics in detail. Retrieved from www.cook-greuter.com

Dawkins, R. (1976). *The Selfish Gene*. Oxford, UK: Oxford University Press.

Dawson-Tunik, T. L., Commons, M. L., Wilson, M., & Fischer, K. W. (2005). The shape of development. The European Journal of Developmental Psychology, 2(2), 163–196.

DeKay, M. (2011). *Integral Sustainable Design: Transformative Perspectives*. London, UK: Earthscan.

De Landa, M. (1995). Homes: Meshwork or Hierarchy? *http://www.mediamatic.net/article-200.5956.html*. Special: Home issue. Retrieved Dec. 4, 2004

De Landa, M. (2006). *A New Philosophy of Society: Assemblage Theory and Social Complexity*. London: Continuum.

Esbjörn-Hargens, S., & Zimmerman, M. (2009). *Integral Ecology: Uniting Multiple Perspectives on the Natural World*. Boston: Shambhala Publications Inc.

Florida, R. (2005). *Cities and the Creative Class*. New York: Routledge.

Florida, R. (2008). *Who's Your City: How the Creative Economy is Making Where to Live the Most Important Decision of Your Life*. Toronto: Random House Canada.

Florida, R. (2017). *The New Urban Crisis: How Our Cities Are Increasing Inequality, Deepening Segregation, and Failing the Middle Class—and What We Can Do About It*. New York: Basic Books.

Gould, J. L., & Gould, C. G. (1988). *The Honey Bee: Scientific American Library*.

Graves, C. (2003). *Levels of Human Existence: Transcription of a Seminar at Washington School of Psychiatry, Oct. 16, 1971*. Santa Barbara: Eclet Publishing.

Gunderson, L. C., & Holling, C. S. (Eds.). (2002). *Panarchy: Understanding Transformations in Human and Natural Systems*. Washington, DC: Island Press.

Hamilton, M. (2006, 7/15/2006). Sustainable Beehives: Lessons and Strategies for Sustainable Cities? Sense in the City 1.8. Retrieved August 24, 2010

Hamilton, M. (2007). Approaching Homelessness: An Integral Reframe. [Philosophy]. World Futures: The Journal of General Evolution, Volume 63(2), 107–126.

Hamilton, M. (2008). *Integral City: Evolutionary Intelligences for the Human Hive*. Gabriola Island BC: New Society Publishers.

Hamilton, M. (2009). How Much Is Enough? Evolving Lessons From the Beehive. Paper presented at the UBC Life and Career Centre.

Hamilton, M. (2010). Meshworking Integral Intelligences for Resilient Environments; Enabling Order and Creativity in the Human Hive. Paper presented at the Enacting an Integral Future Conference.

Hamilton, M. (2011). Monitoring and Releasing the Creative Energy of Cities: A Practical Frameworks for Measuring What Really Makes the Difference [Practical tools]. City, Culture and Society, 2(1), unpublished manuscript.

Hamilton, M. (2017a). Integral City: Meshworking Evolutionary Intelligences for the Human Hive and Eco-Region Resilience. Retrieved from http://integralcity.com/

Hamilton, M (2017b). *Integral City Action & Inquiry: Designing Impact for the Human Hive*. Tucson, AZ: Integral Publishers.

Holling, C. S. (2001). Understanding the Complexity of Economic, Ecological, and Social Systems Ecosystems, Vol. 4, pp. 390–405.

Holling, C. S. (2003). From Complex Regions to Complex Worlds. University of Florida.

Kauffman, S. A. (1993). *The Origins of Order: Self-Organization and Selection in Evolution*. New York, Oxford Press.

Kegan, R. (1994). *In Over Our Heads: The Mental Demands of Modern Life*. Cambridge, MA: Harvard University Press.

Kegan, R., & Lahey, L. L. (2001). *How the Way We Talk Can Change the Way We Work: Seven Languages for Transformation*. San Francisco: Jossey-Bass.

Koestler, A. (1976). The Ghost in the Machine. New York, NY: Random House.

Laloux, F. (2014). *Reinventing Organizations*. Retrieved from http://www.reinventin-gorganizations.com/purchase.html.

Landry, C. (2007). *The Art of City Making*. London, UK: Earthscan Comedia.

Landry, C., & Wood, P. (2008). *The Intercultural City: Planning for Diversity Advantage*. London, UK: Earthscan.

Landry, C., & Murray, C. (2017). *Psychology & the City*. Bournes Green Near Stroud, UK: Comedia.

Laszlo, E. (2004). *Science and the Akashic Field: An Integral Theory of Everything* (2007 ed.). Rochester, Vermont: Inner Traditions.

Lovelock, J. (2009). *The Vanishing Face of Gaia*. New York: Harmony Books.

Maturana, H., & Varela, F. (1987, 1992). *The Tree of Knowledge*. Boston: Shambhala.

Miller, J. G. (1978). *Living Systems*. New York: McGraw-Hill Book Company.

Mitchell, E., & Williams, D. (2001). *The Way of the Explorer: An Apollo Astronaut's Journey Through the Material and Mystical Worlds* (2nd ed.). Buenos Aires: Richter Artes Graficas.

O'Fallon, T. (2010). The Collapse of the Wilber Combs Matrix: The Interpenetration of the State and Structure Stages. Paper presented at the Enacting an Integral Future Conference.

Patten, T. (2018). *A New Republic of the Heart: An Ethos for Revolutionaries (Sacred Activism)*: North Atlantic Books.

Rapaille, C. (2006). *The Culture Code: An Ingenious Way to Understand Why People Around the World Live and Buy as They Do*. New York, NY: Broadway Books.

Rico, G. L. (1983). *Writing the Natural Way*. Los Angeles: Jeremy P. Tarcher Inc.

Sahtouris, E. (1999). *Earthdance: Living Systems in Evolution*. Available from http://www.ratical.org/LifeWeb/

Sahtouris, E. (2010). Celebrating Crisis: Towards a Culture of Cooperation. A *New Renaissance:Transforming Science, Spirit & Society*. London: Floris Books.

Sahtouris, E. (2017). A Tale of Cities and Cells: Our Human Evolutionary Agenda. Retrieved December 7, 2017 https://www.ethicalmarkets.com/a-tale-of-cities-and-cells-by-elisabet-sahtouris/

Taylor, G. (2008). *Evolution's Edge: The Coming Collapse and Transformation of our World*. Gabriola Island, BC: New Society Publishers.

Torbert, W. R., Livne-Tarandach, R., Herdman-Barker, E., Nicolaides, A., & McCallum, D. (2008). Developmental Action Inquiry:A Distinct Integral Theory That Actually Integrates Developmental Theory, Practice, and Research. Paper presented at the Conference—Integral Theory In Action: Serving Self, Community and Kosmos.

Wilber, K. (1995). *Sex, Ecology and Spirituality: the spirit of evolution*. Boston: Shambhala Publications Inc.

Wilber, K. (1996). *A Brief History of Everything*, . Boston,: Shambhala Publications Inc.

Wilber, K. (2000). *A Theory of Everything*. Boston: Shambhala Publications Inc.

Wilber, K. (2006). *Integral Spirituality*. Boston: Shambhala Publications Inc.

Wilber, K. (2007). *The Integral Vision*. Boston: Shambhala Publications Inc.

Winston, M. L. (2014). *Bee Time: Lessons from the Hive*. Boston: Harvard University Press.

THE MASTER CODE OF CARE FOR INDIVIDUAL, COLLECTIVE AND CITY WELLBEING

CHAPTER SUMMARY

This chapter reviews the history of the Master Code: take care of yourself; take care of others; take care of this place; take care of this planet. It considers the practice of mastering the Master Code and frames out its connections to Integral City's 4 Voices and 12 Intelligences with examples from the Master Codes' four scales of manifestation: Self, Others, Place, Planet. It proposes a way to calculate deep happiness as an outcome of living the Master Code simultaneously at all 4 scales and concludes with core rewards of doing so.

Keywords: Master Code, happiness, Voices, Intelligences, Self, Other, Place, Planet

> *Take care of yourself.*
> *Take care of others.*
> *Take care of this place.*
> *Take care of this planet.*

DISCOVERING THE MASTER CODE

When I was writing Book 1 in the Integral City series (*Integral City: Evolutionary Intelligences for the Human Hive*) I had explored all the intelligences except the Evolutionary Intelligence. When I came to write this final chapter, I realized that the twelve intelligences evolved from a Master Code that governed the human hive. According to an urban myth, the essentials of this code had been discovered at the neighborhood scale in a public school where the principal announced to the teachers, administration and students, that the way the school would be managed would be that everyone would follow three rules. The rules were: to take care of their individual selfs, take care of each other and take care of this place. (Was it originally from New Zealand, America, Canada? All had versions of the story.) However, I realized that the code (especially with the addition of the planetary scale) was a fractal intelligence of a species DNA and also a meta-intelligence that guided our wellbeing on all scales from individual to group to city to planet.

When I was writing Book 2 in the Integral City series (*Integral City Inquiry & Action: Designing Impact for the Human Hive*) embracing the Master Code became a key section (with two chapters) in the Placecaring Part I of the book. There I described how practising the Master Code expands our circles of care.

In exploring the Master Code, I have often repeated the question many ask me, "What can our cities do for us?" This inquiry inspired my organization, Integral City Meshworks (in September 2012) to launch a month-long Action Research Inquiry about how the 12 Intelligences of an Integral City could help us develop a new operating system for the city (Integral City 2.0) for the purpose of the city doing more for us.

We brought together 60 Integral City Pioneers—three to five for each of the twelve Integral City intelligences (see Appendix C). Each spoke for the value of that particular intelligence to the city. Thought Leaders explored with us, **What** *is this intelligence?* Designers framed for us, **So What** *is important about incorporating this intelligence into city life?* And Practitioners told us, **Now What** *can we do to implement this intelligence in service to the wellbeing of the Human Hive?*

We used a methodology that was built on the DNA of the Master Code for the human hive as stated at the beginning of this chapter.

It was critical to hear from as many of the 4 Voices as possible in the city. The 4 Voices of the city were introduced in Book I of the Integral City series; and their efficacy explored in Book 2. These 4 Voices represent the core roles that enable the wellbeing of the human hive:

1. Citizens

2. Civil Society

3. Civic Managers (City Government/Institutions)

4. Business/Organizations

The power of bringing together our City Pioneers and our City Voices produced an exponential learning blast. It was like an explosion of WE power that is still circling the earth like volcanic emissions. This kind of blast cast a radically optimistic outfall of evolutionary patterns across our planet of cities.

Our conference started with a passionate question: **How can we design a new operating system for the city that allows us to thrive**—to be fully human? (The conference is fully documented as a report (Hamilton & Sanders, 2013a) and in over 600 pages of the proceedings (Hamilton & Sanders, 2013b).

Why was that question so important to us? I believe it was because we cared so much about life that we could bring our *individual* intelligence(s) to bear on how to add value to it! But when we asked this question in the company of others, it also assumed that collectively we care enough about life that we can bring our *collective* intelligence to bear on how to add value to it.

Here was the trick we discovered—we found in our inquiry that humans can be both as caring and intelligent for ourselves, as for our species and all life on earth. But paradoxically, we discovered that we can only realize this possibility if we *all* have a chance to experience that caring. (In Africa they have an expression for this—Ubuntu—I *am because you are*.)

So, if we are not just to survive, but thrive, we must wake up (at scale), grow up (as activators of city change), goal up and whole up (as noted in the Introduction). This means we take responsibility on all four scales of the Master Code.

Just as the apocryphal principal who set out the code of conduct for his school, we found it to be an equally simple and powerful code of conduct for enabling a thriving city. Thus, we have come to claim it as the **Master Code of Care for the Human Hive**.

The paradoxical and powerful qualities about this Master Code, lead us to explore how to practice it on a regular basis—through meditation, inquiry, action and impact. (We explained how to explore the Master Code through all scales in Book 2, Chapter 3 (Hamilton, 2017)).

Most of us are too busy just living our lives to observe how a "practice" which commits us to a sustained or regular activity can instill a new habit. But, paying attention to what we care about, is one of the first practices worth engaging in (even as we suggested in Book 2—with a playful attitude).

MASTERY OF THE MASTER CODE

We have discovered that beyond the first level of discovery, there is a second level of "mastery" to the Master Code. It lies in the power of practising each level of the code to expand a related "Circle of Care". Each level is more complex than the one before. This means that, as we learn to practise the basics of taking care of our self, then a surprising thing happens—we develop the capacity to take care of each other.

And when we learn well how to take care of each other—on different scales from family, to tribe, to organization, to sector, to community, to city and nation—then we develop even more capacity to take care of this place or city.

And when we learn to take care of our place—whether that is our home (apartment, house), our work place, our neighborhood, or our city, then we can learn to take care of our eco-region, and our planet. Thus, as the scale of the place increases, so do our circles of care.

Finally, we realize that all the elements of the Master Code: take care of yourself; take care of others; take care of this place; take care of this planet—are not really separate from each other. They are not in conflict with one another. In fact, we can acknowledge each element as the same command at different levels of scale. Each of these elements of the Master Code surpasses and includes one another, in a kind of graceful developmental sequence.

INTELLIGENCE IN THE MASTER CODE

When we discovered the transpersonal power of the Master Code, we came to appreciate how this code gave rise to the 12 Intelligences in the City. In turn, we came to recognize how the Master Code synthesizes the Principles of Living Systems (as explored in Chapter 2). We could also link the Master

Code to the relationship of the 4 Voices of the city to each other and to the human hive they serve (as set out in the story of the bees in Appendix E).

This is why, we explored with conference members, in the 2012 Online Conference their relationship to the Voices and their cities of interest. We asked:

How do you see yourself in relation to the city? Which voice is the one you express most often when you are in the city? Maybe you express more than one of these Voices? When you choose one, think about the opportunities that you have to contribute to the intelligence of the city—whether that be as:

Citizen

Civil Society

Civic Manager, or

Business/Organization.

From these simple questions, and the responses shared by conference participants, we came to realize how the circles of care arising through each voice became an expression of one or more Integral City intelligences, that focused the Master Code on the city in a particular way.

Furthermore, when we stood back and took a meta-view of the interaction of the Integral City Intelligences and the Master Code at the three scales internally within the city (self, others, place), we could hear a fifth voice—which was the external exchange between cities. We recognized this fifth voice often manifested as a competitive voice in the modern and post-modern eras of industrial development and early globalization (and even a combative voice in pre-modern cities—something that is still alive in inter-city sports tournaments and as a voice that connects the cities to the land in traditional and indigenous eras). But as the four internal city Voices reached out beyond their own cities first to the regions with which they traded, and then to the ecological regions that supported their environmental footprint, this fifth Voice of the inter-city exchanges moved beyond combat and competition into early forms of collaboration and in some cases coordination. The evolution of the fifth Voice made possible the emergence of the fourth scale of complexity for cities—namely to see themselves not just as individual or even regional entities but as a planet of cities who could thrive more by working together than standing apart. Ultimately our planet of cities is evolving together as we practise the Integral City Intelligences that inevitably expands our circles of care to the scale of the planet of cities. (This is how I believe our cities are evolving into what James Lovelock recognized as Gaia's Reflective Organ (Lovelock, 2009) and ultimately Gaia's Reflective Organ *System*.)

In working with different cities, we have come to see that the 4 Voices demonstrate Integral City Intelligences at all 4 levels of expression of the Master Code.

In the following four tables we build on the examples given in Book 2 (Chapter 4) (Hamilton, 2017) by adding to the self, others and place, the planetary perspective in column 4. This shows how the intelligences can be practised by the 4 Voices at all scales. The fourth column in each table suggests how "taking care of this planet" expands the capacity of the Evolutionary Intelligence in cities. The third row gives city examples.

We start with Table 6 to show four examples of how **Citizens** practice the Master Code and increase the intelligence of the city and planet of cities.

Table 6: Increasing Intelligences from Citizens Caring for Self, Other, Place, Planet

Take Care of Yourself	Take Care of Each Other	Take Care of this Place	Take Care of this Planet
Individuals practise cleansing, connecting, and crowning personal energies for individual and collective clarity of expression.	Leaders improve their effectiveness with the "We" of groups, teams and organizations by integrating structures, cultures and caring for the system.	Activists work together with universities, business and city workers for common wellbeing of the city and the planet.	Link your personal connections in other cities to universities, business and city workers for shared wellbeing of the city in a planet of cities.
This produces Outer Intelligence for acting with authenticity.	This produces Integral Intelligence that allows you to align individuals and groups as you do your work in the city.	This produces Ecosphere Intelligence that makes you aware of the context of the city's eco-region and how it is important to each and all of us.	This increases Evolutionary Intelligence through the actions of individuals that evolves the capacities of Gaia's Reflective Organ in the city, eco-region, continent and planet.
ARGO/IZHEVSK, RUSSIA	DURANT, OK	THE NATURAL STEP/ WHISTLER	MONTERREY, WHEEL OF CO-CREATION

Table 7 shows four examples how **Civic Managers** in Government and/ or Institutions can practice the Master Code and increase the intelligence of the city and planet of cities.

Table 7: Increasing Intelligences from Civic Managers Caring for Self, Other, Place, Planet

Take Care of Yourself	Take Care of Each Other	Take Care of this Place	Take Care of this Planet
Individual designers and architects make their dreams for new city governance real by challenging the status quo with experiments in eco-villages and renewable energy production that engage the many individuals in new forms of engagement to achieve a goal.	Villagers in the developing world (and/or underprivileged city areas) discover how they can mesh themselves and message their story about how climate change affects them, so neighbors learn how to cooperate with each other and local governments, and also national, regional and global institutions.	Investment fund managers using principles based on living systems open up whole new standards for economies, environments, social and cultural pillars of sustainability and resilience at all scales—from public, to private, city, nation, and globe.	Civic Managers can form professional associations to share Best Practices of managing cities based on living systems to grow economies, environments, social and cultural structures for pan-regional sustainability and resilience at all scales.
This produces Structural Intelligence that gives the Designer many new ideas and engages the Residents in co-designing city structures.	This produces Meshworking Intelligence where all the people, priorities, purposes and planet line up—connecting all the dots.	This produces Navigating Intelligence that uses metrics based on living systems, natural capital and strengthens city and citizen alike.	This increases Evolutionary Intelligence at the city scale that expands the impact of cities across regions and the globe as reflective organs of Gaia.
STRATHCONA, CANADA EKURHULENI, S. AFRICA	EL SALVADOR	AQAL INVESTMENT	CITY PROTOCOL SOCIETY, BARCELONA

Table 8 shows four examples how **Business/Organizations** can practice the Master Code and increase the intelligence of the city and planet of cities.

Table 8: Increasing Intelligences from Business Caring for Self, Other, Place, Planet

Take Care of Yourself	Take Care of Each Other	Take Care of this Place	Take Care of this Planet
Leaders have the power to transact, translate, transform and transduce the entire supply chain of business interests and economies.	Private Sector Employers use Appreciative Inquiry to unlock the energy of stakeholders, who: discover they have the wisdom to develop new transportation systems for the city: dream new technology solutions; design ways of changing mobility in the city; and deliver new decision making processes to connect private and public sectors with all city Voices.	Major banks redefine their service to the city in terms of catalyzing generative relationships and revise their collaborative functions accordingly.	The entire private supply chain can make explicit the Purpose of the city in service to a planet of cities and reframe their services to the city in terms of serving the wellbeing of the person, groups, city and planet simultaneously.
This produces Evolutionary Intelligence where the city uses an economic metabolism so matter, energy and information flow through it to sustain prosperity and life.	This produces Inquiry Intelligence that allows for experiments, uncertainty and learning together.	This produces Emergence Intelligence and releases the power of place, so that the intractable problems related to water, food, energy, climate and finance are approached with full human consciousness and greatest cultural values.	This increases Evolutionary Intelligence for economic metabolism at the city, regional and global scale that is aligned and supportive of the flow of energy, matter and information for the wellbeing of individuals, cities, regions and the health of the planet.
EINDHOVEN, NL	EDMONTON, CANADA	RABOBANK— AMSTERDAM, NL	INTERFACE CARPET

Table 9 shows four examples how Civil Society can practice the Master Code and increase the intelligence of the city and planet of cities.

Table 9: Increasing Intelligences from Civil Society Caring for Self, Other, Place, Planet

Take Care of Yourself	Take Care of Each Other	Take Care of this Place	Take Care of this Planet
City faith leaders (from churches, temples and synagogues) invite citizens to see themselves as spiritually empowered contributors to the city.	Civil society members catalyze and support neighborhoods to build together art-based gathering places.	Citizen Observatories convene the collective WE even in bankrupt cities and cities under siege, so people can share how they discover capacities for city change.	Civil Society Faith Communities, Observatories and other NGO's can connect on a regional and global basis to share discoveries about new capacities for city change.
This produces Inner Intelligence for the civil society members and citizens at the same time.	This produces Cultural Intelligence where people tell the stories that bond them together and build community.	This produces Living Intelligence where chaos and crisis can be used to grow resilience in difficult times.	This increases Evolutionary Intelligence where civil societies across the planet of cities connect to one another to grow resilience in the face of volatility, uncertainty, complexity, ambiguity (VUCA).
VANCOUVER— CANADIAN MEMORIAL UNITED CHURCH	SEATTLE— POMEGRANATE CENTER, IMAGINE ABBOTSFORD	LEON, MEXICO	FINDHORN NEW STORY

At the conclusion of the conference, as we analyzed and synthesized our data, we could see how each of the Voices can grow the intelligences that translate into an expansion of the Master Code. This was truly a significant finding!

GROWING CARING CAPACITY

As we contemplated the power of the Master Code and how cities who develop their caring capacity for self, others, place and planet, are cities who also develop their carrying capacity, in other words, their resilience for good times and bad. (Carrying capacity in the field of sustainability has defined concepts and algorithms for the carbon footprint, ecofootprint and resilience equations that describe the limits to growth of how human systems—particularly cities—draw on the natural resource sinks of the planet to aggregate and support life in cities. Here we are using "carrying capacity" to relate to all these approaches in general. (See also Glossary for definition from a four quadrant Integral perspective.)

Communities and cities who care have the capacity to rapidly respond and evolve into new ways of being and becoming together. Research is showing that caring is core to the building of trust across the multiple scales of human systems and impacts the capacity to collaborate and generate impact (Weaver, 2017). (This is frequently evidenced as a shared intelligence when people respond with magnificent acts of generosity and capability, in times of crisis like Hurricane Harvey in 2017, Fort McMurray Fires in 2016, or Gander Newfoundland when the planes landed as a result of the World Trade Center strike in 2001.)

When we connected those intelligences together in the one-month intensive online conference, we could see that if you want to move beyond just the survivability of your city, and improve the thrivability of your city, these 12 intelligences amplify city caring capacity. We could hear resonance to the Master Code through the 60 voices of experts, designers and practitioners—all leaders who revealed the city as the human hive—and the 600 people who joined the conference. Their stories affirmed that the natural power of the Master Code enabled daily life and local and global wellbeing that emerged from demonstrating:

- **Care for self**
- **Care for others**
- **Care for this place**
- **Care for this planet.**

LIVING THE MASTER CODE PRODUCES HAPPINESS INDICATOR OF WELLBEING

We have further come to appreciate that, the outcome of living the Master Code produces a critical indicator of success—namely Happiness. At the conclusion, of Book 2 (Hamilton, 2017) we shared the significance of a Happiness factor which has vertical dimensions of development, aligned with the expanding circles of care and evolutionary levels of complexity. We took special care to link this kind of Happiness to the Master Code (Hamilton, 2017, pp.320–321):

> . . . *happiness studies have produced early evidence for the wellbeing of individuals, cities, cultures and nations (anon; Cummins et al., 2004; Haidt, 2006; Lama & Cutler, 1998; Montgomery, 2014; Wills et al., 2007a, 2007b). This kind of happiness is not merely ego or self-centered, nor is it ethno or regional centered, nor even merely place or planet-centered. Instead this indicator integrates all the scales of possible happiness that arise when our decision sets are aligned. This happens when we live the Master Code—choosing to take care of our Selves, each Other, our Cities/Places and the Planet all at once—simultaneously—an opportunity we have never before experienced in history.*
>
> *Happiness measures the right relationship between Caring Capacity (in the left hand quadrants) and Carrying Capacity (in the right hand quadrants) co-existing and co-emerging at the City scale, like the double helix of emergent cyclical human development that Graves proposed for the individual scale (Graves, 2005). Thus happiness as an evolutionary alignment index of Caring and Carrying Capacities supplies the double wellbeing feedback loop for sustainability and resilience used by the bees.*
>
> *We must learn to notice when our BEEings are depressed (indicating we are unhappy, misaligned, underperforming and poorly rewarded) and what we must do to steward the right relationship of all life in our cities, eco-regions and planet.*

Happiness has been studied for its characteristics, subjective qualities and desirability as a state. Happiness has been declared a right and a responsibility—both of which we agree it entails. But the Master Code shows that happiness goes beyond rights and responsibilities to include results and ratios. Laloux (2014, p. 175, p.261) found that at the organizational scale, complex organizations (like FAVI and Zappos) realized that there was "no performance without happiness."

Happiness is a result of taking care of self, others, place and planet in a way that these systems can survive, connect with one another and regenerate—embracing the basic qualities of a living system (Capra, 1996).

As one expands the circles of care in living the Master Code, happiness naturally expands. In this way, the right to happiness emerges from living and the responsibility for happiness arises from caring for others, place and planet.

These responsibilities then open up as a set of happiness ratios where the nested set of circles of care reveal a kind of calculus of happiness, where each level transcends and includes the ones before as follows (where H represents Happiness):

$$H(self) : H(others): H(place : H(planet)$$

Happiness for Self relates to Happiness for Other relates to Happiness for Place relates to Happiness for Planet. And caring for the Planet transcends and includes caring for Places, Others and Self; as care for Place transcends and includes care for Others and Self; and caring for Others transcends and includes care for Self.

Ultimately, happiness measures the right relationship between Caring Capacity (the combined effect of our consciousness and culture for self, others, place and planet) and Carrying Capacity (the combined effect of our behaviors and systems as self, other, place and planet). Thus living the Master Code produces happiness that is measurable in terms of sustainability and resilience in all 4 quadrants (as set out in Appendix 2, Map 1) .

Happiness is like the 20 kilos of honey produced by the bees (see Appendix E). Happiness supplies the double feedback loop that aligns the effectiveness (or sweet spot) of living the Master Code so that wellbeing in the human hive results at ego, ethno, regional and planetary scales.

Happiness is the ultimate measure of the experience of our aliveness in living the Master Code in all four quadrants of our creative existence (as set out in Chapter 2).

CONCLUSION

The rewards of living the Master Code are multi-fold. They tie together in a sacred embrace the power of Spirituality and the aliveness of Creativity.

We have proposed four rewards as follows (Hamilton, 2017, p.39):

◆

1. We . . . *create a new level of ourselves as caring individuals.*

2. We . . . *augment our capacity to make a positive difference in the world as groups of "others" together.*

3. We . . . *become part of a vibrant community of mutually supportive relationships in our city by connecting to People who Care.*

4. We . . . *release the DNA of our Master Code in our cities as a contribution to the wellbeing of all the cities on our Planet of Cities.*

In this Book 3, we add to these benefits:

5. We discover the secret to Happiness as an ever-evolving condition that is impacted by circles of care, creativity and evolutionary complexity.

6. We strengthen our intelligences as a human hive, when the Master Code amplifies Spirituality and Creativity, thus enabling both sustainability and resilience (aka thrivability).

7. We come to trust the Universe as a caring Source and ourselves as caring Resources whose spiritual energy is refreshed and renewed in a living system embrace.

8. We gain an appreciation for the deep role of caring in all acts of creativity.

Finally, by living the Master Code, we may learn the vital importance of what we discovered in the online conference. The role of cities in the evolution of humans to become Gaia's Reflective Organs and Organ System is critical. Therefore, we should ask both: *"What can our cities do for us?"* as well as: *"What can we do for our cities?"* And we should go one step further and ask: *"What can we do for our planet?"* Because our very survival is symbiotically enmeshed in all four elements of the Master Code.

REFERENCES

Capra, F. (1996). *The Web of Life: A New Scientific Understanding of Living Systems.* New York: Anchor Books, Doubleday.

Hamilton, M. (2008). *Integral City: Evolutionary Intelligences for the Human Hive.* Gabriola Island BC: New Society Publishers.

Hamilton, M. (2017). *Integral City Inquiry and Action: Designing Impact for the Human Hive.* Tucson, Arizona: Integral Publishers.

Hamilton, M., & Sanders, B. (2013a). City-Zen-tricity: A Fractal Non-Local Leap Toward Kosmocentricity Taken With Integral Kosmopolitans on an Evolutionary Mission. *Journal of Integral Theory and Practice, in press.* Retrieved from https://foundation.metaintegral.org/products/volume-9-number-1-june-2014

Hamilton, M., & Sanders, B. (2013b). *Integral City 2.0 Online Conference* 2012 *Proceedings: A Radically Optimistic Inquiry Into Operating System* 2.0 M. Hamilton (Ed.) Retrieved from http://www.scribd.com/doc/120713339/Integral-City-2-0-Online-Conference-2012-A-Radically-Optimistic-Inquiry-into-Operating-System-2-0

Laloux, F. (2014). *Reinventing Organizations.* Retrieved from http://www.reinventingorganizations.com/purchase.html.

Weaver, L. (2017). Turf, Trust, Co-Creation, and Collective Impact. Retrieved December 10, 2017, from Tamarack Institute http://www.tamarackcommunity.ca/library/turf-trust-co-creation-collective-impact

PART 2

Raising Context

Part 2 explores how we wake up to context and gain altitude on the realities of the human hive through: the relationship of cities to other cities and to nations; the invisible cultural roots of urban challenges; and the complexity of security in the human hive.

Chapter 4 is a short chapter, intended to wake us up to the **tension** between two emergent contexts of the human hive: geography and culture. Geographically, cities have geo-spatial locations, but historically many cities have changed geography and the culture of the nations to which they belong. (Some, like Budapest (anon, 2017b), can astonishingly record more than 40 times such changes have occurred through invasion and or colonialization.) The relationship of human hives to their nations has progressed through many eras and now in the 21st century, this relationship varies greatly around the world. The impact of globalization is bringing city-contexting forces into play that demand ongoing recapitulation of the city's relationship to its national contexts as the seats of change in any nation lie in its cities—each of whom is waking up to the multiplicity of powers embedded in its human hive.

Chapter 5 wakes us up to the **invisible** branches of values systems that are the roots of many, if not most, uncomfortable realities in the vast understory of cultural context at play in the human hive. This chapter explores the impact of values as the context underlying the sustainability and resilience of the city and the need for all 4 Voices of the city to make visible the values basis that influence understandings, drive decisions and open or close the relationships that enable sustainability and resilience of the human hive.

Chapter 6 takes a tall stretch into **human security** that is embedded in the complex web of intelligences that are active in cities. It proposes that security in the human hive requires understanding the contexts of planetary evolution (even plate tectonics), biological adaptation, and human development of consciousness and culture.

CITIES ARE PIVOTAL TRIGGER POINTS
AND PLANETARY TIPPING POINTS

CHAPTER SUMMARY

This short chapter considers the relationship of cities to their geographic, cultural and social situations in nations. It considers the new science of cities emerging from complexity science and what enables cities to outlast both organizations and nations. The Integral model reveals the multiple co-arising realities that shape cities and impact individuals and collectives. The capacities of cities to survive, be sustainable and resilient through the evolution of technology, environmental awareness and human development suggest that cities evolve through "eras" such as Traditional, Smart, Resilient and Integral Cities. The internal wellbeing of individual cities appears to be pivotal to the internal wellbeing of other cities, the external wellbeing of their eco-regions and nations, as well as to the overall wellbeing of the planet.

Keywords: science of cities, fractal, Integral, sustainability, resilience, evolution, survival

CITIES ARE FLASH POINTS

Have you noticed that news reports of war or "rumors of war" like to point at countries that are on the cusp of disruption or hostility because it is the traditional "big news" story on the global stage (think Russia/Ukraine and NATO countries; think North Korea and USA; think Turkey and EU)?

However, when I look behind the headlines, as I observe the situations of emerging hostility between nations, I see a pattern where cities are the flash points of anger, fear and concern within nations. If the dissonances in these acupuncture points are not addressed, these cities become the potential trigger points for inflaming the rest of the country. Dysfunction spreads like a contagious virus, because of internal dis-ease and misalignment of information, matter and energy. Thus, disturbed cities expose their nations to many kinds of external threats.

SCIENCE OF CITIES

Searching for the science of cities, when I first published Integral City: Evolutionary Intelligences for the Human Hive, in 2008, I pointed to the science of living systems (Miller, 1978) as a source and framework that gives us lenses to understand the behaviors of cities as living systems, including systems of survival and natural economies (Jacobs 1994, 2001). I looked for new philosophies and sociologies that recognized the complex, non-linear history of human settlement (De Landa, 1997, 2006). Biologist Jared Diamond (2005) had outlined the long view of what makes societies as living systems survive or Collapse and Buzz Holling and colleagues (Gunderson & Holling, 2002) had proposed how resilience emerges in all living systems through a natural Panarchy cycle of four stages of change.

Fast forward ten years and we can add to these sciences a contribution from physics via Geoffrey West's (2011, 2017) proposition that cities concentrate material wealth that generates real economies of scale in energetic functions, as well as amplifies creative capacities (both outcomes demonstrating a non-linear order of efficiency of about 15% reduction or increase respectively).

INTEGRAL PERSPECTIVE

All this science is only comprehensible through a metaview of human systems, offered by an Integral perspective (Wilber 1995, 2000; Hamilton, 2008, 2017). With an Integral framing the scientific constructs can be interpreted through the four lenses (quadrants) of human intention (UL), behavior (UR), cultures (LL) and organizing structures (LR) (see Appendix B, Map 1,). Within each of these quadrants, individual lines of intelligence have been identified, maturing at different rates (or not at all) as inherited propensities and life conditions exert their influence. Moreover, the Integral perspective offers us a lineage of human evolution (that is also reflected in individual development) where the whole person (as well as his/her quadrants and lines) embraces increasing circles of care and compassion, growing capacities from egocentric to ethnocentric to world centric to Kosmocentric—and thereby producing the waves of human development we call traditional, pre-modern, modern, postmodern and Integral (see Chapters 1 and 2 or Appendix B, Map 4).

The elegance of the Integral framing of the human condition is that it is fractal and can be applied at all levels of scale from individuals, to families, teams, organizations, communities, cities, (nations) and eco-regions. Because of its fractal nature, this model then offers us not only a map for humans to track their developmental capacities but also to recognize the zones of greatest probable dissonance. For it is precisely between the quadrants, circles of care and scales of human enterprise, identified in our 5 Integral City Maps (Appendix B) that eruptions are most likely to occur. In these zones, the realities of human existence rub against each other like tectonic plates causing volcanic eruptions of angry worldviews (think of the Middle East), earthquakes of lost territory and despair (remember Iraq, Syria and Rwanda) and tsunamis of overwhelming forces (consider colonizers of all stripes).

CITY SUSTAINABILITY, RESILIENCE, SURVIVAL

Returning to Diamond's (2005) *Collapse* proposition where the key elements that impact a society's survival include: climate, geography, internal culture, friendly neighbors/trading partners and hostile neighbors/trading partners, I would propose that precisely these elements are the deciding factors on whether a city survives or collapses. They are the underlying factors that enable the phenomenon that West points to—that cities outlive organizations. I would also propose the corollary, that cities outlive countries and nations—and their association as voluntarily-formed federations of concentrated urban life and resources, within nations, gives them particular power that is seldom recognized by their own nations until they trigger national instabilities.

The almost universal denial by nations to the phenomenon, that they are only as strong as their weakest cities has been sustained by the great success of cities themselves. As social holons (where a collective center of gravity of developmental stages represented by many entities emerges from the interaction of individuals and their organizations (as discussed below in Part 3)), cities have mirrored the smaller scales of individual human development, maturing through stages of ego-self-centeredness to ethno-nation-centeredness. They have done so within the context of Diamond's climate, geography, friendly/hostile national relationships and most especially from their own internal city cultures.

Now, those (few) cities who have negotiated Diamond's elements most effectively, have entered a stage of world-centeredness that has been enabled by the technologies produced by modernity. (We can look at the world's "best" city lists for candidates of this stage of emergence—they often include New York, London, Seoul, Vancouver, Zurich—but all these cities still exhibit very modern awareness of their world-centricity, with a willingness to demonstrate post-modern sensibilities when responding to emergencies in "sister cities" (like New York's 911 tragedy; Hurricanes Sandy, Harvey and Irma; or Nice/Brussels/Manchester terrorist attacks).

These modern—often called "smart"—technologies have built global bridges that link many lines of development between and within cities—but those technologies are sadly lacking any capacity for awareness of what makes individual cities whole and well, or an awareness of how cities contribute not just to national prosperity but to global sustainability and resilience.

SMART CITY TECH BREAKS DOWN BOUNDARIES

The "smart" digital communication technologies especially have impacted the very qualities of the interstitial zones where quadrants, lines, levels and scales rub against each other. In the traditional pre-modern era(s) those boundaries were usually fixed and closed, monitored by rigid agreements, treaties, militaries and border patrols on the global map. But modern technology has unceremoniously (and generally without asking permission) transformed those boundaries into porous, uncertain and unstable membranes that challenge the functionality of the systems they contain.

Nations are especially susceptible to these boundary breaches (aka challenges)—not so much by the incursion of hostile external neighbors (as in traditional times)—but because of the disintegration of inner cultural certainties (witness the rebellions of Catalonian cities organized to rebel with locally organized referenda, against the federal government of Spain in 2017). Within the densest centers of human settlement, all the assumptions that were the city's former status quo have been disrupted by the in-migration of multiple cultures from rural areas and other countries of the world. (In the developed world, cities hold 90% of the population, while the global average for cities as core population centers now exceeds 50% of the population being in cities).

CITIES AS ORGANS AND TRADING SYSTEMS

To a nation, cities are like the organs of a living system. Traditionally cities are connected most tightly internally (like organ systems)—where the city mirrors, manages and adapts to the smaller scales of human systems within it (Hamilton, 2008). They then are most connected with their trading partners who supply the resources (that West (2011, 2017) has identified) which build its infrastructures, feed its energy and enable creativity. Traditionally those linkages came from other cities within the same nation (or a mother nation or "trade friendly nation-neighbor") but now we are in an era where cities and the organizations within them (in democratic countries) are often totally unconstrained to resource themselves from anywhere in the world—including from countries whom their own nation considers hostile.

Thus, we live at a time when cities have great power to undermine the stability of nations (from which cities have gained much of their cultural and systemic life conditions), but national governance systems have largely shortchanged the capacity of cities to govern themselves to optimize their wellbeing. The tensions are becoming intolerable—and nations need to wake up to the strange but increasingly real possibility that cities may hold the upper hand in the survival game.

CITIES CRITICAL TO RESILIENCE AND SUSTAINABILITY

But before we are too hasty to lay blame at the foot of only one social entity, we must now re-visit the science of resilience and understand how it provides the context for all living systems to live sustainably on the planetary system as a whole.

While our United Nations have skirmished for more than half a century for nations to negotiate their ethno-centric differences, it still struggles to present (let alone gain) any kind of a unified approach to global wellbeing. The human species still battles within itself for ownership/control rights to resources that within a living system context must (if the continued life of the living system is our ultimate value) be superseded by responsibilities to life on the whole planet, which supports all life.

In an attempt to call forth such a world-centric perspective, Integral City has aligned the intelligences that cities need in order to live in service to global wellbeing, into a compass that points to the requisite but flexibly resonant Contexts, as well as Individual, Collective, Strategic and Evolutionary capacities (see Appendix C3).

Paradoxically, in the world today cities need to be freed by nations to optimize life within each city (as a unique human system), while cities need to take the responsibility to serve not just national interests but global sustainability and resilience.

If nations wait too long to enable cities to assume their natural (if not rightful) role in human and planetary evolution, inevitably the pressures that build up within their cities will become the trigger points that cause the tipping points for the very wellbeing of the nations themselves. This neglect in turn has rapid and often uncontrollable consequences that sweep across around the world through both political and environmental breakdowns.

It is time we faced the fact that we have arrived at the stage of human evolution where, individuals, organizations and nations are facing a crisis (Sahtouris, 2010) that demands a new story and a new response. We need to "Ask not what your city can do for you. Ask what you can do for your city . . . and the planet of cities."

REFERENCES

Beck, D. (2002). Spiral Dynamics in the Integral Age. Paper presented at the Spiral Dynamics integral, Level I.

De Landa, M. (1997). A *Thousand Years of Nonlinear History*. New York: Zone Books.

De Landa, M. (2006). A New Philosophy of Society: Assemblage Theory and Social Complexity. London: Continuum.

Diamond, J. (2005). Collapse: How societies choose to fail or succeed (first ed.). New York: Penguin Group.

Gunderson, L. C., & Holling, C. S. (Eds.). (2002). Panarchy: Understanding Transformations in Human and Natural Systems Washington, DC: Island Press.

Hamilton, M. (2008). Integral City: Evolutionary Intelligences for the Human Hive. Gabriola Island BC: New Society Publishers.

Hamilton, M. (2017). Integral City Inquiry & Action: Designing Impact for the Human Hive. Tucson AZ: Integral Publishers.

Jacobs, J. (1994). Systems of Survival New York: First Vintage Books Edition.

Jacobs, J. (2001). The Nature of Economies. New York: First Vintage Books Edition.

Miller, J. G. (1978). Living Systems. New York: McGraw-Hill Book Company.

Sahtouris, E. (2010). Celebrating Crisis: Towards a Culture of Cooperation. A New Renaissance:Transforming Science, Spirit & Society. London: Floris Books.

West, G. (2011). Why Cities Keep Growing, Corporations and People Always Die, and Life Gets Faster: A Conversation With Geoffrey West (5.23.11). In J. Brockman (Ed.), Edge: Edge.org.

West, G. (2017). Scale: The Universal Laws of Growth, Innovation, Sustainability and the Pace of Life in Organisms, Cities, Economies and Companies. New York: Penguin Press.

Wilber, K. (1995). Sex, Ecology and Spirituality: the spirit of evolution. Boston: Shambhala Publications Inc.

Wilber, K. (2000). A Theory of Everything. Boston: Shambhala Publications Inc.

INVISIBLE CITIES:
CONTEXTING URBAN CHALLENGES
FROM THE INSIDE-OUT

By Marilyn Hamilton and Jordan Bruce MacLeod

The first version of this chapter was written for the eBook Invisible Cities *published by the tt30 Club of Rome* (2009).

CHAPTER SUMMARY

This chapter examines the phenomenon that the core realities of consciousness and culture of cities are ostensibly invisible. However, they translate into value systems that impact how individuals, groups and the 4 Voices in cities relate to one another, make decisions and allocate resources. Consideration is given to the holographic realities of the city and how they contribute to the generation of the morphic field as a perpetual influence in the invisible energetic city "record" and "store" of information. The chapter concludes by relating the invisible aspects to the visible realities in the city through the Integral framework.

Keywords: invisible, consciousness, culture, holographic city, morphic field, memes, value systems

Recent scientific research about sustainability has confirmed that each geographic bio-region has limits to its carrying capacity. The idea of an ecological footprint (Rees & Wackernagel, 1994) extrapolated this idea by demonstrating that if all cities used the level of resources currently used in the developed world, we would need four or more planets. While it is only in recent decades that we have encountered these limits, it is now abundantly clear that the window in which we have to confront the challenges of sustainability—in all of its dimensions, including our cities—is narrow and closing.

Some say we should not forget the lessons of history, but we are not sure that humanity has ever intentionally learned them in regard to building and designing intelligent cities. Often it is only the artifacts of our failed experiments that remind us that a lesson was available to be learned. Ironically, the reminders show that the teachable moment has existed just after the peak of the city (or civilization's) existence (Diamond, 2005). Once that tipping point is reached, however, it is usually too late for the city and/or the civilization. There are examples from every habitable continent as found in the archeological records of Uxmal, Anasazi and Easter Island.

Until recently, we have lacked both a philosophy and a science of sustainable human settlement. The State of the World's Cities (United Nations Human Settlements, 2005) should have been able to report not just on the major problems of the world's city infrastructure (like poverty, slums and pollution) for which we have data in excess. It should be able to report not even on just the 'best practices'—mainly because those best practices are simply addressing the greatest problems—but it should be able to report on the relationship of cities to the carrying capacity of their bio-region and the earth as a whole. In order to develop an effective understanding of the dynamics of the whole, the materialist worldviews of the past are proving to fall profoundly short. Even the 2015 Sustainable Development Goals (anon, 2017) fall short of recognizing the significance of human adult development and its impact on worldviews and decision sets. And the revelations of *Scale* (West, 2017) fall short of recognizing the role of consciousness and culture on the emergence of the efficiencies of economies or complexifying of technology.

Recent discoveries in consciousness studies, biology, developmental psychology, sociology and anthropology attest to the essential importance our psychology plays in determining the *quality* of human experiences, relationships, behaviors, cultures and social structures. Yet, this psychology remains largely discounted in current economic, planning, design and management functions. Although we may draw great inspiration and information by measuring our trajectory and thereby determine that humanity is collectively on a disastrous path, there is little that is solely quantitative about the crux of our problem. The converging crises confronting humanity are *qualitative* issues. It is, therefore, primarily a collective crisis about *how* we see our world and its problems. Our response to crisis must move from the center of this new vision and address problems and opportunities from the inside-out.

But, who is responsible for the stewardship of urban resources? With the unfolding of human systems, the answer to that question is largely, "That depends which country you are in." International developer, Gail Hochachka (2005, p. 1) proposes that people's feelings, beliefs and worldviews affect how they are ready and willing to participate in sustainable behaviors. Moreover, she points out traumatic experiences (like natural disasters and war) can damage people and leave them disabled from appropriate responses.

VALUE OF THE INVISIBLE

Although, the psychological realities of a city's population have been largely ignored or discounted because they are subjective, invisible and difficult to study, they are just as real as the exterior physical realties of the city. These psychological realities create an interior environment that has just as many or more layers, contours and textures to it as geographic environments. We have studied them through the lenses of psychology, philosophy and the humanities, but until recently we have not recognized that (like our exterior qualities) these interiors evolve and develop. We map the paleontology of our interiors through the shifts in worldviews that enable the growth of our interior landscapes (and therefore our capacities for response, adaptability and resilience). The key centers of those internalized views are the self, the other (family, clan, place/city) and the world (society, sectors, spheres of influence, regions, planet).

Recent propositions from Florida (2008) and Landry (2017) suggest that indeed, cities do have psychologies (if not sociologies) that must be considered for city planning, but it appears their framing for city psychology is flat and absolutistic—not taking into account what is considered in this chapter, namely the dynamics of psychology in the context of the phenomenon of collective social holons, nor the developmental nature of human psychology across a lifetime of changing life conditions.

Modes of governance span a spectrum from autocratic/dictatorial to democratic. The governance systems reflect the interior worldviews and mindsets of both city leaders and, in most cases, a majority of citizens. They are ever emergent and constantly being re-negotiated because cities are dynamic entities. But one thing is becoming clear: some worldviews are more inclusive and more soundly contexted than others. In other words, the internal life of those who coalesce authority, power and influence contributes largely to the capacity of cities to be coherent, adaptable and sustainable. We are fast becoming aware that sustainability means living in the world with mindfulness about our relationship to the world and its realities.

One of the most perennial proofs of this relationship of the internal human environment to the external environment is the tragedy of the commons (Hardin, 1968). The tragedy of the commons has recently been revived as a persuasive discourse through the writing of authors like Jared Diamond (2005), Ronald Wright (2004) and Thomas Homer-Dixon (2006) who have delved into the startling evidence in the ruins of great civilizations to observe that development can have negative consequences on the local environment. Moreover, they have revealed that the commonly held view is often the view that provides the *least* responsible perspective on how to value and steward a civilization's resources.

Thus, we are learning, that overcoming the tragedy of the commons requires mindfulness, accountability and monitoring of the earth's natural systems. Our internal psychology needs to connect to our external environments, so that we are capable of better governing built environments in a way that both individual and collective human civilization can flourish. If we fail at this task, for instance, favoring the interests of a few, without considering the interests of the many, once again nature has demonstrated to us that we lose diversity in the system and ultimately resilience. Both diversity and resilience are what we need most in the face of any disaster. What's more, diversity is a major contributor to innovation, and the driver of new combinations and inventions (Homer-Dixon, 2006).

Once we see the importance of the mindset and worldview of urban environments then we can see the underpinnings of a city's attitude and relationship to its bio-region. And with the largest view possible—these days viewable from external satellites serving global positioning systems—we can also see what is working (aligned and coherent), what is not working (misaligned and incoherent) and what are the city's next natural opportunities and capacities for change. Then we are able to notice the different lenses that exist in the city because of different levels of expertise. We can see how the urban infrastructure that is managed by expert managers and engineers integrates scientific knowledge and experience. We can also see that despite the value of this expertise and the infrastructure systems, too often the expertise distances citizens from taking ownership and responsibility for their contribution to the healthy operation of the natural earth systems.

Cities are faced with the challenging task of translating this expertise into terms that individuals can comprehend and engage with. This is why we need to monitor the use of resources at the user level, by metering the use of water, fuel, waste production, transportation, land use and CO_2 production. In the path to more sustainable cities we may have to adopt rationing measures for greenhouse gasses, like CO_2 (Monbiot & Prescott, 2007; Hawken, 2017). In the same way that citizens readily adjust their food and housing decisions because they are responsible for paying for them, users of resources who pay as they use, start taking responsibility for waste and inefficiencies that lead to depletion of resources and the tragedy of the commons (Hawken, 2017).

SUSTAINING THE WHOLE CITY

The active field of sustainability studies is challenged by the same spectrum of definitions, worldviews and frameworks as other modern discourses. How individuals understand sustainability is framed by internalities—whether we are thinkers, writers, business people, or merely trying to survive on a daily basis. Urban sustainability presents an additional challenge, namely the sheer scale of the complex adaptive system that a city includes. When you consider the fluid dynamics of behaviors, intentions, relationships and production systems that constitute urban areas, the concept of sustaining a city can become almost an oxymoron.

Archeological excavations in an urban area can demonstrate the trajectory of a city's evolution and illustrate that the layers of a city are not merely ethereal or esoteric, but are literally embedded into the city streets. Although this infrastructure changes more slowly than the people who build or inhabit the urban area, it does change. Moreover, it can change in the direction of more or less complexity. So when we consider sustainable cities we have to ask ourselves: what are we sustaining? Regional planner, Ian Wight (2002) is attracted to the idea that cities arise from the act of placemaking—the integration of all the ways that people interact to create a place. Our Book 2 (Hamilton, 2017) in the Integral City series, differentiates "placecaring" from "placemaking" (in order to focus on consciousness and culture as requiring special focus to bring balance from the left-hand quadrants of the Integral City model (see Appendix B)) into the wellbeing of cities. From both these vantage points, perhaps it is easier to consider that the pervasive quality we could sustain, in as complex a system as an urban area, is the potential to continually evolve. This would be the key to sustaining the city's resilience as a self-correcting cycle of adaptiveness.

Thus, while we may find it somewhat problematic to gain traction with the sustainable city, we may find it much more promising to contemplate the evolving city. Evolution is a characteristic of living systems that arises from the resonance and coherence of the system. Resilience arises from the adaptiveness of the system to its dynamic environment. Resonance emerges when the system is aligned externally to its environment. Coherence arises from the alignment of the elements of the system internally in such a way that energy is optimized. When both resonance and coherence become synchronized new capacities in the system emerge and evolve. We can examine this capacity of evolution from two perspectives. One is holographic and allows us to see how the whole is disclosed from the patterns embedded in its parts. A hologram is a three-dimensional image that arises from the interference patterns of two wave patterns. The hologram carries information about the whole in every part of its composition. The other is morphic fields that emerge from the cumulative repeated activity of like holons and like species.

The Holographic City

Thomas Homer-Dixon (2006), in his book, *The Upside of Down* engages the reader with historical factoids that capture the nature of the holographic city. He derives the nature of three cities from single architectural stones: a foundational stone in the Roman Coliseum; the Temple of Bacchus gate in Baalbek, Lebanon; and the Stone of the Pregnant Woman near Baalbek. Each of these stones provides evidence for the values of the civilization that created them. In that sense they are holographic: a small part of the city which reveals a great deal of information about the city when we consider how they were created, why they were transported there, who did the work, who directed the work, who designed the structures, how they provided the energy to move the matter and the information to communicate the intentions.

Philosopher, Ervin Laszlo proposes that "nature's holograms are cosmic . . . they link . . . all things with all other things" (Laszlo, 2004, p. 71). The evidence for a city as a holographic entity—where a part of the city can reveal insights into the whole of it—is available because the city is a holistic system, which arises from the massive interconnections and entanglements of structures, cultures, intentions and behaviors. In this sense, if we laid our hands on any part of the city and traced the connections of that part to all the other parts of the city, we would discover the sub-systems and systems that make up the city—a holograph.

It is quite possible that the holographic nature of the city reveals the city's capacity for evolution. We see the whole easily, when the holograph suddenly shifts into view from a discrete entry point of a city. This means, for instance, that if we look at the quality of the health care system or effectiveness of the education system, we can obtain a proxy assessment of the quality of life or the capacity for development in the city.

Morphic Fields in Cities

Although we cannot always easily gain the insights that holograms of the city could give us, perhaps we can view the whole city through different filters. If we peer through the lenses that Rupert Sheldrake uses, we can glimpse an intangible reality about human existence that has long been known by people who have the capacity to access it. However, this has also been repressed by those who feel threatened by the existence of anything intangible, regardless of the evidence.

Sheldrake, a biologist, has been curious about how species like homing pigeons, parrots, dogs and horses seem to know how to travel long distances and arrive at specific destinations with pin-point accuracy. Individual animals even seem to be able to access human intentions and be able to anticipate human behavior with a high degree of accuracy (Sheldrake, 1988, 1999, 2003). Sheldrake has proposed that each species over time creates an energetic field, invisible to the naked eye and not registered on any instruments created to date, but, nonetheless, as real as a radio or television signal. His recent research has expanded to include human phenomena like the sense of being stared at, telepathy, foresight and predictive dreams (Sheldrake, 2003, 2012). He refers to these energetic fields as morphic or morphogenetic fields. In the human species it appears that some people have more capabilities than others to access the information in these fields (Hamilton, 2017, Chapters 1 & 2). In some remote tribes in the Amazon and Indonesia, and in some indigenous peoples like the Aborigines of Australia, these capacities are highly developed and widely shared amongst some members of their society.

In the so-called developed world, very few people admit to having skills related to these capacities and little credence is given to those who do practice them (an exception includes some police departments who quietly use people with paranormal capacities to assist them in solving difficult crimes). Nevertheless, as evidence builds to confirm the existence of these fields, it is not difficult to speculate that the city may provide a particularly rich ground for demonstrating the existence of these fields. Nowadays we can measure the amount of physical heat generated by the city. We can also control, radio and Wi-Fi signals so individual receivers can decode the signals into usable messages that inform and entertain us. If Sheldrake is correct about individual people, in the not too distant future we may discover the evidence that confirms every city has a morphic field that reflects (and even transmits) the patterns of consciousness that individuals and groups are generating. (In fact, the Integral City community of practise is already using the technology of Systemic Constellation Work to access the Knowing Field (our name for the morphic field (Hamilton, 2017, Chapters 1 & 2).

Similarly, Laszlo calls the morphic field, the Akashic Record (Laszlo, 2006b)—borrowing from the Sanskrit word for 'sky' or 'space'. Rather than biology he uses the science of physics to suggest that the vacuum of space is not empty, but filled with energy and information that we have simply not recognized nor learned how to access. Accessing it tends to be accidental rather than deliberate, notwithstanding the fact that in most cultures throughout millennia, select individuals have been taught the secrets of doing so. Laszlo suggests that the Akashic field holds a permanent record of human (and earth) activity—just like the brain apparently holds a record of all individual activity since birth (or conception).

The conception of morphic or Akashic fields creates the possibility that we could harness the intelligence that is concentrated in the city to generate much greater (more complex) intelligence capacities. If we could learn how to better think together we would be able to harness the massive leverage of parallel processing that has enabled us to design modern computers and neural networks (like the linking of personal computers for the SETI extraterrestrial life search project). Increasingly, methodologies for thinking together (often called "We-Space") are emerging around the world (Hamilton, Douglas et al in Brabant & Gunnlaugson, 2016). If we can continue to move this forward, we may see a phase shift in human intelligence that will match the analytics of Big Data, to offer urban areas new incentives to improve conditions to better support human existence. In addition, it may offer enhanced capabilities for moving towards sustainability (not over-using resources) and identify emergent opportunities (creating new capacities from existing resources).

VALUE SYSTEMS OF A CITY

Regardless of where people are geographically located, our diverse human cultures demonstrate evidence that when life conditions provoked us to change, society and culture have evolved, generally in the direction of greater complexity. Graves (2005) and Beck and Cowan (1996) have modeled patterns of increasing structural complexities of human systems that have emerged as we have moved from the hearth-based circle of family survival, through the bonding systems of clan and tribe, to the power struggles of chief and king, to the ordering authorities of state and place of worship, to the strategic economies of material exchange, to the accepting embrace of diverse peoples, to the flex and flow of global systems. With each of these levels of historical complexity we have created new artefacts, habitats, structures and forms to structure our human systems. We call the most concentrated and complex of these structures, cities.

The life conditions that stimulated our bodies and brains to adapt and survive were accompanied by an evolving consciousness that enabled the evolution of what it means to be human. Those life conditions contribute to the evolution and the state of well-being of our cities today. The nested hierarchies and patterns of life that manifest and that we extend into the structures of our cities appear in each individual's life. They in turn are interconnected and both inter- and intra-dependent on the system of family, friends, work, health, school and community. Each of which is likewise dependent on the social systems of the city, region, state, and nation and further linked to socio-political and cultural norms and the natural environment (Barnett, 2005; Diamond, 2005; Hamilton, 2017). Thus, who we are depends on who and how we are able to grow the potential of the entangled human condition in each of us. And it is the matching of that human potential to the structures of the built environment of the city, and the social and cultural institutions, that creates a coherence of 'optimal life conditions', which will of course vary for individuals.

MEMES IN THE CITY

In *The Selfish Gene*, Richard Dawkins (1976) coined the term 'meme' to explain the transmission of cultural units of information. Some of the most common memes include ideas, music, architectural styles, art trends, sound bites of politicians, and advertisements. Memes living in the digital age can be instantly communicated and replicated around the world, to millions of human receivers. Furthermore, they are constantly changing (Dawkins, 1976). Using the terminology 'meme' to signify a unit of cultural transmission, 'memeplex' connotes a cluster of relevant and complementary memes that can 'piggyback' off one another to strengthen the meaning of each individual meme. They can also accelerate, enhance and simplify the transmission or replication process by moving together as a group.

While memes explain the content of cultural information, they do not really explain how they evolve or how they reproduce. When we integrate the concept with value systems such as Beck and Cowan's (1996) *Spiral Dynamics*, we can conceive of each emergent value system as a meme generator or 'memetic' operating system. As a value system evolves and its complexity grows, we may readily predict the quality of the memes will also shift. Equally as predictable is the probability that each value system will generally be attracted to and reproduce memes at the same level of complexity and quality.

Cultural infrastructures such as radio, television, print media, email, the internet and social media represent the most obvious memetic super-highways for memes to flow and propagate. With the multiple leverage impacts of replicating memes and cultural technology, it may be possible that morphogenetic fields may be expanded to encode both the invisible and visible patterns that connect cultural information between individuals and groups. An increasing understanding of these processes is opening the door to mapping the invisible dynamics. Armed with an understanding of cultural content (memes) and codes (value systems), we are gaining the abilities to map out the location and flows of information and its *quality*. Detecting these patterns of consciousness enables us to monitor how values interact, change and emerge.

This has not only immense value for identifying historical patterns of consciousness, but also for enhancing and solidifying *anticipatory* planning practices that stimulate both current and near-term values, and also the longer term, emerging patterns of future value systems. Such technologies, when properly aligned, may carry high potential to positively impact the unprecedented complexity of urban centers and the interdependent global commons, and ultimately a planet of Integral Cities. They may also create a grounded pathway to generating an abundance of soft and hard power within urban centers and beyond.

TOWARDS THE 'INTEGRAL CITY'

The recognition of the invisible aspect of cities and its consequent mapping are the necessary next steps towards enabling a compelling and effective integrated approach to planning, managing, designing and building our urban centers. Hamilton (2008, 2017) calls this whole system approach the 'Integral City' or the Human Hive.

An Integral City is a way of looking at the city, regardless of its size to see it as a holistic system—an organic entity that has emerged from an ecology of consciousness, and that includes (but is not limited to) discursive, political and religious/spiritual contexts together with a specific natural environment (such as mountain, sea or prairie), climate and natural ecology. As such, an Integral City is dynamic, adaptive and responsive to its internal and external life conditions.

An Integral City acts much like a complex adaptive human system that concentrates habitat for humans like a hive does for bees or an anthill does for ants. Like a natural system it encounters similar issues, factors and challenges that affect the concentration of life anywhere: sustaining flows of information, matter and energy for the survival of life (Miller, 1978).

The complexity of multiple types of intelligence and value systems brings into focus the evident need for creating resilient internal and external spaces and structures that allow each of these intelligences and systems to find healthy and symbiotic expression. This will require the coordinated efforts of urban planners, leaders, designers and empowerment of individual urban residents.

For this reason, the current dynamic and uncertain global economic realities also depend on creating resilient internal and external "graces, spaces and places" (see Chapter 1) that contribute to both the invisible and visible realities of the Integral City. The present global economic paradigm unabashedly (and unconsciously) discounts the future and rewards myopic values. This naturally leads to the consequent promotion of radical resource inefficiencies, imbalances and vulnerabilities. This economic system will prove constricting and deter the realization of whole systems approaches in our urban centers and to the world's most pressing problems unless it also evolves within a more holistic framework, such as we propose above. Therefore, issues of urban sustainability and emergence must be addressed within the larger context of global economic structures, politics and rule-sets (to be explored in Book 4 of the Integral City series).

REFERENCES

anon. (2017). Sustainable Development Goals. Retrieved December 11, 2017, from Wikipedia https://en.wikipedia.org/wiki/Sustainable_Development_Goals

Barnett, T. P. M. (2005). *The Pentagon's New Map: War and Peace in the Twenty-First Century* (trade paperback ed.). New York: The Berkley Publishing Group.

Beck, D., & Cowan, C. (1996). *Spiral Dynamics: Mastering Values, Leadership and Change*. Malden, MA: Blackwell Publishers.

Dawkins, R. (1976). *The Selfish Gene*. Oxford: Oxford University Press.

Diamond, J. (2005). *Collapse: How societies choose to fail or succeed* (first ed.). New York: Penguin Group.

Florida, R. (2008). *Who's Your City: How the Creative Economy is Making Where to Live the Most Important Decision of Your Life*. Toronto: Random House Canada.

Graves, C. (2005). *The Never Ending Quest: A Treatise on an Emergent Cyclical Conception of Adult Behavioral Systems and Their Development*. Santa Barbara, CA: ECLET Publishing.

Hamilton, M. (2008) *Integral City: Evolutionary Intelligences for the Human Hive*. Gabriola Island, BC: New Society Publishers.

Hamilton, M. (2017) *Integral City Inquiry & Action: Designing Impact for the Human Hive*. Tucson AZ: Integral Publishers.

Hamilton, M., Douglas, D. C., Beck, C., Aurami, A., & Arnott, J. (2016). We-space, Integral City and the Knowing Field. In M. Brabant & O. Gunnlaugson (Eds.), *Cohering the We Space: Developing Theory and Practice for Engaging Collective Emergence, Wisdom and Healing in Groups* (pp. 131–154). San Francisco: Integral Publishing House.

Hardin, G. (1968). The Tragedy of the Commons. *Science* 162, pp 1243—1248.

Hawken, P. (2017). *Drawdown: The Most Comprehensive Plan Ever Proposed to Reverse Global Warming*. New York: Penguin Books.

Hochachka, G. (2005). *Developing Sustainability, Developing the Self: An Integral Approach to International and Community Development*: Polis Project on Ecological Governance, University of Victoria.

Homer-Dixon, T. (2006). *The Upside of Down: Catastrophe, Creativity, and the Renewal of Civilization*. Toronto: Alfred A. Knopf Canada.

Landry, C., & Murray, C. (2017). *Psychology & the City*. Bournes Green Near Stroud, UK: Comedia.

Laszlo, E. (2004). *Science and the Akashic Field: An Integral Theory of Everything* (2007 ed.). Rochester, Vermont: Inner Traditions.

Miller, J. G. (1978). *Living Systems*. New York: McGraw-Hill Book Company.

Rees, W. E. P. D., & Wackernagel, M. (1994). *Ecological Footprints and Appropriated Carrying Capacity: Measuring the Natural Capital Requirements of the Human Economy*. Washington, DC: Island Press.

Sheldrake, R. (1988). *The Presence of the Past: Morphic Resonance and the Habits of Nature* (1995 ed.). Rochester, Vermont: Park Street Press.

Sheldrake, R. (1999). *Dogs That Know When Their Owners Are Coming Home: And Other Unexplained Powers of Animals*. New York: Three Rivers Press.

Sheldrake, R. (2003). *The Sense of Being Stared At: And Other Aspects of the Extended Mind*. New York: Three Rivers Press.

Sheldrake, R. (2012). *Science Set Free*. New York: Deepak Chopra Books, Crown Publishing Group, Division of Random House.

United Nations Human Settlements, P. (Ed.). (2006). *The State of the World's Cities 2006/7*. London: Earthscan.

West, G. (2017). *Scale: The Universal Laws of Growth, Innovation, Sustainability and the Pace of Life in Organisms, Cities, Economies and Companies*. New York: Penguin Press.

Wight, I. (2002). Place, Place Making and Planning. Paper presented at the ACSP.

Wright, R. (2004). *A Short History of Progress* (Avalon ed.). New York: Carroll & Graf Publishers.

6

SECURITY SYSTEMS: EVOLUTIONARY FRAMEWORK FOR THE HUMAN HIVE

A version of this Chapter was originally published under the title Meta-Framework for Security in the Human Hive: Integrally Aligning Sustainability Responses to Trajectory of Evolutionary Threats *in Systems Research and Behavioral Science* Syst. Res. 31, 614–626 (2014)

Published online in Wiley Online Library (wileyonlinelibrary.com) DOI: 10.1002/sres.2310

CHAPTER SUMMARY

This chapter explores human security in the city (aka human hive) within the context of environmental change and proposes an integrated evolutionary framework for designing city-scale human security systems. It explores the Integral City framework for human security and environmental change in the Cosmosphere, Biosphere and Anthroposphere. Five maps reveal how humans in the city impact global environment, and how human security is tightly bound with global evolution and human change. Elements of the maps include subjective/intersubjective and objective/interobjective perspectives; nested holarchies of whole systems; fractal development of holons and social holons; eight levels of complex structures; and evolutionary holistic spirituality. The chapter concludes that the Integral City meta-framework provides a human security system approach that is fractal, scalable, global, local, holistic, comprehensive, pluralistic, interconnected, evolutionary and developmental.

Keywords: meta-framework, human security, Integral city, evolutionary stages, human hive, global environmental change

WHAT IS HUMAN SECURITY?

Human security is the experience of surviving, connecting with one's environment and creating the conditions to reproduce another generation—which are the characteristics of a living system (Capra, 1996; Hamilton, 2008a). Human security relates to species, collective and individual scale (Gasper, 2010, p. 25). Human security in the city, includes being secure about: the environmental context (ecology, adaptiveness, interconnectedness and life cycles); individual thoughts and actions; collective relationships and systems; while one applies strategies for evolutionary adaptation (Hamilton, 2008).

Seeing the city as a living system, like a human hive, in evolutionary terms, implies that the experience of security has shifted as individual and collective capacities for adaptation to the environment have developed along a spectrum of maturity. Graves (1971, 1974, 1981, 2003, 2005) proposed a "double-helix" of human development where human capacities co-evolve with life condition changes; i.e., a system where humans and the environment co-create change in each other.

Being secure (or not) about environmental change has for most of human history appeared to be largely a local condition. However, as our spheres of awareness have widened (even beyond earth), we now recognize its roots as both local and global (and even galactic).

Ironically in terms of critical environmental impact on most cities—the most complex human systems yet created—it appears that all major cities of the world are built on or near the intersection of tectonic plates, or fault lines (for the very good reason that these are the closest point to where the energies and resources arising from the inner core of the planet emerge onto its outer surfaces and provide raw materials for human horticulture, manufacture and city infrastructure (Stewart, 2010)). At the same time, this very juxtaposition of human systems and tectonic forces has required the constant awareness, response and adaptation to these recurring causes of insecurity. A meta-view of human security must consider this as a key factor in city risk assessment, which will persist as long as the planet continues its ever-evolving eruption of "natural disasters" (caused by the shifting of tectonic plates).

Not surprisingly, many human security experts seek a new human security theory that not only embraces both the local and global, but transcends and includes current valuable but partial views of human security. They imagine a full spectrum, holistic, comprehensive, scalable systems approach (including social and biophysical elements) that integrates multiple sustainability paths and short, medium and long-term strategies (Buhaug & al, 2013; Marcotullio & Solecki, 2013; Simon & Leck, 2013).

Global environmental change factors and issues have been documented by many, frequently recognizing the interconnection of core threats (Rockström, Steffen, Noone, & etal, 2009). The Millennium Development Goals (anon, 2000) identified eight threats (poverty and hunger, lack of universal primary education, gender inequality, child mortality, maternal health, HIV/AIDS, environmental unsustainability, absence of global partnership for development). The Millennium Project identified fifteen challenges (sustainable development and climate change, clean water, population and resources, democratization, long-term perspectives, global convergence of IT, rich-poor gap, health issues, capacity to decide, peace and conflict, status of women, transnational organized crime, energy, science and technology, global ethics (Glenn, Gordon, & Florescu, 2011a, 2011b)). Recently in the Integral City 2.0 Online Conference, five major threats to human populations in cities were identified as critical (climate, energy, water, food, finance) (Hamilton & etal, 2013; Hamilton & Sanders, 2013). The Sustainable Development Goals (anon, 2017) aimed to target 17 goals to attain by 2030 (including no poverty, no hunger, wellbeing, quality education, gender equality, clean water and sanitation, clean energy, economic growth and work, industry innovation and infrastructure, reduced inequalities, sustainable cities/communities, responsible consumption/ production, climate change, life in water and on land, justice/peace and partnerships). However, these taxonomies, despite recognizing the interconnection and multi-directionality of the threats (implied in the goals), are not viewed within a systemic framework that tracks environmental risks along with the bio-psycho-cultural-social factors of human systems reflected in all the taxonomies.

Thus, if for no other reason than the necessity to adapt to ever-changing life conditions, humans and cities are permanently locked into a never-ending learning cycle, to create ever-more complex adaptations to protect increasingly more complex cities. So, in service to city evolution, human security systems must evolve risk assessment lenses, methodologies and measures for cities. Table 10 (col.1) charts four major levels of system complexity in human systems: self, socio, world and "Kosmo" centric levels of complexity (Greiving, Wanczura, Vossebuerger, Sucker, & Fourman, 2007, p. 18). As they interact with life conditions, humans at these levels of complexity express increasingly complex systems of values (col. 2) that transcend and include one another, while manifesting requisite economic structures (col. 3) to enable survival. As human systems adapt and complexify (col. 1, 2, 3), they develop the capacities to expand their boundaries of space and time (col. 4) from local to global. Within this evolutionary matrix, the focus of human security has matured (col. 5) from sensing the natural environment, to honoring spiritual practices, to protecting power tyrants, to following authorized ways, to organizing for strategic results, to serving community justice and diversity, to designing systems that flex and flow to supporting the principles of life on the planet.

Table 10: Human Security Evolution and Maturity Levels

Adapted from Beck and Cowan (1996), Eddy (2003, 2005), Wilber (1996), Hamilton (2011)

1. Level of System Complexity	2. Related Values Systems	3. Historical Economic Structures	4. Space/Time Boundaries	5. Maturity of HS Focus
Traditional: Self	1. Basics of life	Gatherer	Local	Sense HS in the city's land, sea, air and life forms
	2. Family	Gatherer/Hunter	Local Extended	Honor HS through spiritual practices that honor places and ancestors
Modern: Socio	3. Power	Hunter/ Horticultural	Region/Territory	Protect HS through "tyranny of Power"
	4. Authority	Horticultural/ Agrarian	State	Rule HS through authorities of "One Right Way"

1. Level of System Complexity	2. Related Values Systems	3. Historical Economic Structures	4. Space/Time Boundaries	5. Maturity of HS Focus
Modern-Post-Modern: World	5. Competition	Industrial	Nation	Organize for HS results through logic, science and strategy
	6. Social Safety	Industrial/ Informational	Multi-Nation	Serve HS as community justice caring for all (including diverse) members
Integral: Kosmos	7. Systems Flexibility	Informational/ Systemic	Eco-Region	Design HS systems that flex and flow
	8. Global Holism	Ecosystem/ Global	Globe	Enable HS as a global process related to all life on earth

A META-FRAMEWORK FOR EVOLUTIONARY CHANGE

Global Environment as the Cosmosphere and Biosphere

Eddy (2003) reframed the study of geography as a history of the universe and world, within an Integral model and ecosystem science. He provides an evolutionary view within which to examine both global environmental change and theories of human security. Eddy (2005) starts with the Big Bang and reveals the evolutionary strata that culminate in human civilization as in Figure 5.

Eddy grounds the study of global environmental change within three differentiated strata: The Cosmosphere that spans the universe; the Biosphere that includes the living global environment; and the Anthroposphere that embraces the human condition. He groups the study of these into a spectrum of "pure and applied (CBA or ABC) sciences": Earth and Planetary Sciences; Life Sciences; and Social Sciences as set out in Table 11.

A Brief History of the World

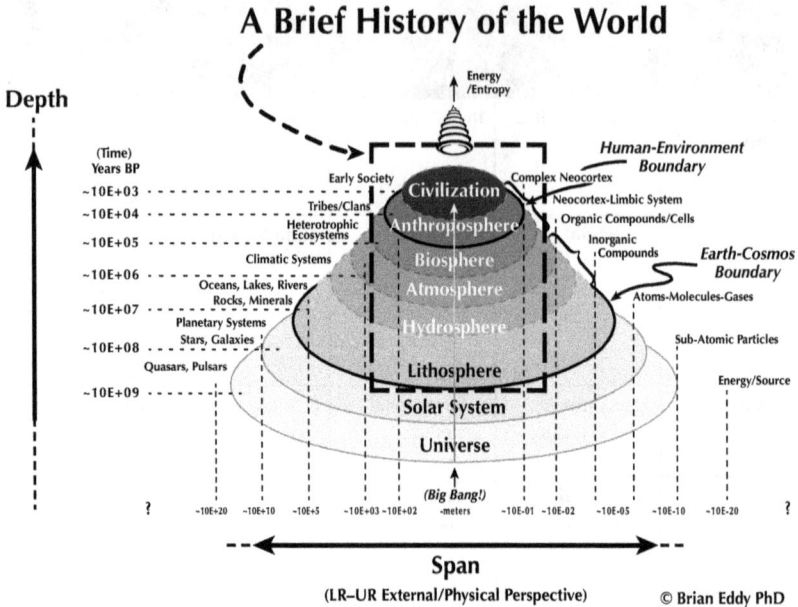

Figure 5: Brief History of the Universe and World. Source (Eddy, 2005)

Table 11: The ABC of Integral Geography (*adapted from Eddy, 2005*)

Science Cluster	Disciplines	Relevant Geographic Spheres
Earth and Planetary Sciences:	Math, Physics, Chemistry Astronomy Geology Hydrology Meteorology etc.	Cosmosphere: Universe Earth Matter
Life Sciences	Biology Microbiology Zoology Botany etc.	Biosphere: Life Living Environment
Social Sciences	Psychology Sociology Anthropology etc.	Anthroposphere: Human Individual Collective

Eddy's evolutionary ABC framework builds on Wilber's framing of holons and holarchies (Wilber, 1995, 1996a, 2000b, 2007) and effectively integrates the human condition within global environmental change , showing the three spheres as evolving one from the other and massively entangled at all scales and times, co-creating conditions where now it is evident that the A-sphere is impacting both the B and C-spheres; for example reducing biodiversity in the B-sphere (Esbjörn-Hargens & Zimmerman, 2009) and changing the hydrological cycle in the C-sphere (Linton, 2010).

More recently, Hamilton (2011, 2014) using Eddy's Figure 5, integrated global environmental change issues within an evolutionary analysis of key literature, to identify the strata critical to global wellbeing:

- Psycho-Cultural-Social (Diamond, 2005; Hamilton, 2008a; Wilber, 1995; Wright, 2004)
- Bio-Genetic-Ecological (Esbjörn-Hargens & Zimmerman, 2009; Hamilton, 2008a; M. E. Zimmerman, 2005)
- Food Scarcity (L. Brown, 2008; McKibben, 2007, 2011; Taylor, 2008)
- Climate (Adger, Aggarwal, Argawala, Alcamo, & etal, 2007; Diamond, 2005; McKibben, 2011; M. Zimmerman, 2010)
- Water (L. Brown, 2008; Diamond, 2005; Linton, 2010)
- Energy (Monbiot & Prescott, 2007)

Taylor (Taylor, 2008) elegantly mapped the evolutionary incursion of human activity on earth's natural capital, embraced by the Biosphere and Cosmosphere. But the evolutionary connections to the B and C-spheres that underpin our security (and sustainability) dilemmas more effectively emerge when they are situated on Eddy's vertical History of the World Map as in Figure 6. Figure 6 makes the direct linkages, of Energy threats to degradation of the Lithosphere; Water threats to degradation of the Hydrosphere; Climate threats to degradation of the Atmosphere; Food threats to degradation of the Biosphere; and Psycho-Cultural-Social threats to degradation of the Anthroposphere.

Through this lens, we can see that global environmental change is not just horizontally observable and quantifiable (in the taxonomies previously mentioned), but undoubtedly has deep interdependent evolutionary roots which we humans are ignoring at the cost of human security. Hamilton's application of Eddy's map integrates the threats of global environmental change with the issues of human security. Because the most evolved strata of this Threat Map is human civilization, which is now predominantly located in cities (anon, 2011a, 2011b; Glenn et al., 2011a; Taylor, 2008) this evolutionarily aligned Threat Map provides a meta-frame to explain the concurrency of influences embedded in human security in the city. The meta-frame of the Integral City model (Beck & Cowan, 1996; Hamilton, 2008a; Wilber, 1995), now suggests an evolutionarily aligned strategy for addressing these threats. (It should be noted that this alignment is stratified, but non-linear. Each strata transcends and includes the strata below, but as noted above, the progressive entanglements and feedback loops between strata amplify the impacts of change as increasing complexity emerges. Thus, while the A-sphere is the most complex it not only impacts B and C-spheres, it too is impacted in turn by any changes originating in the B and C Spheres—just as Graves double helix model proposes.)

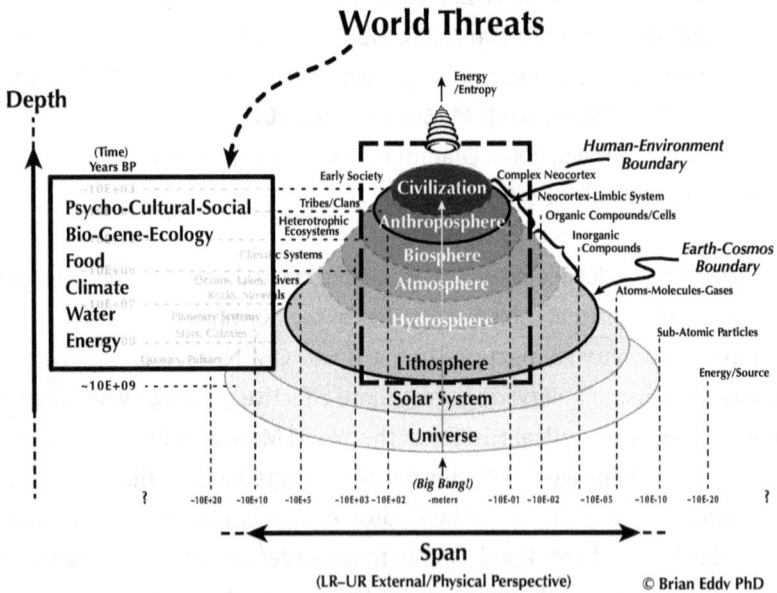

Figure 6: Threats to World Spheres in Evolutionary Trajectory

GLOBAL ENVIRONMENT AS THE ANTHROPOSPHERE: 5 MAPS THAT REVEAL HUMANS IN THE CITY AS GLOBAL ENVIRONMENT

The Anthroposphere can be appreciated through a meta-theory that integrates five essential maps of the most concentrated human system—the city (Hamilton, 2008a). Each map gives us a different view of human life in the whole city and eco-region (and thus human security as defined above) and helps us to understand the interrelationship of individuals, groups, sectors and communities. Although each map offers only a partial perspective, together they can be conceptually (and technologically) hyperlinked to give a more comprehensive picture of the human hive as interconnected, fractal, holographic and alive. A brief description of the value of each map follows (with graphic illustrations and full descriptions in Appendix B: Integral City Maps (1–5)).

Map 1: The City as Holon—The Four Quadrant, Eight Level Map

Map 1 is analogous to a "plan view" of human life and provides the perspective and altitude coordinates for what Wilber calls "Kosmic addresses" (Wilber, 2006).

The value of Map 1 to seeing human security in the city is that it situates not only perspectives but methodologies (that are designed using Integral methodological pluralism (Wilber, 2006)) for seeing the city as a whole living system (Wilber, 2006). It locates the parts, partial views and fragments of the city so that they can inform one another. By viewing the quadrants as an integrated city system we can see, for instance how the LL cultural values can be linked to the LR systems of safety, family law and recreational facilities, as well as individual UL beliefs and UR actions. Map 1 has a series of "growth rings" that spiral out from the center along the diagonal axis of each quadrant, representing the eight stages of complexity discussed in Table 12 and Map 4 (below). The outward pointing arrows on Map 1 indicate these vectors of change, expanding the four quadrants of the whole city outward from the core.

Map 2: The Nested Holarchy of City Systems

The city as a human system is a nest of systems made up of centers (Alexander, 2004), holons (Koestler) or nested holons (Sahtouris, 1999). The systems have orders of complexity (as discussed above), so that the holons, wholes and centers are nested into holarchies (Wilber, 1996c) or panarchies (Gunderson & Holling, 2002) where levels of complexity (and scale) emerge over time.

The value of Map 2 to human security in the city is that it reveals that every individual is a member of multiple city sub-systems or sectors (e.g. family, workplace, education system(s), healthcare system(s), place(s) of worship, neighborhood, city hall, and environment). Connections amongst individuals and sub-systems create spheres of influence, networks, communities of practice and meshworks as they become densified and aligned (Hamilton, 2010c). This map also reveals the progression of expanded time and space dimensions that correlates with larger and larger social holons (Table 12).

Map 3: The Scalar Fractal Relationship of Micro, Meso and Macro Social Holons

Map 3 shows the city as a social holon. Map 3 conveys how capacity development in an individual contributes to capacity in all the social holons of Map 2, while also revealing the reality of capacity dilution and amplification in the social holons of groups, organizations and communities.

Map 3 reveals that human security in the city is dynamic, arising from the tension between levels of development in collectives and individuals. This tension is only resolved when a critical mass of individual behaviors in the collective becomes coherent (for example, a minimum critical number of youths start online gaming so that it becomes socially accepted and then culturally contagious). Likewise, one group or cohort in a sector will find it difficult to be successful until a critical mass of groups also commits to the same practice (for example, conflicting faith systems collaborate to create a trans-organizational ministerial council). Complexity science reveals that, only 10 to 15 percent of a population need change, in order that the whole system shifts towards that change (Gladwell, 2002; Hamilton, 2008).

Map 4: The Complex Adaptive Structures of Change

Map 4 makes visible how the city's (Map 1, Lower Right) organizational structures evolve over time. (They also act as proxies for the commensurate Upper Right neural structures developing in individual brains as in Maps 1 and 3.)

The value of Map 4 to human security is that it provides a map of structural complexity for a multiplicity of human security practices, expressed at all eight levels of complexity. This allows us to correlate all the Traditional, Modern, Post-Modern (and emerging Integral) discourses operating in the 21st century city.

Map 5: Spirituality in the City

Map 5 conveys the qualities of spirituality in the city. Its zones of Grace, Space and Place reveal where the core spiritual values of Goodness, Truth and Beauty are manifested. The Kosmic addresses of these core spiritual values of the Integral City have both vertical and horizontal locations.

The value of Map 5 to human security is that it transcends and includes the other 4 Maps so we can see the location and contribution of Goodness, Truth and Beauty in both an involutionary and evolutionary context. Map 5 unpacks how the Master Code energizes all scales of human systems as Care, Context and Capacity flow through them. Map 5 shows the dynamics of the core Evolutionary Intelligence that empowers the city to be Gaia's Reflective Organ. When the zones of Grace, Space and Place are aligned through the lived values of Goodness, Truth and Beauty then living human systems (at any scale) can survive, connect with their environment and regenerate. When the spiritual zones and values are misaligned at any scale, the effect of that misalignment ripples throughout all the scales of human systems included in the Integral City. Map 5 unpacks the spiritual elements of what makes all human systems secure at all scales.

COMBINING THE MAPS INTO A HUMAN SECURITY INFORMATION SYSTEM

Combining the five city maps allows us to access evolutionary lenses to view human security and create resilient human security solutions sufficient to the level of complexity facing human systems. One can organize them into an Integral City Human Security Information System (ICHSIS) that reveals the tetra-arising, holarchical, evolutionary, developmental, adaptive dynamics of human security in the whole city.

To illustrate such an approach, Table 12 shows the fate of various cities related to all the categories of global threats (illustrated in Figure 6) in just the years 2010–17.

Table 12: Global Threats in Cities 2010–17

Threat (Figure 6)	Manifestation	City
Psycho-Cultural-Social	Terrorism Economic Meltdown Political/Cultural Clashes	Oslo, Paris, Brussels, Barcelona Manchester Athens, Rome Cairo + Arab Spring Cities
Bio-Genetic-Ecological	Avian Flu Ebola Zika Virus HIV	Jakarta & other cities in Indonesia Africa North America
Food Scarcity	Famine	Mogadishu, Somalia South Sudan
Climate	Hurricanes Sandy, Harvey, Irma Ice Melting	New York, Houston, Miami, USA Antarctic Ice Shelf Detaching
Water	Flooding	Brisbane, Australia Houston Bangladesh
Energy	Nuclear Meltdown Fire	Sendai, Japan Fort McMurray
Lithosphere	Earthquake	Christchurch NZ, Jiuzhaigou China, Kathmandu Nepal, Mexico City, Chilean Cities

While it is easy to inventory the threats as they occur in multiple cities we tend to miss their stratified interconnectedness in individual locations, because the immediacy of responding to local conditions can easily obscure the global patterns from which they arise (as initial news coverage of the above events tended to do).

When examining human security in any particular city, an ICHSIS can use a meta-security approach to design appropriate responses for threat adaptation, mitigation and/or prevention. If a design fails to align solutions along the evolutionary trajectory, the threats in Table 12 will continue to re-occur—usually worsening on each re-occurrence. (For instance, the downstream effects of the unresolved issues relating to the nuclear meltdown in Japan are still being experienced. To name just a few—it has impacted water quality and fish stocks around the Pacific, air quality, food crops, economy and cultural tourism in Japan.)

The meta-theory proposes that the most effective place to engage and design a human security system, is to start at the top of the threat chain; i.e., within the city leaders and stakeholders themselves (B. Brown, 2011). The human security challenge is to re-frame stakeholder mindsets to recognize they are part of the very human security paradigm, with which they are called to engage. Expanding paradigms to embrace the ABC sequence of threats will give human security systems the greatest leverage for change (Meadows, 2008) because the system will gain an "overview" (anon, 2014) perspective. Such a whole system, integrated approach begins the process called "meshworking"—which meshes or weaves together responses to the ABC issues, without omitting any key factor. Core principles of meshworking (Hamilton, 2010, 2017; Sahtouris, 2010, 2017) to create an ICHSIS include aligning the following elements.

Principle 1. Honor Spheres

1. Identify the change severity of the ABC spheres of the city container.

Principle 2. Respect Threat(s)

2. Name and evolutionarily map the ABC environmental threat(s) in the system.

3. Identify the purpose for human security change. Facing the ABC threat provides the impetus or catalyst to change. Create the vision for changing human security from what to what; e.g. mitigate, adapt or eliminate threat?

Principle 3. Engage Stakeholders

4. Use an Integral map to find the agents for human security change—engage as many stakeholders in the process as possible—actively seek out diversity and make room for difference.

5. Enable leadership to emerge to address the threat(s) at the appropriate level of complexity.

Principle 4. Facilitate Processes

6. Amplify the threat to human security so others can see it.

7. Integrally identify the resources needed to facilitate the change and invite and involve stakeholders to contribute them.

Principle 5. Design Integral Methodologies

8. Co-design Integral methodologies for human security change that self-organize passion, purpose, priorities, people, and planet. Expect it to be messy.

Principle 6. Learn from Feedback Loops

9. Create target-based feedback loops and Integral vital signs monitors so that participants can self-correct and develop operational human security structures that work.

10. Make the feedback accessible to all by publication and display; e.g. community newspapers, online media, real time intelligence display systems.

11. Pay forward to other stakeholders, cities, eco-regions, the Integral learning for prevention, mitigation and/or adaptation.

Principle 7: Practise the Master Code

12. Take care of Self, so that you can care for Others, so together we care for our Place(s), and all of us can care for our Planet.

Such an Integral human security approach reveals how to integrate partial responses and meshwork spheres, threats, stakeholders, processes, methodologies and feedback loops into whole system, multi-level flexible strategies.

CONCLUSION: HELPFUL SIGNS

In conclusion, we propose that human security for city systems have to be integrated into evolutionary sequences. Human security without adaptation to global environmental change is futile if not impossible. Leaders in sustainability progress through the understanding of the kind of deep evolutionary change, to which we are pointing, in terms of security, sustainability and resilience, by first working *on* the system, then working *with* the system, and finally working *as* the system (B. Brown, 2011). As each leader's worldview expands, they become more closely identified with environmental change evolving in themselves along with their capacity to survive and develop a spectrum of adaptive human security systems. With this Integral approach, it then becomes possible to shift from the fragmentation inherent in traditional reductionism, modern management and post-modern social safety nets, to an Integral human security system that is globally designed but locally adapted because it is fractal, scalable, holistic, comprehensive, pluralistic, interconnected, evolutionary and developmental.

A final note of optimism comes from returning to the threats we noted in Table 12. We offer a final Table 13 where those threats are being addressed by sciences of resilience and living systems, Integral leadership practices, plans for food abundance, framing an Integral discourse for climate change, recognizing our relationship with water is both physically and intellectually evolutionary and institutionalizing eco-footprints into ISO city standards (Peirce, 2014). All these responses contribute to an ICHSIS approach as part of a new science of cities (West, 2011, 2017).

Table 13: Helpful Signs

Threat	Integral Manifestation & Response	Integrally Informed Researchers & Authors
Psycho-Cultural-Social	Resilience Paradigm Shift Reinventing Organizations	Holling, Bloom, Hamilton Meadows, Laszlo, Wilber, Beck, B. Brown, Laloux
Bio-Genetic-Ecological	Living Systems	Miller Sahtouris
Food Scarcity	Plan B 4.0	L. Brown
Climate	World in 2050 Rethinking the Climate Change Debate	Smith Zimmerman
Water	Story of Water	Linton
Energy	Evolution's Edge Eco-Footprint	Taylor Rees, Wackernagel ISO City Standard
Lithosphere	All major cities are built beside faults—it gives them access to resources from Earth's core	Iain Stewart, "Hot Rocks" Geographer

(D. Beck, 2010; Bloom, 2000; B. Brown, 2011; L. Brown, 2008; Hamilton, 2008a; Hamilton, 2011a; Laszlo, 2006d; Linton, 2010; Rees & Wackernagel, 1994; Smith, 2010; Stewart, 2010; Taylor, 2008; West, 2017; M. Zimmerman, 2010)

Ultimately the application of an Integral City approach to human security creates a methodology of care at all three ABC spheres, which is Principle 7—the Master Code of the human hive.

Principle 7. Master Code

Take Care of Yourself—in the Anthroposphere
Take Care of Life—in the Biosphere
Take Care of this Place/Planet—in the Cosmosphere.

REFERENCES

Adger, N., Aggarwal, P., Argawala, S., Alcamo, J., & etal. (2007). Climate Change 2007: Impacts, Adaptation and Vulnerability, Summary for Policy Makers. Retrieved from http://www.ipcc.ch/

anon. (2000). Millennium Development Goals. Retrieved November 8, 2011, from UN: http://en.wikipedia.org/wiki/Millennium_Development_Goals

anon. (2011a). Global Report on Human Settlement 2011 Hot Cites: Battle-Ground for Climate Change. Retrieved December 29, 2017, from UN Habitat http://mirror.unhabitat.org/downloads/docs/E_Hot_Cities.pdf

anon. (2011b). World Health Organization Global Alert and Response (GAR). Retrieved November 7, 2011: http://www.who.int/csr/don/en/

anon. (2017c). Sustainable Development Goals. Retrieved December 11, 2017, from Wikipedia https://en.wikipedia.org/wiki/Sustainable_Development_Goals

anon. (2017d). Overview Effect. Retrieved December 13, 2017, from Wikepedia https://en.wikipedia.org/wiki/Overview_effect

Beck, D. (2000). MeshWORKS™: A Second Tier Perspective & Process. The Spiral Dynamics Group.

Beck, D. (2010). Natural Designs for Meshworking. Retrieved from Gaiaspace, Meshworking, Private.

Beck, D., & Cowan, C. (1996). *Spiral Dynamics: Mastering Values, Leadership and Change*. Malden, MA: Blackwell Publishers.

Bloom, H. (2000). *The Global Brain: The Evolution of Mass Mind from the Big Bang to the 21st Century*. New York: John Wiley & Son Inc.

Brown, B. (2011). *Conscious Leadership for Sustainability: How Leaders with a Late-Stage Action Logic Design and Engage in Sustainability Initiatives*. Fielding, Santa Barbara.

Brown, L. (2008). *Plan B 3.0*. New York: W.W. Norton & Company.

Buhaug, H., Urdal, H., & Ostby, G. (2013). Sustainable Urbanization and Human Security. In L. Sygna, K. O'Brien, & J. Wolf (Eds.), *A Changing Environment for Human Security: Transformative Approaches to Research, Policy and Action*. Abingdon, Oxon, OX: Routledge.

Capra, F. (1996). *The Web of Life: A New Scientific Understanding of Living Systems*. New York: Anchor Books, Doubleday.

De Landa, M. (1995). Homes: Meshwork or Hierarchy? *http://www.mediamatic.net/article-200.5956.html*. Special: Home issue. Retrieved Dec. 4, 2004

Diamond, J. (2005). *Collapse: How societies choose to fail or succeed* (first ed.). New York: Penguin Group.

Eddy, B. (2003). Sustainable Development, Spiral Dynamics, and Spatial Data: A '3i' Approach to SD. Paper presented at the Spiral Dynamics integral, Level II, Ottawa, 2003.

Eddy, B. (2005). Place, Space and Perspective. *World Futures, 61*, 151–163.

Esbjörn-Hargens, S., & Zimmerman, M. (2009). *Integral Ecology: Uniting Multiple Perspectives on the Natural World*. Boston: Shambhala Publications Inc.

Gasper, D. (2010). *The Idea of Human Security Climate Change, Ethics and Human Security*. Cambridge, UK: Cambridge University Press.

Gladwell, M. (2002). *The Tipping Point: How Little Things Can Make a Big Difference*. New York: Back Bay Books.

Glenn, J. C., Gordon, T. J., & Florescu, E. (2011a). *State of the Future 2011*: The Millennium Project.

Glenn, J. C., Gordon, T. J., & Florescu, E. (2011b). State of the Future 2011 Electronic Research CD pp. (8000).

Graves, C. (1971). A systems conception of personality: Levels of existence theory. Paper presented at the Washington School of Psychiatry.

Graves, C. (1974). Human Nature Prepares for a Momentous Leap. *The Futurist*, 8(2), 72–78.

Graves, C. (1981). Summary statement, The emergent, cyclical, double helix model of the adult human biopsychosocial systems. (Publication no. http://www.clarewgraves.com/articles_content/1981_handout/1981_summary.pdf). Retrieved July 3, 2002.

Graves, C. (2003). *Levels of Human Existence: Transcription of a Seminar at Washington School of Psychiatry, Oct. 16, 1971.* Santa Barbara: Eclet Publishing.

Graves, C. (2005). *The Never Ending Quest: A Treatise on an Emergent Cyclical Conception of Adult Behavioral Systems and Their Development.* Santa Barbara, CA: ECLET Publishing.

Greiving, S., Wanczura, S., Vossebuerger, P., Sucker, K., & Fourman, M. (2007). *Multidimensional Integrated Risk Governance: Scalable Resilience and Risk Governance Concept Including Guidelines on Stakeholder Involvement.* London, UK: UNIDO, IKU.

Gunderson, L. C., & Holling, C. S. (Eds.). (2002). *Panarchy: Understanding Transformations in Human and Natural Systems.* Washington, DC: Island Press.

Hamilton, M. (2008). *Integral City: Evolutionary Intelligences for the Human Hive.* Gabriola Island BC: New Society Publishers.

Hamilton, M. (2010). *Meshworking Integral Intelligences for Resilient Environments; Enabling Order and Creativity in the Human Hive.* Paper presented at the Enacting an Integral Future Conference 2010.

Hamilton, M. (2011). *Big Picture for Sustainability Leadership: Life Conditions for Leading from our Deepest & Widest Perspectives.* Paper presented at the Embody Integral Leadership Conference.

Hamilton, M. (2013). *Meta Security in the Human Hive: Integrally Aligning Sustainability Responses to Trajecectory of Evolutionary Threats.* Paper presented at the International Society Systems Science 2013, Haiphong, Vietnam.

Hamilton, M. (2014). Meta-Framework for Security in the Human Hive: Integrally Aligning Sustainability Responses to Trajectory of Evolutionary Threats. *Systems Research and Behavioral Science, Syst.Res.* 31, 614–626. Retrieved from doi:10.1002/sres.2310

Hamilton, M. (2017). *Integral City Inquiry and Action: Designing Impact for the Human Hive.* Phoenix, AZ: Integral Publishers.

Hamilton, M., & etal. (2013). Integral City 2.0 Online Conference 2012 Appendices: A Radically Optimistic Inquiry Into Operating System 2.0—36 Interviews. In M. Hamilton (Eds.) Available from http://www. scribd.com/doc/123005653/Integral-City-2-0-Online-Conference-2012-Appendices-A-Radically-Optimistic-Inquiry-into-Operating-System-2-0-36-Interviews

Hamilton, M., & Sanders, B. (2013). Integral City 2.0 Online Conference 2012 Proceedings: A Radically Optimistic Inquiry Into Operating System 2.0. In M. Hamilton (Eds.) Available from http://www.scribd.com/doc/120713339/Integral-City-2-0-Online-Conference-2012-A-Radically-Optimistic-Inquiry-into-Operating-System-2-0

Laloux, F. (2014). *Reinventing Organizations* Retrieved from Electronic Book.

Laszlo, E. (2004). *Science and the Akashic Field: An Integral Theory of Everything* (2007 ed.). Rochester, Vermont: Inner Traditions.

Laszlo, E. (2006). Ten Benchmarks of an Evolved Consciousness *The Chaos Point: The World at the Crossroads* (pp. pp. 80–81). Charlottesville, VA: Hampton Roads Publishing.

Linton, J. (2010). *What is Water? The History of a Modern Abstraction.* Vancouver, BC, Canada: UBC Press.

Marcotullio, P., & Solecki, W. (2013). Sustainability and Cities: Meeting the Grand Challenge for the Twenty-First Century. In L. Sygna, K. O'Brien, & J. Wolf (Eds.), A *Changing Environment for Human Security: Transformative Approaches to Research, Policy and Action.* Abingdon, Oxon, OX: Routledge.

McKibben, B. (2007). *Deep Economy: The Wealth of Communities and the Durable Future.* New York: Time Books Henry Holt and Company, LLC.

McKibben, B. (2011). 350.Org. Retrieved December 13, 2017, from 350.Org: http://www.350.org/

Meadows, D. (2008). *Thinking in Systems.* White River Junction, VT: Chelsea Green Publishing.

Monbiot, G., & Prescott, M. (2007). Heat: *How to Stop the Planet From Burning.* Toronto: Anchor Canada.

Peirce, N. (Producer). (2014, July 7, 2014) Finally, clear performance data for comparing the world's cities. article retrieved from http://cityminded.

org/finally-clear-performance-data-comparing-worlds-cities-1173?utm_source-ReviveOldPost

Rees, W. E. P. D., & Wackernagel, M. (1994). *Ecological Footprints and Appropriated Carrying Capacity: Measuring the Natural Capital Requirements of the Human Economy.* Washington, DC: Island Press.

Rockström, J., Steffen, W., Noone, K., & etal. (2009). Planetary Boundaries: Exploring the Safe Operating Space for Humanity. art32. Retrieved from http://www.ecologyandsociety.org/vol14/iss2/art32

Sahtouris, E. (2010). Celebrating Crisis: Towards a Culture of Cooperation. A *New Renaissance:Transforming Science, Spirit & Society,* . London: Floris Books.

Sahtouris, E. (2017). A Tale of Cities and Cells: Our Human Evolutionary Agenda. Retrieved December 7, 2017 https://www.ethicalmarkets.com/a-tale-of-cities-and-cells-by-elisabet-sahtouris/

Simon, D., & Leck, H. (2013). Cities, Human Security and Global Environmental Change. In L. Sygna, K. O'Brien, & J. Wolf (Eds.), A *Changing Environment for Human Security: Transformative Approaches to Research, Policy and Action.* Abingdon, Oxon, OX: Routledge.

Smith, L. G. (2010). *The World in 2050: Four Forces Shaping Civilization's Northern Future.* New York: Dutton.

Stewart, I. (Writer). (2010). "Hot Rocks" Geography [TV]. In BBC (Producer): Knowledge Network.

Taylor, G. (2008). *Evolution's Edge: The Coming Collapse and Transformation of our World.* Gabriola Island, BC: New Society Publishers.

West, G. (2011). Why Cities Keep Growing, Corporations and People Always Die, and Life Gets Faster: A Conversation With Geoffrey West (5.23.11). In J. Brockman (Ed.), *Edge:* Edge.org.

West, G. (2017). *Scale: The Universal Laws of Growth, Innovation, Sustainability and the Pace of Life in Organisms, Cities, Economies and Companies.* New York: Penguin Press.

Wilber, K. (1995). *Sex, Ecology and Spirituality: the spirit of evolution.* Boston: Shambhala Publications Inc.

Wilber, K. (1996). A *Brief History of Everything,* . Boston,: Shambhala Publications Inc.

Wilber, K. (2000). A *Theory of Everything.* Boston: Shambhala Publications Inc.

Wilber, K. (2006). *Integral Spirituality*. Boston: Shambhala Publications Inc.

Wilber, K. (2007). *The Integral Vision*. Boston: Shambhala Publications Inc.

Wright, R. (2004). A *Short History of Progress* (Avalon ed.). New York: Carroll & Graf Publishers.

Zimmerman, M. (2010). *Changing the Conversation: Rethinking the Climate Change Debate from an Integral Perspective.* Paper presented at the Enacting an Integral Future Conference.

Zimmerman, M. E. (2005). Integral Ecology: A perspectival, developmental, and coordinating approach to environmental problems. *World Futures, Volume 61, Issue 1 & 2 January 2005, pages 50—62 (Issue 1 & 2),* 50—62

PART 3

Widening Capacity

The original framework for Book 1 in this series (*Integral City: Evolutionary Intelligences for the Human Hive*) was fractal; it depended fundamentally on the concept of the scale of human systems. It offered a framework of 12 Intelligences that cities must use to become and remain sustainable and resilient. The 12 Intelligences (as outlined in Appendices C1, C2, C3) are habits or capacities that enable the dynamics, interrelationships and coherence of cities for their sustainability and resilience; namely, 5 sets of intelligences that are: Contexting, Individual, Collective, Strategic and Evolutionary.

Part 3 explores in four sections how capacity in the human hive widens at progressively larger scales:

- **Leader**
- **Organization**
- **System**
- **City**

SECTION 1:

Widening Capacity
at Leader Scale

Chapter 7 explores how **individual leaders grow** through eight successive stages that progressively widen their capacities to influence the dimensions of morality, time and space.

Chapter 8 explores how the peculiar but necessary role of the **Diversity Generator** in the human hive sparks creativity and enables both sustainability and resilience.

Chapter 9 offers the **case study of leadership by an architectual partnership** which enacts personal sustainability leadership while working in the interstitial zones of conflicting nations, evolving cities and intermingled cultures.

LEADERSHIP TO THE POWER OF 8: LEADING SELF, OTHERS, ORGANIZATION, SYSTEM AND SUPRA SYSTEM

*Originally published in **Integral Leadership Review** 2012 and in revised shorter version in **WiPsi**, 2012 as* LEADERSHIP TO THE POWER OF 8: LEADING SELF, OTHERS, ORGANIZATION, SYSTEM AND SUPRA-SYSTEM

CHAPTER SUMMARY

This chapter explores the qualities of leadership to the "Power of 8". It offers a definition of leadership that can be recalibrated across a spectrum of complexity. It proposes the Integral paradigm as a source for framing, measuring, mapping and tracking leadership across four levels of complexity. The article examines evidence from three sets of leaders at three progressively more complex levels of leadership, considering their capacities related to moral influence, space and time, within the contexts of organizations, systems and supra-systems. The chapter concludes that the Integral model is a valid model for framing and/or understanding leadership and summarizes its key advantages.

Key words: Leadership to the Power of 8, Integral model, leadership context, moral influence, space, time

INTRODUCTION

. . . leaders with increasing capacity are more equipped to engage with the complexity, paradox, non-linear stresses, ambiguity and multitude of perspectives. . . . The [peer teachers of integrally informed leadership who] have tested their theories

through the lenses of Integral frameworks using multiple methodologies and gathered data with a plurality of methods: interviews, observation, self/peer/coach evaluations, introspection, action inquiry, and inter-organizational comparisons . . . all conclude that the need for advanced leadership development is critical in today's complex world and that the resources to deliver leaders with advanced capacities are not sufficient to the current demands that we face from: global, multi-scale, unsustainable, stressful, cross-sector complicities, productivity challenges, resource depletion and generational values shifts. (Hamilton, 2008b)

DEFINING LEADERSHIP

For the last twenty-five years, my "pracademic" inquiry into leadership has ranged from teaching and publishing a multi-construct leadership typology (Anderson, 1992, p. 115; Anderson & Ford, 1998; Hamilton, 2000), to doctoral research seeking to understand the relationship between leadership and learning in a self-organizing online community (Hamilton, 1999) to performing as a positional leader in my communities of interest and location, to serving as a professor in a School of Leadership (Hamilton, 2001, 2008b). Definitions for *Leadership* and *Communities* in my leadership research and positional experience have progressed from "leader as coach" in the adult developmental and coaching frameworks of Anderson et al and Egan (Anderson, 1992; Anderson & Ford, 1998; Egan, 1990); to "leader as visionary or team leader" in the leadership systems models of Senge (Senge, 1994; Senge, Kleiner, Roberts, Ross, & Smith, 1994) and Flood (Flood, 1999); to "leader as anyone who wants to help at this time" in the complexity and living systems framings of leadership by Wheatley (Wheatley, 2006; Wheatley & Kellner-Rogers, 1996); to "leader as agent of change" in the change discourse (Eoyang & Olson, 2001); and finally to "leader as a values-based organizational change agent" in a model that seemed able to contain all of these frameworks, namely the Integral model of reality developed by Ken Wilber coined AQAL (Wilber, 2006, 2007). In the last decade I have refined my understanding of the Integral leadership framework with a study of Graves' adult development model (Graves, 1971, 1974, 2003, 2005) and Spiral Dynamics (Beck & Cowan, 1996; Beck & Linscott, 2006).

While my original research question focused on discerning which came first, leaders or the communities they lead, my early quest was inspired by the elegant simplicity of Jaworski's (1996) definition of leadership as: "a journey to wholeness for an individual". That simple statement seemed to imply the kind of unfolding that had occurred with my examination of leadership across a spectrum of increasing complexity. Wilber's AQAL model provided a template to observe, track and evaluate the performance of leaders in a wholistic frame composed of four lenses (quadrants). Table 14 illustrates them as: Upper Right (UR) exterior individual action, Upper Left (UL) interior individual reflection, Lower Left (LL) interior collective relationships and Lower Right (LR) exterior collective systems. For the purposes of this chapter, an acting definition of leadership is: "the dynamic bio-psycho-cultural-systemic capacity of a person to adaptively lead human systems at multiple scales of complexity to achieve some outcome".

Table 14: AQAL Quadrants

	Interior	Exterior	
Individual Upper Left	psycho reflection	bio action	**Individual Upper Right**
Collective Lower Left	cultural relationships	system structural	**Collective Lower Right**

INTEGRAL MODEL—AN EFFECTIVE MODEL FOR RESEARCHING LEADERSHIP

This definition can be applied across increasing scales of complexity that can be termed: ego-ethno-world-Kosmic. Thus leadership capacity can be tracked during the lifetime of the leader through four performance lenses of wholeness or holons. Both Wilber (1995, p. 18), and Beck and Cowan (1996, p. 289) borrowing from Koestler (1976), termed the quality of this wholeness as "holonic", meaning that systems and sub-systems are both parts of larger systems while being whole systems in themselves. Such a frame introduces the concept, dynamics and complexity of systems thinking to wholeness as a holarchy of nested holons (where an individual leader belongs simultaneously to family, teams/groups, organizations, communities, city, society/culture and finally species).

Within the Integral frame we encounter the quality of fractalness. Fractal patterns of human development repeat themselves at different scales in the holarchy. The fractal qualities of the four quadrants and the four evolutionary levels of development enable the application of this model not only to individual holons but to social holons (the collective of individuals in any multi-person grouping). Thus the fractal patterns offer ways of grasping individual systems that persist and/or develop along with the exponential levels of dynamic complexity of human systems. Over time my own research and writing has attempted to unpack the application and implications of the leadership definition to the collective scales of community and city, where a fractal definition of community becomes: "the dynamic bio-psycho-cultural-systemic capacity of a groups to adaptively develop human systems at multiple scales of complexity to achieve some shared outcome." (Hamilton, 1998, 1999).

In addition to Wilber (Wilber, 2001, 2006), Beck (Beck, 2000b, 2001, 2002a), Cook-Greuter (Cook-Greuter, 1999, 2002) and Kegan (Kegan, 1994; Kegan & Lahey, 2001, 2009) have explicated similar waves of human development, which help explain the situational variants of leadership development.

Table 15 illustrates one version of this trajectory.

Table 15: Leadership Development Levels and Basic Motives

ᵛMeme Symbol	Developmental Level	Basic Leadership Motives
BEIGE	1	Staying alive through innate sensory equipment.
PURPLE	2	Belonging to blood relationships; conjuring mystical spirits in a magical and scary world.
RED	3	Enforcing power over self, others, and nature through exploitive dependence.
BLUE	4	Commanding absolute belief in one right way and obedience to authority.
ORANGE	5	Inventing and possibility thinking, focused on making things better for self.
GREEN	6	Sharing equality and seeking the well-being of people; building consensus as highest priority.
YELLOW	7	Adapting flexibly to change through connected, systemic views.
TURQUOISE	8	Attending to Whole-Earth dynamics and macro-level actions.

Note: *This is a simplified description of the eight* ᵛMemes; *the developmental levels not only of individuals, but also the evolution of societies. Adapted from Beck and Cowan* (2006)

These developmental waves or levels locate individuals (and the groups they lead) within the four quadrants as noted above situated at a "center of gravity" (COG) level. This COG spans multiple levels (generally three) of development as a person or group's capacity expands through increasingly complex layers of development, with varied weightings of quadrant development. (It must also be noted that the same map can chart the contraction to lesser levels of complexity if the environment imposes life conditions that force a contraction to earlier levels of development for the sake of survival (e.g. in the face of natural disaster, famine or disease.)

Thus the developmentalists chart the map of potential human (and leadership) growth, while Graves and Beck, in particular, point to the contexting of this within an understanding of complex adaptive systems— where the environmental life conditions must always be considered a triggering factor and become the context for increasingly complex forms of organization (as identified in Table 16).

Table 16: Organizational Environments as Leadership Contexts

Level of Complexity	Structure of Organization
Level 1 (BEIGE)	Hearth circle
Level 2 (PURPLE)	Tribal gathering circle
Level 3 (RED)	Power-based hierarchy
Level 4 (BLUE)	Authority-based hierarchy
Level 5 (ORANGE)	Strategic hierarchical system
Level 6 (GREEN)	Social network
Level 7 (YELLOW)	Self-organizing system
Level 8 (TURQUOISE)	Global noetic field

Note. *Adapted from Hamilton* (2008) *and Beck & Cowan* (1996)

LEADERSHIP TO THE POWER OF X

One of the discoveries of developmental theorists is that humans develop intelligences that can increase in both quantity and quality. Quantity relates to the multiple intelligences identified by Gardner (Gardner, 1999) and quality relates those intelligences to a trajectory of development that is emerging in terms of leadership effectiveness defined as Intelligence Quotient (IQ), Emotional Quotient (EQ) (Goleman, 1997), Values Quotient (VQ) (McIntosh, 2007) and Spiritual Quotient (SQ) (Wigglesworth, 2002, 2004, 2011, 2014)(Gauthier & Fowler, 2008).

Graves proposed that intelligences emerge in humans in response to triggering events in their environments (Graves, 1971, 2003, 2005). His proposition was that the potential for development was inherent in the healthy human, and the quality of intelligences emerges as the individual encounters increasingly more complex environments. Similar theories have emerged that track the levels of complexity of adults (Cook-Greuter, 1999, 2002; Dawson-Tunik et al 2005; Kegan, 1994; Kegan & Lahey, 2001; Torbert et al, 2008).

Thus the potential for leadership is released in the context of any given leader's environment. As noted in (Hamilton, 2008a, p. 103) those environments can be calibrated essentially as shown in Table 17.

Table 17: Summary of Leadership Calibrations

- **Self aware**
  - ° Self manage
  - ° Self learn/lead/teach
    - **Other aware**
      - ° Other manage
      - ° Other learn/lead/teach
        - **Context aware**
          - ° Context manage
          - ° Context learn/lead/teach
            - **System aware**
              - ° System manage
              - ° System learn/lead/teach

These calibrations (adapted from the measurement system used by Dawson et al (2005) for the tracking of leadership lines of specific expertise) effectively map the lifecycle of leadership learning stages: entry-awareness, practitioner-management and exemplar-teacher.

As leaders learn to manage and then lead self, other, context and system, they become of necessity increasingly attentive and increasingly intentional. While becoming increasingly attentive and intentional, the leader becomes an increasingly capable contributor to the intelligence of larger and larger environments. A leader who has higher capacities of emotional, mental and interpersonal intelligences has the potential to contribute to many complex social holons, including families, groups, teams, organizations, communities, cities and nations at larger and larger scales. (Hamilton, 2008a, p. 103)

In essence the development of leadership capacity (UL) can be measured as performance (UL) that leads effectively in contexts of ever increasing metrics of space (LR), time (LR, LL) and moral influence (LL) [3]. This means that as the leader matures through levels of complexity their spheres of influence grow from:

> **space** measured as very near (home turf) to very far (global influence)
>
> **time** measured as impact of decision horizons defined in months to decades (Beck & Cowan, 1996, pp. 53, 169; Dutrisac, Fowke, Koplowitz, & Shepard, nd; Gray, Hunt, & McArthur, 2007, p. 108; Hamilton, 2008a, pp. 174–175)
>
> **moral influence** measured as the number (and levels of complexity) of people (from few to many and from less developed to highly developed) who are impacted by direct and indirect decisions (UL), actions (UR), policies (LL) and systems (LR) (Beck & Cowan, 1996, pp. 62, 123).

It is this combination of leadership calibrations and reach that gives us the metrics for noticing the trajectories of Leadership to the Power of 5, 6, 7 and 8. But before we examine this span in particular, let us look at the capacity of leaderships to all the powers that we are currently examining.

3, In chapter 1 I have written about how spiritual leadership can also be calibrated in terms of the qualities of beauty, goodness and truth. However, for the purposes of this chapter I wanted to select metrics that could be quantified.

SUMMARY OF ALL LEADERSHIP FOCI

(It should be noted that each level of leadership from 2 to 8 recalibrates the preceding levels.)

Leading Self (Ego)

Leadership to the Power of 1 is only able to focus on the self. It is the root of the egocentric stage of leadership development.

Leadership to the Power of 2 focuses on leading the family or clan.

Leadership to the Power of 3 completes this egocentric wave. Leaders to the Power of 3 focus on the power of "might as right". This is the apex of the dominator model and focus of leadership.

Leading Others (Ethno)

Leadership to the Power of 4 focuses on hierarchical order, based on merit and measurable standards, rules and authority.

Leading Context (World1)

Leadership to the Power of 5 focuses on the power of individual success, organizational results and sectoral competition.

Leadership to the Power of 6 focuses on the development of social justice, tolerance of differences and recognition of equality within social systems.

Leading System (World2)

Leadership to the Power of 7 focuses on the emergence of multiple perspectives that can value all prior levels of development. It sees the world within the context of complex systems and operates with flexibility and flow.

Leading Supra-System (Global)

Leadership to the Power of 8 focuses on the world as an integrated evolutionary whole. Through interconnection and cross-collaboration on a truly global scale, we can see that Leadership to the Power of 8 enables the global flow of people, energy, security and resources. (Hamilton, 2008a, p. 115). As noted elsewhere (Hamilton, 2005) leadership to the Power of 8 focuses an ecological, political and global perspective and presence.

In summary, *Leadership to the Power of* 8 operates with the infinite qualities of adaptiveness that enable human systems to thrive (and reproduce themselves) in endlessly changing life conditions as set out in Table 18.

Table 18: Summary of Leadership Maturity Qualities

Level	Calibrations	Moral Influence	Space Span	Time Impact (Years)
1	Self, Manage	Ego—self	Here	<1
2	Self, Manage, Learn/Lead/Teach	Ego-family	Here	1–2
3	Self, Manage, Learn/Lead/Teach	Ego-clan	Here	2–4
4	Self, Manage, Learn/Lead/Teach	Ethno-Nation	Near	4–8
5	Self, Manage, Learn/Lead/Teach	Context—Sector	Near	8–13
6	Self, Manage, Learn/Lead/Teach	Context—Social	Far	13–21
7	Self, Manage, Learn/Lead/Teach	System	Far	21–44
8	Self, Manage, Learn/Lead/Teach	Supra-System	Global	44–65+

OBSERVING LEADERSHIP DEVELOPMENT IN ACTION

In order to illustrate the development of leaders from Level 5/6 to Level 8, for this article, nine leaders, three at each stage of advanced development, act as examples of applied Integral leadership.

The first trio are graduates of a Leadership degree program at Royal Roads University (RRU), where the author has taught for the last 19 years. This two year program was designed using constructivist, adult learning, cohort-based, competency, problem-framed approaches (Hamilton, 2001). As a result, the hundreds of graduates have been observed through the interactions of teaching, coaching and comparative evaluation. In particular the more than 60 students, whose theses this researcher has supervised have provided an ongoing set of living case studies to observe leadership development. Three of those students (identified by pseudonym) will provide the evidence to support observations about Leadership to the Power of Levels 5 and 6. They are called **Ann, Betty and Carl**.

The second trio, comes from an engagement in the last ten years with the Integral Community through collegial exchanges, presentation and attendance at two Integral Theory Conferences (ITC). Engaging with these peers has affirmed and triangulated the experience of teaching leadership at RRU. Within this community of integrally-informed peers, the researcher has reviewed three books authored by members of the Integral community. These three authors (identified by pseudonym) will provide the evidence to support observations about Leadership to the Power of Level 7. They are named **Lorna, Max and Norman**.

The third trio are peers to key leaders, teachers and mentors (Margaret Wheatley, Ken Wilber and Don Beck) who provided to this author, a discourse on leadership through complexity science, the Integral model and human values development respectively (Wheatley, 1992; Wheatley & Kellner-Rogers, 1996; Wheatley & Kellner-Rogers, 1998; Wheatley & Nickerson, Aug-98); (Wilber, 1995, 1996a, 2000a, 2000b, 2001, 2006, 2007; Wilber, Patten, Leonard, & Morelli, 2006); and (Beck, 1999, 2000b, 2001, 2002b, 2006; Beck & Cowan, 1994, 1997, 1996). Building on the wisdom of these leaders, the works of evolutionary biologists, political scientists and global journalists have inspired the conclusion that "Leaders to the Power of 8 lead through informed ecological action, massive, continuous and Integral connection, continual adaptation and respect for all living systems" (Hamilton, 2007).

For the purposes of this chapter three such Leaders (identified by pseudonym) provide the evidence to support observations about Leadership to the Power of 8. They go by the names of: **Xena, Yolanda and Zoe**.

(Note: I have masked the names and field for all leaders to preserve anonymity.)

AUTHOR'S LEADERSHIP QUALIFICATIONS

One lesson that the Integral model offers that is relevant to the study of leadership is that the center of gravity of the leader/evaluator must be disclosed in order to identify the filters the observer is using to evaluate other leaders. Based on analysis in a conference paper (Hamilton, 2008b, 2008c), the researcher situates herself in a center of gravity (COG) between Leadership Level 6 and Level 8. This gives her levels of confidence in her ratings of others that range from high for Level 6 and Level 7 and moderate for Level 8.

LEADERSHIP TO THE POWER OF 5 AND POWER OF 6

Using the landscape of multiple levels of leadership as our foundation, let us look now at three actual leaders whose leadership practise was observed while they were students in the RRU Masters of Leadership program. In particular let us consider the period of six months when they were undertaking their final action research project.

The design of action research (Coghlan & Brannick, 2007; Glesne, 1999; Stringer, 1996, Torbert, 2004) places the researcher into a co-researching, co-participant role where he/she becomes part of the system of interest that he/she is studying. This is a form of research that can be designed with both qualitative and/or quantitative methods and therefore integrates well with Integral quadrants (where left hand quadrants reveal qualitative epistemologies and right hand quadrants align with quantitative epistemologies).

The three candidates, Ann, Betty and Carl entered the research stage of their MA with centers of gravity in the range of Leadership to the Power of 5. The evidence for this included:

Moral Influence—they managed, consulted or lead organizations at middle manager level with spheres of influence numbers ranging from the tens to the hundreds for employees; tens to the hundreds for suppliers; and hundreds to thousands for clients/users.

Time—the impact of their decision horizons spanned from one year to five years.

Space—their range of influence spanned department within a city (Carl), culture within a province (Ann) and sustainability pillar sector within a nation (Betty).

Each was capable of self-assessing for contributions measured in various weightings related to bottom line: priorities (Betty), financial results (Ann) and employee performance (Carl).

When each embarked on their Major Project, no one had experience of this kind of research system (LR), this quantity of data collection (UR), the Masters' quality of participatory analysis (LL), nor the academic style of action research reporting (UL). Thus for each person their projects were a significant leadership stretch in all four quadrants. In Gravesian terms they had set themselves up for an environmental trigger that would grow their leadership capacities. In Integral terms they were experiencing new capacity stretches in each of the four quadrants. In developmental terms their research design would demand that they shift from a scale of team or department impact to one of transorganizational, intersectoral and/or transcultural influence.

The research question that each person had framed was both personally interesting and also significant to their system of study. In the case of these researcher/leaders they chose Integral and/or Spiral Dynamic framings to frame literature review; collect, organize and analyze data; and present conclusions and recommendations. The psycho-active nature of the Integral/spiral models along with the participatory action research worked internally on how the researchers thought, externally on how they tabulated their results and collectively as they shared the outcomes with their client organizations.

Thus by the time they had concluded their projects they had a lived experience that they were able to frame in bio-psycho-cultural-systemic terms. Their 130+ page papers were illustrated with images, tables and themes that explicitly demonstrated their command of a new mindset that as a minimum could be defined at Level 6 (and in many cases Level 7).

At the conclusion of their projects, each of these leaders had to self-reflect their own developmental journey resulting from completion of the project. Each was able to frame it in terms of the four quadrants, providing evidence based on insight (UL), literature (LL), systemic integration of evidence and theory (LR) and commitments for future action (UR).

Moreover, in all cases, subsequent to their MA graduation the three leaders moved into leadership positions with greater span in all three definable arenas:

Moral Influence—they managed, consulted or lead organizations at senior manager or director level with spheres of influence numbers ranging to the high hundreds for employees or contractors; tens to the hundreds for suppliers; and thousands to hundreds of thousands for clients/users.

Time—the impact of their decision horizons expanded to five to ten years (or longer).

Space—their range of influence caused each of them to move into new positions that included a new city in a new region (Carl), multiple cultures across a regional geography (Ann) and increased visibility of sectoral contribution to sustainability pillars on a national level (Betty).

Thus these three Leaders to the Power of 6 provide for us three stories as evidence of how to apply the Integral model for measuring the development of leadership competence and capacity as a result of focused study and action research.

LEADERSHIP TO THE POWER OF 7

Let us now move on to the second trio of leaders and consider their leadership qualities.

Lorna, Max and Norman are distinguished by their shift from expert practitioners in their respective fields to producers and teachers. In other words, they had mastered leadership behaviors calibrated at self management and other management, committing to extended years of study with mentors and teachers in the Integral movement (including but not limited to Wilber, Beck, Kegan, Cook-Greuter and Edwards). Each of them were teaching in accredited institutions (Lorna and Norman) and/or with prestigious global peer groups (Max). Each had been recognized by peer review for published articles and/or been selected for special presentations at international conferences.

These were the defining characteristics of this Leadership Cluster at the beginning of their Leadership shift from exit Level 6 to entry Level 7. One could describe their capacities in these terms.

Moral Influence—they taught others in institutions where student impact could be measured as spheres of influence in the hundreds to thousands for graduate students over multiple years; and to teaching peers measured in the tens to hundred.

Time—the impact of their decision horizons (as defined by their course designs) ranged from five to twenty years (or longer).

Space—their range of influence was the city, province, state or country where they taught in institutions (Lorna, Norman, Max respectively); the country and region of the developed world where they presented at conferences (all three in the USA; Max in Europe); and the virtual global reach they influenced through their published articles (all three).

In the last five years, each person of this trio has elected to write a book and been successful in proposing it to a publisher. Two of the books have been released (Max and Norman) and the third is in editorial review (Lorna). In all three cases having read and/or reviewed the books, this researcher has observed evidence of these leaders' next stage of development.

The conception, design, writing, editing and publication of a book, like the MA students who experienced action research projects, provides an environmental trigger that demands from the author a whole person response in order to complete the project. In this case the authors were not writing about trivial topics, but had set out to reframe whole discourses of interest into a new Integral paradigm (aesthetics for Lorna; economics for Max; and sustainability for Norman). Thus the authors were called to work at a meta-paradigmatic level that transcended and included the earlier versions of their chosen discourses. This demanded that they have an understanding of Traditional (Level 4), Modern (Level 5) and Post-Modern (Level 6) discourses in their respective fields and then go beyond those levels to offer a whole new framing within an Integral (Level 7) framing.

In comparison to the Leaders at Level 5 and 6, this pattern of leadership represents a progression not only within the calibration levels (self, manage, learn/lead/teach) but across the contexting calibrations (self, others, organization, system) as set out in Table 17. The authors have shifted from leading context for organizations or sectors into leading within a systems context a whole field of discourse.

As many (if not most) authors can relate, the writing of a book is a major project because of the scope and scale of the physical and mental organization of the project. In the case of these authors, their practise as leaders in the Integral movement meant the experience went much deeper than the production of copy or the delivery of a manuscript. They related (in person and in their book Introductions) how the experience was a four quadrant, bio-psycho-cultural-systemic experience that demanded more of them than they had ever had to provide in their prior career experience. What is more, as leaders in the Integral movement (i.e. each produced a book that was a bellwether contribution to the discourse of focus) they accomplished this while continuing with alternative lives (e.g. to support families, generate cashflow, fulfil contractual commitments). This illustrates their multi-disciplinary capabilities. Furthermore, as pioneers they lacked peer support of any significant kind, because few peers were available to counsel them—either in their field of discourse or in the Integral movement. Thus these Leaders to the Power of 7, were exploring systems on a mission "where no one had gone before".

Their accomplishments are very recent, but in terms of leadership, I observe the shift in their capacities to be definable as follows.

Moral Influence—each has produced a seminal non-fiction literary work that is rigorously substantiated by references, citations and examples. Each has used an Integral and/or spiral/developmental/evolutionary framing to re-define the paradigm of their field. In the case of Lorna and Norman their writing and illustrations go beyond workmanship into high aesthetic qualities in their own rights. (In the case of Norman his work has been independently reviewed by peers in his field with high praise that corroborates the extensive review that I wrote.) Max, as the youngest of these three has drawn on his multi-disciplinary background to make arguments for economic change that are unusually grounded not only in truth, but in beauty and goodness as well.

The measures of influence for this leadership trio, now span potentially thousands to hundreds of thousands of readers around the world in English speaking countries (with future potential for translation into other languages).

Time—the impact of their decision horizons (as defined by their book designs) ranges from ten to fifty years (or longer). The seminal nature of their books position the books and the authors to be classics in the Integral paradigm in each of their fields.

Space—their range of influence is now the English speaking world on a global basis—with a projected propensity for those countries which have most embraced a systems-based view of the world. Max's focus on economics may have an earlier uptake because of the world's economic woes. Norman's focus on sustainability may also attract an audience that is larger than the English speaking world as that discourse matures because of accelerating interest in global climate change. And Lorna's process for aesthetic transformation, may well morph outside the English speaking world because the Integral design process she describes enables transcultural participation.

Thus these three Leaders to the Power of 7, are by inner competence (UL), collegial relations (LL), outer capacity (UR) and systemic creativity (LR) on a different scale of performance, as measured by all four quadrants, than the Leaders to the Power of 6. Indeed, as they season (along with the audience they serve) to the potential generated by their authorship, they will position themselves not just to speak to, but also to lead and teach at the Complexity Level 7. Given time, commitment and circumstance each seems to have the qualities that will allow them to mature into Leaders to the Power of 8. And that is now where we turn our attention.

LEADERSHIP TO THE POWER OF 8

Our last trio of leaders, Xena, Yolanda and Zoe are an unusual set of leaders—not only because they can demonstrate Leadership to the Power of 8, but because forty years ago, as friends they conducted an inquiry that was only recently published as a book.

What is striking in this book is not only that they revealed how they were pioneers of their fields at the time it documents, but, they also recognized their pivotal role in shifting the capacity of the human species from their gender perspectives. If the Leaders to the Power of 7 are ploughing new fields with little support from peers, because they do not yet exist, these three exemplars of Leaders to the Power of 8 had even fewer systems of support.

So, in effect they filled this vacuum by creating their own cohort amongst themselves, despite the fact that their fields of interest were distinctively different from one another. Xena was an early pioneer of the human potential movement. Yolanda had the temerity to challenge the entire field of traditional economics. Zoe committed to evolutionary consciousness long before multiple sciences proved this was not merely a metaphor.

Thirty-five years ago these three created the conditions for developmental, evolutionary, complex adaptive framings in entirely new fields of knowledge. They were instrumental in breaking new ground where possibilities had not even seemed to exist before. In terms of our calibrations this was how their leadership playing fields were defined.

Moral Influence—each was defying the gatekeepers of the power structure that was entrenched in their field of interest. Xena sidestepped legal challenges to her research using psycho-tropic drugs and gained access to funding for research that revolutionized the Integral paradigm of human consciousness. Yolanda took on the even more impervious power structure of global financial institutions and economic power brokers by challenging assumptions about capital formation and resource creation. Zoe gained unexpected entry into private foundation funding that sponsored a series of conferences, prototyped organizational formats and entry into the plenaries of political process.

The measures of influence for these three leaders, spanned thousands in America to hundreds of thousands (before the internet and now millions with the internet) of citizens around the world.

Time—the impact of their decision horizons (as defined by their life purpose) ranged from twenty to fifty years (or longer). The seminal reframings of their fields of interest meant short-term constraints but long term recognition (if they could stay the course).

Space—their range of influence started in the English speaking world on a regional basis with their students and followers, but slowly became global in scope as others from many different countries, cultures and languages recognized the relevance of their new paradigms to their lives, organizations and countries.

With the opportunity to observe, read, learn and co-present with each of these three leaders the author notes that she first encountered Yolanda's work on community wellbeing thirty years ago with her influence on the World Health Organization's Healthy Community initiatives. About fifteen years ago, she encountered Xena's impact on the human potential movement through a personal development journey, her books and participating in a new intensive she developed 5 years ago. And finally she met, studied with, and co-created a workshop with Zoe over the last five years.

First-hand observations in the last four years has revealed how each of these Leaders has come into her Leadership to the Power of 8. It seems that their insights, commitment to change and risks to pioneer new ways of being, acting, relating and creating in the world has finally matured them into a stage where each leader is being recognized, sought after and invited to ground Integral practise in their chosen fields. (Interestingly even those who claimed and named the "Integral Movement" have had to back track and recognize how much earlier these three leaders had not just adopted but defined what "Integral" means in their spheres of influence.)

When we fast forward to today we can see in the lived practise of these three exemplars, the qualities of Leadership to the Power of 8.

Moral Influence—each of the leaders is now a published author multiple times over. Moreover, they have sophisticated websites; and sponsored, produced and/or directed video and multi-media productions. They have travelled the world presenting at conferences, framing policy initiatives and teaching Leaders to the Power of 4, 5, 6, 7 and 8. Thus their measures of influence have grown beyond casual encounters to thousands of well qualified experts on the most complex end of the spectrum to hundreds of thousands to millions of citizens, and multiple languages around the world on the less complex end of the spectrum.

Moreover, these three leaders have redefined the meaning of "moral impact" in creating whole new categories of ethical investments (Yolanda); ways of learning (Xena); and transdisciplinary collaborations (Zoe).

Time—the impact of their decision horizons (as defined by their multiple callings) ranges from fifty to 100 years. In their respective fields each is an ambassador for sustainable living and resilient systems, so they think in deep evolutionary time and regularly access the wisdom of history and the energetic fields of the future, breaking all the traditional framings even related to time. Their legacies already transcend "normal" lifetimes and reach far into future generations, because each of these leaders is directly influencing at least four generations while their collected authorship will reach many more. In addition, because of their access to and use of electronic media, they meet with people both synchronously and asynchronously, while also being adept practitioners of being deeply present.

Space—their range of influence, which started in the English speaking world, now spans the physical globe and also infiltrates the energetic airwaves of all forms of electronic media. This means that like the expansion of time, they have transnational, transcultural and pan-global spheres of influence that reach inside the highest elected offices and into the youngest minds in classrooms. (This is not speculative. Records exist of their coaching in the USA White House; running for Vice Presidential office; and influencing the World Economic Forum as just three examples.)

Their influence on space can be defined in truly Integral terms—you could say that they have co-created the conditions to occupy mind space (UL), brain space (UR), cultural space (LL) and structural space (LR).

Effectively these Leaders to the Power of 8 are leading not simple systems—but have created a new calibration at the Supra-System Level (a category defined by Miller (Miller, 1978, p. 903) in his transdisciplinary research of living systems). Thus to Table 17 we must add another calibration level as set out in Table 19.

Table 19: Supra-System Calibration for Leadership to the Power of 8

- **Supra-System aware**
  - Supra-system manage
  - Supra-system learn/lead/teach

These Leaders to the Power of 8 are not inappropriately immodest about their accomplishments (for each has paid a heavy price for her achievements); at the same time each of them is humble about her understanding of how much more exists to discover. As pioneers of Supra-System leadership, they are constantly experimenting with managing (is that an oxymoron for Supra-Systems?), learning, leading and teaching in this global context. Yet, their continued output, itineraries and schedules bespeak amazing energy, contagious humor and inspiring joy. Together and severally they are exemplars of Leaders to the Power of 8 and work tirelessly to remove barriers and enable the flow of people, energy, security and resources for wellbeing on a global level.

SUMMARY OF THE PATH TO LEADERSHIP TO THE POWER OF 8

In summary then we can recapitulate the leadership journeys of the three sets of leaders. In overviewing the real stories of real leaders (and not just the theory that predicts such performance) we can see that there are levels of maturity that one can correlate to age: our Leaders to the Power of 5 and 6 were in the age range of 30–40 years old; our Leaders to the Power of 6 were in the range of 40–60 years old; and our Leaders to the Power of 8 were in the range of 70–80+ years old. However, we know from both theory and practise that it is not age alone that enables leadership power to progress, but the life conditions that trigger expanded moral, time and space capacity and hence influence. Each power is exponentially greater than the one before it and transcends and includes the earlier powers.

Table 20: Summary of Leadership to Powers 5, 6, 7, 8 sets out the trajectory of leadership as it develops across the levels of complexity that we have called the Power of 5, 6, 7, 8.

Table 20: Summary of Leadership to Powers 5, 6, 7, 8

Power	Calibrations	Moral Influence	Space	Time (Years)
5	Self, Manage, Learn/Lead: Organization	organizations at middle manager level 10–1000's	City department Province culture National pillar	1–5 years
6	Self, Manage, Learn/Lead: Sector	organizations at senior manager or director 10–100,000+	Whole city Regional & multiple cultures National sustainability	5–10 years+
7—entry	Self, Manage, Learn/Lead/ Teach: System	Teach in institutions 100–1000	City, province, state or country Published articles Country, region Virtual globe	5–20 years
7—maturing	Self, Manage, Learn/Lead/ Teach: System	Book 1000's–100,000's	Global English world	10–50 years
8—entry	Self, Manage, Learn/Lead/ Teach: System	Books influencing Sectoral Pioneer 1000's–Xmm	Global English and non-English	20–50+ years
8—maturing	Self, Manage, Learn/Lead/ Teach: Supra-System	1000 Experts 1mm+ citizens New categories of ethics	Multiple languages around the world Transnational, transcultural and pan-global Mind space (UL), brain space (UR), cultural space (LL) and structural space (LR)	50–100 years + history & future time Synchronous & asynchronous time

In reviewing this table one can notice that as the Powers of Leadership increase the spheres of moral influence not only increase in numbers but they intensify in complexity. Thus the measure of influence is not only expanded by the total span or number of people reached, but by the depth of quality or level of leadership that it influences.

INSIGHTS FROM APPLICATION OF INTEGRAL MODELS TO STUDY OF LEADERSHIP DEVELOPMENT

Returning to the questions which engendered this chapter we can now offer some conclusions about the value of using the Integral model to study the development of leadership. The four quadrants and eight levels of the Integral model offer observational and methodological dimensions that transcend and include leadership frames from traditional, modern, post-modern and even post-post modern discourses. While each of those frames are useful within their respective contexts, the Integral model gives us a framework to align the capacities they reflect within quadrants of reality, holarchies of influence and levels of complexity. In this way Integral allows us to appreciate leadership to each Power of emergence and the apparently natural path of unfolding from one to the other, caused by triggers in the life conditions, that demand complex adaptive leadership response(s).

The Integral model appears to be useful for framing the journey of Leadership because:

1. It integrates four perspectives of bio-psycho-cultural-systems views of leadership.
2. It is developmental in multiple ways:
    c. across discreet stages (8 levels),
    d. waves (4—ego, ethno, world, Kosmic) and
    e. within stages (entry, intermediate, exit)
3. It is evolutionary, enabling the contexting of leadership development within historical and social contexts and discourses.
4. It is holonic, allowing one to track individuals as holons and collectives as social holons.

5. It is quasi-fractal which means that one can note the self-same patterns of development at different scales of leadership influence (while taking into consideration the dynamics of social holons versus individual holons).

6. It is systemic, meaning that leadership can be viewed within the context of changes in the cultural and social (and natural) environments as a complex adaptive system.

7. It is transcultural. This means that the deep patterns of leadership development can be noticed regardless of cultures because they are based on the hierarchy of complexity (which means surface differences might exist but underlying patterns will apply across cultures.)

8. It allows for the study of leadership in trans-disciplinary contexts. Although the individual practices of leadership will vary from discipline to discipline (and even between specialized areas within disciplines) the general hierarchy of complexity is transferable.

This chapter concludes that the theory of the Integral model offers a useful framework to measure, map and track observable leadership performance. As a pracademic, charged with grading and/or supervising evidence for leadership competency, the Integral model has even permitted the translation of competencies across frameworks (e.g. grading assignment marks for the modern university; assessing academic research quality for the post-modern School of study; coaching individual leadership performance for post-postmodern competency review; and supporting high quality teamwork as collective outcomes in an Integral context). The analysis in this chapter of three sets of leaders, at different "Powers of Leadership" has illustrated the value of using an Integral model to track the emergence of Leadership from the Power of 5/6 to the Power of 8. Moreover, the theory appears to provide a resilient framework to continue to map emergent leadership capacities that Graves (2003, 2005) predicted would emerge beyond the Power of 8.

REFERENCES

Anderson, T. D. (1992). *Transforming Leadership: New Skills for an Extraordinary Future*. Amherst, Mass: HRD Press, Inc.

Anderson, T.D., Ford R., Hamilton, M. (1998). *Transforming Leadership: Equipping Yourself and Coaching Others to Build the Leadership Organization*, Second Edition. CRC Press, Taylor & Francis Group: Boca Raton, FL.

Beck, D. (1999). The Search for Cohesion in the Age of Fragmentation: From the New World Order to the Next Global Mesh. Paper presented at the State of the World Forum.

Beck, D. (2000). Stages of Social Development: The Cultural Dynamics that Spark Violence, Spread Prosperity and Shape Globalization. Paper presented at the State of the World Forum.

Beck, D. (2001). Human capacities in the integral age: How value systems shape organizational productivity, national prosperity & global transformation. Paper presented at the International Productivity Conference. Retrieved from http://www.integralworld.net/beck7.html

Beck, D. (2002a). The Color of Constellations: A Spiral Dynamics Perspective on Human Drama. Paper presented at the Bert Hellinger Constellation Conference.

Beck, D. (2002b). Spiral Dynamics in the Integral Age. Paper presented at the Spiral Dynamics integral, Level I.

Beck, D. (2006). Spiral Dynamics Integral, Level I Course Manual. Denton, TX: Spiral Dynamics Group.

Beck, D., & Cowan, C. (1994, 1997). The Future of Cities. Unpublished Article. The National Values Center, Inc.

Beck, D., & Cowan, C. (1996). *Spiral Dynamics: Mastering Values, Leadership and Change*. Malden, MA: Blackwell Publishers.

Beck, D., & Linscott, G. (2006). *The Crucible: Forging South Africa's Future* (hardcover ed.). Columbia, MD: Cherie Beck, Coera.us, Center for Human Emergence.

Coghlan, D., & Brannick, T. (2007). *Doing Action Research in Your Own Organization* (2nd ed.). Thousand Oaks, CA: Sage Publications Ltd.

Cook-Greuter, S. (1999). *Postautonomous ego development: its nature and measurement.* Unpublished Doctoral dissertation, UMI Dissertation Information Services UMI #9933122, Harvard Graduate School of Education, Cambridge, MA.

Cook-Greuter, S. (2002). The development of action logics in detail. Retrieved from www.cook-greuter.com

Dawson-Tunik, T. L., Commons, M. L., Wilson, M., & Fischer, K. W. (2005). The shape of development. *The European Journal of Developmental Psychology*, 2(2), 163–196.

Dutrisac, M., Fowke, D., Koplowitz, H., & Shepard, K. (nd). *Global Organization Design: a dependable path to exceptional business results based on Requisite Organization principles*. Toronto: Global Organization Design Society.

Egan, G. (1990). *The Skilled Helper*. Pacific Grove, CA,: Brooks/Cole Publishing Company.

Eoyang, G., & Olson, E. (2001). *Facilitating Organization Change: Lessons from Complexity Science*. San Francisco: Jossey-Bass Pfeiffer.

Flood, R. (1999). *Rethinking the Fifth Discipline: Learning Within the Unknowable*. London: Routledge.

Gardner, H. (1999). *Intelligence Reframed; Multiple Intelligences for the 21st Century*. New York,: Basic Books, Perseus Books Group.

Gauthier, A., & Fowler, M. (2008). Integrally-Informed Approaches to Transformational Leadership Development. Paper presented at the Conference—Integral Theory In Action: Serving Self, Community and Kosmos.

Glesne, C. (1999). *Becoming Qualitative Researchers: An Introduction*. New York: Longman.

Goleman, D. (1997). *Emotional Intelligence*. New York: Bantam.

Graves, C. (1971). A systems conception of personality: Levels of existence theory. Paper presented at the Washington School of Psychiatry.

Graves, C. (1974). Human Nature Prepares for a Momentous Leap. *The Futurist*.

Graves, C. (2003). *Levels of Human Existence: Transcription of a Seminar at Washington School of Psychiatry*. Oct. 16, 1971. Santa Barbara: Eclet Publishing.

Graves, C. (2005). *The Never Ending Quest: A Treatise on an Emergent Cyclical Conception of Adult Behavioral Systems and Their Development*. Santa Barbara, CA: ECLET Publishing.

Gray, J., Hunt, J., & McArthur, S. (Eds.). (2007). *Organization Design, Levels of Work & Human Capability: Executive Guide*. Toronto: Global Organization Design Society.

Hamilton, M. (1998). Ethnographic Codebook Developed for Doctoral Research *The Berkana Community of Conversations: A Study of Leadership Skill Development and Organizational Leadership Practices in a Self-Organizing Online Microworld* (2007 ed., Vol. 1). Abbotsford, BC: TDG Holdings Inc.

Hamilton, M. (1999). *The Berkana Community of Conversations: A Study of Leadership Skill Development and Organizational Leadership Practices in a Self-Organizing Online Microworld.* Unpublished doctoral dissertation, Columbia Pacific University, Novato, California.

Hamilton, M. (2000). How Building a Leadership Organization Prepares the Way for Learning. In T. Anderson (Ed.), *Every Officer is a Leader: Transforming Leadership in Police, Justice, and Public Safety.* Boca Raton: St. Lucie Press.

Hamilton, M. (2001). Review, revise, reframe, MALT program design review: Discussion paper. Royal Roads University.

Hamilton, M. (2007). Leadership to the Power of 8: Leading Integrally in the 21st Century. *Sense in the City,* July.

Hamilton, M. (2008a). *Integral City: Evolutionary Intelligences for the Human Hive.* Gabriola Island BC: New Society Publishers.

Hamilton, M. (2008b). Leadership Development: Accelerating the Development of Post-Conventional Leaders. *Sense in the City,* October.

Hamilton, M. (2008c). Integral Methods from the Margins: Finding Myself in the Research—A Retrospective of Integral Leadership Development Methods Using Online Dialogue Analysis, a Competency Development Framework and Action Research. Paper presented at the Conference—Integral Theory in Action: Serving Self, Community and Kosmos, John F. Kennedy University.

Hamilton, M. (2010). Integral Spirituality in the Human Hive: A Primer. *Trialog,* 2010(4), 10–17.

Jaworski, J. (1996). *Synchronicity: The Inner Path of Leadership.* San Francisco: Berrett-Koehler Publishers.

Kegan, R. (1994). *In Over Our Heads: The Mental Demands of Modern Life.* Cambridge, MA: Harvard University Press.

Kegan, R., & Lahey, L. L. (2001). *How the Way We Talk Can Change the Way We Work: Seven Languages for Transformation.* San Francisco: Jossey-Bass.

Kegan, R., & Lahey, L. L. (2009). *Immunity to Change: How to Overcome It and Unlock Potential in Yourself and Your Organization.* Boston, MA: Harvard Business Press.

Koestler, A. (1976). *The Ghost in the Machine*. New York, NY: Random House.

McIntosh, S. (2007). *Integral Consciousness and the Future of Evolution: How the Integral Worldview is Transforming Politics, Culture and Spirituality*. St. Paul, Minnesota: Paragon House.

Miller, J. G. (1978). *Living Systems*. New York: McGraw-Hill Book Company.

Senge, P. M. (1994). *The Fifth Discipline: The Art and Practice of the Learning Organization*. New York,: Currency Doubleday.

Senge, P., Kleiner, A., Roberts, C., Ross, R., & Smith, B. (1994). *The Fifth Discipline Fieldbook: Strategies and Tools for Building a Learning Organization*. New York: Currency Doubleday.

Stringer, E. T. (1996). *Action Research: A Handbook for Practitioners*. Thousand Oaks, CA: Sage Publications Inc.

Torbert, W., & Associates (Eds.). (2004). *Action Inquiry: The Secret of Timely and Transforming Leadership*. San Francisco: Berrett-Koehler Publishes Inc.

Torbert, W. R., Livne-Tarandach, R., Herdman-Barker, E., Nicolaides, A., & McCallum, D. (2008). Developmental Action Inquiry:A Distinct Integral Theory That Actually Integrates Developmental Theory, Practice, and Research. Paper presented at the Conference—Integral Theory In Action: Serving Self, Community and Kosmos.

Wheatley, M. (1992). *Leadership and the New Science: Learning about Organization from an Orderly Universe*. San Francisco: Berrett-Koehler.

Wheatley, M. (2006). *Leadership and the New Science: Learning about Organization from an Orderly Universe*. San Francisco: Berrett-Koehler.

Wheatley, M., & Kellner-Rogers, M. (1996). *A Simpler Way*. San Francisco: Berrett-Koehler.

Wheatley, M. J., & Kellner-Rogers, M. (1998). *The Promise and Paradox of Community*: Jossey-Bass, Inc.

Wheatley, M. J., & Nickerson, J. E. (Aug-98). *Cape Cod Lectures*: Private Notes.

Wigglesworth, C. (Producer). (2002, December 14, 2017). Spiritual Intelligence and Why It Matters. Retrieved from http://www.godisaserialentrepreneur. com/uploads/2/8/4/4/2844368/spiritual_intelligence__emotional_intel- ligence_2011.pdf

Wigglesworth, C. (Producer). (2006, December 14, 2017). Why Spiritual Intelligence Is Essential to Mature Leadership. Retrieved from http://

www.godisaserialentrepreneur.com/uploads/2/8/4/4/2844368/spiritual-intelligence-n-mature-leadership.pdf

Wigglesworth, C. (2011). Deep Intelligence & Spiritual Intelligence: Why is Relevant for You? For Leaders? For the World. On *Integral Leadership Collaborative*: Integral Leadership Review.

Wigglesworth, C. (2014). SQ21: *The Twenty-One Skills of Spiritual Intelligence*. New York: SelectBooks.

Wilber, K. (1995). *Sex, Ecology and Spirituality: the spirit of evolution*. Boston: Shambhala Publications Inc.

Wilber, K. (1996). A *Brief History of Everything*. Boston: Shambhala Publications Inc.

Wilber, K. (2000a). *Integral Psychology*. Boston: Shambhala Publications Inc.

Wilber, K. (2000b). A *Theory of Everything*. Boston: Shambhala Publications Inc.

Wilber, K. (2001). *Marriage of Sense and Soul*. New York: Random House.

Wilber, K. (2006). *Integral Spirituality*. Boston: Shambhala Publications Inc.

Wilber, K. (2007). *The Integral Vision*. Boston: Shambhala Publications Inc.

Wilber, K., Patten, T., Leonard, A., & Morelli, M. (2006). *Integral Life Practice: A 21st Century Blueprint for Phsycial Health, Emotional Balance, Mental Clarity and Spiritual Awakening* (1 ed.). Boston, MA: Integral Books.

8

DIVERSITY GENERATORS: RESILIENCE
INNOVATORS OF THE HUMAN HIVE

CHAPTER SUMMARY

Diversity is a natural phenomenon of the most complex system yet created by humans—the city. Diversity Generation as the complement of Conformity Enforcement enables adaptation, emergence and evolution. The city is a social holon whose complexity is so dynamic that we need a wholistic Integral Map to reveal how interlocking fractals in human ecologies play a critical role in the city's coherence, creativity and resilience. Diversity Generators tap into the diversity naturally embedded in the city biologically, psychologically, culturally and structurally, offering solutions to challenges, barriers and seemingly intractable problems as a necessary contribution to the city's survival. Although migration has created hyperdiversity in the city that Conformity Enforcers attempt to control, it is likely that Diversity Generators will innovate strategies that spawn new collaborations, communities of practise, constellations, institutionalization of new systems and governance that can bridge today's silos, stovepipes and solitudes.

Key Words: diversity generator, conformity enforcer, complexity, Integral City, innovation, resilience

Cities are tolerant of extraordinary diversity . . .

—(West, 2011)

Diversity: for all the attraction of strange, exotic and even novel characteristics the word conjures up, the dictionary definition is surprisingly mundane: "a range of different things" (diversity"Oxford Online Dictionary," 2011). Even Thomas' definition of "any mixture of elements characterized by differences and similarities" (Thomas, 1996, p. 5) masks the dynamics that Gregory and Raffanti (2009) explore. It is only when you examine diversity's etymology that a glimmer of the potential power that lies behind the definition shows through. "From diversitas, from diversus 'divers', past participle of divertere 'turn aside' (see divert)." ("Oxford Online Dictionary," 2011).

Diversity Generation (DG) is the complement of Conformity Enforcement (CE) and "turns aside" conformity to norms that no longer serve the city's survival, to enable adaptation, emergence and evolution. The role of DGs is to trigger the cycle of change in the city so that the city not only survives or sustains itself but adapts to ever changing life conditions in a resilient way.

This chapter on Diversity Generators (DGs) in the Integral City (Hamilton, 2010a) is the story of how diversity is a natural phenomenon of the most complex system yet created by humans—the city. It should be noted that the city, as I define it, is a fractal of the individual human systems (embracing all the human brain, body, mind and values). The city is effectively the human system writ large and as such replicates every system of the human individual and articulates them, so a collection of individuals may live in close proximity in a specific environmental habitat. Cities come in a spectrum of sizes from villages to megalopolises. The reason the city is a fascinating system through which to observe the dynamics of diversity generation, is because like all systems it has boundaries within which the agents of the system interact (Eoyang, 1997; Eoyang & Olson, 2001; Hamilton, 2008a; Midgley, 2000; Midgley, Munlo, & Brown, 1998; Ulrich, 2000). It is precisely because the population of a city continues to change through life cycles, migration, deaths and births that it offers a rich vessel for learning about diversity in all four Integral quadrants and levels of complexity as proposed below.

In the discussion that follows I have drawn terminology from the fields of micro-biology, physics, systems thinking, complexity and Integral models. (The Glossary of Definitions offered at the end of the book can assist readers who are not familiar with key words.)

5 MAPS OF THE CITY

The city is a social holon whose complexity is so dynamic that a holistic framework like the Integral model is needed to map and understand its individuals, cultures and nature (Beck & Cowan, 1994, 1997, 1996; Beck & Linscott, 2006; DeKay, 2011; Esbjörn-Hargens & Zimmerman, 2009; Hamilton, 2006, 2007, 2010a, 2010c; Wilber, 2006). In fact, we propose that five maps reveal the meta dynamics of the city, each from a different perspective within the four quadrants of the "classic" Integral model proposed by Wilber (1995, 1996, 2000b, 2007).

Diversity in the city can be tracked through the shift in perspective that each map offers. Taken together the five maps could be conceptually (and technologically) hyperlinked to give us a more comprehensive picture of diversity in the human hive. A brief description follows of the contribution each map reveals in the city (with illustrations and full explanations in Appendix B).

Map 1: City as Holon—The Four Quadrant, Eight Level Map of Diversity

This map shows that reality (and its expression through diversity) in the city arises from both an individual/collective and an interior/exterior expression (Wilber, 1995). The intersection of these two polarities reveals four city realities as shown in Table 21.

Table 21: Integral Map: Four Quadrants

UPPER LEFT (UL): INDIVIDUAL BELIEFS	UPPER RIGHT (UR): INDIVIDUAL ACTIONS
interior/internal/subjective/intangible	exterior/external/objective/tangible
LOWER LEFT (LL): COLLECTIVE CULTURE	**LOWER RIGHT (LR): COLLECTIVE SYSTEMS**
interior/internal/intersubjective/intangible	exterior/external/interobjective/tangible

Our institutions of higher learning have organized the domains of knowledge into four perspectives (or voices). This pattern may have emerged as a natural extension of the phenomenon, that these voices appear to be common to all languages (I, We, It and Its, shown in Table 22) (Wilber, 1995, 2006; M. E. Zimmerman, 2005).

Table 22: Domains of Knowledge and Related Voices

Upper Left (UL) aesthetics and fine arts (I)
Lower Left (LL) humanities (We)
Upper Right (UR) life sciences (It)
Lower Right (LR) social sciences (Its)

Interestingly in academia, where faculties have institutionalized these domains of knowledge, the scientific method has created a culture where research methodologies have continuously challenged the models and paradigms of the very academic knowledge base they arise from—thus institutionalizing the act of diversity generation. Paradoxically the faculties also represent the bastions of conformity enforcement of the current knowledge base, with institutionalized resistance to rapid change. Thus a tension between DG and CE exists at the core of academic institutions.

Map 1 is analogous to a "plan view" of diversity in the human hive and provides the coordinates for what Wilber calls "Kosmic addresses"(Wilber, 2006). **The value of Map 1 to see diversity is that it locates perspectives, methodologies, parts, partial views and fragments of the city.** Thus they can inform one another and be viewed as an integrated system where what happens in the LL cultural values of the city can be linked to the LR systems of safety, organizational forms and infrastructure, as well as individual UL beliefs and UR actions. It has a series of "growth rings" that spiral out from the center along the diagonal axis of each quadrant, representing the eight stages of complexity that have emerged as diversity generation has enabled the system to adapt to and co-create the life conditions discussed in Map 4. This map (like the others is fractal) includes lines of intelligence, types, and states—all of which have been well explored within a dynamic diversity maturity context (Gregory & Raffanti, 2009).

Map 2: Nested Holarchy of City Systems

The city as a human system is a nest of systems made up of centers (Alexander, 2004), holons (Koestler, 1979) or nested holons (Sahtouris, 1999). The systems have orders of complexity, so that the holons, wholes and centers are nested into holarchies (Wilber, 1996) or panarchies (Gunderson & Holling, 2002) where levels of complexity emerge over time.

The value of Map 2 to the understanding of diversity in the city is that it reveals the scales in which diversity can simultaneously emerge in the city—because every individual is a member of multiple city subsystems at different scales (family, workplace, education, healthcare, place(s) of spiritual practice, neighborhood, city hall, and environment). Interconnections amongst individuals and sub-systems create spheres of influence, networks, communities of practice and meshworks as they become densified and aligned to achieve goals and purposes (Hamilton, 2010c)—all of which contribute to enforcement of conformity or divergence from norms.

Map 3: Scalar Fractal Relationship of Micro, Meso and Macro Social Holons

Map 3 shows the city as a social holon—a group of people whose capacities are not summative but dynamically non-linear that come from the unique contributions of each individual holon in the social grouping.

The value of Map 3 for comprehending diversity generation is that it conveys how capacity development in individuals contributes to capacity in families, organizations and communities, while also revealing the reality of capacity dilution and amplification in social holons—a core measure of conformance or diversity.

As a natural system, the dynamics of social holons can be expressed by the non-linear mathematics of fractal geometry — the elegant, patterns created by the repetition of simple rules of relationship, at multiple levels of scale that predict both behaviors and infrastructures (West, 2011, 2017). It appears that at every level of scale, fractal patterns of citizen thoughts, behaviors, relationships and creations are deeply embedded in the capacity of individual holons and the social holons they belong to (as noted in Map 2).

Diversity in Map 3 reveals emergent patterns that arise from the tension between levels of development in collectives (where norms tend to prevail) and individuals (where diversity tends to be initiated). Such tensions only become resolved when a critical mass of individual behaviors in the collective becomes coherent (e.g., the many Americans identified as Cultural Creatives (Ray & Anderson, 2000) who are active in politics, the arts (Florida, 2005, 2008) and sustainability (L. Brown, 2008)). Complexity sciences reveal that only 10 to 15 percent of a population need change, in order to shift the whole system (Gladwell, 2002; Hamilton, 2008, West, 2017). This implies that one group or cohort will find it difficult to be successful until a critical mass of groups commits to similar practise (e.g. reducing, reusing and recycling becoming a common sustainability practise in the 1990's in North America). However, it also reveals the tremendous power of DGs to change a system by persisting in their divergent worldviews, behaviors, cultures and systems until they become the new practise.

Map 4: Complex Adaptive Structures of Change

Map 4 conveys the stages of structural organizational change in the city. Living human systems in the city are constantly in the flux of adapting to life conditions. Adaptations arise from both external causes (like geo-climatic incidents) and from internal causes related to bio-psycho-cultural-social triggers.

The directions of change are best pictured as vectors (or developmental lines) expanding the four quadrants of the whole city outward from its core as shown by the outward pointing arrows on Map 1. Map 4 makes visible the city's LR quadrant in Map 1, revealing how complexifying organizational structures emerge over historical time along a trajectory that our domains of knowledge refer to as: Traditional, Pre-Modern, Modern, Post-Modern and Integral. These structures emerge as responses to challenges that face the social holons in the city as it evolves.

One can think of the eight structures illustrated in Map 4 as being clustered into four major "change centers": Levels 1–2 are ego-centric; Levels 3-4-are ethno-centric; Levels 5–6 are world-centric; and Levels 7–8 (and 9 not shown) are Kosmo-centric.

Map 4 gives us a trajectory of potential structural change, with the caution of no guarantees of an ever-upward shift. In times of long term instability and uncertainty, cities (and their organizations) risk down spiraling into less complex structures in order to find older more stable "comfort zones" (particularly after natural or revolutionary disasters like those in New Orleans, Sendai Japan or Middle East cities torn apart by war).

The direction of change up or down depends on the capacities of the individuals and groups (reflected in Map 3) to adapt to challenges (like the turbulent chaos of Cairo and Tripoli in the 2011 Arab Spring or Mosul and Aleppo in 2016) or breakthrough stabilizing conditions (like Beijing in the 2008 Olympics).

In fact, the organizational genealogy in Map 4 is mostly hypothetical, because although all the eight iconic organizational forms exist, they are generally connected in very non-linear ways, creating fragments, gaps and breakdowns when different organizational formations interact.

However, the value of Map 4 to understanding diversity generation is that it shows that diversity in the city has emerged historically in waves of increasing complexity (or maturity (Gregory & Raffanti, 2009)) and can be organizationally expressed at multiple levels of structural complexity. Moreover, each LR structure can be related to a LL value system which gives us insights to the diversity (or coherence) dynamically impacting all the ego-ethno-world-Kosmo-centricities alive in the 21st century city (Beck, 2012; Bloom, 2000).

Map 5: Spirituality in the Integral City

Map 5 conveys the qualities of spirituality in the city. Its zones of Grace, Space and Place reveal where the core spiritual values of Goodness, Truth and Beauty are manifested. The Kosmic addresses of these core spiritual values of the Integral City have both vertical and horizontal locations. Spirituality itself responds through these qualities and values in a holographic way. (For more details see Chapter 1: Spirituality in the Human Hive: Involutionary & Evolutionary Cycle of Love".)

The value of Map 5 to understanding diversity generation is that it reveals that diversity is not only manifested in the external world of objective and interobjective place and planet, but it exists powerfully in

the subjective and intersubjective world of consciousness and culture.
Map 5 allows us to point to the infinite expression of diversity in aesthetic
expression of Beauty; the variety of ways we can offer Goodness or compassion; and the discoveries and creations we make from the Truth or insights
of life sciences and systems sciences. Map 5 also implies the impulse for
diversity through the cycle of involutionary diversity imagination and evolutionary diversity generation (both in relation to conformity enforcement).

The Value of an Integral City Framework for Seeing Diversity

With such an integrated framework, it becomes possible to see the
fractal nature of diversity generation in the city that is evident through:

- mapping individual and collective Kosmic addresses that allow us to
  see where different members of the population locate conformance
  and diversity (Beck, 2012; Bloom, 2000).
- the interlocking scales of individual, family, neighborhoods, workplaces, sectors, institutions, governance systems and ecologies
  (Hamilton, 2008a).
- interdisciplinary research in the study of living systems (Gunderson
  & Holling, 2002).
- fundamental laws of fractal relationships in physics (Abrams & Primack,
  2006; West, 2011) and through interdisciplinary research in resilience
  studies (Gunderson & Holling, 2002) that reveal the patterns of order
  and diversity generated in living systems.

We can look at an example of diversity generation through the 4 quadrants in a particular city like Vancouver, BC, described in the Inset below.

THE ROLE OF DIVERSITY GENERATION IN THE RESILIENCE CYCLE

Geoffrey West says that organizations die, but cities persist (West, 2011,
2017). By simple reference to the volume of systems within systems in the
city, cities have more diversity than organizations, but while this seems
obvious, it is not always apparent that diversity generation plays a critical role in the city's persistence through the emergence of collaboration,
coherence and constellation. In comparing the "human hive" of the most

EXAMPLES OF DIVERSITY GENERATORS SHIFTING THE CITY OF VANCOUVER FROM MODERN TO POST-MODERN WORLDVIEWS

City media may be one of the best trackers of DGs in the city—simply because basic media design focuses on the reporting of news events that differ from the norm—through natural selection, resistance, hostility, conflict and/or disaster. (As noted Gregory & Raffanti (2009)).

Recent examples illustrate DGs in each of the quadrants of Map 1 relating stories of the change by Post-Modern DGs against Modern life conditions— as illustrated in one city, Vancouver, Canada (rated as one of the most livable cities in the world (anon, 2017a)).

Upper Left (UL): individual beliefs, intentions, psychology

Perhaps an unusual example of the inner life of city leaders can be gleaned from some of the public trials that mayors suffer in the face of unpredictability? From the 1990's the city of Vancouver has benefitted from a series of mayors, each of whom has been associated with strongly expressed personal platforms of leadership, spanning Modern to Post-Modern. In the 1990's Mike Harcourt, a community-based store-front lawyer, brought the post-modern beliefs of civil society in defense of the economically marginalized (homeless, disenfranchised cultures) to the mayor's office. He was succeeded by Gordon Campbell a Modernist with strong connections to the pro-development sector, who promoted (and succeeded) that Vancouver be the Olympics 2010 site. He was succeeded by two strong Post-Modernists (Larry Campbell and Sam Sullivan) who brought institutional experience respectively from the coroner's office and city council to the chair, but neither of whom were re-elected after their first term as the global economy made the electorate shy of their more free-thinking proposals and free-spending budgets. The mayor of 2011–17 (Gregor Robertson) brought a mix of beliefs and intentions from a generation younger than his predecessors (Generation X—a term coined by Vancouverite Douglas Coupland), an entrepreneurial background, and experience in provincial left-wing politics. He attempted to bridge Modern and Post-Modern views (hinting at a more Integral perspective to come).

The high visibility of the mayor's belief systems as they lead a city clearly generates divergent expectations of the mayor's leadership, reflecting the electorate's sense of what and who is most needed during different life conditions that impact the city from the larger scales of the eco-region and the world. These conditions create the backdrop for the diversity response that a mayor can offer to the CE status quo. At each election the worldviews of the mayoralty candidates become public DG knowledge available to the larger city system. As a result the electorate responds by making choices it deems best serve both individuals and the collective in the human hive (Beck, 2012; Hamilton, 2008).

Upper Right (UR): individual actions, biology, physical traits

The issue of gender identity became a point of contention in the 2012 Miss World Contest in Canada, when Vancouver contestant, Jenna Talackova revealed that she had undergone transgendered sexual surgery. The contest sponsor at first rejected her application and then reversed their decision (Szaklarksi, 2012) causing both consternation amongst traditional contestant candidates and approval amongst more liberal supporters. However, as pointed out by a well-informed columnist nature's qualities tend not to be discrete but to occur along a spectrum (McKnight, 2012). Thus he contends there

is no such thing as a "natural born woman" (or man) (Baron-Cohen, 2003; Moir & Jessel, 1991). In this example we see the Diversity Generation in the UR actions of the transgendered contestant and the UL views of the media authors. They may have been the first examples of Diversity Generation in the beauty contest arena, but they gave publicity to the results of decades of research redefining sexual diversity (Moir & Jessel, 1991) that influence how and with whom people define sexuality and related interactivity in the city. Fast forward to 2017 and the conversation had exploded (in the process of "normalization") into the LGBTQ discourse where the city's own website (anon, 2017b) declares, "Vancouver is home to the largest lesbian, gay, bisexual, transgender, and queer (LGBTQ) community in Western Canada".

Lower Left (LL): collective culture, relationships, beliefs

Relationships in the city are perhaps the most dynamic of Diversity Generation zones, because every time an individual connects with someone outside their usual sphere of influence in the family, work place, place of worship, community or recreation facility, miniature exchanges of belief, values and culture occur—creating whirlwinds like micro-climates in the city. Each of these unique exchanges is a potential generator of diversity. When the exchange is amplified by feedback loops, as others replicate the relationships, these micro-climates can gather energy and become zones of viral activity in their ability to generate diversity (Eoyang & Olson, 2001).

In Vancouver a perfect illustration of diversity generation occurred after the annual Stanley Cup Hockey play-offs in Vancouver in 2011 (anon, 2017c), when the city's beloved Canucks lost a seventh playoff game to rival city Boston Bruins. The Vancouver citizens who had so prided themselves on a successful and worldview-changing view of the city as a global, proud, beautiful center of sports excellence and fair play, deteriorated in the time of a hockey game into an apparently dangerous, riot zone. Police lost control, over 100 citizens were injured and property was attacked and severely damaged. The city's post-modern face to the world, in fact was blackened by warring clans of pre-modern DG hooliganism who willfully broke the usual public peace. The public shame of this situation was somewhat mitigated by the compassionate and generous acts of volunteers who appeared on the streets on the morning after the riot with brooms and waste-bins to clean up the results of the previous night's ugliness in

an attempt to restore the norms of CE modernism and postmodernism. However, in a paroxysm of ineffective modernist and post-modernist justice, 4 years later more than 800 charges had been laid. As a result, the entire city felt some redress after the first two years of impotent stalemate in the face of the attacks by the DG underbelly. A team of justice investigators from city hall, police, emergency response and justice systems, caused shifts in the whole city's expectations about how to create lawful ways of being together during emotionally heightened (and/or provoked) situations.

Perhaps, through such generational tensions between DGs and CEs city governance is being redefined. Howe and Strauss (Howe & Strauss, 1992; Strauss & Howe, 1997) considered revolution to be a mark of a particular generational cohort. They proposed that revolutionaries were characteristic of the fourth generation in a four generational cycle. However, the protestors in Vancouver, who were primarily members of the Generations dubbed "Y and Z" did not seem to match this profile well. (Rather they seemed to be throwbacks to the anarchical Gen X soccer rioters from Europe.) Nevertheless other research (Consumers of Tomorrow: Insights and Observations About Generation Z, 2011) describes the life conditions of Generation Z as "born into an environmentally conscious world, and with greater exposure to a wide range of resources, they are expected to be more socially responsible. . . . Characterized as tech-savvy, flexible and smarter, and tolerant of diverse cultures this cohort of young adults has been able to work around the assumption of older generations (X and Boomer) because of their agility with their internet technology that interconnects them." This makes them DGs who practise an emerging form of collective intelligence not easily practised by their elders—and perhaps it is this modernist technology that enabled the pre-modern collective riot to end-run the CE authorities so easily?

Ironically the Boomer elders that the Gen Z's are defying were the DGs of the 1960's who broke the social and cultural taboos of the modern world, ushering in the civil rights movement, women's rights, birth control and a strong suspicion of anyone over 30, as they blasted open the relationship doors of the post-modern world (Wilber, 2002).

Lower Right (LR): collective systems, structures, infrastructures

Structures and infrastructures in the city may be the slowest elements of the city to change. They seem to survive for centuries like the Coliseum in Rome, or the narrow streets of medieval Freiberg or the planned city of Paris. However, diversity generation may well be more the norm for city structures than we are willing to be-lieve, because according to geologist, Iain Stewart most cities of the world are located beside the great tectonic rifts where the most resources occur (Stewart, 2010). Vancouver certainly fits this mold as it lies on the edge of the great Juan de Fuca fault, in the Fraser valley, below Mount Baker—one of the great volcanoes that forms the North American Pacific Ring of Fire. Despite the fact that the media reports periodic reminders of Vancouver's ecologi-cal vulnerability (making parallels to the great tragedies to city structures, infrastructures and environments when natural disasters have ripped the levees out of New Orleans, the nuclear meltdown of Fukishima Japan and burned the town of Fort McMur-ray, Alberta to the ground in 2016). In the face of such calamitous threats, the role of Diversity Generation is a neces-sary one for survival for the fabric of the city. Eco-aware DG's clearly need to generate responses so that CE's can make the necessary emergency plans to respond and rebuild with new solu-tions to address the possible and prob-able impacts of floods, earthquakes, volcanic eruptions or fire.

As a designer DG, Mark DeKay has examined the qualities and conditions of Integral sustainable design (DeKay, 2011) needed to build and rebuild the city using the Integral model including: the perspectives of Integral design using the four quadrants; levels of complexity in city design; the developmental path of designers and their designs; ecological design thinking that embraces the design journey from linear to non-linear perceptions; and the relationship of design to nature from ego, ethno, world, Kosmocentric and spiritual views.

advanced species of vertebrates (homo sapiens sapiens) to the "bee hive" of the most advanced species of the invertebrates (apis mellifera), the surprising role of DGs as critical role players in an ecological survival strategy, becomes more visible (see Appendix E).

Both species exist in life conditions that are incessantly changing, because of the interaction of the population with landscape, climate, ecology, and/or other groups within the population (i.e. cultures or hives within the eco-region). Ironically in order to survive, cultures within the city are forced to adapt as they interact with one another or die. Survival is each culture's (and species') ultimate goal but adaptation through diversity generation is the secret to why cities persist.

The pattern of resilience in human cities seems to follow a similar cycle to that of the bees (described in Appendix E). Resilient systems appear to cycle through four distinct stages (Gunderson & Holling, 2002; Hamilton, 2008):

1. Conservation—where the system is structured into a fairly steady state, able to optimize resource access and deployment in replicatable operations (which have so far occurred in cities at Traditional, Modern and Post-Modern forms, with Integral now showing early signs of coming online.)

2. Breakdown—where the system tips into a state of disequilibrium unable to adapt resource access and/or deployment to changing life conditions (which occurs when order in the previous cycle

breaks down and dis-order (resistance, revolution, impasse) becomes prevalent.

3. Resource Redistribution—where the system breaks apart into constituent elements that self-organize into divergent and incoherent exchanges (a stage of anarchy and hyper-divergence).

4. Exploitation—where the system self-organizes into convergent and coherent exchanges enabling exploitation of new structures for resource access and deployment (a stage of new hope, high expectations, great innovation).

In each of the stages of resilience the relationship of DGs to CEs differs. (While, in the beehive, it appears to be the role of Resource Allocators (RAs) and Inner Judges (IJs) to reward the appropriate balance of behaviors between DG and CE bees so that 20 kilos of honey can be produced (Beck, 2012; Bloom, 2000; Hamilton, 2008). At this stage of evolution of the human hive, the clarity of what constitutes the equivalent of the 20 kilos of honey remains obscure—although we appear to be approaching core algorithms expressed in terms of eco-footprints and GHG emissions (Taylor, 2008), the ratios of certain behaviors to population size as discussed in Chapter 15 (West, 2011, 2017), the economics of health, productivity and happiness (Robinson, 2012), and livability indexes (anon, 2017a).

The Integral model has demonstrated how diversity dynamics are biologically, psychologically, culturally and structurally embedded in the people of the city (Gregory & Raffanti, 2009). People act, think, relate and produce within the life conditions they co-create, responding to the interactive relationship of CE's with DG's. When CE's encounter seemingly intractable problems that drain resources from the system on a large enough scale, eventually the contribution of DGs to overcome dissonances, challenges, blocks and barriers becomes critical to the city's survival and evolution. (It becomes effectively the dissonance trigger to transformative change (Graves, 1974; Gregory & Raffanti, 2009)). However, such decisions and actions to issues like homelessness (see Chapter 13), can take a surprisingly long time to realize because of the power of the CE's to resist change.

. . . the dominant behaviors [of social systems in cities], arise in response to life conditions (as one would expect from any complex adaptive system (Holling (2001); Stevenson and Hamilton, 2000; Capra, (Capra, 1996) 1996)). So each level of existence behaves with increasing levels of complexity in order to maximize the organizing principle (or value) of the current life condition. This behavior results in a tendency to protect the status quo at its current level of complexity . . . [which] could be interpreted as conformity enforcement (of the organizing principle / value).

Thus a tension in favor of the values and behavior that is most coherent with the current life conditions [called in complexity theory, the "fitness landscape"], will be demonstrated as conformity enforcement. The flip side of this behavior is that the dominant culture will also protect itself against diversity generation, until such time as life conditions require the solutions that diversity generation can offer to the problems created by maximizing the values and organizing principles in play at any level of existence. Moreover, we can see the natural evolutionary cycles emerge at all levels of scale: individual, family, organization, society.(Hamilton, 2007)

When considering the Resilience Cycle it appears that CE's and DG's have the following relationships at the four stages (as illustrated in Figure 7).

1. Conservation—CE's are strong (+); DG's are weak (-)

2. Breakdown/Release—both CE's and DG's are weak (-), conflicted in their connections

3. Redistribution/Reorganization—CE's are strong (+) and DG's are strong (+), conflicted in their potentializing

4. Exploitation—CE's are weak (-) and DG's are strong (+) in a stage where innovation and entrepreneurial behavior is necessary for new systems to come of age.

Each of the stages of the resilience cycle embraces CE's and DG's at different levels of strength (strong or weak). These tensions keep the system dynamic and adaptive, able to optimize the phase of resilience the system needs to stabilize. In its own way each role contributes to the rising trajectory of diversity/differentiation in the Reorganizing and Exploiting Stages and the rising trajectory of conformity /integration from the Exploitation to Conservation stages. The war of the roles (strong opposing forces creating great tension) in the Breakdown or Release phase helps to explain why they are such uncomfortable, unproductive, unstructured, misaligned, fragmented, disincentivizing stages.

Resilience Cycles & 4 Roles (*Panarchy*, Gunderson & Holling, 2002, Hamilton, 2012

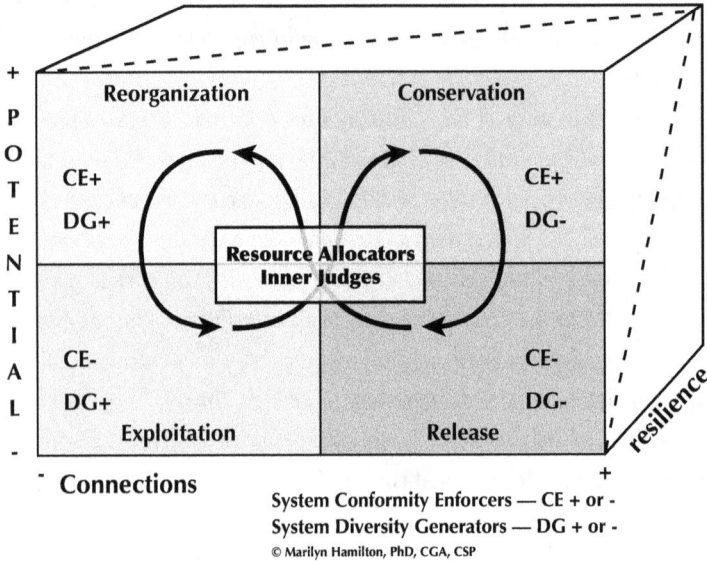

System Conformity Enforcers — CE + or -
System Diversity Generators — DG + or -
© Marilyn Hamilton, PhD, CGA, CSP

Figure 7: Resilience Cycle & Role Strength

Diversity Generation is optimized in the low connection stages of Reorganization and Exploitation stages and minimized in the Conservation and Release Stages. Whereas CE's are optimized primarily in the Conservation stage where their effectiveness at structuring and systemization allows the resilience cycle to optimize the distribution of resources within the system.

Within the Redistribution phase of the cycle of resilience DG's are the first individuals to initiate connections in a new network of people sharing a common interest (e.g. the emergence of performance coaches in the 1990's). If this network becomes densified over time (in the Exploitation phase), then we observe that the DG initiative emerges into a collaborative association when a group of individual practitioners evolve professional standards (e.g. the advent of coaching associations). As life conditions stabilize and the Exploitation phase matures, it is typical for these associations to develop professional competencies; ensure that quality standards change to match new discoveries, technologies, territories and customer demands; and shift the collaborative orientation from just establishing norms to seeking results and realizing bottom line objectives (e.g. the establishment of institutionalized coaching universities, accreditation and conferences). So DG collaborations (and/or associations) eventually evolve, in the Conservation phase, into CE associations who enforce coherent practices, standards and even examinations. If they are successful enough, communities of practice (COP) will result who may even join with other COPs into constellations of COPs—essentially creating a powerful field of influence (e.g. when performance, quality of life and executive coaches create federations that work with Human Resource, Organizational Development and Accounting Professional Associations). When this occurs a strong set of CE, RA's and IJ's will have replaced the DG's and institutionalized what was once a divergent practise.

These behaviors will continue until life conditions trigger a shift into the Breakdown phase, where the institutionalized behavior cannot adapt to new circumstances (e.g. coaches of the future may not be able to compete with artificial intelligence/robo-guides and Internet-Cloud capacity expansion technology).

Meanwhile other DG's will be creating new innovations, that if successful will follow a similar trajectory from initiation to institutionalization (e.g. meshworkers bridging multi-organizational collaborations within the city).

As a species, homo sapiens sapiens, has survived through optimizing adaptation to current life conditions, co-creating unstable life conditions and developing solutions to overcome the lack of stability and new structures that re-stabilize the human system within its life conditions. In this way a panarchy of resilient solutions has emerged across evolutionary time.

The pattern of emergence in human cities (or communities) seems to follow a similar sequence to that of the bees (described in Appendix E), although the great capacity of human consciousness has already emerged the four eras noted above (Traditional, Modern, Post-Modern and Integral). These eras themselves have characteristics where Traditional and Post-Modern eras appear to be framed more by cultures where the values of the group are enforced. On the other hand, Modern and Integral eras appear to be framed where the values of individuals are enforced.

Over time, we realize that both the human stages influenced by individuals and those influenced by groups are vital to the long term survival of cities (and indeed the human species) as noted in Map 4. We can also see, in response to the increasing complexity of life conditions, that each era and its culture emerges a greater complexity of community expression. The culture's rules, laws, rituals, structures, roles, learning competencies, assets and physical capacities are integrated outcomes and expressions of the relationship between the group and the individual, as complexity increases. The relationship is dynamic, because life conditions are dynamic—in terms of complexity science we would say that the city is a nest of complex adaptive systems, in states ranging from stable to chaotic (Hamilton, 2008, p. 31), depending on what stage of resilience the neighborhood or city finds itself.

EARLY RESEARCH

In statistical analysis, DGs will show up as outliers on the bell curve of population behaviors. They are inevitably the Early Adopters (if not the inventors) of new behavior. As such they are typically attempting to attract others, rather than being courted. Within the city the role and recognition of DGs can vary vastly from one cultural grouping or neighborhood to another. My research (see Inset below) has shown that the resilience cycle co-exists in many population sub-groups of the city (each at its own distinctive stage) and that it is only by identifying the value systems, of each group that one can discern who are the CE's and DG's (as well as the Inner Judge/Integrators (IJ's) and Resource Allocator/Administrators (RA's)). Moreover it is critical to understand this not only to appreciate, engage and influence sub-populations appropriately, but also to grasp the intergroup rivalries that exist between such groups (Hamilton, 2010b).

DIVERSITY GENERATION AS SOURCE AND PROCESS OF INNOVATION

In a world where migration has created "mongrel cities" of "unnatural" diversities (Sandercock, 2000; Sandercock & Lyssiotis, 2003), the Integral approach reveals how strategies that generate, embrace and harness diversity can encourage creativity that is not simply type related, such as how Florida characterizes the Creative City (Florida, 2005, 2008) or even plurally psychologically defined as Landry explores (Landy & Murray, 2017) but that is All Quadrants, All levels, All Lines (AQAL) framed, as in the Integral City (Hamilton, 2007, 2008, 2010b, 2017; Wilber, 1995, 2007).

From a metaview, we realize that the self-organizing creative contributions influenced by DG's and then structurally enshrined by CE's are both vital to the long term survival of the human hive (and indeed the species) (Appendix E). Where changing life conditions have required adaptive responses (e.g. to the 2008–2012 global economic meltdown), the four internal roles of the beehive (and the fifth external role of inter-city tournaments) can be seen operating in the human hive to create the necessary adaptations for city survival. The economies, environments, social and cultural capacities that express the relationship between the group and the individual, are formed and reformed as life conditions change and complexity upskills into new capacities or

THE FOUR ROLES AT WORK IN THE CITY

When the city is stable the work of CEs (usually recognized as Workers, Producers, Administrators) is at its peak. When the city is in chaos the work of DGs (usually recognized as Entrepreneurs, Developers, Inventors and Innovators— such as Steve Jobs, Elon Musk and Richard Branson) responds to new opportunities, threats and possibilities that enable firstly their own survival, and then as their innovations gain traction, enable the survival of the greater population. During times of transition between stability and chaos and back to stability our Inner Judges (IJ) and Resource Allocators (RA) (often recognized as Financiers, Investors, Bankers, Mayors, Councilors, Judges and elders) respond to life's complexities and changes attempting to integrate and mediate the opposing forces (e.g. of smart phones, driverless cars and cheap travel).

downgrades into earlier levels of comfortable expression (e.g. the formation of Homeland Security after 911 in the USA to enforce national domestic security in the face of terrorism; or Erdogan's repressive reactions following the military coup in Turkey in 2016).

The relationship of intelligences that emerge in a trajectory of complexity, from role interaction in the human hive is thus dynamic, because life conditions are dynamic. The work of our IJs and RAs is to respond to life's complexities and changes by adjusting the performance of the CE's and DG's so that rewards support behavior that sustains life. At some level (in these days through frenetic social media exchanges, but in less complex times through story telling exchanges) the IJs and RAs are taking stock of what is happening to internal city cultures in relationship to critical survival contexting factors: climate change, environmental damage, hostile neighbors, friendly trade partners in order to shape the appropriate individual and social response in the city (Diamond, 2005; Hamilton, 2008).

Thus self-organizing diversity generation, emerges new patterns and processes as innovations which become hierarchically structured in the city. Zooming out from the scale of the individual, to groups, organizations and the city itself, we can appreciate that without the natural self-organizing operating system that produces diversity we would not be able to adapt or respond or expand our capacities through ever complexifying emergence.

We could say that the city is populated by complex adaptive systems whose diversity generation capability enables the social holon of the city to reorganize and recalibrate itself to be more internally resonant and externally coherent with life conditions.

Without the convergent structuring operating system that CEs provide to counter-balance the diversity generation system, the city would waste energy resources in unfettered impulses of divergence.

Therefore, to be effective, the innovation that results from diversity generation must be harnessed to systems and structures and eventually be institutionalized (as noted above in the discussion of resilience). This happens by reinforcing the energy for existing conformity enforcement which actually dampens creativity (e.g. in the post 2008 financial meltdown in the USA financial institutions shied away from bundling mortgage backed securities and became reluctant to buy houses with unsustainable mortgages) or releasing energy so that it can be redirected to diversity generation thus encouraging creativity (e.g. creating new kinds of online banking or ethical mortgage funds).(See Chapter 2.)

Key steps to harness effective diversity generation in a city change process could include:

1. Recognize and name the dissonance in the system—explore how to dance with that dissonance and even amplify it rather than attempting to overcome the dissonance. Such an exploration can discover the impetus or catalyst to change.

2. Identify the purpose for harnessing DGs—create the vision for changing from what to what?

3. Find the DG's who are the agents for change—enable leadership to emerge from the DG's who have the passion for solving the catalyzing dilemma and/or attaining the vision.

4. Support the DG's to amplify the dissonance/catalyst/impetus for change, so others can see it.

5. Engage as many diverse stakeholders in the process as possible—actively seek out diversity and make room for difference. Ask: *who else should be here?*

6. Create reflective feedback loops with the CEs in the system so that both DG's and CE's can self-correct and develop co-operational structures that work.

7. Make the feedback accessible to all by publication and display for further amplification; e.g. community newspapers, online media, real time intelligence display systems.

(It should be noted that these steps are complementary to caring creativity described in Chapter 2; Book 2's inquiry, action and impact of the Master Code (Hamilton, 2017); and the process of Meshworking where both self-organizing DG operating systems are aligned with structuring CE operating systems.) (Hamilton, 2010c)

CONCLUSIONS

Diversity generation appears to be a key factor in the persistence of cities. Five maps of the city help us to view diversity through biological, psychological, cultural, systems and spiritual lenses; track the holarchy of nested human systems from individuals to communities all of which simultaneously express diversity; understand the developmental cycle of coping with diversity in relationships; and appreciate a trajectory of increasingly diverse and complex structures and energies in the city. When we see the tensions between ego-ethno-world-and-Kosmocentric circles of care and the divergent interpretations of Traditional, Modern, Post-Modern and Integral discourses, we realize the city is a microcosm and seed bed of the world's Diversity Generators.

The tensions between individual and collective values systems create forces that ebb and flow in a resilience cycle, allowing the diversity generation that is counter to the norm to act as a self-organizing alternative option generator. The greater the diversity of interests, values and capacities in the city, the greater the dynamics and natural generation of diversity. However, the chaos that too much diversity can generate is kept in check by the domination of the CEs as long as they offer the greatest coherence to the life conditions. When the CE behaviors, beliefs, relationships and structures no longer enable the optimum stability, then the role of the DG's becomes critical to the survival of the city as the DG's supply (sometimes a spectrum of) possibilities that enable a complex adaptive shift to a better match with the life conditions.

At this time of mongrel cities, faced with the intransigence of rebellious youth, warring ethnicities, fragmented sectors and resistant bureaucracies, we experience an increase in the conditions of breakdown. However, with a recognition that this is merely one of four stages of the resilience cycle, the existence of DGs in the Integral City gives us a resource that can be accessed and an expectation that new strategies and systems can evolve to integrate the silos, stovepipes and solitudes (Dale, 2001) that stymie us today. Cities appear not only to be extraordinarily tolerant of diversity but actually dependent for their survival on the diversity generation that enables them as complex adaptive systems to survive.

REFERENCES

Abrams, N. E., & Primack, J. R. (2006). *The View from the Centre of the Universe: Discovering our Extraordinary Place in the Cosmos.* New York: Riverhead Books, Penguin Group.

Alexander, C. (2004a). *The Luminous Ground* (September 1, 2004 ed. Vol. 4). Berkeley, CA: Center for Environmental Structure.

anon. (2017e). https://www.economist.com/blogs/graphicdetail/2017/08/daily-chart-10. *The Economist,* (August 16, 2017). Retrieved from http://www.economist.com/node/21542773?fsrc=scn/tw/te/ar/bossesunderfire

anon. (2017f). LGBTQ Community. Retrieved December 15, 2017, from Vancouver City website http://vancouver.ca/people-programs/lgbtq-community.aspx

anon. (2017g). 2011 Vancouver Stanley Cup riot. Retrieved December 15, 2017, from Wikipedia https://en.wikipedia.org/wiki/2011_Vancouver_Stanley_Cup_riot

Baron-Cohen, S. (2003). *The Essential Difference: The Truth About the Male and Female Brain.* New York: Basic Books.

Beck, D. (2012). The Integral Dance: How a Master Code Pollinates and Preserves the Culture of Bumblebees. *Integral Leadership Review,* (June). Retrieved from http://integralleadershipreview.com/7174-the-master-code-spiral-dynamics-integral

Beck, D., & Cowan, C. (1994, 1997). The Future of Cities. Unpublished Article. The National Values Center, Inc.

Beck, D., & Cowan, C. (1996). *Spiral Dynamics: Mastering Values, Leadership and Change.* Malden, MA: Blackwell Publishers.

Beck, D., & Linscott, G. (2006). *The Crucible: Forging South Africa's Future* (hardcover ed.). Columbia, MD: Cherie Beck, Coera.us, Center for Human Emergence.

Bloom, H. (2000). *The Global Brain: The Evolution of Mass Mind from the Big Bang to the 21st Century.* New York: John Wiley & Son Inc.

Brown, L. (2008). *Plan B 3.0.* New York: W.W. Norton & Company.

Capra, F. (1996). *The Web of Life: A New Scientific Understanding of Living Systems.* New York: Anchor Books, Doubleday.

Consumers of Tomorrow: Insights and Observations About Generation Z. (2011). Grail Research, A Division of Integreon.

Dale, A. (2001). *At The Edge: Sustainable Development in the 21st Century.* Vancouver: UBC Press.

DeKay, M. (2011). *Integral Sustainable Design: Transformative Perspectives.* London, UK: Earthscan.

Diamond, J. (2005). *Collapse: How societies choose to fail or succeed* (first ed.). New York: Penguin Group.

Eoyang, G. (1997). *Coping With Chaos: Seven Simple Tools.* Cheyenne, Wyoming: Lagumo Corp.

Eoyang, G., & Olson, E. (2001). *Facilitating Organization Change: Lessons from Complexity Science.* San Francisco: Jossey-Bass Pfeiffer.

Esbjörn-Hargens, S., & Zimmerman, M. (2009). *Integral Ecology: Uniting Multiple Perspectives on the Natural World.* Boston: Shambhala Publications Inc.

Florida, R. (2005). *Cities and the Creative Class.* New York: Routledge.

Florida, R. (2008). *Who's Your City: How the Creative Economy is Making Where to Live the Most Important Decision of Your Life.* Toronto: Random House Canada.

Gladwell, M. (2002). *The Tipping Point: How Little Things Can Make a Big Difference:* Back Bay Books.

Graves, C. (1974). Human Nature Prepares for a Momentous Leap *The Futurist.*

Gregory, T. A., & Raffanti, M. A. (2009). Integral Diversity Maturity: Toward a Postconventional Understanding of Diversity Dynamics. *Journal of Integral Theory and Practice,* 4(3), 41–58.

Gunderson, L. C., & Holling, C. S. (Eds.). (2002). *Panarchy: Understanding Transformations in Human and Natural Systems* Washington, DC: Island Press.

Hamilton, M. (2006). Integral Metamap Creates Common Language for Urban Change. [Research Paper]. *Journal of Organizational Change Management,* 19(3), 276–306.

Hamilton, M. (2007). Approaching Homelessness: An Integral Reframe. [Philosophy]. *World Futures: The Journal of General Evolution,* Volume 63(2), 107–126.

Hamilton, M. (2008). *Integral City: Evolutionary Intelligences for the Human Hive.* Gabriola Island BC: New Society Publishers.

Hamilton, M. (2010a). Integral City: Meshworking Evolutionary Intelligences for the Human Hive and Eco-Region Resilience. Retrieved August 25, 2010, from http://integralcity.com/

Hamilton, M. (2010b). Mapping the Values of Abbotsford and Developing a Prototype for an Integral Vital Signs Monitor of City Wellbeing. Victoria, BC, Canada: Canada-British Columbia Immigration Agreement, Welcome BC.

Hamilton, M. (2010c). Meshworking Integral Intelligences for Resilient Environments; Enabling Order and Creativity in the Human Hive. Paper presented at the Enacting an Integral Future Conference.

Hamilton, M. (2010d). Integral Spirituality in the Human Hive: A Primer. Trialog, 2010(4), 10–17.

Hamilton, M. (2012). Meshworking Evolutionary Intelligence for the Human Hive. Paper presented at the Building Sustainable Communities 5. Kelowna, BC.

Hamilton, M. (2017). *Integral City Inquiry and Action: Designing Impact for the Human Hive*. Phoenix, AZ: Integral Publishers.

Howe, N., & Strauss, W. (1992). *Generations: The History of America's Future, 1584 to 2069*. New York: Harper Perennial.

Koestler, A. (1976). *The Ghost in the Machine*. New York, NY: Random House.

Landry, C., & Murray, C. (2017). *Psychology & the City*. Bournes Green Near Stroud, UK: Comedia.

McKnight, P. (2012). No Such Thing as a Natural Born Woman. Retrieved from http://www.vancouversun.com/health/mcknight+such+thing+natural+born+woman/6647696/story.html

Midgley, G. (2000). *Systemic Intervention: Philosophy, Methodology, and Practice*. New York: Kluwer Academic/Plenum Publishers.

Midgley, G., Munlo, I., & Brown, M. (1998). The theory and practice of boundary critique: Developing housing services for older people. Journal of the Operational Research Society, 49:5, pp. 467–478. https://ezproxy.royalroads.ca/login?url=http://links.jstor.org/sici?sici=0160–5682%28199805%2949%3A5%3C467%3ATTAPOB%3E2.0.CO%3B2-S. *Journal of the Operational Research Society*, 49:5, pp. 467–478. Retrieved from https://ezproxy.royalroads.ca/login?url=http://links.jstor.org/sici?sici=0160–5682%28199805%2949%3A5%3C467%3ATTAPOB%3E2.0.CO%3B2-S

Moir, A., & Jessel, D. (1991). *Brain Sex*. New York,: Dell Publishing.

Oxford Online Dictionary. (2017). Retrieved December 15, 2017: http://oxford-dictionaries.com

Ray, P., & Anderson, S. R. (2000). *The Cultural Creatives: How 50 Million People Are Changing the World*. New York: Harmony Books Member Crown Publishing Group, Random House Inc.

Robinson, J. (2012). Personal Communication: Tour of the UBC Centre for Interactive Research in Sustainability. In M. Hamilton (Ed.) (John's tour of CIRS building identified 7 factors of sustainability: 4 quantitative— energy, water, structural, GHG/emissions and 3 soft—health, productivity, happiness ed.). Vancouver.

Sahtouris, E. (1999). *Earthdance: Living Systems in Evolution* Retrieved from http://www.ratical.org/LifeWeb/

Sandercock, L. (2000). When Strangers Become Neighbours: Managing Cities of Difference. *Planning Theory and Practice*, 1(1).

Sandercock, L., & Lyssiotis, P. (2003). *Cosmopolis II: Mongrel Cities of the 21st Century*. London: Continuum International Publishing Group.

Stewart, I. (Writer). (2010). "Hot Rocks" Geography [TV]. In BBC (Producer): Knowledge Network.

Strauss, W., & Howe, N. (1997). *The Fourth Turning: An American Prophecy, What the Cycles of History Tell Us About America's Next Rendezvous with Destiny*. New York: Broadway Books.

Szaklarksi, C. (2012). Too soon to say if other pageants will follow Miss Universe Canada's transgender precedent: official. Retrieved from http://news.nationalpost.com/2012/05/19/too-soon-to-say-if-other-pageants-will-follow-miss-universe-canadas-transgender-preceden-official/

Taylor, G. (2008). *Evolution's Edge: The Coming Collapse and Transformation of our World*. Gabriola Island, BC: New Society Publishers.

Thomas, R. R. (1996). *Redefining Diversity*. New York, NY: AMACOM.

Ulrich, W. (2000). The 12 Critically Heuristic Boundary Questions. In G. Midgley (Ed.), *Systemic Intervention: Philosophy, Methodology, and Practice* (pp. 141). New York, NY: Kluwer Academic/Plenum Publishers.

West, G. (2011). Why Cities Keep Growing, Corporations and People Always Die, and Life Gets Faster: A Conversation With Geoffrey West (5.23.11). In J. Brockman (Ed.), *Edge*: Edge.org.

West, G. (2017). *Scale: The Universal Laws of Growth, Innovation, Sustainability and the Pace of Life in Organisms, Cities, Economies and Companies*. New York: Penguin Press.

Wilber, K. (1995). *Sex, Ecology and Spirituality: the spirit of evolution*. Boston: Shambhala Publications Inc.

Wilber, K. (1996). A *Brief History of Everything*. Boston,: Shambhala Publications Inc.

Wilber, K. (2000). A *Theory of Everything*. Boston: Shambhala Publications Inc.

Wilber, K. (2002). *Boomeritis: A Novel That Will Set You Free*. Boston: Shambhala Publications Inc.

Wilber, K. (2006). *Integral Spirituality*. Boston: Shambhala Publications Inc.

Wilber, K. (2007). *The Integral Vision*. Boston: Shambhala Publications Inc.

Zimmerman, M. E. (2005). Integral Ecology: A perspectival, developmental, and coordinating approach to environmental problems. *World Futures, Volume 61, Issue 1 & 2 January 2005, pages 50–62* (Issue 1 & 2), 50–62

9

INTEGRAL INTELLIGENCES: PRACTISING PERSONAL SUSTAINABILITY LEADERSHIP

CHAPTER SUMMARY

This chapter illustrates the twelve intelligences identified in *Integral City: Evolutionary Intelligences for the Human Hive* (Hamilton, 2008a) through the leadership of architect Teddy Cruz and political theorist Fonna Forman. The chapter discusses their socially responsible research-based architectural practice in terms of each intelligence and demonstrates how they transcend and include traditional, modern and postmodern mindsets into an Integral evolutionary paradigm.

Keywords: socially responsible, architecture, political theory, sustainability, Integral City Intelligences, interstitial zone, transcultural, transnational

"As we try to define robust R&D for urban sustainability, when does it get personal?" I had been curious about this question from the MC, before the beginning of the Elevate 09 Conference in Boulder Colorado in February 2009. Architect and expert in Sustainable Integral Design, Mark DeKay (2011, p. 129) had been waking me up to the look for the qualities of designers who listen to multiple perspectives arising from "cultural, individual, ecological [and] technical" realities.

Thus, I had designed for the conference, a methodology to look for the personal and the sustainable, based on the lenses of the twelve intelligence from my book, Integral City: Evolutionary Intelligences for the Human Hive (Hamilton, 2008). My job (for a wrap-up panel) was to listen, observe, reflect and reframe Elevate 09's presentations on sustainable real estate, land use and economic development. This gathering of developers, architects, planners, policy makers, lawyers and business professionals marked the inauguration of University of Colorado's Initiative for Sustainable Development, sponsored by the LEEDS School of Business and the Colorado Law School. I crafted data gathering observation summaries (based on the intelligences summarized in Appendix C2) and duly made observations from each panel related to "Regulating and Developing for Sustainability" in this century of the city (Pierce, Johnson, & Peters, 2008). While presenters were all intensely committed to their academic, regulatory and planning roles, the person who most energized the answer to the question about the intersection of the personal with the sustainable, was architect Teddy Cruz.

For this chapter, I have returned to Cruz and his professional partner Fonna Forman as exemplars to illustrate what these intelligences can look like in practitioners at the leading edge of combining the personal and the sustainable. (Note that I have placed square parentheses [I#] relating to each intelligence and each chapter from Book 1 (Hamilton, 2008) mapped from Appendix C1 in the narrative that follows).

PERSONAL LEADERSHIP PRACTISE OF INTEGRAL CITY INTELLIGENCES

Currently, Professor of Pubic Culture and Urbanism, Department of Visual Arts at University of California, San Diego, Cruz is known for his architecture of social responsibility [I8 Cultural], derived from his experience in the water shed of the Tijuana River, which flows north out of the cultural chaos of Mexico into the socially structured zones of San Diego. In the years since the Elevate '09 event, Teddy has partnered with Fonna Forman, Professor of Political Theory, University of California, San Diego, and Director of the UCSD Center on Global Justice. Their research-based practice, Estudio Teddy Cruz + Fonna Forman is committed to integrating the realms of theory and practice, ethics and space, and mediating between top-down and bottom-up intelligences and capacities in the city (Forman & Cruz, 2015).

Their curiosity and deep respect for the natural and human ecologies enliven both their commentary and visuals of the ecosphere [I1 Eco], which has called them to notice emergent life in the interstitial zones influenced by the river wetlands, the tidal flats, the estuary flows, the international border and the human migrations. Originally from Guatemala, Cruz has a genuine empathy with the newcomer, with ecological invasions, political clashes and ambiguous spaces. He sees the degradation of the environment reflected in social and political degradation and vice versa. Forman is a political theorist best known for her revisionist work on Adam Smith, recuperating the ethical, social, spatial and public dimensions of his thought (as editor of the Adam Smith Reviews), and grounding her research through engaging issues at the intersection of ethics, public culture, policy and the city (including human rights at the urban scale, climate justice, border ethics and equitable urbanization).

Cruz + Forman give voice to the value of emergent complexity [I2 Emergent]—not with aesthetic judgment at the rough and ready changes that continually surprise, but with delight in the co-existence of contradictory conditions like the San Diego gated community whose existence depends on immigrant housekeepers, child minders and landscape workers, crossing the border from Mexico.

Cruz + Forman see new life and new possibilities because local conditions on both sides of the border are being radicalized [I2 Emergent]. On the north side of the international divide people are the invading species, pixilating the carefully zoned American landscape with their lively Latin routines of daily work, travel, art and home life. On the south side of the same crossing, they admire the ingenuity of repurposing building materials like garage doors imported from San Diego suburb renovations, that become the primary exterior cladding for buildings made entirely of garage doors.

What is the role of architect in such a fluid time and space? [I9 Inquiry] It is the designer who sees the possibilities for modular steel frames that enable the shapeshifting of devalued, atypical land spaces, and the evolution of building clusters imagined as an unfolding series of purposes, with plural dimensions and a variety of co-designing users.

Cruz + Forman are masters of complex adaptive design—negotiating ambiguity at multiple scales [I3 Integral]. They see the potential for nests of whole systems to serve both individual and collective needs—whether that be a tradesman, his family, his shop, a neighbor's retail store or the meeting space for the street [I6 Outer, I7 Social]. Consider: a building with ground floor living rooms, transmuting into a 2nd floor home, with a working garage underneath it, and a father-in-law flat behind, bordered by living quarters for a brother's new family and artisan shop.

Cities who talk about density, too often offer it as a clinically static benchmark of urban life. Cruz + Forman, on the other hand, consider density merely a resulting condition of negotiating shared intention, social responsibility and economic opportunities. [I4 Living, I11 Navigating] Density for them has become flexible and fluid. The duo considers that regulation ought not to lock in density as a permanent condition but keep the social condition responsive and adaptive, so that density is a healthy and intelligent result of active participation in urban life. [I2 Emergent, I4 Living]

Listening to and watching Cruz + Forman convey their story of intelligent design, is an entertaining, breathtaking, provoking and challenging experience. Don't expect to sit still because they invite you to examine your assumptions. [I9 Inquiry] How can you use the natural conflicts that come up about land use to enable creativity to flourish? Why shouldn't the house/ workplace dweller be an active participant in street/city design? What politics of zoning assure hardening of the legislative arteries? When will we embrace the fact that all resources have a natural flow and lifecycle—whether they be human resources or natural resources or recycled window frames? [I4 Living]

Cruz says, "My education came out of phenomenology in the '80s [I5 Inner], and it stressed that we all engage in the reality of the world through our perceptions [I6 Outer] and interpretations [I5 Inner, I8 Cultural] of that reality. At the same time, I feel the poetics in architecture remain too isolated from the politics of the construction of the city. [I5 Inner, I8 Cultural] And somehow many of these images should be bridges to reconnect the poetic and the political." (Sokol, October 2008)

The urbanism of *Estudio Teddy Cruz + Fonna Forman* has been described as "bricollage". Philosopher Andy Clark proposes that "our minds are a kludge (or bricollage) of different kinds of intelligence . . . some . . . arise out of decentralized and parallel processes; others from centralized and sequential ones." (De Landa, 1995). Cruz + Forman seem to be natural meshworkers—those who facilitate self-organizing hierarchies and hierarchies of self-organization (Hamilton, 2008a). [I10 Meshworking] They cross boundaries, enabling the co-existence of differentiated wholes (or holons), so that healthy integration and complex emergence can happen. [I10 Meshworking] They are not merely networkers, or replicators but catalysts to self-organizing design. They penetrate the center of conflicts like zoning bylaws and lending requirements and discover the new intelligences that come from transcending and including old structures so that new processes and patterns can happen. They demonstrate the mutually beneficial values of pixilated land use zoning, economic micro-loans, and an aesthetic fabric that emerges from peoples' involvement in stitching together the co-design of their urban life. They dance on the margins where the exchanges between the old traditional ways, the modern strategies and the socially responsible approaches recombine into living systems energized by hope, action, engaged culture and growing social capacity. [I12 Evo]

CONCLUSION

In the century of the city (Pierce et al., 2008), architect Teddy Cruz and political theorist Fonna Forman make urban sustainability personal, by living all twelve of the Integral City intelligences in a totally evolutionary way. [I12 Evo]. They reaffirm DeKay's (2011, p. 129) injunction that designers of integrally-informed sustainability must naturally embrace "rich human experiences, significant cultural meaning, high technological performance and true ecological sense."

Cruz and Forman exemplify the highest leverage point for changing a system, identified by systems pioneer, Donella Meadows (Meadows, 2008); namely, changing mindsets. But, not only do they create the conditions for changing mindsets, they transcend old paradigms through their personal commitment to bridging the poetic and the political. In doing so they seem to live by the Integral City Master Code: Take care of yourself, Take Care of Each Other, Take Care of this Place / Planet (see Chapter 3). Teddy Cruz showed us how to do this at Elevate 09, by sharing his passion, his calling and his challenge for all to co-create personal sustainability design practice. Today with his partner Fonna Forman they are enacting these practices in collaboration with immigrant communities across the San Diego-Tijuana border region.

REFERENCES

Cruz, T., & Forman, F. (2017a). Latin America and a New Political Leadership: Experimental Acts of Co-Existence. In J. Burton, S. Jackson, & D. Wilsdon (Eds.), *Public Servants: Art and the Crisis of the Common Good* (pp. 71–90). Boston, MA: MIT Press.

Cruz, T., & Forman, F. (2017). Un-walling Citizenship. *Avery Review: Critical Essays on Architecture,* 21(Winter), 98–109.

DeKay, M. (2011). *Integral Sustainable Design: Transformative Perspectives.* London, UK: Earthscan.

De Landa, M. (1995). Homes: Meshwork or Hierarchy? http://www.mediamatic. net/article-200.5956.html Special: Home issue. Retrieved December 28, 2017.

Forman, F., & Cruz, T. (2015). Changing Practice: Engaging Informal Public Demands. In H. Mooshammer, P. Mörtenböck, T. Cruz, & F. Forman (Eds.), *Informal Markets Worlds—Reader: The Architecture of Economic Pressure.* Rotterdam: nai010 Publishers.

Forman, F., & Cruz, T. (2017b). The Cross-Border Public. In G. Urbonas, A. Lui, & L. Freeman (Eds.), *Public Space? Lost and Found* (pp. 172–195). Cambridge: MIT Press.

Hamilton, M. (2008). *Integral City: Evolutionary Intelligences for the Human Hive.* Gabriola Island BC: New Society Publishers.

Meadows, D. (2008). *Thinking in Systems.* White River Junction, VT: Chelsea Green Publishing.

Pierce, N., Johnson, C., & Peters, F. (2008). *Century of the City.* New York: The Rockefeller Foundation.

Sokol, D. (October 2008). Repositioning Practice: Teddy Cruz. Retrieved December 28, 2017, from Architectural Record http://archrecord.con-struction.com/features/humanitarianDesign/0810cruz-1.asp

SECTION 2

Widening Capacity through Reinventing Organizations

C hapter 10 wakes us up to the roots of **wellbeing in organizations** and how that is related to the very aliveness of people and organizations that underpins the capacity to widen organizational effectiveness in the city.

Chapter 11 opens the organizational door further by inquiring into the **capacity of organizations to reinvent themselves**. Is it possible for organizations to skip from modern to an Integral organization without developing the web of relationships that emerge from working on purpose, in the context of your city? And how is it possible to widen the city's capacity without first reinventing its organizations?

10

IMPROVING ORGANIZATIONAL WELLBEING

CHAPTER SUMMARY

This chapter considers organizations as living systems within the larger living system of the human hive or city. We look at sick and well organizations in the context of a metaview of the lifecycle of organizations. We differentiate between organizations in transition and those that are not well. Diagnosing the state of organizational health is followed up by ten key steps to improve organizational health.

Keywords: organization, living system, organizational stages, transitions, wellbeing, improvements

Sick buildings were a major complaint of the workplace in the last century. In the new century, people are complaining about working in sick or toxic organizations. Their complaints reflect their desire for a well organization. How can you tell if your organization is well or ailing?

A SICK ORGANIZATION SUFFERS

A Sick Organization suffers from the following challenges:

Identity issues: the organization does not really know what business it is in. As a result, people in it do not have a clear understanding of the significance of their work, their roles or contributions, or who the organization serves.

Relationship issues: the organization has client complaints, supplier difficulties, employee apathy, investor misunderstanding, community distrust, or a combination of these ailments. Leadership, management, personnel and/or union problems may be regular occurrences. Materials may be difficult to obtain on time, or at all. Shipping and receiving may cause major challenges.

Information issues: the organization never has the information it needs in a timely manner (this may be from internal or external causes). Information is inaccurate or inaccessible. Information doesn't get to the people who would be able to use it most effectively. Information is blocked across departments or between organizational levels.

A WELL ORGANIZATION THRIVES

A Well Organization thrives because of the following qualities.

Effective processes: the organization's systems "metabolize" energy from the environment (such as investment dollars, people skills, information, raw material), and produce useable, useful, and efficient outcomes (such as services, products, and ideas).

Resilient structure: people, information, work, and places are connected for optimal relationships—not just in good times, but during change and difficult circumstances, as well.

Continuous learning: the organization continuously learns from its experiences in processing and structural encounters with the environment. It explicitly notices, interprets, uses, and applies trends and patterns affecting its relationships, information, and identity.

Organizations are complex adaptive systems

Organizations are complex adaptive systems (social holons) that emerge from the agreements of people, who are also complex adaptive systems. In fact, in a legal sense, organizations are recognized as separate legal entities. They have rights, responsibilities, liabilities, and legal structures that give the illusion they are rather permanent and unchanging. We treat organizations as if they were people (and suffer the consequences of the misalignment between such legal fabrications and living systems principles (Korten, 2015)).

But, just as no person stays the same from one moment to the next, neither do organizations. As complex adaptive systems, organizations are alive, dynamic, and ever-changing. In fact, when you consider the levels of dynamic complexity within organizations, you might conclude that control of an organization is totally illusory. Under such circumstances, perhaps wellbeing might be, also.

While control of an organization, of its people, or its wellbeing might be impossible, order within an organization is not. Just as a flock of birds have devised methods for orderly flight—or a hive of bees for orderly production of honey or rush-hour traffic for orderly (usually!) flow—so organizations can develop guidelines for Organizational Wellbeing.

Wellbeing Behaviors

An organization exhibits wellbeing behaviors and patterns when it exhibits the basic acts of aliveness: surviving, connecting with its environment and regenerating.

Survives:

An organization must attract resources that serve a purpose that in some way supports organization and life outside itself. Attracting the resources of funds, people, ideas, and materials and adding value by re-combining (self-organizing) them in some way, to serve others, ensures the survival of an organization. Paradoxically the organization is able to support (ensure the survival of) the funds, people, ideas, and materials it uses internally, by organizing these elements for the benefit of some good outside itself. Survival is not necessarily of the "fittest" organization, merely an organization that is able to "fit" into its environment. Thus as the world complexifies, organizations may survive by serving their customers in more and more specialized ways; e.g., niche markets and/or because they discover how to attract and combine elements of diversity into new levels of complexity, such as online recruitment or teaming. (However, we have received serious warnings from West (2017) that the scale of the organization (and also the nation) does not have the longevity of cities; so perhaps we need to respect the more tenuous nature of organizations as we tend to their wellbeing?)

Connects with its environment:

An organization cannot survive for long if it does not connect with its environment. By definition, every resource an organization uses comes from outside its organizational boundaries (including the human resources who form its social holon). Thus, its very lifeblood depends on the organization's ability to find all of the input for its internal processes from its environment. Likewise, an organization must deliver its output (and what it does not use for itself) back into its environment, as a service and/or product and/or waste. This part of the environment is the organization's market. In a larger context, the organization must connect with a regional or global environment to understand the effects of the flow of using resources, and any byproducts of such process. For instance, a power generation plant connects with its environment by using a fuel source (hydro, coal, gas, oil, nuclear); produces waste water that flows into the ground and/or a waste water system; emits airborne gases and/or particles into the air-shed; produces spent fuel that requires storage which impacts environmental systems; connects with an electrical grid for distribution; and collects finances from its investors and payments from its users.

Regenerates:

An organization may be able to survive and connect with its environment for a fixed period of time, but unless it has a means of regeneration, it will not survive beyond the life of the individual people in the organization (West, 2017). As in the biological world—where trees propagate from seed, roots, cloning, or grafting—organizations may have multiple regeneration strategies. Here are examples of organizations with a regeneration strategy.

- Reinventing its identity, (as Phillips did, in moving from an industrial manufacturing company to a health information company).
- Purposely creating new organizations (the way Magna International creates new organizations every time a critical mass of 150 people outgrow a current one or creates a Lattice of relationships and sponsors).
- Purposely pruning old product divisions and creating new ones (as 3M did, and the way the Canadian banking system divested community banks to the Credit Unions).
- Developing a succession plan (as the Baby Boomer generation enters retirement).

HOW A METAVIEW REVEALS ORGANIZATIONAL PATTERNS

The insights from Spiral Dynamics (Beck, 1996) give us a metaview that allows us to see patterns in the organizations of the human hive that seem similar to patterns in other complex living systems (like the honey bees described in Appendix E). Several decades before Bloom (2000) contemplated the wisdom of bees, Clare Graves (1971, 1974, 2003, 2005) in the 1960's and 1970's conducted an 18 year study that ended in a theory that explained the "evolutionary complex levels of human existence". Graves' research, showed that human behaviors arising out of one set of conditions created problems of existence that could not be solved at that level. As a result, he proposed that new adaptive behaviors are called into existence.

Graves identified an individual-centric cluster of behaviors he called "express self" values; and a group-centric cluster of behaviors he called "sacrifice self" values. Moreover, his research showed that these behaviors adapted and alternated with one another at an ever-increasing level of complexity, as life conditions changed. Graves used a set of identifiers to represent life conditions (designated by letters from the first half of the alphabet) and bio-psycho-social human existence (designated by letters from the second half of the alphabet) (see Table 23). Beck and Cowan (1996) and Beck (2001, 2002b; Beck & Linscott, 2006) devised the Spiral Dynamics system of color codes to identify each level of complexity: beige, red, orange, yellow (i.e. warm colors) relate to "express self" versions of existence; purple, blue, green, turquoise (i.e. cool colors) relate to "sacrifice self" versions of existence. They also applied these patterns to human systems at the individual, organizational and society scales.

Table 23: Levels of Complexity (adapted from Beck, 2002)

Express Self	Organizing Principle Of Life Condition	Sacrifice Self	Organizing Principle Of Life Condition
1. AN—Beige	Survival		
		2. BO-Purple	Belonging
3. CP—Red	Command & Control		
		4. DQ—Blue	Authoritarian Structure

Express Self	Organizing Principle Of Life Condition	Sacrifice Self	Organizing Principle Of Life Condition
5. ER—Orange	Economic Success		
		6. FS—Green	Humanitarian Equality
7. GT—Yellow	Systemic Flex & Flow		
		8. HU—Turquoise	Planetary Commons

It should be noted that these levels of existence can be clustered into the discourses of creativity that are often called Traditional (Levels 1/ Beige, 2/Purple); Pre-Modern (Level 3/Red, Level 4/Blue); Modern (Level 5/Orange, early Level 6/Green); Post-Modern (mature/late Level 6/Green); and Integral (Level 7/Yellow and Level 8/Turquoise). On an individual level, each of these levels transcends and includes the prior levels. (B. Brown, 2005a, 2005b, 2005c; Hamilton, 2008).

Holling (Gunderson & Holling, 2002; C.S. Holling, 2001; C.S. Holling, 2003) suggested that humans as complex adaptive living systems are evolving a "panarchy" of capacities. He explained that a panarchy is the "hierarchical structure in which systems of nature . . . and humans . . . as well as combined human-nature systems . . . and social-ecological systems are interlinked in never-ending adaptive cycles of growth, accumulation, restructuring and renewal". Like Wilber (1996) and Graves (2003), Holling proposed that these transformational cycles are nested at ever-increasing scales of complexity. He suggested that wealth (potential), controllability (connectedness) and adaptive capacity (resilience) are the "properties that shape the responses of ecosystems, agencies and people to crisis".

The basic resilience loop in Holling's model describes two separate objectives: maximizing production and accumulation (stages 1 and 2—and similar to Bloom's conformity enforcement) followed by maximizing invention and reassortment (stages 3 and 4—similar to Bloom's diversity generation). Holling proposed that the success at achieving one objective sets the stage for success at achieving the next objective in an endless figure 8 "panarchic" cycle. He defines a panarchy as "a hierarchy [of] nested sets of adaptive cycles. The functioning of those cycles and the communication between them determines the sustainability of a system." (2002, p. 396) (See Figure 7 in Chapter 8.)

To translate this into terms related to our exploration of organizations, we could propose that because the dominant behaviors arise in response to life conditions at each level of existence, the roles that organizations play, cause the city to behave with increasing levels of complexity in order to maximize the organizing principle (or value) of the current life condition. This behavior results in a tendency for the city and its organizations to protect the status quo at its current level of complexity. In Bloom's terms this could be interpreted as conformity enforcement (of the organizing principle/value).

It seems that, the human hive as a living system will exhibit a tension in favor of the values and behavior that is most coherent with the current life conditions, and its organizations will implement this as conformity enforcement (see a discussion of this related to the phenomenon of home-fulness in Chapter 13). The flip side of this behavior is that the dominant culture in the human hive (like the beehive) will also ignore and/or protect itself against the information produced by organizational roles operating as diversity generators, until such time as life conditions require the cre-ative solutions that diversity generation can offer to the problems created by maximizing the values and organizing principles in play at any level of existence. This very natural process can set up the conditions for the healthy, evolutionary, upshifting emergence of organizations (and the human hives in which they are located) or the unhealthy, chaotic, downshifting degeneration of organizations (that can even be masked as mono-cultures or sectoral monopolies (like communication systems or food distributors) that discourage creativity and innovation).

Indeed, the exploration by Jared Diamond (2005, p. 11) of the condi-tions for sustainable human existence, details a long history of failure by humans to understand that their societies, cities, organizations, homes and very lives depend on the deep and tangled interconnections of five factors: climate change, environmental damage, hostile neighbors, friendly trade partners and society's response. Diamond cites the repeated blind-ness of societies to grasp the implications of their short-term behaviors for their long-term survivability and describes in horrific detail the histories of societal "collapse" from the south Pacific to the north Atlantic to Latin

America. He warns that these historical instances may be more than metaphorical warnings for the continuation of life on earth.

From a metaview, we realize that the creative contributions influenced by diversity generators and those contributed by conformity enforcers are both vital to the long-term survival of organizations, (and the human hive and even the species as discussed in Chapter 8). They both have a function to play in aligning care within and between organizations so that they can in turn contribute to the healthy functioning of the human hive (including to its purpose as a reflective organ as discussed in Part I). The economies, environments, social and cultural capacities (including rules, laws, rituals, structures, energy exchanges, roles, learning competencies, assets and physical capacities) that express the relationship between the group and the individual, are formed and reformed as life conditions change, care is recapitulated and complexity increases.

The relationship of care, intelligences and capacity that emerge from organizational interaction in the human hive is thus dynamic, because life conditions are dynamic. The work of our organizations is to respond to life's complexities and changes by adjusting performance so that rewards support behavior that sustains life (especially life that cares). At some level (in these days often through social media interactions, but in less complex times through story telling exchanges) the alert organizations are also noticing what is happening in Diamond's key contexting factors. Aware organizations notice they must align themselves for city wellbeing, climate change, environmental damage, hostile neighbors and friendly trade partners. Effectively, this attempt of organizations to align with all the key factors affecting city life, orders and shapes the response of individual holons (aka people) and by association the responses of the social holons (aka collectives, organizations) and altogether the response-ability of the human hive. Using these (implicit and explicit) guides for alignment, capacity in the city is either inhibited or encouraged.

With each city having its own history of development and evolution, each city will have its own bandwidth of organizational expression (typically spanning three levels of complexity (as set out in Graves' research in Table 15) that represent older systems that gave birth to current realities; current expressions; and new systems coming on stream through early adopters). The forms that organization take in each city depend on the stage of the city's development—both for expressions of placecaring and placemaking (Hamilton, 2017). These days, the more advanced cities have organizations with centers of gravity that span Traditional, Modern, Post-Modern and early Integral. Organizations arise at any level of development, within any quadrant of reality. However, organizational systems that can emerge into a thriving economic ecosystem, depend on the degree of complexity of the caring systems that are at the center of gravity of the city (see Part 1). Moreover, sufficient order needs to be established and sustained in predecessor systems of placecaring and placemaking to support the infrastructure that the organizations require for realizing their full potential at any given level.

AN ORGANIZATION IN TRANSITION IS NOT SICK

While considering the indicators of organizational wellbeing then, it is useful to observe that a sick organization is not the same as an organization in transition. An organization in transition is transforming **naturally** into a different phase—just like the human body transforms over a lifetime, from fetus (initial investment) to baby (startup), to child (young organization), to teenager (maturing organization), to adult (mature organization), to senior (fading organization) (Adizes, 1999, Hamilton, 2008 p. 87). Sometimes organizations may have even more radical transformations like the life of a butterfly—where the egg, the caterpillar, the chrysalis, and the butterfly seem to have little in common with one another's outward appearance—like SpaceX moving from space delivery services to building a colony on Mars, or a grocery wholesaler becoming an e-commerce business (or vice versa as in Amazon buying Whole Foods).

Whether the pattern we recognize as transformative is human or butterfly, we know, from a scientific perspective, that these life forms are embedded within the DNA of the individual, the collective/organization and the species. We have also learned that even this DNA sequence is the emergent result of the creature, as a complex adaptive system, surviving, staying connected with its environment (even changing its environment), and regenerating. In other words, the DNA is co-creative with its environment (Lipton 2005).

In a time of massive global change, such as the period of history in which we live, it is often difficult to know whether organizations are well and merely metamorphosing (i.e., maturing from one stage to another) or whether they are actually sick. Sometimes the symptoms look the same. Just as sleeping could indicate natural cycles OR sickness, one organization may be purposely (and healthily) delaying its entry into a new market until the right time, while another may be procrastinating because it is undercapitalized (i.e., lacking the requisite energy). Another example of similar symptoms could be re-structuring through downsizing. That same symptom could be healthily appropriate to a mature organization downsizing on purpose in a thriving industry, compared to an indication of illness, in a sick sunset manufacturer in a rustbelt location laying off a work shift.

DIAGNOSING ORGANIZATIONAL HEALTH

Diagnosing an organization's condition of health depends on the viewer's understanding of its context as a complex adaptive system embedded in complex adaptive systems—its environments. As discussed above, growing numbers of researchers are concluding that different kinds of organizations have emerged in different periods of history, in response to different life conditions or environments (Laloux, 2014). Like biological organisms in the natural environment, organizations have emerged increasingly complex properties over time. We can identify these major organizational forms (which are represented in Map 4, Appendix B).

- Families and clans
- Tribes and regions
- Feudal states
- Early nations and bureaucracies
- Industrial empires and modern states
- Environmental services and global alliances

Organizations from each level of complexity still remain evident around the world today, though in some parts of the world, they may have died away. Here are some examples.

- Gleaning parties
- Ethnic allegiances and sports teams
- Military organizations; raiding parties
- Civil services; churches/religions; universities; hospitals
- Limited companies; health care; education; big business; big government
- International corporations; United Nations; environmental and peace groups; just-in-time organizations; virtual organizations
- Pan-global organizations: International space station

Until recently, these evolving kinds of organizations have been separated by geography, as well as time. Although each type of organization evolved from different life conditions, each kind that still exists today has been able to continue as a complex adaptive system, because in some way, its organizing principles have met the conditions of survival. It isn't that one form of organization is right and another wrong. Rather, it seems that each surviving form of organization is appropriate because it has adapted to and contributes in some way to life's continuing conditions.

As discussed above, each kind of organization is built around different organizing principles which manifest in organizations as sets of values or worldviews. Understanding an organization's wellbeing depends on an understanding of the organization's history, roots, and adaptiveness, and therefore the organizing principles embedded in its purpose, identity, processes, and structure. It also critical to understand how these principles impact the organization's physical, cultural, and social environment.

Considering these contexts, it becomes obvious that assessing an organization's wellbeing is itself a complex process.

- An organization may have different symptoms of sickness or wellbeing at each of its natural transition stages (regardless of its values base).
- An organization exists within an industry or sector. The industry or sector may be in various stages of transition (sunrise to sunset). The industry or sector may also be sick or well.

- An organization (and its industry or sector) exists within a series of overlapping environments (physical, cultural, social). These environments may be sick or well, and/or transitioning.
- An organization is made up of people, each of whom, as a complex adaptive system, carries both DNA and values systems, which may be sick or well.

Thus attaining and maintaining organizational wellbeing is a process and an outcome of a myriad of complex interactions. Organizational wellbeing is more likely to be a mystery or a miracle to be appreciated than a problem to be solved, or a sickness to be treated.

In the end, improving organizational wellbeing is not a challenge for the faint of heart. But it is a challenge that will engage the heart, along with the entire body, mind, and soul of any organizational wellbeing specialist, along with everyone in the organization, because it is critical to organizational survival, connectedness, regenerativity, and the health of the environment.

TEN KEYS TO IMPROVE ORGANIZATIONAL WELLBEING

To position an organization for wellbeing here are key actions to take.

1. Acknowledge that **organizations are living, complex adaptive systems**, and not "just" well-oiled machines with replaceable parts. As such, they are often unpredictable and surprising. Appreciate that; don't resist that.

2. Define and **share the organization's purpose, identity and reason for being** with all people inside and outside the organization. Find ways to do this playfully, as well as seriously.

3. **Align processes, structures, and relationships** with the organization's identity and purpose. Dispense with or recalibrate the ones that aren't aligned.

4. **Structure the organization** in ways that serve the organization's stage of development, its internal processes and the external environment. Consider the value of hierarchies for command and control, and the benefits of virtual networks for collaboration and innovation.

5. Identify and **maintain the vital connections** of the organization—to and with its environment—physically, culturally, and socially. For starters, explore the natural connections that already exist through employees' personal, recreational, and professional networks.

6. Create an **open system of information-sharing that connects** as much of the organization's subsystems and parts to one another as possible. Make information-sharing rewarding, fun, authentic, and respectful.

7. Accept responsibility, and develop **strategies for organizational regeneration** appropriate to the organization's purpose, survival, stage of development, and connection to its environment. Create opportunities for leaders to explore different survival scenarios, (at all levels: personal, organizational, community), without requirements for commitment.

8. Recognize that leadership must **continuously care for, nurture, anticipate, and respond to changes in balance** of the organization's subsystems with the whole—and its environment(s). Oftentimes, this may involve experimentation, uncertainty, and messiness.

9. See that **organizational relationships are more important** than the things, ideas, people, and situations themselves. This means treating relationships as important foreground phenomena, instead of background phenomena that we take for granted.

10. **Balance relationships** between things, ideas, people, and situations. Sometimes this means taking the organization less seriously, and seeing it in a context of "possibility, probability, and play."

REFERENCES

Adizes, I. (1999). *Managing Corporate Lifecycles*. Paramus, NJ: Prentice Hall Press.

Beck, D. (2001). Human capacities in the integral age: How value systems shape organizational productivity, national prosperity & global transformation. Paper presented at the International Productivity Conference. Retrieved from http://www.integralworld.net/beck7.html

Beck, D. (2002). Spiral Dynamics in the Integral Age. Paper presented at the Spiral Dynamics integral, Level 1.

Beck, D., & Cowan, C. (1996). *Spiral Dynamics: Mastering Values, Leadership and Change*. Malden, MA: Blackwell Publishers.

Beck, D., & Linscott, G. (2006). *The Crucible: Forging South Africa's Future* (hardcover ed.). Columbia, MD: Cherie Beck, Coera.us, Center for Human Emergence.

Bloom, H. (2000). *The Global Brain: The Evolution of Mass Mind from the Big Bang to the 21st Century*. New York: John Wiley & Son Inc.

Brown, B. (2005a). Theory and Practice of Integral Sustainable Development— An Overview, Part 1: Quadrants and the Practitioner. AQAL Journal, 1(2).

Brown, B. (2005b). Theory and Practice of Integral Sustainable Development— An Overview, Part 2: Values, Developmental Levels and Natural Design. AQAL Journal, 1(2).

Brown, B. (2005c). Theory and Practice of Integral Sustainable Development—An Overview, Part 3: Current Initiatives and Applications. AQAL Journal, 1(2).

Capra, F. (1996). *The Web of Life: A New Scientific Understanding of Living Systems*. New York: Anchor Books, Doubleday.

Csikszentmihalyi, M. (1993). *The Evolving Self: A Psychology for the Third Millennium*. New York: Harper Perennial, Harper Collins.

Dawkins, R. (1976). *The Selfish Gene*. Oxford, UK: Oxford University Press.

Diamond, J. (2005). *Collapse: How societies choose to fail or succeed* (first ed.). New York: Penguin Group.

Graves, C. (1971). A systems conception of personality: Levels of existence theory. Paper presented at the Washington School of Psychiatry.

Graves, C. (1974). Human Nature Prepares for a Momentous Leap *The Futurist*.

Graves, C. (2003). *Levels of Human Existence: Transcription of a Seminar at Washington School of Psychiatry, Oct. 16, 1971*. Santa Barbara: Eclet Publishing.

Graves, C. (2005). *The Never Ending Quest: A Treatise on an Emergent Cyclical Conception of Adult Behavioral Systems and Their Development*. Santa Barbara, CA: ECLET Publishing.

Gunderson, L. C., & Holling, C. S. (Eds.). (2002). *Panarchy: Understanding Transformations in Human and Natural Systems*. Washington, DC: Island Press.

Hamilton, M. (2008). *Integral City: Evolutionary Intelligences for the Human Hive*. Gabriola Island BC: New Society Publishers.

Holling, C. S. (2001). Understanding the Complexity of Economic, Ecological, and Social Systems Ecosystems. *Vol.* 4, pp. 390–405.

Holling, C. S. (2003). *From Complex Regions to Complex Worlds*. University of Florida.

Korten, D. (2015). *When Corporations Rule the World*. San Francisco: Berrett-Koehler Publishers.

Laloux, F. (2014). *Reinventing Organizations*. Retrieved from http://www.reinventingorganizations.com/purchase.html.

Lipton, B. (2005). *The Biology of Belief: Unleashing the Power of Consciousness, Matter and Miracles*. Santa Rosa, CA: Mountain of Love/Elite Books.

Miller, J. G. (1978). *Living Systems*. New York: McGraw-Hill Book Company.

West, G. (2017). *Scale: The Universal Laws of Growth, Innovation, Sustainability and the Pace of Life in Organisms, Cities, Economies and Companies*. New York: Penguin Press.

Wheatley, M. (1992). *Leadership and the New Science: Learning about Organization from an Orderly Universe*. San Francisco: Berrett-Koehler.

Wheatley, M. (2006). *Leadership and the New Science: Learning about Organization from an Orderly Universe*. San Francisco: Berrett-Koehler.

Wheatley, M., & Kellner-Rogers, M. (1996). A *Simpler Way*. San Francisco: Berrett-Koehler.

Wilber, K. (1995). *Sex, Ecology and Spirituality: the spirit of evolution*. Boston: Shambhala Publications Inc.

Wilber, K. (1996). A *Brief History of Everything*, . Boston,: Shambhala Publications Inc.

Wilber, K. (2000). A *Theory of Everything*. Boston: Shambhala Publications Inc.

11

ORGANIZATIONS WILL
REINVENT THE CITY

CHAPTER SUMMARY

This chapter considers the evolutionary trajectory of organizational development. It examines the implications of Appendix B Map 4 that illustrates the levels of complexity through which organizations evolve, with a particular focus on level 7 or "tier 2". The connection between individual development and organizational development is considered through the lens of evolutionary purpose. Organizations who pioneer reinventing themselves have the opportunity to influence other organizations in the city to develop thrivability strategies through enacting the Integral City Intelligences of Inquiry, Meshworking and Navigating.

Keywords: reinventing organizations, tier 2, Level 7, complexity, evolution, thrivability, Integral City Intelligences, inquiry, meshworking, navigating

HOW MIGHT REINVENTING ORGANIZATIONS REINVENT THE CITY?

How might an integrally informed city learn from an integrally informed re-frame that reinvents organizations? Frederic Laloux's book, *Reinventing Organizations* (2014), examines the emergence of Integral organizations ("Teal" in the Wilber-Integral lexicon, "Yellow" in Spiral Dynamics integralese). Laloux's exploration of reinventing organizations is based on research in eleven organizations who are demonstrating the qualities and capacities of second tier (or Level 7 based on Appendix B, Map 4) operations.

From the perspective of Integral City this is excellent news. Organizations are vital to recalibrating three of the 4 Voices in the city—Civic Managers, Civil Society and Business. And if that kind of recalibration were possible, the ripple effects would necessarily engage the fourth Voice of Citizens because the majority of citizens are working in one or more of the "organizing Voices".

So *Reinventing Organizations* offers a meso-scale of impact with enormous leverage for changing the whole system of the city. It seems to me that the ideas reported in *Reinventing Organizations* offers a fractal resonance to the larger scale of the city, where learning within organizations and between organizations will necessarily shift the complexity of the city upwards towards the emergence of an Integral City, operating with all its evolutionary intelligences (Hamilton, 2008).

ON-PURPOSE ORGANIZATIONS SEED ON-PURPOSE CITIES

Reinventing organizations at the second tier (level 7 and beyond on Appendix B Map 4) rests on a core organizational process that is centered on evolutionary purpose.

When organizations are seen as living entities within an evolutionary worldview, it is natural that they discover the purpose that they are alive to serve. Organizationally they are answering the question: **How *does our organization serve what customers, located where, for what purpose*?**

This purpose emerges from fitting the organization's function to serve a larger ecology of organizations. Such an ecology is usually called an "economy", but from Integral City's perspective this ecology is the city itself. The ecology is made up of the 4 Voices of the City dynamically interacting with each other as an evolutionary living system (and interacting with the fifth Voice of other cities in the larger ecology of our planet of cities).

If we are using the fractal patterns of living systems to notice the scaling role of purpose, we can see that at the **micro-scale**, individuals within the city also enact a purpose. (We have written about the interconnections of individual and leadership purpose, passion, priorities and prosperity in Chapters 7, 8 and 9.)

When we tap into the wisdom of living systems through the science of biomimicry, we can relate purpose at the macro or city scale—what I call the human hive—to the function that the beehive serves within its eco-regional ecology. The beehive seems to have evolved the purpose of pollinating and recycling the biological energy sources from which it gathers the raw ingredients (nectar and pollen) to produce the 20 Kilos of honey that it needs to sustain itself.

Within the city, organizations emerge at the meso-scale, because groups of individuals organize themselves to serve a purpose. At the second-tier evolutionary stage, Laloux (2014) suggests that, the organization is not merely formed to work for efficiencies, effectiveness, productivity or social enterprise—but for a purpose that is evolutionary.

Laloux proposes that organizations with a second-tier purpose act as if competition is irrelevant. So-called competitors—aka other organizations—have their own purposes. All can co-exist in the organizational ecology/economy to pursue purposes that support life.

We can notice organizations have entered this stage of evolution, when we see that everyone in the organization is acting as a kind of sensor (to the inner and outer environments). They are asking the question—**What is happening in here and out there that we need to be aware of?** Individual actions are subsumed into large group processes—where collective intelligence can emerge and we discover that the multiple sensors, sensing each other, expand the base of intelligence that we work from.

Within organizations who are operating on purpose, individual inner processes are encouraged and enabled through shared consciousness and cultural practices like meditations, guided visualizations, visioning and values discoveries.

At the same time the organization becomes spontaneously able to respond to requests and prompts from the outside world. This happens at every level of the organization because the purpose is a shared intelligence throughout the organization.

When we consider the possibility of many organizations working on purpose within a city, it becomes conceivable that they might work together towards an even higher purpose. What would happen if many organizations within the city, discovered they could embrace a purpose for the city itself?

What are the evolutionary stages that individual cities progress through in order to discover that they serve an evolutionary purpose that might be in service to the whole planet (and in fact, a whole planet of cities)?

Can we reinvent cities to serve such a planetary life-giving purpose, without reinventing organizations so they discover their purpose? How would such organizations then connect with each other through a group purpose? And how would these on-purpose clusters then connect with each other, as they move the scale from individual organization to many organizations? This would seem to be a necessary precursor to a city who is living on purpose.

CITY AS DOJO FOR REINVENTING ORGANIZATIONS

However we invent tier 2 organizations, we will need to consider them as being embedded in an ecology and economy of tier 1 organizations.

This is vital to realize because as we reinvent organizations and thus reinvent the city, we can recognize that so-called tier 2 organizations cannot exist without the competencies of the workers and capacities of the tier 1 organizations in which they are currently and necessarily embedded.

All the organizations that Laloux explores have gained their capacities from the contributions of individuals who have learned basic skills and grown their capacities to organize, team, partner and collaborate in the tier 1 systems.

If we fail to recognize the essential "background" support of this ecological space (of the city) we will be blind to the functions offered by the city as a living system. The city is like a mega-dojo where players can learn their way through a series of organizational practices that earns them the privilege and freedom to articulate those competencies like a black-belt master (who thereby reinvents organizations). In most cities, a whole spectrum of tier 1 organizations offers a series of dojos where players can learn the rudiments of reinventing themselves, their teams and organizational forms. If for no other reason than to gain the advantages of building on our skill sets, we must thank the spectrum (and holarchy) of tier 1 organizations that co-exist in our cities who accomplish these competency outcomes as a by-product of their existence. (Our gratitude goes to the spectrum of organizations who manifest in our cities as families, sports teams, military and para-military organizations, professional associations, social networks, systems innovators, environmental invigorators and global connectors).

All living systems must be able to survive, connect with their environment and reproduce (see Chapter 10). These conditions are axiomatic to a circular economy. If we consider organizations to be living systems, then we must recognize the necessary and inextricable connections each organization has with all the other organizations and people that exist—especially because they provide the very context of (mostly) tier 1 (and a few tier 2) capabilities, in which they do business.

We cannot reinvent the city, if we do not respect the fundamentals of the circular economy and the dojos where our human hive learns how to manage self, others, organizations and the system.

ORGANIC STRATEGIES REINVENT INTEGRAL CITIES

Eleven organizations contributed to the research behind the book *Reinventing Organizations*, by author Frederic Laloux (2014). Although these eleven were selected as exemplars from the population of cities studied, it is apparent that very few organizations can pass the filter of tier 2 qualifications. Therefore, we must wonder if will we have to wait centuries for enough organizations to mature to this stage before we can reinvent our cities?

That is a sobering thought—and one that should motivate us to get on with the work of growing our capacities as individual leaders and redesigning our organizations so that we can expand the circles of care and thrivability from tier 1 to tier 2.

But the Integral City has three natural Strategic Intelligences that can accelerate the maturing processes of organizations and communities—the WE-space of the city.

Inquiry Intelligence opens us up to learning, discovery and innovation.

Meshworking Intelligence creates the conditions where self-organizing capacities in the city combine with structuring capacities to create a scaffold that enables a hierarchy of complex organizations and individuals to co-create a resilient ecology.

Navigating Intelligence gives us the systemic feedback that lets us know if we are proceeding in the right direction to achieve our purpose (and correct our course of action in order to achieve our intended goals).

Reinvented organizations can play special roles as actors, agents and catalysts of Strategic Intelligences within their cities of operation.

As **Inquirers**, they can take the lead in "calling the question"—*How can we do this differently (e.g. redesign a mature neighborhood). Who else should be here? How can we call the 4 Voices of the City into this conversation?*

As **Meshworkers**, they can call together the 4 Voices of the City (*Citizens, Civic Managers, Civil Society, Business*) and help other organizations, economic sectors and communities identify the purpose that they serve in common. They can facilitate and/or call in facilitators who can help reveal the life conditions and align the values of the community for resilient outcomes.

As **Navigators**, they can co-create feedback loops that inform everyone of the city's progress, through designing Vital Signs Monitors that track wellbeing and resilience for communities and the city (see Hamilton, 2017, Chapter 8).

If city halls, as key organizations in the City's Voices that we call "Civic Managers", choose to reinvent themselves, they can quicken the reinvention of the whole city. City halls who reinvent how they conduct the business of the city, must draw on the Strategic Intelligences of an Integral City either implicitly or explicitly. If you want to look at how one city has chosen to implement such a strategy to reinvent its mature neighborhoods—look at how Strathcona has implemented Integral City Strategic Intelligences, engaging facilitators to engage the 4 Voices of the City to complete the groundwork that may incubate the reinvention of the city as a whole.

Pioneering projects like **Strathcona Mature Neighborhood Strategy** (see Hamilton, 2017, Chapter 14), are necessary models, for us to learn the early stages of how applying Integral City Strategic Intelligences, in the service of reinventing organizational patterns can reinvent the city.

Now I am curious—as the study of complex adaptive living systems teaches us—if we change 10% of the city's key organizations would that be the tipping point for shifting the whole city into Integral City operational territory? Pursuing the answer to that question may be the key impetus to wake up our city's organizations so they can wake up the city itself.

REFERENCES

Gladwell, M. (2002). *The Tipping Point: How Little Things Can Make a Big Difference.* Back Bay Books.

Laloux, F. (2014). *Reinventing Organizations*. Retrieved from http://www.reinventingorganizations.com/purchase.html.

Hamilton, M. (2008). *Integral City: Evolutionary Intelligences for the Human Hive*. Gabriola Island BC: New Society Publishers.

Hamilton, M. (2017). *Integral City Inquiry and Action: Designing Impact for the Human Hive*. Tucson, Arizona: Integral Publishers.

SECTION 3

Widening Capacity through the Emergence of City Systems

Chapter 12 widens our capacity to see the city through the lens of **systems thinking**. The chapter offers a short primer that is based on the Integral geographical filters of Anthro-Bio-Cosmological lenses (that link it back to Chapter 6, and our exploration of security systems for the Integral City).

Chapter 13 wakes us up to the **city as home**—and how the conditions of homefulness and homelessness are inextricably interwoven systems in the human hive.

SYSTEMS THINKING:
A PRIMER FOR CITY CAPACITY BUILDING

CHAPTER SUMMARY

This chapter is a short primer for the basics of systems thinking. It draws on the ABC (Anthroposphere-Biosphere-Cosmosphere) frame developed by Eddy (2003, 2005) as a metaview of major types of systems that impact the city. The city as a living system is explored and readers are asked to find themselves and their perspectives by thinking through the context of seeing themselves as a system embedded in systems and how that impacts their motivations for change.

Keywords: systems, systems thinking, anthroposphere, biosphere, Cosmosphere, living system, change

WHAT ARE SYSTEMS?

Systems thinking is fundamental to understanding systems. So to understand systems thinking, let's start with exploring, what are systems?

Systems are evolutionary structures. They are characterized by boundaries that contain system elements. Those elements have evolved across deep time, from the Big Bang until now. The basic evolutionary strata that we can point to on our planet can be classified as A—B—C (as we explored in more depth in Chapter 6 (Eddy, 2003, 2005). Explaining this backwards . . . **C is for Cosmosphere**—containing Universe, Earth and

Matter. We study this with Physical Sciences like Astronomy, Cosmology, Math, Physics, Chemistry, Geology, Hydrology, Meteorology.

B is for Biological Systems—containing the living environment and life. We study these with Life Sciences like Microbiology, Biology, Botany, Zoology.

A is for Anthropocentric Systems—or human systems. We study these with Social Sciences like Psychology, Sociology, Anthropology, etc.

As humans we are the most complex systems on Earth and we not only depend on all the ABC systems but we ARE those systems. We are in effect Awake Boisterous Cosmic-dust.

An interesting characteristic of systems, is when you combine two different systems a surprising result can happen that is not necessarily evident from looking at the two original systems separately. For instance, if you look at Hydrogen and Oxygen as two separate elements, you would not predict that combining them as $H2O$ would produce water—with qualities that neither Hydrogen nor Oxygen possess on their own. (We call this propensity of systems for unexpected outcomes—emergence.)

The **B & A Systems** contain the **Living systems**. They are wholes that not only have boundaries, but the elements they contain co-exist within the boundary symbiotically—that is the existence of each element is dependent on the co-existence and adaptability with other elements.

LIVING SYSTEMS

Systems are considered alive if they can do three things:

1. They can sustain themselves.
2. They connect with their environment (or adapt).
3. They reproduce.

When we consider how all these **ABC** systems have evolved together we can see that they make the world sustainable—as we know and need it to be. Energy, Water, Climate, Food, Bio-genetic Ecology and Human Systems are all necessary to sustain our life and all other life on the planet.

When we consider how these systems impact on one another we can see the major *Threats* that our global systems face today. Because human systems have become so successful, we are impacting on Ecology, Food Systems, Climate, Water, Energy and Geology in ways that are eroding these system as non-renewable resources or if they are renewable living systems, we are eroding their capacity to adapt and regenerate themselves.

Living systems evolve in complex organic hierarchies (or holarchies)— which means as they evolve, they become more complex as they contain more and more systems.

Basic systems start with atoms, that make up molecules, that make up cells, that make up organelles, that make up organs, that make up organ systems, that make up bodies, that make up ecologies.

As a whole living system, the human body is the system we are most familiar with.

But even our bodies become parts of larger human systems: like families, teams, organizations, neighbourhoods, communities and cities.

Interestingly each of these systems is made up of other systems and we say they are "fractal" meaning they exist at different scales; that is they retain similar patterns, but each system is larger than the ones that make it up. The larger the system is, the greater is its sphere of influence. The concept of scale lets us zoom in and zoom out to see systems with the same patterns at different magnifications.

City as Living System

My great interest is in the most complex human system that we have yet created—the city—because it contains all these systems co-existing in dynamic relationship.

In fact, I believe we are in an era when even cities are being superseded by yet a larger system—that I call the planet of cities.

In human systems we need to consider not only what makes up our bodies physically—but also what makes up our minds consciously—and how we relate to others in group cultural systems and to the environmental and built systems.

SYSTEMS THINKING

So this brings us back to systems thinking. When we can see systems—in other words, recognize a whole with a boundary containing elements—we are starting to think in the basics of systems thinking. When we can see how different systems are interconnected, we are progressing our systems thinking to a more complex level. When we use our consciousness to design new systems we are demonstrating our evolutionary human capacity to adapt through being innovative and creative.

As we design new systems, we eventually produce systems of systems— like those controlling water; first by carrying it in portable water vessels, then irrigation channels, then viaducts, then water canals and locks; then building reservoirs and dams; and then creating plumbing systems; and finally recreating portable vessels as bottled water.

But the challenge of systems thinking is not just to see one system in isolation of other systems—but to see the whole trajectory of ABC systems as an evolutionary supra-system. Then our thinking must consider the consequences of our innovations, designs and creations. True systems thinking embraces our responsibility for initiating change that impacts all earth systems—taking responsibility not only for our intended conse- quences—but the unintended ones.

One of the great values of systems thinking is that it is critical to being able to shift our perspectives.

A perspective represents a point of view and in order for us to change in any way, we must shift our perspective.

A shift in perspective assumes that a change in my view occurs. Learning to shift requires the answers to 4 basic questions:

1. What is my current perspective?
2. Why would I change it?
3. How can I change it?
4. When will I shift my perspective?

The first question—what is my perspective?—is the fundamental starting point of any change—**become aware** of where you stand, thus providing an awareness of yourself and the systems of which you are a part.

The second question—why change my perspective?—relates to **internal motivation** – should you choose (voluntarily) to shift your perspective? Or do **external circumstances** give you no choice? Have you been knocked off your current position by outside systems—literally pushed aside by person(s), thing(s), idea(s) or systems changes?

The third question—how can I change?—**brings our resources for shifting** perspective into play—such as **soft technologies** like inquiry, play or experimentation (as you negotiate perspectives with other human systems like individuals, groups, competitors, neighbourhoods). It might also include **hard technologies** like using smart phones, microscopes, telescopes or satellites (to gain insights about data, biota, geography or GIS mapping systems).

The fourth question—when will I shift my perspective—involves **timing** that may allow for change to emerge **gradually, orderly, chaotically, unexpectedly or instantly**. Such timing may mean the difference between shifting perspective on your own terms (like seeing that bottled water wastes resources) or without agreement (like unknowingly drinking water from a polluted water system).

Each of these questions reveals a quality of systems thinking that we can use to help ourselves and others shift perspectives. Each question supports us to see (and respect) ourselves as a whole living system, in relationship to other whole living systems, within the larger context of environmental systems and ultimately the earth as a whole planetary system.

Thinking in systems impacts how we can shift perspectives and thus how we are able to adapt and innovate, design and lead, and grow and expand our capacity for caring, for the living systems we are, that we relate to and that we co-create.

The question we want to leave you with is: **What perspective do you hold today and how can systems thinking help you shift this perspective?**

REFERENCES

Capra, F. (1996). *The Web of Life: A New Scientific Understanding of Living Systems*. New York: Anchor Books, Doubleday.

Eddy, B. (2003). Sustainable Development, Spiral Dynamics, and Spatial Data: A '3i' Approach to SD. Paper presented at the Spiral Dynamics integral, Level II, Ottawa, 2003.

Eddy, B. (2005). Place, Space and Perspective. *World Futures*, 61, 151–163.

Esbjörn-Hargens, S., & Zimmerman, M. (2009). *Integral Ecology: Uniting Multiple Perspectives on the Natural World*. Boston: Shambhala Publications Inc.

Gladwell, M. (2002). *The Tipping Point: How Little Things Can Make a Big Difference*. New York: Back Bay Books.

Graves, C. (1971). A systems conception of personality: Levels of existence theory. Paper presented at the Washington School of Psychiatry.

Gunderson, L. C., & Holling, C. S. (Eds.). (2002). *Panarchy: Understanding Transformations in Human and Natural Systems*. Washington, DC: Island Press.

Hamilton, M. (2008). *Integral City: Evolutionary Intelligences for the Human Hive*. Gabriola Island BC: New Society Publishers.

Linton, J. (2010). *What is Water? The History of a Modern Abstraction*. Vancouver, BC, Canada: UBC Press.

McKibben, B. (2007). *Deep Economy: The Wealth of Communities and the Durable Future*. New York: Time Books Henry Holt and Company, LLC.

McKibben, B. (2011). 350.Org. Retrieved December 13, 2017, from 350.Org: http://www.350.org/

Meadows, D. (2008). *Thinking in Systems*. White River Junction, VT: Chelsea Green Publishing.

Miller, J. G. (1978). *Living Systems*. New York: McGraw-Hill Book Company.

Sahtouris, E. (1999). *Earthdance: Living Systems in Evolution*. Retrieved from http://www.ratical.org/LifeWeb/

West, G. (2017). *Scale: The Universal Laws of Growth, Innovation, Sustainability and the Pace of Life in Organisms, Cities, Economies and Companies*. New York: Penguin Press.

Wilber, K. (1995). *Sex, Ecology and Spirituality: the spirit of evolution*. Boston: Shambhala Publications Inc.

Wilber, K. (2000b). *A Theory of Everything*. Boston: Shambhala Publications Inc.

REFRAMING HOMEFULNESS BY REFRAMING HOMELESSNESS

A *version of this chapter was originally published as*: Hamilton, M. (2007). Approaching Homelessness: An Integral Reframe. *World Futures: The Journal of General Evolution*, Volume 63(2), 107–126.

CHAPTER SUMMARY

This chapter explores a metaview of the many bright faces of homefulness in contrast to the dark faces of homelessness. It analyzes an evolutionary meaning of home and suggests that ever-complexifying life conditions influence how societies enforce conformity to the status quo of homefulness. It goes on to describe how homelessness might be reframed as a complex adaptive form of survival for diversity generators who cannot or will not conform to the status quo of home. The chapter proposes an Integral framework on which intervention strategies could be structured to provide evolutionary, appropriate and flexible ways to build homefulness.

Key Words: homefulness, homelessness, complexity, evolution, adaptation, maladaptation, Integral interventions

The homeless and mentally ill are mostly ignored. Many rarely see their families. Many have no family. Friendship can be transient and even service workers often hurry

their clients due to their overwhelming caseload. So my main practice is to slow down, listen to the contents of these people's hearts (no matter how distorted) and attempt to connect. (McQuade, 2005)

WHAT ARE THE ROOTS OF HOMEFULNESS?

An examination of homefulness requires a study of the contexts within which the condition occurs. For those who study the evolution of the individual (e.g. through psychology; (Wilber, 2000; Beck 2002b; Beck and Cowan, 1996) or the group (e.g. through family systems, sociology or anthropology (Beck 2002a; Beck, 2000b; Graves, 2003; Diamond,1992, 2005) homefulness can be viewed within an ever unfolding "hierarchical differentiation and complexity" (Holling, 2001). A growing volume of literature, across disciplines shows an emergence of patterns in the human life cycle that can cast some light on understanding both homefulness and its counterpart homelessness.

Such an evolutionary approach demonstrates that homefulness (and homelessness) could mean different things at different levels of emergent complexity. As complex adaptive systems, humans, at each level of complexity, seek resonance, coherence and emergence as indicators of the health of their human systems (Stevenson & Hamilton, 2001).

- **Resonance** means that the individual is healthy, self-reliant, responsive and balanced on a subjective (inner) and objective (outer) level.
- **Coherence** means that the individual exists in balance with his/her environment. How the individual lives is coherent or aligned with the larger context of family, workgroup, society.
- **Emergence** means that individuals within the context of their primary groups of association (family, work, cultural and social systems) are supported to evolve their capacities throughout their life and learning cycles.

As humans develop the complexity of both their consciousness and their societies, the expression of resonance, coherence and emergence changes. Humans are forever adapting to changing life conditions. Each change in life conditions essentially redefines the meaning of "home" (and its obverse: "homelessness").

Moreover, it appears that humans as complex adaptive living systems are evolving a "panarchy" of capacities. Holling (2001) explains that a panarchy is the "hierarchical structure in which systems of nature . . . and humans . . . as well as combined human-nature systems . . . and social-ecological systems are interlinked in never-ending adaptive cycles of growth, accumulation, restructuring and renewal". Like Wilber (1996) and Graves (2003), Holling proposes that these transformational cycles are nested at ever-increasing scales of complexity. Graves (2003) proposed that these human cycles are constantly attempting to survive within two major sets of complex conditions: one where the group controls the status quo and a second where the individual controls the status quo.

Bloom (2000) proposes a view of human systems, which he sees as patterns similar to other natural life systems (including insects and animals), where people are constantly balancing two sets of values. The first set of values enforces conformity of meaning and behavior amongst groups and individuals. The second set of values generates diversity for the benefit of individuals and groups. These two major sets of beliefs and behaviors both generate survival values for the human species and appear to have a dynamic relationship with one another.

In a resonant manner, Holling (2001) suggests that wealth (potential), controllability (connectedness) and adaptive capacity (resilience) are the "properties that shape the responses of ecosystems, agencies and people to crisis". He identifies the four stages of the cycle contained by these properties as:

1. Exploitation (low potential, low connectedness)
2. Conservation (high potential, high connectedness)
3. Release (low potential, high connectedness)
4. Reorganization (high potential, low connectedness)

The basic resilience loop in Holling's model (see Appendix G) describes two separate objectives achieved in a looping figure 8 sequence: maximizing production and accumulation (stages 1 and 2—and similar to Bloom's conformity enforcement) followed by maximizing invention and reassortment (stages 3 and 4—similar to Bloom's diversity generation). Holling proposes that the success at achieving one objective sets the stage for success at achieving the next objective in an endless cycle. He defines a panarchy as "a representation of a hierarchy as a nested set of adaptive cycles. The functioning of those cycles and the communication between them determines the sustainability of a system." (p. 396)

Several decades earlier than either Bloom or Holling, Graves in the 1960's and 1970's (2003) conducted an 18-year study that came to be known as the "evolutionary complex levels of human existence". Graves' research, showed that human behaviors arising out of one set of conditions created problems of existence that could not be solved at that level. As a result, new adaptive behaviors are called into existence. Graves identified a group-centric cluster of behaviors he called "sacrifice self" values; and an individual-centric cluster of behaviors he called "express self" values. Moreover, his research showed that these behaviors adapted and alternated with one another at an ever increasing level of complexity, as life conditions changed. Graves used a set of identifiers to represent life conditions (designated by letters from the first half of the alphabet) and bio-psycho-cultural-social human existence (designated by letters from the second half of the alphabet) (see Table 24). Beck and Cowan (1996) and Beck (2002) devised a system of color codes to identify each level of complexity: beige, red, orange, yellow (i.e. warm colors) relate to "express self" versions of existence; purple, blue, green, turquoise (i.e. cool colors) relate to "sacrifice self" versions of existence.

Table 24: Levels of Complexity (adapted from Beck, 2002)

Express Self	Organizing Principle Of Life Condition	Sacrifice Self	Organizing Principle Of Life Condition
AN—Beige	Survival		
		BO—Purple	Belonging
CP—Red	Command & Control		
		DQ—Blue	Authoritarian Structure
ER—Orange	Economic Success		
		FS—Green	Humanitarian Equality
GT—Yellow	Systemic Flex & Flow		
		HU—Turquoise	Planetary Commons

Because the dominant behaviors arise in response to life conditions (as one would expect from any complex adaptive system (Holling, 2001; Stevenson and Hamilton, 2000; Capra, 1996), each level of existence behaves with increasing levels of complexity in order to maximize the organizing principle (or value) of the current life condition. This behavior results in a tendency to protect the status quo at its current level of complexity. In Bloom's terms this could be interpreted as conformity enforcement (of the organizing principle / value).

Thus a tension in favor of the values and behavior that is most coherent with the current life conditions, will be demonstrated as conformity enforcement. The flip side of this behavior is that the dominant culture will also protect itself against diversity generation, until such time as life conditions require the solutions that diversity generation can offer to the problems created by maximizing the values and organizing principles in play at any level of existence. Moreover, we can see the natural evolutionary cycles emerge at all levels of scale: individual, family, organization, society. Thus, this very natural process can set up the conditions for the evolutionary redefinitions of "homefulness" and "homelessness".

For the purposes of this chapter, homefulness (and homelessness) will be contexted at the level of scale of the family (with reference to larger contexts where appropriate).

To illustrate the insights that can be gained by this line of argument, we will trace the meaning of home within the level of complexity that produces a particular social structure, organizing principle and key value; the purpose of the family; benefits of that social structure to the family; and how the dominant culture protects its status quo and enforces conformity to its preferred behaviors through penalties. Of necessity, this discussion will span both the emergence of complex human systems across historical time, but which are all still present in family life today. (For the purposes of this discussion we will designate the levels of complexity by the color codes used by Beck and Cowan in Spiral Dynamics (1996).)

WHAT IS THE MEANING OF HOME?

Starting with the most fundamental level of complexity, **Beige**, the social structure is primarily focused on the nucleic family and the key value is survival. The meaning of **home centers around shelter** from the elements of climate and environment for the purpose of family survival. The family structure enables the short term collection and/or assembly of basic survival necessities of food, clothing and shelter. In the long term the family structure enables the emergence and survival of not only individuals but multiple generations. In this most basic structure of human systems, the culture enforces conformity to its needs and behaviors by abandonment of individuals who do not or cannot contribute or conform. We see examples of this in street life where mothers who cannot support their newborns, abandon them. We hear of it in the apocryphal stories of Inuit who separate the old, unwanted or infirm on ice flows. And we learn of it from the extreme endeavors of those who climb Mt. Everest, where the infirm are abandoned by their teammates to enable others to summit and/ or return to base camp.

When the Beige system succeeds (evidenced by the expansion of human families and population, who place more demands on their surrounding environment), life conditions demand a more complex structure to organize people in relation to available resources. Thus the **Purple** level of complexity emerges, evidenced by clans with bonding practices and rituals. The meaning of **home becomes attached to belonging** to this identifiable clan. It may be ritualized as a spirit home, and the purpose of the family will not only be to provide the necessities of life but to practise and pass on the rituals that signify clan belonging. The value to the family of this structure is that it enables continued expansion and propagation, because of increased capacity from shared living, resourcing and ritualized communications. This belonging culture enforces conformity to its shared practices by physically ejecting anyone who does not support the collective way of life from the shared home(land). We see examples in modern day of parents who eject teenagers from homes where the youth refuse to conform to family ways. We see it in countries threatened by "guest workers" who are extradited because their traditions, behaviors, attitudes and/or beliefs do not match the country where they work. Cults also physically eject those who refuse to conform to their rituals (we can suggest examples as varied as the ejection of Rajneesh dissidents and the ostracism practised by Quakers and Seventh Day Adventists).

As the Purple system loses its effectiveness to provide protection to people through its belonging rituals, the **Red** level of complexity emerges, with a strong leader who can offer protection in return for obedience and/ or fealty. The meaning of **home is related to the protective fortress** whose boundaries are defended by a ruler who commands troops who can protect the family from invaders. A ruler with such troops has the power to enforce his/her will. Might is right. But the level of protection from outside forces and/or the invasion into other territories enables the expansion of the "kingdom". This commanding culture enforces conformity to the ruler by physical punishment and/or death. The most typical example we see of this fortress way of life is in the street gang (or on a country scale a repressive dictatorship). On a multi-cultural scale, it is clearly the modus operandi of the Mafia family, whose punishment of offenders of its status quo are perennial subjects of crime news, laws, fiction and crime fighting. On an even larger scale we witness these punishments meted out on whole nations by zealots of all stripes.

As the Red system becomes ineffective to respond to more complex life conditions resulting from both the accumulation of wealth and/or rising chaos (wars) that result from the practise of Red offenses, the **Blue** level of complexity arises. Here order, laws and organization create a village, town or city where the meaning of **home is related to a person's place within the social hierarchy** or caste system. Such a position is often justified by an elite system of education that trains, reinforces and justifies the ordered distribution of resources according to class or caste. The value to the family is that life becomes stabilized and predictable. In this level of complexity, the collective has more value than the individual, but the relative social stability allows for the organization of justice, wealth and resources that was never available under the chaotic conditions of the Red level of complexity. Within a Blue level of complexity, laws and rules enable a more stable home life. On the other hand, they also codify and institutionalize the costs of non-conformity, creating prisons for containing unacceptable physical, mental and emotional expression. As examples, we can point not only at formal prisons, but mental institutions and many forms of institutionalized emotional repression (aka manners, protocols) and also segregated school and health systems.

The very success of the Blue level of complexity, opens up the life condition for the **Orange** level. Ironically the Blue system creates the conditions where the expression of personal merit, success, and self-confidence can flourish first within the stability established by the Blue social hierarchy. Eventually however the Blue level of complexity stagnates within its own rules and the demand for engineering to be combined with entrepreneurial flair creates the urban center where the meaning of **home is a branded status symbol** that reflects the success criteria of the person who occupies it. Thus the value to the family of the home is as beneficiary of the consumption patterns and success of the individual whose wealth has "won" it in a competitive world. Though the Orange family will defend the boundaries that give its home special protections as being rightfully earned, the status quo is protected by a socially sanctioned technology-enforced form of exclusion and/or rehabilitation. Those who do not conform to Orange's idea of home and values, will be socially excluded, imprisoned and/or technically processed. Examples abound in socially and economically separated neighborhoods, gated communities, school systems, and the largely privately operated American prison system.

The individual driven Orange level of complexity, eventually encounters the limits to growth, that resurrect the values of the collective that are needed when Orange consumption patterns exceed the cultural and social environments' capacities to remain responsive and resilient. Thus emerge **Green**'s renewed appreciation for peoples' rights, the removal of barriers to human development and the acceptance of differences and diversity. Under Green, the meaning of **home is a shared community of cooperative interests**, that enables people to live and work together in socially conscious ways, redistributing wealth to those most in need, and removing barriers created by class and competition. Green values are "exclusively inclusive", to the extent that those who don't share such wholesale acceptance, are excluded. Thus Green accepts (often without judgment) the non-conformists from all the less complex human systems. Homelessness itself is accepted as one choice of many diverse ways of living. Consideration is even given to enable people to be homeless, often without regard to their capacity to provide for self or others' survival, belonging, protection, order or success. A review of news archives from the 1960's to the 1990's will disclose the stories of people released from mental institutions onto the streets who became psycho-physical destitutes—a whole new group of marginalized homeless. This time frame also saw the rise of squatters' camps in condemned buildings and homeless tent cities on the lawns of city halls (which continue to this day).

With the levels of complexity that have emerged in the prior six stages, it is now becoming evident that one of the most important solutions to the human condition, is to gain the capacity of systems thinking. This represents the core capacity of the **Yellow** level of complexity which values the flex and flow of natural systems, the ecological realities of environmental carrying capacities and the interconnection of human systems to all of life. At this evolutionary level, the meaning of **home is a natural habitat for human systems, appropriate to the ecological life conditions**. This approach to home, ensures a conscious awareness of the health of individuals and families together with the larger social systems of which they are a part, in relation to the 17 geo-climatic habitats that exist on earth (Fernandez-Armesto, 2001). As the Yellow level of complexity is still emerging we have not completely stabilized how this individual-based system will enforce conformity to an ecological view of life, but early indications are that eco-transgressors (and/or eco-terrorists) will be publicly identified, severely fined, rehabilitated if possible, and required to redress their wrongs. Some of these systems are now emerging in the form of eco-footprinting, reporting and monitoring; e.g., reporting companies who pollute the environment; criminally trying individuals who knowingly spread AIDS; and defending the eco-system in court. As the system matures, homelessness that encroaches maladaptively on to the environment may not be tolerated.

Finally, the most complex level of human existence to date, has been identified as **Turquoise.** Like Yellow it has not fully emerged, but as a collective system, its interests transcend Yellow's individual focus with a recognition that not only do we have 17 natural habitats on earth but that they exist on one indivisible planet and are massively interconnected. Not only human life, but all life on earth is interdependent. The meaning of **home is Gaia, planet earth, "the only one we've got"** (to quote the Wombat

(Able, 2005)). The value to families is the capacity to survive, despite the massive increase of human population and/or the decrease of resources. This requires a level of consciousness that recognizes lack of conformity to respecting life on earth, is a threat to survival for all life. It anticipates the rise of Vital Signs Monitors, that can inform human systems that all homes are healthy and when, where and what kind of homelessness is a threat and how to remedy it.

Table 25 summarizes the meaning of home across eight levels of complexity.

Table 25: The Meaning of Home at Eight Levels of Complexity

The emergence of homefulness across eight levels of complexity is presented in the following Columns.

1. The level of complexity in the human environment (using the levels developed by 3in the early 1970's (2002) and defined by Beck and Cowan (1996)).

2. The meaning of home at this level of complexity is defined.

3. The social structure, organizing principle or value contributing to a healthy family for this definition of home (this equates to family resonance)

4. The purpose of the family—what values, benefits, goals it offers family members and society. (These indicators relate to healthy family coherence or alignment of the family with other related social values in the same life conditions).

5. The outcomes of maximizing the social structure. These are indicators of healthy emergence: survival, sustainability and/or thriving.

6. How the Dominant Culture enforces conformity to the social structure. These are the penalties used by society to maintain the status quo. These behaviors indicate what the dominant culture (family, clan, society, government, guardian) will do to protect itself against failure to conform to the meaning of home, value of the social structure, purpose of the family and achieve the outcomes of the family structure.

1. Level of Complexity in Social Structure	2. Meaning of Home	3. Social Structure, Organizing Principle / Key Value	4. Purpose of Family	5. Outcomes of Social Structure on Family	6. How Dominant Culture Enforces Conformity to Social Structure— Penalty to Protect Status Quo
Beige	Family Survival, Shelter from Climate, environment	Family survival	Enough food, Clothing, Shelter	Multiple generations	Abandonment
Purple	Clan Survival, Spirit Home Group Belonging	Traditions of clan belonging are practised	Ritual practices: Food, clothing, shelter	Clan thrives, propagates, expands	Physical ejection
Red	Protective Fortress, Castle, Kingdom, commanded by ruler	Obedience to rules of ruler's home	Might is right; obedience guarantees protection from invaders	Kingdom expands	Physical punishment
Blue	Town home in neighborhood, village, city under rule of law	Everyone in his/her place / caste; all according to rules of elite	Ordered social system creates different classes of homes for different castes	Stable, predictable life conditions	Imprison to contain physical mental & emotional expression
Orange	Branded city residence in engineered city	Homes allocated by meritocracy, competition & success criteria thru logical cause & effect	Mechanics of justice create conditions for individuals to accumulate wealth. Home is status symbol of individual success	Brand, wealth, success, excess, home demonstrates capacity as consumer	Emotional, mental, physical "gating"; zoning; secure boundaries thru legislation, technology, keys, passwords; exclude the unwanted; technically excise
Green	Cooperative housing, Community home, sharing of public property	Acceptance of differences; social consciousness; tax redistribution for social housing	Egalitarianism; leveling of playing field; sharing of common property for common good	Shared decision processes; removal of barriers based on "isms"; opening to assault by less complex values	Inclusivity; excludes those who don't agree with egalitarianism; political correctness
Yellow	Efficient, effective, eco-friendly housing	Individual family units appropriately housed to suit circumstances & local resources; small and simple is beautiful/ elegant	Multiple co-existing, complementary shelter formats; ecologically friendly; allows both individual expression and technological connectivity	Misalignments visible through Vital Signs Monitors for informed to see; resource allocation; responsive systems & structures	Make responsible individual and local choices to correct systemic allocations of resources; individual & family monitoring & accountability

1. Level of Complexity in Social Structure	2. Meaning of Home	3. Social Structure, Organizing Principle / Key Value	4. Purpose of Family	5. Outcomes of Social Structure on Family	6. How Dominant Culture Enforces Conformity to Social Structure— Penalty to Protect Status Quo
Turquoise	Natural energy recycling housing systems; eco-regional appropriate human habitats; varies by region	Individuals & groups / family units appropriately housed by matching with eco-regional resources; global responsibility	Eco-regional housing appropriate to each of 17 habitats and bio-psycho-cultural-social life conditions	Common Regional Good; Regional thriving through Vital Signs Monitor for all to see resource use & availability	Make responsible eco-regional choices to ensure eco-regional survival with awareness of global interconnection; eco-regional monitoring, reporting, & accountability.

WHAT IS HOMELESSNESS?

In many places the condition of homelessness is a daily reminder that most of the so-called developed world has not yet discovered, how to create human habitats where all may experience life conditions for thriving—let alone, life conditions that integrate subjective, intersubjective, objective and interobjective qualities.

Homelessness has become a conundrum faced by cities from small to large around the world. Ironically, Able (2005) and Taylor (2008) remind us that we only have one world as our home. Yet on this planet, some condition of homelessness displaces many of us from our connections to our life conditions and to one another.

Indeed the poignant exploration by Jared Diamond (2005, p. 11) of the conditions for sustainable human existence, details a long history of failure by humans to understand that their societies, homes and very lives depend on the deep and tangled interconnections of five factors: environmental damage, climate change, hostile neighbors, friendly trade partners and society's (cultural and structural) response to life conditions. Diamond cites the repeated blindness of societies to grasp the implications of their short term behaviors for their long term survivability and describes in horrific detail the histories of societal "Collapse" from the south Pacific to the north Atlantic to Latin America. He warns that these historical instances may be more than metaphorical warnings for the continuation of life on earth.

In a series of articles in 2004 entitled *"No Fixed Address"*, the *Vancouver Sun* concluded that "homelessness can't be eradicated through a single, one-size-fits-all solution. The problems require a set of solutions that are sensitive to the variety of people living on the street and to the different causes and consequences of homelessness." ("No Fixed Address," 2004).

As Inglis and Steele (2005) noted, "Research conducted by the Vancouver Sun journalists led them to the clear conclusion that homelessness is "not a single problem but a complex set of problems". People become homeless for different reasons. People experience homelessness in different ways. Therefore, it is difficult, if not impossible to pin down a specific definition of 'homelessness'". Glaser and Bridgman (1999) used an anthropological approach to studying homelessness and affirmed the variety of definitions of homelessness. They noted that international conceptualizations of homelessness included: "lack of shelter . . . cutoff from a household or other people . . . homeless street children . . . squatter settlements" (p. 12). In North America, Glaser and Bridgman remarked that homelessness was linked to:

"Rural to urban migration
Chronic alcoholism or substance abuse
Deinstitutionalization of the mentally ill
Gentrification, decreased government support for social housing, service economy" (p. 12)

Not only is a single definition of homelessness a seeming impossibility, when we consider who is offering the definitions, it becomes apparent that the worldview of the definers is as relevant to consider as the subject of the definitions. McQuade (2005) proposed that that many of the mentally ill living on the streets had only developed to a stage of rational cognition, while many others are living at even lower levels, where "the streets fragment any budding sense of self, tax the few psychical resources available, strain relationships, destroy the physical body, and expose the vulnerable self to untold dangers." By the same token, McQuade's experience suggests that many serving the homeless population are not equipped to translate their service into the developmental needs of those being served.

It therefore has become apparent that, however we try to understand the roots of homelessness, intervention strategies cannot be effective if they are designed as "one size fits all".

MALADAPTATIONS AND PATHOLOGIES OF HOMELESSNESS AS COMPLEX ADAPTIVE BEHAVIOR

The previous section summarized the meaning of "home" and the penalty within the family system for threatening the value of "home" at that level of complexity of existence. This section discusses, the roots of homelessness and the evolutionary nature of homelessness that results from the protection of the status quo at each level of complexity. In other words, it is proposed that the very actions that the dominant culture takes to protect its values of "home" set up the conditions that lead to homelessness. The effects can be seen in both individual health and family structures. As the dominant culture evolves through the natural stages of complexity, those precipitating conditions also complexify. Moreover, as each new stage emerges, the prior levels of complexity do not disappear, but continue to exist in a kind of cultural/social "ecology". Thus, as complexity increases so do the variations of homelessness in this ecology.

By the same token, when life conditions are undermined, the social structure and family are forced to adapt to a lower level of complexity. The family structure tends to downshift. Holling (2001, p. 398) refers to this tendency as "remembering"—the downshift to a less complex (but faster) cycle. The individual cycle could also "remember" and down shift or conversely, "revolt" and upshift to a more complex but slower cycle. This affects both individuals and the family unit itself. When the conditions change because of social forces at the national and/or cultural level, the family may disintegrate to the level of dissonance, incoherence and violence embodied now in the horrifying story of the Ik people (Turnbull, 1972) who were disinherited from their lifestyle (dependent on elephant migrations) and homelands by other African nations. We see potential similar fates in the more recent displacements of whole peoples in Rwanda. Jane Jacobs' (2004), feared for the sustainability of even the North American family because of the effects of the automobile on dissipating community energy and the impossible demands of modern life made on the adult anchors of the family.

In a similar manner to how the complexification of home was traced above, now the precipitating maladaptive or pathological life conditions on the family at each level (that lead to homelessness) are described in extreme circumstances, while for the individual we propose the "revolt" adaptation that shifts them to a more complex cycle. Using the insights from Spiral Dynamics integral, to disclose the individual's internal and external state, we also identify their subjective experience and objective effect as Integral influences on individual complex adaptive behaviors. (We note that McQuade (2005) suggested that shockingly from her experience in Denver, most people on the streets are mentally ill; however, for the purposes of this discussion we widen the lens to consider the possibility of all sources of homelessness so that a full Integral spectrum of remedies can be considered.) Nevertheless, we attempt to trace the cycle right through from Beige to Turquoise, because Graves reminded us that the human journey is a "never-ending quest".

The **cause of homelessness at Beige** is the endangerment of shelter (and the basics of life it holds) through fire, flood, earthquake or some other turbulent condition. This threatens the organizing principle of family survival and/or endangers the actual health and/or life of family members, causing it to disintegrate. The subjective experience of individuals is fear, accompanied by the objective loss of basic necessities of life. The natural complex adaptive behavior is escape from the life conditions to survive.

At **Purple** the conformity enforcers change life conditions for the diversity generating individual through ostracism from the family home. The clan refuses to accept individual innovation and suppresses individual expression. The effects on the family are to lose the capacity of the non-conforming member(s). The subjective experience of the individual is rejection and the objective effect on both the family and the individual is separation (disavowal of belonging). The complex adaptive behavior for the individual is to reject the clan and strike out on one's own.

At **Red** when the conformity enforcing "head of the family" removes protection from the divergent individual, the family can be threatened through association with the offending individual. In the long term this can lead to disobedience by the family to the ruler and the eventual breakup of the family home (kingdom). The subjective experience of the individual is that of victimization and the objective effect can be the creation of rival factions who challenge the ruler. The complex adaptive behavior for the individual is to rebel (against the king, father, ruler, dominator, etc.)

At **Blue** when the conformity enforcers deny opportunities for individual expression, they set up conditions where eventually the diversity generators will incite revolution (or downshift back to their Red power base). However, initially it is highly probable that the family rules might rigidify. The subjective experience for the individual is shame and the objective effect can be denial of status and resources by the authorities. The complex adaptive behavior for the individual is to organize revolution, culturally, physically, mentally and/or emotionally.

At **Orange** when the conformity enforcers relentlessly expect competitive results from every individual, they set up the conditions for win/lose scenarios where variations of guerrilla warfare can effectively undermine order and property values, encourage looting, ruthlessness, and sniping. Family life disintegrates (as so cogently described by Jane Jacobs (2004)). The subjective experience for the divergent (unsuccessful) individual is failure and the objective effect can be strategic manipulation, loss of property and dog-eat-dog competition. The complex adaptive behavior for the individual can be to become coercive, move underground and turn to or create organized crime and/or a black market. Intelligent passive aggressiveness can also arise.

At **Green** when the conformity enforcers demand that one size fits all, they conflate individual capacities and impede group effectiveness. The effects on family structure can be dissonance, disagreement and judgment of political incorrectness. The subjective experience of the individual can be depression and withdrawal, and the objective effect is frustration with decisions on behalf of the common good. The complex adaptive behavior can be infighting, emotional blackmail, and public embarrassment of perpetrators.

At **Yellow** (speculatively as this is still emerging) when the conformity enforcers systemically undermine individual outlaws they might impede the optimization of individual contributions. The effects on family structure might be a form of cultural/social auto-immune breakdown resulting in chaotic conditions. The subjective experience of the individual might be betrayal (and anger) and the objective effect may be systemic intrusion and/or obstruction.

The complex adaptive behavior might be unplugging from the system, going underground and/or locating and clustering with those of like mind.

At **Turquoise** (speculatively as this is still emerging) when the conformity enforcers realize that groups and/or individuals might be causing eco-regional threats to human survival they will take counter-action. The effects on the family who disagrees with such action might be to suffer the loss of their eco-regional habitat in defense of their non-conforming beliefs. The subjective experience of the individual could be despair and/or vengeance, and the objective effects could be the loss of substantial regional habitat. The complex adaptive behavior might be to develop and enforce trans-habitat agreements for survival at regional and planetary levels.

Table 26 summarizes the precipitating conditions of homelessness across eight levels of complexity.

Table 26: Precipitating Conditions of Homelessness.
Conditions of homelessness are summarized as follows in each column.

1. The level of complexity of social structure (using the levels defined by Beck and Cowan (1996)

2. The life conditions that give rise to homelessness at this level of complexity. Note that the reason for homelessness is linked to the penalty enforced by the same level of enforcement of conformity shown in column 6 of Table 25.

3. The outcomes of the change in life conditions on the family. (These indicators show the loss of resonance and coherence for the family home caused by the disintegration of life conditions. This results in the lack of sustainability of the home under life conditions identified in Column 2.)

4. Subjective (inner) experience of the individual arising from the change in the life conditions. This results in loss of individual resonance and sets up the inner conditions for the individual to adapt as noted in Column 6.

5. Objective (outer) effects of the life conditions causing homelessness on the individual in the family. (These are indicators of lack of

resonance or loss of resilience for the individual as a result of the change in life conditions.)

6. Individual adaptive behavior resulting from the change in life conditions and conformity enforcement (identified in Table 25, Column 6) and family structure. (Table 25 Column 3). These behaviors are what result in the different definitions of homelessness at each level of existence.

Precipitating Conditions of Homelessness at Eight Levels of Complexity

1. Level of Complexity in Social Structure	2. Change in Life Conditions Causing Homelessness	3. Effects on Family Social Structure, Organizing Principle / Key Value	4. Subjective Experience of the Individual Arising from Change in Life Conditions	5. Objective Effects on the Individual in the Family	6. Individual Adaptive Behavior re Change in Life Conditions & Family Structure
Beige	Shelter is dangerous or endangered by: fire, flood, earthquake, war, substance abuse, etc.	Family disintegrates; family health &/or numbers decline	Fear for life	Basics not available, esp. food	Escapes to survive
Purple	Ostracism from family home	Clan blind to individual innovation; Individual suppression	Rejection	Ritual exclusion; individual rejection	Anger, Fear, Reject the Clan
Red	Protection removed	Breakup of kingdom; disobedience to ruler; opportunity for change to ruler	Victimization	Rival factions	Rebel against the King (father, ruler, dominator, etc.)
Blue	Deny opportunity for individual expression, privacy denied, repressed, ignored	Revolution; overthrow head of the family; Revolt against rules	Shame	Denial of status and resources to lower orders/ castes/ generations by higher orders/ elite/parents/	Organize revolution— cultural, physical, mental and/ or emotional

1. Level of Complexity in Social Structure	2. Change in Life Conditions Causing Homelessness	3. Effects on Family Social Structure, Organizing Principle / Key Value	4. Subjective Experience of the Individual Arising from Change in Life Conditions	5. Objective Effects on the Individual in the Family	6. Individual Adaptive Behavior re Change in Life Conditions & Family Structure
Orange	Relentless competition; Denial of the rule of law	Consumerism, looting; black market; undermines family values; guerilla warfare; sniping; ruthless competition for property values	Failure	Manipulation of property values; strategic plotting	Organized crime; black market, underground, manipulation, coercion
Green	One size fits all; Inability/refusal to see the mix of individual needs	Holier than thou factions; dissonance, disagreement, judgment	Withdrawal, depression	Frustration with decisions on behalf of common good	Infighting, emotional blackmail, public embarrassment of others
Yellow	Systemically undermine individual systemic resource allocations	Systemic cultural/social auto-immune breakdown; disagree with systemic individual choices	Betrayal, anger	Systemic malevolence, invasion, intrusion, obstruction	Unplug from the system; go underground to survive; locate others of like mind
Turquoise	Eco-regional threat to human survival	Substantial breakdown of inter-related eco-regional habitats and/or life conditions e.g. loss of water, forest, food supplies; disagree with systemic eco-regional choices	Despair, vengeance	Substantial die off of regional species, habitats and/or life conditions at geo-bio-noetic levels	Develop and enforce trans-habitat defense agreements for survival at regional and eventually planetary conditions for survival

ECOLOGY OF HOMELESSNESS

As noted above, it appears that an ecology of homelessness emerges, where some or all the meanings of home, maladaptations and pathologies of homelessness co-exist. Thinking about the protectionism and adaptation that emerges as society complexifies, it could be proposed that the dignity of "home as habitat suited to life conditions" is matched by the disaster of "homelessness as loss of habitat, because of change of life conditions".

Thus "homelessness" emerges not just from a horizontal continuum of differences amongst people's choice of shelters, but from a verti-cal evolution of the complexities of habitats, life conditions, individual choices, capacities and social enforcements. This means that the meaning of homelessness changes as life conditions and people change (both as individuals and groups). The capacities and values people enforce and the choices they make all contribute to a myriad of complexifying, entangled roots of homelessness.

Indeed, homelessness does emerge from the relationship between individuals and their family/ groups/cultural and social relationships. It is also both an inner and outer phenomenon, arising from people's emotional, mental, spiritual and belief systems, as well as their housing technology, systems and engineering infrastructures (Anderson, 1997).

APPRECIATING HOMEFULNESS TO REFRAME HOMELESSNESS: WHERE DO WE START?

McQuade (2005) noted that many of the problems she saw in social ser-vices for the homeless arose from service providers failing to understand "their own developmental position and not understanding the position of the person being served" (p.14). She suggested (and my own experience would corroborate) that many of the people serving in social services have a center of gravity ranging from Blue to Orange to Green.

So, the place to start, for any city or municipal governance system faced with the dilemma of finding solutions to homelessness, is by examining their basic assumptions about both homefulness and homelessness.

- What are the worldviews of service providers? What levels of devel-opment can they see in themselves? In others?

- How do we map out the developmental levels of the panarchy or ecology of homefulness and homelessness?
- How do people define and/or value "home"?
- How do people define and/or understand "homelessness"?
- How do different life conditions support homefulness and/or cause homelessness?
- How can we discover a plurality of solutions to support homefulness and address or prevent homelessness? i.e. what different solutions exist for different life conditions?
- How do homefulness and homelessness express these qualities as resources or scarcities?
  - ° Subjective experience: emotional, mental, spiritual
  - ° Economic realities: food, shelter, clothing
  - ° Cultural roots: belonging, beliefs, relationships
  - ° Social and technological resources: shelter systems, engineering, technology
  - ° Contextual conditions: habitat, life conditions, eco-systems, economic flows
- How can we design supports for homefulness and approaches to homelessness that address both the individual and the family/social contexts?

When we attempt to answer these questions we discover the extent to which we take for granted the needs to support homefulness. We also reveal the ineffective interventions we have tried to address homelessness. The causes of failure and the outcomes we desire demand effective responses that include subjective, intersubjective, objective and interobjective approaches.

It should be noted that in reviewing these options, at each level of complexity, the effective supports and interventions must subsume and include all the intervention strategies that precede it. In other words, support and intervention will be less effective if all supports and interventions are not in place up to and including the relevant level of complexity.

Furthermore, we have learned that support or intervention responses will not be effective if used from a higher level of complexity to address a lower level of complexity; e.g. one cannot use a green intervention to address a red cause. (Social democracy interventions in the developing world have shown such a strategy is both harmful and unethical, and precipitates unhealthy dependencies, pathologies and barriers that worsen the situation instead of improving it. (Beck, 2000, 2002)).

ACHIEVING INTENDED OUTCOMES: REPLACING INEFFECTIVE HOMELESSNESS APPROACHES WITH EFFECTIVE HOMEFULNESS SUPPORTS AND INTERVENTIONS

At **Beige**, overcoming homelessness depends on restoring family and/or creating a pseudo-family as a survival unity. Typical but ineffective interventions have been to remove people from the street and provide food and shelter. However effective this might be for emergency responses, in the long term failure to develop family capacity leads to the dependency of individuals and families on a charitable system. They might receive "fish for a day" but the circumstances are not created where they can learn to "fish for a lifetime" and support themselves. The better response is to create safe conditions for shelter; restore family groups capable of maintaining safe shelter and enable them to obtain, through some value exchange the basics of survival: food, water, clothing.

At **Purple**, overcoming homelessness depends on the restoration of group belonging and/or placement in protective care until members can rejoin or create their own belonging clans. Typical but ineffective interventions include classifying all homelessness as lack of basic food and shelter; simply removing people from the street; solely offering individuals food and shelter; or providing a food bank. Failure to address Purple values is caused by lack of recognition that home has a spiritual component. This can be exacerbated by neglecting the need for a healing ceremony that recognizes the damage inflicted by emotional and/or spiritual abuse or the loss of unique cultural values. Effective responses for Purple homelessness can come from creating ceremonies to heal spiritual rifts; conducting cleansing rituals to appease damage to conditions of belonging; honoring elders and ancestors; restoring sacred places and relationships connected within the home.

At **Red** overcoming homelessness requires restoration of protective care and relationships. Ineffective responses to Red homelessness classify the homeless as victims. Individuals or families are given temporary shelter with no requirement for responsibility, or worse still they are returned to abusive social conditions that encourage a recurrence of Red pathologies. The causes of these failures are centered as much in the interveners' worldview as the homeless themselves. When individuals are considered victims, they are not expected to take responsibility for their life conditions; e.g. alcoholism, substance abuse, sex dependencies, etc. Solutions need to offer supportive conditions for individuals to protect themselves, and learn to accept responsibility. The family needs to be treated, as well as the community where norms and laws support family life and the family in turn supports the individual. Effective interventions for Red homelessness might require unusual approaches, even including repairing the protective influence of a "head of the family" as long as they do not invade the protective rights of other "family heads"; ensuring adequate life conditions for physical, cultural/social, and economic survival; installing peacekeeping forces if necessary (e.g. other family members, community members, social workers, police); and supporting the enforcement of the rule of law. Solutions to Red homelessness need to avoid "shaming" and enable small successes. A good example is the Dignity Village in Portland (anon, 2000).

At **Blue** overcoming homelessness means establishing some authority for social housing norms while offering creative outlets for individual expression. Interventions for Blue homelessness have failed because individuals and/or families have so often been uprooted from community support systems and relocated in coop housing units where "lawlessness" is endemic. Failure has resulted because (as Jane Jacobs (1994) so early recognized) of a lack of awareness that even in stable slums, informal community support systems create resilience against homelessness. These support systems are often (like) extended families, with elders able/willing to look out for youth and children. Effective interventions will not only provide shelter, but heal physical and emotional scars; restore the rule of law; relocate individual(s) (if necessary) from group repression to a place (if possible) where they can establish their own rule of law; and offer the discipline of community run systems like 12 step kinds of programs to create responsibility and discipline frameworks. Informal and formal sports and arts facilities should also be provided so individuals (especially youth) can creatively channel their energy.

At **Orange** overcoming homelessness involves developing a strategy for success, not only through restoring the individual to an appropriate residence but to one where they will be able to earn a living to maintain the residence. Ineffective interventions address homelessness at this level of complexity by offering subsidized or coop housing, when the individual really needs to be challenged to experience success. Failure arises because of the assumption that by throwing money at the problem it will be solved, while failing to recognize the individual sense of accomplishment that needs to accompany this level of development. More effective intervention would rehabilitate and/or educate individuals to cope with success-based life conditions; and provide job and housing renewal programs to build personal and family capacity to be self-sustaining.

At **Green** overcoming homelessness might mean offering shared housing and/or access to eco-friendly space for complex group experiences. The importance of peer group interaction and learning is enabled. Ineffective interventions tend to ignore the need for shared community, which requires a different approach to public spaces than solutions at Orange. Interventions fail at Green because people are victimized by a one-size-fits all classification system and at the same time a lack of accountability. Failure to see that individuals and families have different needs, forces everyone into the same housing solution and misallocates resources. Effective interventions recognize that not everyone needs or wants the same living area; housing density; or quality of housing. Needs vary by age, interests, work, size of family, stage of family. Utilizing Green's preference for sharing and caring, the parties involved can be facilitated to use interest based negotiation to develop new agreements for housing options. Supporting peer groups to help themselves can be very effective as long as they are required to demonstrate outcomes, accountability and results (as well as relationships).

At **Yellow** overcoming homelessness could mean the restoration of eco-friendly space for complex individual expression and/or access to local friendly co-housing; it could involve residents in housing design. Ineffective interventions would involve government payouts for minimum housing standards; attempts to make all parts of the urban landscape the same. Failure would probably result from failure to recognize the systemic (anthropological) relationship between people, housing, infrastructure and habitat. A failure to understand that a city will always have an ecology of housing options and a failure to recognize the lifecycles of housing options would also lead to ineffectiveness with Yellows. More effective interventions would facilitate self-discovery and commitment to systemic conditions for wellbeing, including criteria for "home". All stakeholders would recognize that needs vary by age, gender, culture, experience, etc. (An early example of Yellow success on an experimental level could be Burning Man (Hamilton, 2008, pp.88–89).

At **Turquoise** overcoming homelessness might entail the restoration of eco-regional agreements for complex adaptive conditions for human habitats in long term balance with other species in the region (and other regions). Probably few or no typical interventions can yet be identified as ineffective at this level of complexity, but one might speculate that ineffectiveness would arise from trying to treat human habitats in all regions the same. Causes of ineffectiveness would arise from failure to recognize that human habitat must co-evolve with eco-regions, along with a failure to bring individual and group intelligence to urban housing challenges. Effective interventions might involve facilitating group accord for creating and maintaining systemic conditions for eco-regional wellbeing (including criteria for home life conditions) of all species.

COMPLEX ADAPTIVE APPROACHES FOR EMERGING HOMEFULNESS

The foregoing discussion demonstrates that homefulness is a natural evolutionary condition of the healthy human system; by contrast, homelessness can be viewed as a maladaptation or pathology of a healthy human system. Both these systemic views suggest that indicators that could serve as "vital signs monitors" for homefulness and "early warning signs" for homelessness. Using the resilience monitor from Holling's Panarchy, we can notice the natural cyclic patterns of homefulness. With this overview of homefulness we can gain the clarity of what is needed to keep our human systems healthy at each stage of development (and evolution).

In addition to this Panarchy cycle we could reframe what have seemed to be the futilities of homelessness approaches as the emergence of homelessness traps—for example, where poverty and homelessness become so locked into the cycle that they are resistant to the normal influences of cyclic change. Likewise, we can notice the emergence of "rigidity traps" where service providers are so locked into service provision through one mode, that they become unresponsive and ineffective.

With a more optimistic approach, it is apparent from the natural evolution of homefulness that the multi-variate causes that underlie homelessness indicate that a "one size fits all" approach to address homelessness, will never be sufficient. Homelessness clearly arises from the complex adaptive nature of the human species as we respond to our life conditions. To have any hopes at changing the condition of homelessness, we need to context it in relation to homefulness, considering:

- the levels of complexity at which it arises
- the life conditions, including natural and human-made habitat
- the interconnections between the levels of complexity (and how many of them may be simultaneously in play)
- both individuals and the larger society contribute to the condition through the interplay of individual choice, family dynamics and social norms.

We need to accept the complexity of both homefulness and homelessness as bio-psycho-cultural-social phenomena and abandon paradigms that see linear cause and effect approaches as appropriate solutions (Inglis & Steele, 2005). Without an Integral vision of homefulness no amount of programs and money will ever be effectively applied to overcome homelessness,

This means taking action to prevent homelessness before those who experience it, become entrenched as an outlier social caste. To do so, we can:

- **create action research cycles ((Stringer, 1996) and learn from the actual outcomes of action compared to the intended outcomes.**

- **continue to learn how to improve our knowledge of the patterns of human systems dynamics ((Eoyang & Olson, 2001).**
- **design and offer ongoing supports to strengthen homefulness**
- **intervene to end homelessness** by healing, restoring, educating, facilitating: individuals, families, neighborhoods, cities and societies.

With this in mind, by learning from the resources and interventions proposed above, we can encourage homefulness (and approach homelessness) by meshworking solutions (Beck, 2004; Hamilton, 2008, 2012), so that we:

- **scan our cultures (both urban and rural)** to understand the levels of complexity that exist in families, neighborhoods, the city and the region
- **learn more about the patterns in natural human systems** e.g. the dominant values; expressions of conformity enforcement and diversity generation; and sacrifice self vs express self systems.
- **introduce vital signs monitors** to create feedback and feed forward loops
- **work together across disciplines to enable strategic foresight, scenario planning, and formulation of strategies that support homefulness and address and prevent homelessness.**
- **take intervention actions**

In supporting homefulness we will strengthen individuals, families and cultures so that together we can make a major impact on addressing homelessness. Both home-FULL and home-LESS strategies require us to embrace expertise on the human condition that arises from at least the following knowledge domains:

- Bio-physical Sciences
- Health and Healing Modalities—both Allopathic and Alternative; Individual and Family Systems Therapy
- Psychology
- Evolutionary psychology

- Culture
- Law
- Sociology
- Anthropology
- Human settlements (architecture, engineering, construction trades)
- Economics
- Ecology

By meshworking in a whole system, transdisciplinary, evolutionary way, we might even mature as a species so that any instance of homelessness becomes a leading indicator for us to automatically correct our actions and interactions with one another and our habitat. By so doing we might avoid Diamond's (2005) all too vivid description of societal "Collapse" and learn to survive and thrive on the only home we ultimately have: planet Earth. (To remind yourself why this is important, I return you to the message of the Wombat (Able 2005): http://www.globalcommunity.org/flash/wombat.shtml).

REFERENCES

Able, J. (2005). Wombat. Retrieved December 19, 2017, from Foundation for Global Community http://www.globalcommunity.org/flash/wombat.shtml

anon. (2000). Dignity Village. Retrieved December 19, 2017, from Wikipedia https://en.wikipedia.org/wiki/Dignity_Village

Anderson, R. (1997). Street as Metaphor in Housing for the Homeless. Journal of Social Stress and the Homeless, Vol. 6.(No. 1).

Beck, D. (2002a). The Color of Constellations: A Spiral Dynamics Perspective on Human Drama. Paper presented at the Bert Hellinger Constellation Conference, Germany.

Beck, D. (2002b). Spiral Dynamics in the Integral Age. Paper presented at the Spiral Dynamics integral, Level 1, Vancouver, BC.

Beck, D. (2000b). Stages of Social Development: The Cultural Dynamics that Spark Violence, Spread Prosperity and Shape Globalization. Paper presented at the State of the World Forum, New York.

Beck, D., & Cowan, C. (1996). *Spiral Dynamics: Mastering Values, Leadership and Change*. Malden, MA: Blackwell Publishers.

Bloom, H. (2000). *The Global Brain: The Evolution of Mass Mind from the Big Bang to the 21st Century*. New York: John Wiley & Son Inc.

Capra, F. (1996). *The Web of Life: A New Scientific Understanding of Living Systems*. New York, Anchor Books, Doubleday.

Diamond, J. (1992). *The Third Chimpanzee: The Evolution and Future of the Human Animal*. New York: HarperCollins Publishers.

Diamond, J. (2005). *Collapse: How societies choose to fail or succeed* (first ed.). New York: Penguin Group.

Eoyang, G., & Olson, E. (2001). *Facilitating Organization Change: Lessons from Complexity Science*. Jossey-Bass Pfeiffer.

Fernandez-Armesto, F. (2001). *Civilizations: Culture, Ambition and the Transformation of Nature*. New York: Touchstone.

Glaser, I., & Bridgman, R. (1999). *Braving the Street: The Anthropology of Homelessness*. New York: Berghan Books.

Graves, C. W. (Ed.). (2003). *Levels of Human Existence*. Santa Barbara: Eclet Publishing.

Hamilton, M., & Stevenson, B. (2001). How Does Complexity Inform Community? How does Community Inform Complexity? Emergence, 3(No. 2), pp.57—77.

Hamilton, M. (2007). Approaching Homelessness: An Integral Reframe. *World Futures: The Journal of General Evolution, Volume* 63(2), 107–126.

Hamilton, M. (2008). *Integral City: Evolutionary Intelligences for the Human Hive*. Gabriola Island BC: New Society Publishers.

Hamilton, M. (2012b). Meshworking Evolutionary Intelligence for the Human Hive. Paper presented at the Building Sustainable Communities 5, Kelowna, BC.

Holling, C. S. (2001). Understanding the Complexity of Economic, Ecological, and Social Systems Ecosystems, Vol. 4, pp. 390–405.

Inglis, J., and Steele M. (2005). Approaching the Complexity of Homelessness. *unpublished manuscript*.

Jacobs, J. (1992). *The Death and Life of Great American Cities*. New York: Vintage Books.

Jacobs, J. (2004). *Dark Age Ahead*. New York: Random House Canada.

McQuade, A. (2005). Reviving our Interiors: Serving the Mentally Ill Living on Our Streets. AQAL, Vol. I(No. 4).

No Fixed Address. (2004, January 24—31, 2004). Vancouver Sun.

Stringer, E. T. (1996). *Action Research: A Handbook for Practitioners*. Thousand Oaks. CA: Sage Publications Inc.

Taylor, G. (2008). *Evolution's Edge: The Coming Collapse and Transformation of our World*. Gabriola Island, BC: New Society Publishers.

Turnbull, C. (1972). *The Mountain People*. New York: Touchstone Simon Schuster.

Wilber, K. (1995). *Sex, Ecology and Spirituality: the spirit of evolution*. Boston: Shambhala Publications Inc.

Wilber, K. (2000a). *Integral Psychology*. Boston: Shambhala Publications Inc.

SECTION 4

Widening Capacity at City Scale

Chapter 14 inquires why **city governance** deserves unique design elements for this most complex human system. It suggests that cities cannot simply be privatized and run like an organization. It explores the conjectures that Jane Jacobs offered to counter this notion as well as proposing an evolutionarily more complex framework than her proposition that dangerous and toxic hybrids emerge from combining the government and private sectors.

Chapter 15 explores the field of **international development** as an energizing opportunity for waking up the human hive. It uses the metaframework that has served us so well to understand this new paradigm of the city by demonstrating how their capacities vary around the world depending on their national contexts—based on both demographic realities and values systems.

14

INTEGRAL CITY SYSTEMS OF SURVIVAL: WHY NOT JUST PRIVATIZE THE GOVERNMENT?

*Originally published in **Integral Life** November, 2012*

CHAPTER SUMMARY

Why not privatize city government? Jane Jacobs described two moral syndromes necessary for a human social system to survive—one called Guardian and the other called Commercial. She argued that mixing their ethics created "monstrous hybrids" that were immoral and subversive to life. Reframing these syndromes from an Integral perspective allows the retention of the collective dignities of Purple and Blue in the Guardian syndrome to be re-aligned with the innovation dignities of Red and Orange in the Commercial syndrome, while avoiding the unhealthy misappropriation of the disasters inherent in Jacobs' moral codes. This transcendence and inclusion in evolutionary social systems requires commitment to a purpose-driven, planet-centric set of life-giving principles (captured in the Integral City's 12 Evolutionary Intelligences and Elisabet Sahtouris' 15 principles of living systems). Essentially when the health of all the holarchies in the city (and the planet of cities) is contexted with the health of all living systems, a superordinate goal for city governance emerges. Integrally informed organizing practices like Holacracy™, Biomimicry Investment Codes and Almere City Principles are all experiments that demonstrate how healthy hybrids based on life-giving principles are emerging in human systems. They suggest ways to develop integrally-informed city governance that avoids monstrous hybrids because they are based on evolutionary life-principles as requisite levels of complexity for survival.

Keywords: systems of survival, Jane Jacobs, monstrous hybrids, guardian, commercial, city governance, Integral City Systems, evolution, living systems

WHY NOT JUST PRIVATIZE THE GOVERNMENT?

Back in the days of my impressionable (but contrarian) 1960's youth, I followed the Objectivist philosophy of Ayn Rand with some considerable zeal. I was an avid free-enterpriser and imagined that we would be better off without most government—certainly everything connected with Big Government.

In recent years I have listened to some strong arguments from members of the Integral movement making very similar propositions—that we should privatize many government departments so that competition would theoretically improve service and reduce costs.

As I have mellowed, travelled the world wide and far, and cogitated on the writings of city observer Jane Jacobs, I have come to question my assumptions about the role of government in civilized society. Jane, the author of *Systems of Survival* (Jacobs, 1994, p. 93) and most noted for her first book *The Death and Life of Great American Cities* (Jacobs, 1992), proposed that two moral syndromes had evolved that contributed to the wellbeing of cites, namely the syndrome of the Guardian and the Syndrome of the Commercial.

Since writing *Integral City* Book 1, and identifying 12 integrally informed intelligences for enabling the city as an evolutionary living system, I have been curious how an Integral reframe might bring new light to the arguments favoring divestment of government functions to the private sector. How might they include Jacobs' proposition but transcend it into more life giving principles?

Jacobs' Two Syndromes

Jacobs' two syndromes differentiated between the "Right Morals" of the private sector and the government sectors. My observations about the challenges of city development suggest that the distinctive qualities of the "syndromes" are worth considering in terms of systems thinking and the distinctive stakeholder roles who have a vested interest in the governance of the city. (The syndromes are set out in Table 27 below.)

Table 27: Jane Jacobs' Moral Syndromes

The Commercial Moral Syndrome

- Shun force
- Come to voluntary agreements
- Be honest
- Collaborate easily with strangers and aliens
- Compete
- Respect contracts
- Use initiative and enterprise
- Be open to inventiveness and novelty
- Be efficient
- Promote comfort and convenience
- Dissent for the sake of the task
- Invest for productive purposes
- Be industrious
- Be thrifty
- Be optimistic

The Guardian Moral Syndrome

- Shun trading
- Exert prowess
- Be obedient and disciplined
- Adhere to tradition
- Respect hierarchy
- Be loyal
- Take vengeance
- Deceive for the sake of the task
- Make rich use of leisure
- Be ostentatious
- Dispense largesse
- Be exclusive
- Show fortitude
- Be fatalistic
- Treasure honor

Jacobs had deep respect for the values of these lineages and a moral repugnance at intermixing the two. She called such an animal a "monstrous hybrid" (Jacobs, 1994, p. 93) and warned that a mixed set of Commercial and Guardian values would create such conflicts of interest that undue power, authority and influence would result to the detriment of a balanced and thriving society.

REFRAMING WITH AN INTEGRAL COMPLEXITY LENS

When I take an Integral lens (using the Spiral Dynamics (Beck & Cowan, 1996) framework as set out Chapter 13) to Jacobs' Guardian syndrome I see the worldview and values of Level 4 (Blue). The Guardian syndrome appears to me to be the natural expression of healthy authority, order, merit and discipline. In it rests the authority of our institutions of justice, all the professions and well-honed bureaucracies. This syndrome provides the structures and infrastructures that make cities manageable. It is essentially the pre-modern culture that recalibrates traditional (Purple) values and power hierarchies (Red) into Blue obedience based on the rule of law and authority derived from "prowess" or meritorious standards.

On the other hand, the Commercial syndrome appears to me to be the natural expression of healthy strategic, goal oriented, entrepreneurial activity. It embodies the worldview and values of Level 5 (Orange). While the Guardians "shun trading", the Commercials depend on voluntary exchange for productive purposes. The Commercials recalibrate from Red the unlawful piracy and involuntary seizures of property and person into the Orange creative, thriving, collaborative habitat for commercial exchange.

It appears that Jacobs could see the evolutionary lineage of the Purple values systems needing recalibration and realignment, while controlling the excesses of the self-centered Red values systems, and that evolved into the Guardian Syndrome.

In the Commercial Syndrome, on the other hand, it is as if she could also see that the merits of the individual power and expression of the Red values systems needed the discipline and agreements of the Blue values systems to emerge the Orange Commercial Syndrome's optimistic capacity for industry and production.

And what does she suppose happens to produce a Monstrous Hybrid? Such an animal arises when either syndrome borrows values from the other syndrome (without recalibrating or re-aligning the systems), producing a kind of cloned trans-species monster and unintended consequences. Jacobs gave examples that have become all too common front page news—such as: the moral bankruptcy of accounting firms who accepted payments for solvency letters; corporations that solve their dilemma of debt overextension by callously laying off employees; guardian governments investing in the military machine at the cost of their citizens' wellbeing; quota-incented police forces rewarded for fabricated arrests.

The monstrous hybrids seem to arise from both intentional and unintentional misalignments of values. They appear to describe a toxic mix of unhealthy Blue (can't support the structures or management needed), unhealthy Orange (attempt to produce results at the expense of over-consumption and/or over-extension of resources), and unhealthy Green (where the lack of appreciation of the evolutionary hierarchy of values, capacities and capitals systematically erodes the wealth-generating capacity of Orange Commercials and the order-creating capacity of Blue Guardians).

TRANSCEND AND INCLUDE

If we follow the logic of Integral thinking, can we consider the possibility of a Healthy Hybrid? What would that look like? Instead of shifting into the shadows of prior levels of complexity, we could look to the lessons of systems thinking from the Yellow complexity level of worldview. That might mean that we would acknowledge both the civilizing contributions of Blue management structures and the wealth-generating contributions of Orange production structures. We would also include the people-enhancing priorities of Green social and cultural structures. But in the systems view of the world, the process of goal attainment becomes nested within an ecology of ecocentric, worldcentric and Kosmocentric contexts. Purposes are no longer merely egocentric or ethnocentric. Rather, both the individual and the organizational goals would transcend mere authority, profit or people considerations. They would operate in service to a higher level purpose where their relationships would become symbiotic for the wellbeing of all the entities and relationships within the ecology. Thus both Guardians and Commercials would become recalibrated so their purposes were driven and flexed and flowed in service to such purpose.

Of course the question then becomes, how would we define such a purpose in a way that was not just a totalitarian or utopian frame? I would suggest that purposes like these are defined in terms of the health and wellbeing of the system in the context of the world as a living system. James Lovelock called this world system *Gaia* (Lovelock, 1972, 1991, 2009).

IMPLICATIONS OF LIVING SYSTEMS FOR GOVERNANCE

If we are going to recalibrate the Guardian and the Commercial syndromes into a living system, then what principles can offer life-giving direction?

Evolution biologist Elisabeth Sahtouris (1999, 2017) defines 15 principles that are organically foundational to the 12 intelligences of an Integral City. (These are explored in some depth in Chapter 2.)

Her last two principles suggest how the evolutionary process of transcending and including can be applied to retain the foundations of good management from the Guardians, the innovation capacities of the Commercials and the people enhancement capacities of the Green level of development. Sahtouris suggests that we conserve what works well, and innovate, create and change what does not work well. Thus she reinforces the evolution of a city as a learning system.

If we are curious about how cities can integrate such life-giving principles into their way of doing business, we might visit the Dutch city of Almere, which developed a set of life-giving principles based on architect William McDonough's (McDonough & Braungart, 2002).

Cradle-to-Cradle design principles which sets out a full life-cycle framework for the flow of materials right down to the bio-chemical level (Hamilton, 2011). The seven Almere Principles are intimately connected with "an act of culture and the expression of an optimistic approach of the future (Hamilton, 2011)". Like the Integral City intelligences, the Principles describe the need for Contexting, Capacity Building, Strategy and Evolution.

Recently, other living system approaches that could inform integrally designed governance systems have emerged.

Evidence for New Systemic Hybridizers

Holacracy (Robertson, 2017) is one such system that has been developed for the governance and operation of organizations. It is designed to remove the negative and shadow sides of egocentric and ethnocentric worldviews that can hijack an organization wanting to work as a living system. Core elements of Holacracy offer distinctive alternatives to Guardian and Commercial enterprises, starting with identification of and commitment to a clearly defined purpose of the organization. Roles in a holacratic organization are defined solely in terms of how they serve the accomplishment of the purpose and the people (souls). They in turn accept the responsibility of the roles and accept that their role and their soul are both in service to the whole that emerges from the organizational purpose. This new form of organization uses systemic holarchies (for team relationships and interactions), rather than hierarchies, to accomplish its goals. The Holacracy framework (a Yellow organizational design) has developed a series of governance and operational decision making processes that enable everyone's voice to be heard (Green) while dynamically steering towards goals (Orange) within agreements that establish and ensure high standards (Blue).

Despite the fact that I can't yet identify any cities specifically applying Holacratic principles within their institutional operations (although Laloux (2014) has identified 10 more organizations that have reinvented themselves using similar principles as explored in Chapter 11), it appears to me that this framework offers possibilities for the radical reform of Guardian-Commercial standoffs that are too often present in public hearings and town hall meetings.

Another reframing of an old set of standards is emerging around the proposition of the Commons. Commons are both public and private resources held in common by communities. They can include natural resources (air, water, biosphere), land, intellectual property economics, business, politics, democracy, culture and technology, trusteeship, interest rates, systems theory and spirituality. The principles of caring for the Commons extend beyond the Guardian role of regulation into stewarding, social cooperation and thinking about succeeding generations. This kind of systems thinking, relating, thinking and doing applies norms that prevent parasitism, bond communities for the good of all life and create whole new principles of economic exchange (Quilligan, 2008, 2009a, 2009b). Thus Commoning is expanding governance frames from rigid Blue rules, past opportunistic Orange contracts and beyond porous collective Green Unrests (Hawken, 2007) into a recognition that an Integral approach could emerge a caring wise hybrid. (And to me this rather sounds like the Shambhala warrior who emerges at crisis times like now, wielding a sword of compassion and a sword of wisdom on behalf of Life.)

The last hopeful hybrid I want to notice is the Life Giving Investment Principles that have emerged from the conjoint work of solar economist

Hazel Henderson (H. Henderson, 1997; Hazel Henderson, Lickerman, & Flynn, 2000) and biomimicry pioneer Janine Benyus (Benyus, 1997). They issued a manifesto for transforming finance (Henderson & Benyus, 2012), based on life's principles, that is founded on the axiom "that the human species is interdependent with all other life forms on Planet Earth. Therefore, human societies, cultures, values and belief systems that are informed by and modeled on . . . Life's Principles . . . should provide the basis for all production and exchange of goods, community structures and services."

Thus their principles re-frame the arguments about whether we should privatize government roles and/or avoid monstrous hybrid consequences. The life-giving investment principles basically embrace energy from all four Integral quadrants (consciousness, culture, bio-physical and systems/structures). They affirm in no uncertain terms that life-giving investment embraces all human exchange (and thus city exchange) including the "design of monetary systems, investments, banking, financing, bartering, reciprocal exchange, payments, crowd funding, compensation and unpaid gifting, sharing, cooperatives, reproduction of future generations, provision of public goods, infrastructure, collective health, education and life-supporting services." The crux of their six life-giving investment principles is:

1. Evolve to survive
2. Be resource (material and energy) efficient
3. Adapt to changing Conditions
4. Integrate development with growth
5. Be locally attuned and responsive
6. Use life-friendly chemistry

Clearly these six principles align well with Sahtouris' 15 Principles of Living Systems, McDonough's cradle-to-cradle principles and the 12 intelligences I propose for Integral City (Hamilton, 2008).

New Hybrids for Integral City Systems of Survival

We can now return to the "let's privatize government" proposition and Jane Jacobs' original contention that monstrous hybrids emerge from the confusion and/or recombination of Guardian and Commercial syndromes. With an Integral frame on the governance dilemma that she proposes, it seems to me that it is possible to consider evidence for the emergence of *Healthful* or *Thriving Hybrids* at higher orders of complexity.

These hybrids don't arise from the unmindful or mechanical combination of cloning two polarized systems (the Blue Guardians and Orange Commercials) even if they are ineffectively mediated by a well-intentioned but ill-informed social embrace (Green Caregivers). Rather they evolve a whole new evolutionary system with new DNA that carries forward what works (leaving behind what no longer appropriately serves life) and is systems-aware, emergent, adaptive and able to flex and flow in new contexts and variations of the environment. We know we need something that is not simply applying Orange free-enterprise band-aids to higher orders of complex human systems. We can see evolutionary evidence for what we seek in organizational Holacracies; full lifecycle structural production; and life giving economic/metabolic flows. In all cases these are naturally emergent hybrids (at different levels of scale) that transcend and include what works from all previous levels of complexity. They also let go of the toxic elements that can no longer work in the cities or world that are now so complex.

The underlying governance system that is starting to emerge appears to serve a worldcentric purpose, based on life-giving principles that enable a healthy ecology for all life. This new syndrome appears to be defining qualities that enable the creation and sustainability of healthy resilience in the face of change.

For, as the changing life conditions in the world continue to accelerate at an exponential rate, the kind of governance we now need in our cities must be able to respond to the hard truths of life (Rockström et al., 2009). As Elisabet Sahtouris (2010, 2017) has pointed out however, it is precisely these chaotic conditions that have presented life with the opportunities to evolve over the last 4 billion years. These conditions are now triggering our learning about how to develop governance that avoids the path of the monstrous hybrid by developing the principles of life-giving syndromes. And that is what cities using an Integral paradigm seek as their requisite systems for survival.

REFERENCES

Beck, D., & Cowan, C. (1996). *Spiral Dynamics: Mastering Values, Leadership and Change*. Malden, MA: Blackwell Publishers.

Benyus, J. M. (1997). *Biomimicry: Innovation Inspired by Nature*. New York: William Morrow and Company Inc.

Hamilton, M. (2008). *Integral City: Evolutionary Intelligences for the Human Hive*. Gabriola Island BC: New Society Publishers.

Hamilton, M. (2011, April 20, 2011). Almere Principles Guide City Growth. *Integral City Blog*. Retrieved from http://marilyn.integralcity.com/2011/04/20/almere-principles-guide-city-growth/

Hawken, P. (2007). *Blessed Unrest: How the Largest Social Movement in History is Restoring Grace, Justice and Beauty to the World*. New York: Penguin Books.

Henderson, H. (1997). Looking Back From the 21st Century. *New Renaissance, Vol. 7*(No. 2). Retrieved from http://www.ru.org/backis.html

Henderson, H., Lickerman, J., & Flynn, P. (Eds.). (2000). *Calvert-Henderson Quality of Life Indicators*. Bethesda, MD: Calvert Group, Ltd.

Henderson, H., Benyus, J. (2012). Statement on Transforming Finance Based on Ethics and Life's Principles. *New Renaissance, Vol. 7* (No. 2). Retrieved from http://www.ethicalmarkets.com/statement-on-transforming-finance-based-on-lifes-principles/

Jacobs, J. (1992). *The Death and Life of Great American Cities*. New York: Vintage Books.

Jacobs, J. (1994). *Systems of Survival*. New York: First Vintage Books Edition.

Laloux, F. (2014). *Reinventing Organizations*. Retrieved from http://www.reinventingorganizations.com/purchase.html.

Lovelock, J. (1972). Gaia As Seen Through the Atmosphere, Atmospheric Environment, (Vol. 6, p. 579).

Lovelock, J. (1991). *Healing Gaia*. New York: Harmony Books.

Lovelock, J. (2009). *The Vanishing Face of Gaia*. New York: Harmony Books.

McDonough, W., & Braungart, M. (2002). *Cradle to Cradle: Remaking the Way We Make Things*. New York: North Point Press.

Quilligan, J. B. (2008, Fall Winter). Global Commons and Society as Global Commons Organizations. *Kosmos*, VIII, p.26.

Quilligan, J. B. (2009a, Spring Summer). The Commons and Integral Capital. *Kosmos*, VIII, pp. 30–35.

Quilligan, J. B. (2009b, Fall Winter). People Sharing Resources: Toward a New Multilateralism of the Global Commons. *Kosmos*, IX, pp. 30–35.

Robertson, B. (2017). Holacracy How It Works. Retrieved from http://www.holacracy.org/how-it-works/

Rockström, J., W. Steffen, K. Noone, Å. Persson, F. S. Chapin, III, E. Lambin, T. M. Lenton, M. Scheffer, C. Folke, H. Schellnhuber, B. Nykvist, C. A. De Wit, T. Hughes, S. van der Leeuw, H. Rodhe, S. Sörlin, P. K. Snyder, R. Costanza, U. Svedin, M. Falkenmark, L. Karlberg, R. W. Corell, V. J. Fabry, J. Hansen, B. Walker, D. Liverman, K. Richardson, P. Crutzen, and J. Foley. (2009). Planetary boundaries: exploring the safe operating space for humanity. *Ecology and Society*, 14(2), 32.

Sahtouris, E. (1999). *Earthdance: Living Systems in Evolution*. Available from http://www.ratical.org/LifeWeb/

Sahtouris, E. (2010). Celebrating Crisis: Towards a Culture of Cooperation. A *New Renaissance: Transforming Science, Spirit & Society*. London: Floris Books.

Sahtouris, E. (2017). A Tale of Cities and Cells: Our Human Evolutionary Agenda. Retrieved December 7, 2017 https://www.ethicalmarkets.com/a-tale-of-cities-and-cells-by-elisabet-sahtouris/

CAPACITY BUILDING AT THE CITY SCALE WITH EVOLUTIONARY DEVELOPMENT PRINCIPLES

CHAPTER SUMMARY

This chapter applies the Integral City paradigm to design developmental strategies in existing cities as well as for new cities. It examines the Master Code as an essential reframe of city building codes. It considers the 12 intelligences of the Integral City as the source of growing capacities for contexting, individual development, collective development, developmental strategies and evolutionary resilience. It builds out a metaframework of city systems, arising from the Cosmosphere, Biosphere and Anthroposphere, and links them to the five maps that reveal the Integral City as a whole system of systems. Population demographics from cities located in countries traversing four different levels of Anthropospheric maturity reveal the natural patterns of the human hive as it develops from Traditional, to Modern, to Post-Modern to Integral capacities. These patterns and driving values reveal the most appropriate developmental strategies for cities at any stage of demographic maturity. Design questions are proposed for neo-cities and neo-civics based on the Integral City framework. The Action Research designs from Book 2 are proposed as detailed processes for designing developmental strategies. In conclusion, the chapter suggests that this spectrum of strategies might be relevant to any city with a plurality of immigrant cultures or new cities that will have to design for the interconnected multi-scalar trajectory of human system development.

Key words: Integral City design elements, evolution, sustainability, intelligences, global threats, developing cities, developed cities, new cities, neo-cities, neo-civics

"Humans are Gaia's reflective organ."

—James Lovelock (2009)

DESIGN ELEMENTS FOR DEVELOPING CITIES

This penultimate chapter of Book 3 builds on the power of the Master Code discovered in Book 1 and put to service in Book 2 (Hamilton 2008, 2017). It reflects back on the 12 intelligences for the human hive explored in Book 1 (Hamilton, 2008) and the five maps developed in Books 1 and 2 and Chapter 1 of this book. It contexts the development of cities within the Anthroposphere, Biosphere and Cosmosphere. This chapter reprises the design processes of placecaring and placemaking mapped out in Book 2 (Hamilton, 2017) and offers questions for city designers, developers and planners to consider as they create the space for capacity building at the city scale. (The design elements offered here are peculiar to the Integral City framework, but it should be noted that at least two other authors are developing a series of books that offer integrally-informed design compendiums—especially Paul Van Schaik (2016, 2107a-g) with his Hub 1–8 Series on Thrivable Cities and Charles Landry (2017; Landry & Murray, 2017; Wood & Landry 2008) with his explorations of culture, psychology and the art of placemaking.)

Master Code as Building Code

Paris, San Bernardino, Brussels, Ferguson, Nice, Orlando, Dallas, Lahore, Baton Rouge, Istanbul. The threats that the world's cities face from within and without give us clues about what is needed to develop existing cities and design new cities.

When Integral City sponsored the Online Webinar 2012 (Hamilton & Sanders, 2013), we learned the five major threats that all cities faced were: climate, energy, water, food and finance. Since then we have added a sixth threat that trumps them all—and that is culture.

Culture is the collective expression of values, worldviews and belief systems that holds each city together. It is woven one thread at a time by each person, family, group, street, neighborhood and community until the city's cultural cloth of warp and woof becomes substantial enough and resilient enough for the weavers to walk across without thought to its existence. Culture in a city is largely invisible but utterly vital to the living dynamic of its wellbeing and existence.

Culture arises from practice of what we call the Master Code:

- **Take care of yourself**
- **Take care of each other**
- **Take care of this place**
- **Take care of this planet.**

The Master Code has an evolutionary thrust to it that naturally emerges hierarchies of complexity within the city (see Appendix B, Map 2). Enabling care of self, others, place and planet is a universal code that transcends and ought to include a multiplicity of belief systems. Practice of the Master Code at each level of complexity weaves the tensile strength for individuals in the city to practice at the next level of complexity. In other words, taking care of one self enables taking care of others; taking are of others enables taking care of place; taking care of place enables taking care of planet.

The Master Code has an involutionary thrust to it as a natural complement to the evolutionary thrust. Each city has emerged from the life conditions supplied by the planet at its distinctive geological location. The life conditions of the city create the context for the capacity for families and groups to care for one another; and the capacity of families to care creates the primal hearth for caring for individuals who learn first in the family to care for themselves.

The terrible irony and truth of the Master Code is that its evolutionary practice depends utterly on its involutionary sustainability and resilience.

The reverse orders of enabling care for the planet and enabling care in the city depends on the institutions that our city cultures have created to keep us safe, secure and supported so that we can care—at any level of complexity (see Chapter 6 for a full discussion).

Effectively the Master Code is the fundamental "building code" for any integrally informed city—whether we are designing new cities or developing existing cities regardless of where they are located (in the developed world or developing world).

12 Intelligences as Capacities for the City Scale

Geoffrey West (2011, 2017) says companies die, whereas cities persist. How do cities evolve and what characteristics enable them to persist and why is it critical to learn this now?

City life, challenged by global and local security, sustainability threats and resilience meltdown, needs a new paradigm for wellbeing (Hamilton, 2011). The city is now home to more than 50% of humanity and its old operating system is fragmented by traditional reductionism, modern management and post-modern social safety nets.

Integral City is a new paradigm for looking at cities that reveals their bio-psycho-cultural-structural evolutionary roots. An Integral City:

- Responds to critical contexts that situate the city in its eco-region as a living human system on planet Earth
- Creates the bio-psycho-cultural-social climate to build capacity in individuals
- Develops habitats for the prosperity of the collective
- Integrates strategies that bridge and mesh sectors, silos, stovepipes and solitudes
- Continuously evolves intelligences that integrate optimal conditions for city emergence and eco-regional sustainability.

Each of these five capacities derives from the practise of intelligences that are supported by key principles for creating and sustaining the wellbeing of an Integral City. These principles were explored at some depth in Chapter 2, referencing their close relationship to

Sahtouris' Principles of Living Systems (Sahtouris, 1999, 2010, 2017) The five capacities which emerge from the practice of twelve intelligences are organized into an Integral City Compass (Appendix C3) that provides direction and alignment for an integrated operating system for the "human hive". (The core principles for wellbeing are summarized in Appendix C2: Integral City Intelligences).

Figure 8: Integral City Compass: 5 Sets of 12 Intelligences

The five sets of capacities encompassed in an Integral City operating system are these.

I. **Outer Ring: Contexting Intelligences:**

1. **Ecological Intelligence** is an awareness and capacity to respond to the realities of a city's climate and eco-region environment. Just as honey bees adapt themselves to different geographies (see Appendix E), Integral Cities in different locations must adapt different solutions to the same infrastructure problems.

2. **Emergent Intelligence** is the capacity to look at the city as a whole, through the lenses of *aliveness, survival, adaptiveness, regeneration, sustainability and emergence.*

3. **Integral Intelligence** uses five essential maps to integrate city life:

   a. the four quadrant perspectival map of reality (bio-psycho-cultural-social)

   b. the nested holarchy of city systems

   c. the scalar fractal relationship of micro, meso and macro human systems

   d. the complex adaptive dynamic stages of change

   e. the involutionary and evolutionary cycle of spirit

4. **Living Intelligence** relates to the aliveness of each citizen through each of his/her lifecycle stages and the aliveness of the city through its lifecycle stages. Living intelligence asks: how can we align and optimize the life of people in the city at each stage of life? How can we align and optimize the lifecycle stage of the city with its people?

2. **Inner Ring Upper: Individual Intelligence**

   1. **Inner Intelligence** is the "I" space of each citizen. It is the seat of intentional consciousness, attention, interior experience and intelligences or lines of development, e.g. emotional, cognitive, spiritual.

   2. **Outer intelligence** is the biological "It" space of the citizen — the space where the body acts and behaves. Behaviors demonstrate our intelligence in action. Demographics are key determinants of our intentional, cultural and social capacities, because they represent the bodies through which our intentions, cultures and systems are delivered.

3. **Inner Ring Lower: Collective Intelligences**

   1. **Cultural (or Storytelling) Intelligence** represents the "We" life of the city. It considers the relationships in the city which transcend boundaries that both contain and separate, including: the individual and the group voice; multiple levels of values; and city cultures and rural cultures.

   2. **Social (Structural) (or Building) Intelligence** represents the "Its" space of the city. This intelligence connects us to the realities of the

city, that we see, feel, hear, smell, touch and taste. It gives us the capacity to structure and systematize our environment.

4. **Middle Ring: Strategic Intelligences**

 1. **Inquiry Intelligence** asks key questions that reveal the meta-wisdom of the city:

 a. What is important to you?

 b. What's working in your life, family, community, school, health system, city?

 c. What's not working in your life, family, community, school, health system, city?

 d. What is your vision of the optimum in your life, family, community, school, health system, city?

 e. Where do you source your bio-psycho-cultural-social energy in the city?

 2. **Meshworking Intelligence** creates a "meshwork" by weaving together the best of two operating systems — one that self-organizes, and one that replicates hierarchical structures. The resulting meshwork creates and aligns complex responsive structures and systems that flex and flow.

 3. **Navigating Intelligence** monitors and discloses the wellbeing or general condition of the city. It uses a vital signs monitor as a reporting mechanism or protocol which monitors and discloses the health of the city. It includes five key indicators for an Integral dashboard:

 a. Climate change

 b. Environmental health

 c. Society's responses to environmental problems

 d. Positive economic relationships

 e. Incongruent neighbors ((Hamilton, 2008, p. 11)

5. **Centre Ring: Evolutionary Intelligence**

 Evolutionary Intelligence is the spiritual impulse that gives us the capacity to transcend and include the intelligences we currently demonstrate, in order to allow new intelligences to emerge. Evolutionary intelligence looks backward at our evolutionary history and forward to our evolutionary future. It assumes that life conditions will continue to change and the human species will change and adapt and evolve with such changes.

Using an Integral City paradigm has many advantages for understanding the evolution of cities. It engages the voices of experts to share leading edge insights that align us. It meshes diverse thought leaders into transdisciplinary dialogues that build bridges across sectors. It enables policy makers to learn from transectoral conversations that assist continuous exchanges of knowledge and practices. It facilitates citizen responsibility that activates people on the margins as well as those in the center of city life.

Our Integral City paradigm can recalibrate the energy of cities in the developed world. But, this paradigm also offers evolutionary developmental explanations of the functioning of cities everywhere.

In Book 2, Chapter 5 and Appendix C2 (Hamilton, 2017) we formulated an Assessment Worksheet to take a Discovery Tour of existing cities that reveals the levels of development for each of the intelligences and also the degree to which the Master Code is practised. It can be used in cities in the developed world as well as the developing world.

5 Maps that Reveal Anthroposphere in the City

The impact of the intelligences in the city (Hamilton, 2008) can be tracked through the five maps that give us five views of city (and eco-regional) life, revealing the interrelationship of individuals, groups, sectors and sections (as set out in Appendix B). Although each map offers only a partial perspective (Hamilton, 2008, 2014), together they give a comprehensive picture of the "human hive" as interconnected, fractal, holographic and alive. A brief description of each map follows (with illustrations and full descriptions in Appendix B: Integral City Maps (1–5)) with a particular focus on what value it offers to understand city development.

Map 1: City as Holon—The Four Quadrant, Eight Level Map

This map shows how civilization in the city arises from both an individual/collective and interior/exterior expression (Wilber, 1995). Map 1 is analogous to a "plan view" of human life and provides the coordinates for what Wilber calls "Kosmic addresses" (Wilber, 2006).

The value of Map 1 for city development is that it situates perspectives and methodologies for seeing the city as a whole living system. It locates the parts, partial views and fragments of the city so that they can inform one another. Map 1 provides the common denominators to compare one city with another, especially through the measurement of capacity in each quadrant and each level of development. (This has also been well applied to research on retail supply chains at an international scale by Hochachka (2015)).

Map 2: Nested Holarchy of City Systems

The city as a human system is a nest of systems made up of centers (Alexander, 2004), holons (Koestler) or nested holons (Sahtouris, 1999). The systems have orders of complexity, so that the holons, wholes and centers are nested into holarchies (Wilber, 1996c) or panarchies (Gunderson & Holling, 2002) where levels of complexity (and scale) emerge over time.

The value of Map 2 for city development is that it reveals the core relationships in the city particularly arising because every individual is a member of multiple city sub-systems or sectors (e.g. family, workplace, education system(s), healthcare system(s), place(s) of worship, neighborhood, city hall, and environment). Relationships and connections amongst individuals create sub-systems and spheres of influence, networks, communities of practice and meshworks that reveal how densification and/or alignment emerge in the city (Hamilton, 2010).

Map 3: Scalar Fractal Relationship of Micro, Meso and Macro Social Holons

Map 3 shows the city as a social holon. A social holon is any group of people. Its qualities are not summative but dynamic capacities that come from the unique contributions of each individual holon in the social grouping. Map 3 conveys how capacity development in an individual contributes to capacity in all the holons of Map 2, while also revealing the reality of capacity dilution and amplification in the social holons of groups, organizations and communities.

The value of Map 3 to city development is that it reveals the city as consciousness and culture that is dynamic, arising from the tension between levels of development in collectives and individuals. Resolution of these tensions emerges when critical mass of individual behaviors in the collective becomes coherent (for example, a minimum critical number of women choose to demand the vote). Likewise, one group or cohort in a sector will find it difficult to be successful until a critical mass of groups also commits to the same practise (for example, the traditional crafts created by women create an economic strategy for a city to develop micro-financing for craft-based eco-tourism). Complexity science reveals that only 10 to 15 percent of a population needs to change, in order for the whole system to shift towards that change. (Gladwell, 2002; Hamilton, 2008).

Map 4: Complex Adaptive Structures of City Change

Map 4 conveys the stages of structural organizational change in the city. (This map is also a proxy for the organization of the brain as it structurally complexifies.) Living human systems in the city are constantly adapting to life conditions. Adaptations arise from both external causes (like tectonic shifts) and from internal causes (like bio-psycho-cultural-social triggers such as social media use).

The value of Map 4 to city development is that it provides a map of structural complexity for a multiplicity of organizational practices, expressed at all eight levels of complexity. This allows city developers to correlate and meshwork all the Traditional, Modern, Post-Modern and Integral structures co-existing and operating in the 21st century city.

Map 5: Spirituality in the City

Map 5 conveys the qualities of spirituality in the city. Its zones of Grace, Space and Place reveal where the core spiritual values of Goodness, Truth and Beauty are manifested. Spirituality responds through these qualities and values in a holographic involutionary and evolutionary cycle, through three levels: Resource, Field and Source. (For full discussion, see Chapter 1: Spirituality in the Human Hive: Involutionary & Evolutionary Cycle of Love, and for the illustrated graphic and explanations see Appendix B: Integral City Maps (1–5)).

The value of Map 5 to city development is that it transcends and includes the other 4 Maps so we can see the invisible energies of the city (and as a result reveal the Kosmic location and contribution of Goodness, Truth and Beauty in both an involutionary and evolutionary context). Map 5 unpacks how the Master Code energizes all scales of human systems as Care, Context and Capacity flow through them. Map 5 shows the dynamics of the core Evolutionary Intelligence that empowers the city to be Gaia's Reflective Organ. When the spiritual zones and values are misaligned at any scale, the effect of that misalignment ripples throughout all the scales of human systems included in the Integral City. Map 5 unpacks the spiritual elements of what contributes to development in all human systems at all scales.

These five maps give us a technology to navigate design and development in the Integral City whether it is located in the developed world or the developing world. But before we apply these lenses to examine their functionality in particular cities, let us return to the Biosphere and Cosmosphere to appreciate the life conditions that the Anthroposphere has co-created on the globe.

A Meta-Framework for Tracing the Evolutionary Roots of Cities

As discussed in Chapter 6, Eddy (2003) (see Appendix D) reframed the study of geography as a history of the universe and world, within an Integral model and ecosystem science. His frame contexts the evolution of city systems within three strata: the Cosmosphere that spans the universe; the Biosphere that includes the living global environment; and the Anthroposphere that embraces the human condition. Eddy's map effectively integrates the human condition within the three spheres as massively entangled at all scales and times. His research underpins the five capacities and twelve intelligences in the Integral City as set out in Table 28.

ANTHROPOSPHERE MATURING

In purely biological terms, the success of the Anthroposphere can be measured by the rise in global population. Figure 9 illustrates the exponential rate at which human population has grown and is anticipated to continue to grow.

Table 28: Summary of Eddy Spheres & Integral City Intelligences

Integral City Intelligence	Cosmosphere	Biosphere	Anthroposphere
Contexting: Ecological Emergent Integral Living	 X X X X	 X X X X	 X X X X
Individual: Inner Outer		 X	 X
Collective: Cultural Social		 X	 X
Strategic: Inquiry Meshworking Navigating			 X X X
Evolutionary	X	X	X

A SHORT HISTORY OF POPULATION   POPULATION IN BILLIONS OF PEOPLE

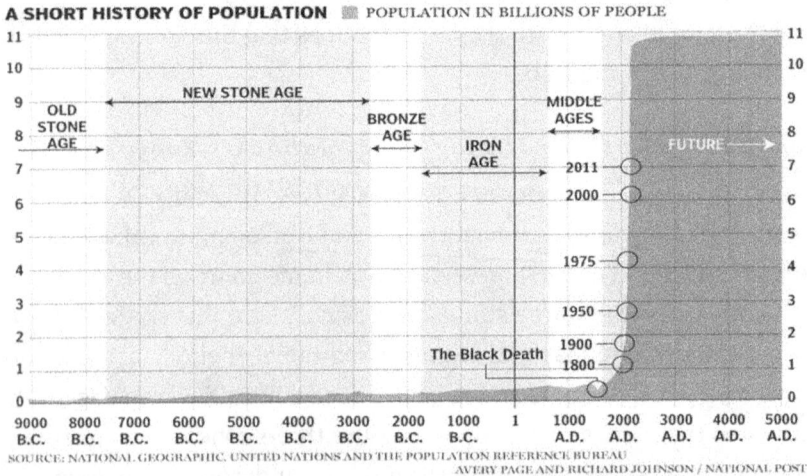

SOURCE: NATIONAL GEOGRAPHIC, UNITED NATIONS AND THE POPULATION REFERENCE BUREAU
AVERY PAGE AND RICHARD JOHNSON / NATIONAL POST

Figure 9: Human Population Growth Past & Future (Page & Johnson, 2011)
Material republished with the express permission of: National Post, a division of Post-media Network Inc. Data in this material was sourced from the United Nations and is shared with permission from the United Nations. Source: https://nationalpost.com/news/graphic-how-human-population-growth-may-plateau

In relating this population growth to cities we can date the first city with over 1 million inhabitants in 1800 (Beijing). By 1900 the world's 10 largest cities had populations in the range of 1.4 to 6.4 million. By 1950 the world's 10 largest cities had populations in the range of 4.8 to 12.4 million. By 2000 the world's 10 largest cities had populations in the range of 14 to 33 million. (All figures from VanSustern (2007).) As a corollary to the global population data, recent analysis of regional demographic profiles shows changes to worldviews and human capacities as the society matures in complexity (Page & Johnson, 2011). Figure 10 shows the demographic profiles of four societies: Traditional/Pre-Industrial, Pre-Modern/Boom Time, Modern (Industrial)/Still Rising and Post Modern-Early Integral/The Plateau. The clear trend is that as societies become more complex (measured in terms of wealth and/or development), population fertility rates drop, life spans lengthen and total population size stabilizes or reduces.

POPULATION GROWTH

PHASE 1: Preindustrial	PHASE 2: Boom time	PHASE 3: Still rising	PHASE 4: The plateau
Disease, poor living conditions, and warfare can lead to a high death rate that exceeds the birth rate.	Better sanitation, health care and food supply cause the death rate to drop.	Birth rates decline as women gain access to education	Birth rate drops. The population stabilizes or even declines.

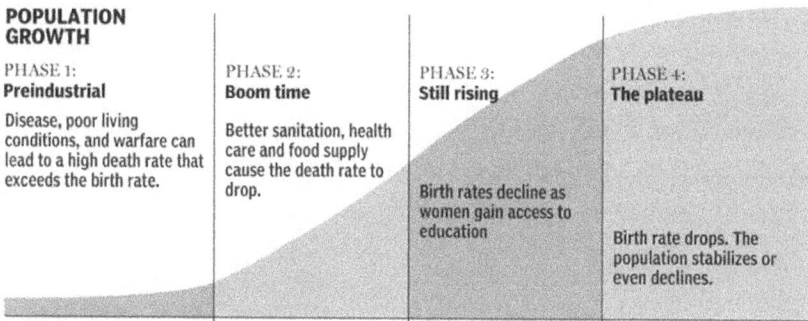

Source: National Geographic, United Nations and the Population Reference Bureau, Avery Page and Richard Johnson/ National Post, August 13, 2011

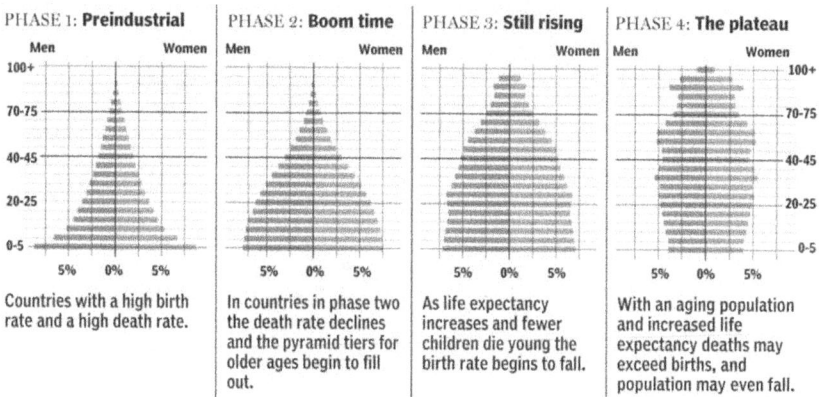

PHASE 1: Preindustrial	PHASE 2: Boom time	PHASE 3: Still rising	PHASE 4: The plateau
Countries with a high birth rate and a high death rate.	In countries in phase two the death rate declines and the pyramid tiers for older ages begin to fill out.	As life expectancy increases and fewer children die young the birth rate begins to fall.	With an aging population and increased life expectancy deaths may exceed births, and population may even fall.

Source: National Geographic, United Nations and the Population Reference Bureau, Avery Page and Richard Johnson/ National Post, August 13, 2011

Figure 10: Demographic Profiles of Four Societies (Page & Johnson, 2011)
Material republished with the express permission of: National Post, a division of Postmedia Network Inc. Data in this material was sourced from the United Nations and is shared with permission from the United Nations. Source: https://nationalpost.com/news/graphic-how-human-population-growth-may-plateau

Beck (nd) has proposed that in large scale human systems such changes in complexity impact the political systems, economics and wellbeing of societies. Beck (nd) draws a global map of stratified complexity distribution where less developed and/or low income countries show cultural profiles in the 21st century related to developmental levels 1 to 4 (with larger bulges at Level 2 and Level 3 for less developed countries), while more developed and/or high income countries show cultural profiles with bulges in the Level 5 to 6 range (with indications of Level 7 coming on stream in Northern Europe and Singapore). Beck makes the point that democracy as a governance system comes in many forms that align with the stages of maturity of a country.

We would propose that cities are the key zones where each of these core society profiles (Traditional, Pre-Modern, Modern, Post-Modern/Integral) emerge. The profiles seen in the sample Figure 11 nations (less and more developed) and Figure 12 (low and high income) effectively make visible the demographic shapes of the human hive at ever increasing stages of complexity in the years 1950, 2017, 2050 and 2100.

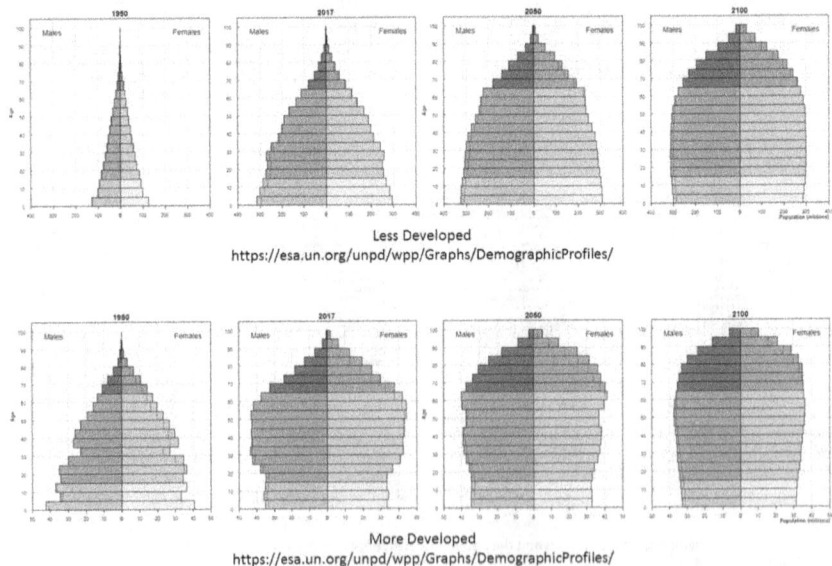

Less Developed
https://esa.un.org/unpd/wpp/Graphs/DemographicProfiles/

More Developed
https://esa.un.org/unpd/wpp/Graphs/DemographicProfiles/

Figure 11: Demographic Profiles of Less & More Developed Nations
Population pyramids from World Population Prospects 2017 for Less Developed and More Developed Regions (retrieved from: https://esa.un.org/unpd/wpp/Graphs/DemographicProfiles/). Copyright c 2017. United Nations. Reprinted with the permission of the United Nations.

Low Income
https://esa.un.org/unpd/wpp/Graphs/DemographicProfiles/

High Income
https://esa.un.org/unpd/wpp/Graphs/DemographicProfiles/

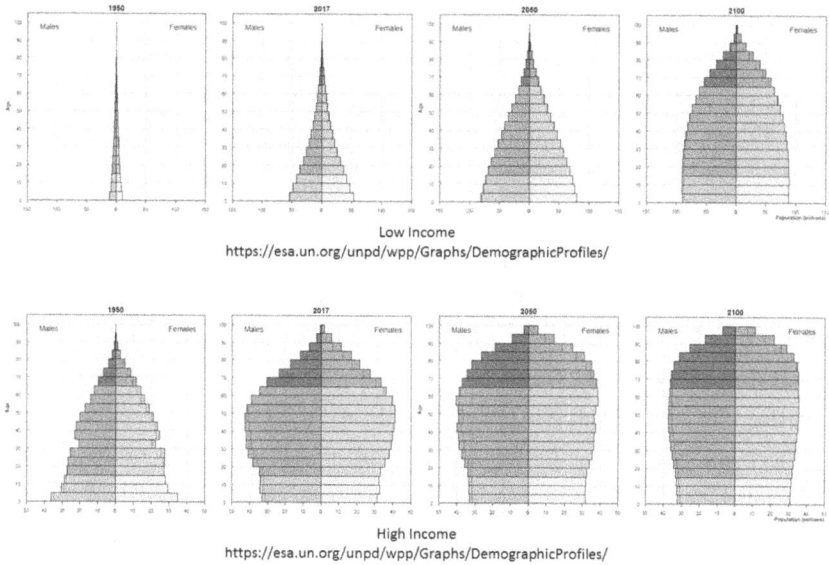

Figure 12: Demographic Profiles of Low & High Income Nations
Population pyramids from World Population Prospects 2017 for High Income and Low Income Countries (retrieved from: https://esa.un.org/unpd/wpp/Graphs/DemographicProfiles/). Copyright c 2017. United Nations. Reprinted with the permission of the United Nations.

As we explored in Chapter 6, along with these evolving population profiles, life conditions have also shifted in cities around the world, producing a toxic mix of interconnected threats. The relationship of natural capital to human endeavor has been effectively mapped by Taylor (2008), who demonstrates in total that human society (in the industrial and post-industrial world) is almost bankrupt because it no longer utilizes the renewable resource "interest" produced by natural capital, but is now consuming Earth's capital at a dangerous and unsustainable rate. As noted by Rees and Wackernagel (1994) over two decades ago, living at this rate of consumption demands the equivalent of three to four planets.

From an economic perspective, the trajectory of threats to our cities (as detailed in Chapter 6) translates the relationship of natural capital to human endeavor (Taylor, 2008) , within Eddy's evolutionary ABC contexts. In this view (Figure 6), it is apparent that city (and global) threats have deep interdependent evolutionary roots. Furthermore, it demonstrates that the resolution of these issues demands an evolutionary solution—especially if we want to build "new cities".

Implications for Development of Existing Cities

As we have seen in Chapter 6, an evolutionary analysis of sustainability threats tells us that cities in the developing world face different categories of risk than cities in the developed world. These measures of risk can be related to both the internal ways of thinking, cultural beliefs and visions of the city (by individual holons and collective social holons), as well as in the external behaviors and structures and systems of the city. Greiving et al offered a new paradigm for risk assessment and management using an Integral model that demonstrated a spectrum of strategies would be more resource and outcome effective (Greiving et al., 2007) than any single strategy. These integrally defined categories (essentially representing the four quadrants of realities that are captured in the Integral Map 1 (in Appendix B: Integral City Maps (1–5)) become more intertwined as the levels of complexity emerge.

Resilience of Developed City Sendai, Japan

For instance, the (lithospheric) magnitude 9 tectonic quake in 2011 in post-modern Sendai, Japan impacted energy, water, climate, food production, ecology destruction and psycho-cultural-social strata with ripple effects that were felt around the world because of the advanced interconnection of Japan's economy with the global economy. Remarkably one year later in 2012, although the nuclear energy threat was still ongoing, most of the other impacts had been addressed and life had returned to a post-modern norm because the city, the nation and the global emergency response systems had deep, complexly developed, evolutionary capacities to build on. On the other hand, evidence in 2017 indicated the ongoing impacts of the event on the environment as floating debris and alien biosystems washed up on the shores of North America (anon, 2017b).

Vulnerability of Less Developed City Port au Prince, Haiti

By comparison, the (lithospheric) magnitude 7 tectonic quake in 2010, in traditional/pre-modern Port Au Prince Haiti generated the same ripple effect of stratified decapacitation. However, seven years later, life in Haiti had not even been restored even to the traditional/pre-modern norms prior to the earthquake, because the city, the nation and the global emergency response agencies had only limited, evolutionary, developmental capacities to build on, and they were all further challenged by the series of tropical storms that set back progress in the following years.

Ecological Implications for City Sustainability & City Development

When threats to sustainability occur that are as dire as these earthquakes, it becomes apparent that restoring city capacities depends on strategies that must be evolutionarily appropriate to the level of complexity of the city while keeping in mind its ecology, climate and natural capital load (Esborn-Hargens & Zimmerman; Zimmerman 2010, 2005).

These examples of disaster-based meltdowns, are dramatic scenarios that condense the focus of demands and responses needed by "normal" city development. However, they dramatically illustrate the dilemma of development in the developed world (Sendai) compared to the developing world (Haiti).

Where the threats are less dramatic, for example where deterioration has occurred over extended time frames, the results may be no less drastic. For instance, in countries where industrialization has not been supported by social equity for workers' or citizens' health and safety, toxic soups of physical and chemical deterioration endanger human survival. We can consider many current conditions of polluted cities from cold-war Russia; the electronic and shipping recycling dumps in China and India; and the maquiladoras in Mexico and southern Asia. These cities are stuck in life conditions that have long ago threatened the health of the local Biosphere and toxified the Cosmosphere sufficiently to imperil the health of the Anthroposphere. These same threats are now increasing regional and global deterioration, including global temperature increases, CO_2 emissions, terrorism, corruption, refugee displacement and governance participation; and are clearly impacting any clear resolution of deforestation, democratization of large cities, non-fossil fuel adoption and unemployment (Glenn et al., 2011a, p. 3; 2011b).

Reframing with Systems Thinking

This becomes the starting point for framing the challenges of development in terms of priority and with systems thinking lenses (which emerge from Level 7 consciousness). Meadows (Meadows, 2008) long ago worked out the core leverage points to intervene in a system as (from least effective at the rating of 12 to most effective at the rating of 1):

12. Numbers
11. Buffers
10. Stock-and-Flow Structures
9. Delays
8. Balancing Feedback Loops
7. Reinforcing Feedback Loops
6. Information Flows
5. Rules
4. Self-organization
3. Goals
2. Paradigms
1. Transcending Paradigms

Keeping the most effective leverage points in mind as the paradigms in use and how to transcend them, we discover in the Integral City Map 4 (Appendix B) clues to understanding what are the driving values of the Traditional, Pre-Modern/Modern, Post-modern, and Integral paradigms as shown in Table 29.

Table 29: Paradigms & Levels of Complexity (adapted from D. Beck with permission)

Level of Complexity	Who is Center of the Universe?	What is Driving Value
Integral	Globe	Global Wellbeing
	Natural System	Flex/Flow
Post-Modern	Social Network	Caring & Sharing
	World Economy	Performance
Pre-Modern/Modern	Nation/State	Authority
	Kingdom	Power
Traditional	Family/Clan/Tribe	Belonging
	Individual	Survival

In effect Table 29 (and Map 4 Appendix B) shows us a relationship between the worldviews (which define who is the center of the universe), driving values and the level of complexity. The more advanced levels of complexity (Integral, post-modern and modern) act as the amplifiers to the capacity of the structures in cities in the developed world (like Sendai). On the other hand, the less complex levels of complexity (traditional and pre-modern/modern) act as the limiters and filters to complexity and capacity of the structures in cities in the developing world (like Port Au Prince).

With this combination of insights from the evolutionary, stratified map of the ABC/CBA spheres (Table 11), the map of the stratified threats (Table 12), and the map of helpful signs (Table 13), we have input that can enable us to design a strategy for city development that aligns development with the systems embedded in the people, place, priorities and planet who will be impacted.

With such an approach to existing cities in mind and hand, let us now look at the challenges for designing whole new cities.

DESIGNING NEW CITIES

Beyond the challenges of bringing new lenses to the development of existing cities, we are now asked to consider how to design Neo-Cities such as those imagined by Yury Lifshits (2016) and Elon Musk (Titcomb, 2017).

Questions for Neo-Cities as Human Hives

Lifshits conceptual approach seems very aligned to designing human hives. By all accounts his team designs in many elements that give the city beauty, fitness to the environment and alignment with the intentions of the people who will potentially live there.

The proof of this design approach, will be that these new cities will actually be designed WITH the people who will live there. (Even though I have reservations, when the target market for such neo-cities are imagined to be an elite group who will choose to live in a city that enables them to co-exist with others who share interests.)

The questions we need to ask designers, investors and developers focuses on how they might step out beyond merely projecting their own intentions and expectations onto their designs (instead of just imagining these new cities will exist apart from the Traditional, Pre-Modern, Modern and Post-Modern/ cities that already exist)? Here are some questions to ask these stakeholders:

- How is a Neo-City just the leading edge of cities of the future? Do we expect them to emerge as the logical next step for cities?
- The Neo-City assumes that it is possible to create a specialized habitat for humans with select interests. But I have some questions that beg to be answered:
  - ○ How will Neo-Cities learn from the Masdar or Dubai effect— where construction and maintenance workers cannot afford to live there?
  - ○ How do Neo-Cities administer themselves democratically?
  - ○ How do the voices of non-elite workers and residents get equally heard with those of the elite?
  - ○ How do Neo-Cities avoid developing caste systems (internally or in comparison to external cities)?

Internal Requirements of Neo-Cities

Thinking about the Neo-Cities of Lifshits (or Elon Musk's plan for a city on Mars) is undeniably exciting, especially when they seem to be really designed with the external requirements of the human hive in mind.

But, when viewing the ghost cities in China which have been built and stand virtually empty without residents, we must be curious if designers of Neo-Cities have considered any of the internal requirements of the human hive; such as:

- Considering that humans go through a developmental cycle, how have they built into the design of the city, the fact that we all start out at a basic developmental stage and must learn our way through a series of such stages?
- Do the designers recognize vertical development in themselves? Have they made allowances for continuous learning and the need/opportunity for the city to change? (DeKay, 2011)
- What happens if assumptions about the city's environment (both internal and external) are drastically altered by events not under the designer's control (e.g. natural disasters, or man-made invasions)?

- How do Neo-Cities respond to the need to defend themselves from external invaders? How do they defend themselves against envy, greed, power-plays?
- What is the right relationship of Neo-Cities to other Neo-Cities and Traditional, Pre-modern/Modern, Post-Modern Cities?

Neo-Cities Need Neo-Civics

With Neo-Cities on the drawing boards—and even before Investor Boards, I wonder if the investors will consider similar aspects of investing in cities as they do in entrepreneurial start-ups, especially remembering the importance of the organizational team? (In the last year alone, I have encountered intentions for creating new city projects in the USA, Canada, UK, Spain, Russia for such projects).

In entrepreneurial ventures the quality of the people generally outweighs the most clever of ideas or the most unusual patents. I suggest the same considerations for team quality ought to be true of Neo-Cities. But how will that be done? Here are more questions to consider:

- Will there be an application process for citizens? Will the investors form a recruitment team for desirable citizens?
- What criteria will they use to choose the initial citizens?
- Will the criteria hold the same seeds of disaster that many an intentional community has sown?
- How will the recruiters separate their own biases from the needs of the Neo-City?
- How will the designers build in the appropriate form of governance? Will they design the first stage and then expect neo-politicians to take over the subsequent stages of developing governance—like condominium/strata corporations?
- Will the state become involved in setting standards for Neo-Cities?
- Will Neo-Cities exempt themselves from state interference through economic separation of banking and transactional exchanges?
- Does a Neo-City need a neo-civics? Would that evolve out of Integral City's 4 Voices and 4 Roles???

- Might the Integral City 4 Voices provide the stem-cells for such a neo-civics?

ACTION RESEARCH FOR DEVELOPMENTAL DIRECTION

Integral City developmental meshworking has already been unpacked and described in considerable detail in Book 2 (Hamilton, 2017). There we used an approach of Action Research/Inquiry/Learning to describe the steps to take for designing placecaring and placemaking with impact.

Book 2 walks Integral City developers through the steps of designing participatory processes for accessing the Knowing Field, embracing the Master Code, assessing the 12 intelligences, discovering and mapping city values and vital signs, engaging the 4 Voices, prototyping designs, meshworking people, place, priorities and planet, and evaluating impact.

DEVELOPMENT STRATEGIES

In summarizing a developmental strategy for an Integral City we start with an Integral lens to design appropriate responses first of all for threat adaptation, mitigation and/or prevention as outlined in Chapter 6 (Hamilton, 2011). Then we look for the opportunities for city development that are revealed by the city's levels of complexity, worldviews and values (Hochachka, 2005, 2015). We call this Integral approach "meshworking", as it meshes or weaves together all the opportunities (and responses to all of the ABC capacities and threats) in an evolutionarily compatible way.

Not surprisingly the roots of our designs for city wellbeing that were explored in relation to creativity in Chapter 2, offer us a way of imagining the human hive that we can explore with the core principles of living systems, the 12 intelligences, 5 maps and 4 Voices. Appendix F provides a summary for imagining why, how and when the principles can be implemented to initiate the design strategy.

Essentially these core principles of meshworking for city development build on Books 1 and 2 (Hamilton, 2010, 2017) and include the following:

Implement the Master Code

1. Create an *Agreement to Work Together* with the Formation Team (including all 4 Voices), based on the Master Code: Take care of Self, so

that you can care for Others, so together we care for our Place(s), and all of us can care for our Planet.

Honor the Spheres

2. Identify the change condition of the ABC spheres of the city container (Figure 5).

Recognize Threat(s)

3. Name and evolutionarily map the environmental threat(s) in the system—overcoming the dissonance that provides the impetus or catalyst to change (Figure 6).

Develop with Purpose

4. Identify the purpose for developmental change—create the vision for changing the city from what to what (e.g. Traditional to Modern; or Modern to Post-Modern; or Post-Modern to Integral)?

Engage Stakeholders

5. Use Integral City maps 1,2,3,4,5 to find the agents for developmental change—engage all the 4 Voices (as many stakeholders in the process as possible)—actively seek out diversity and make room for difference.

6. Enable leadership to emerge to champion the development and address the threat(s) at the appropriate levels of complexity (Figure 6 & Table 12).

Facilitate Change Processes

7. Amplify the resources available for development from all 5 maps (in Step 4) so others can see them (e.g. in scenario planning).

8. Amplify the threat(s) to development so others can see it/them (Figure 6).

9. Integrally identify the resources needed to facilitate the change and invite and involve stakeholders to contribute to them (Figure 6 & Table 13).

Design with Integral Methodologies

10. Use Integral City Master Code, Compass, Intelligences and Principles as checklists to determine "right action".

11. Co-design Integral methodologies for developmental change that self-organize passion, purpose, priorities, people, and planet. Expect it to be messy.

Learn from Feedback Loops

12. Create reflective feedback loops and Integral vital signs monitors (based on Navigational Intelligence) so that participants can self-correct and develop operational structures that work.

13. Make the feedback accessible to all by communication, publication and display; e.g. community gatherings, community newspapers, online media, real time intelligence display systems.

14. Pay forward to other stakeholders, cities, the Integral learning for development, evolution and adaptation.

Practise the Master Code

15. Take care of Self, so that you can care for Others, so together we care for our Place(s), and all of us can care for our Planet.

CONCLUSIONS

This chapter suggests that developmental change starts with a commitment to practising the Master Code. A spectrum of strategies is needed to effectively align city development with Earth's evolutionary strata.

Applying our evolutionary intelligences is likely to be a necessary commitment to actually ensure the survival of the human species long enough for us to mature beyond the over-consumption of our natural capital in every eco-region on this planet.

Thus we have many decades (if not generations) of Integral City capacity building ahead of us to create self-sustaining human habitats on our home planet. This will require us to grow the capacities of collaboration, community, and urbanization beyond any context the human system has ever evolved. We will need to work at multiple scales simultaneously—as the preceding chapters explore the scales of human systems nested within the city as a whole: communities, organizations, families/groups and individual leadership.

Furthermore, applying evolutionary strategic design will not just be useful for considering different approaches to cities in the developed and developing worlds with a plurality of immigrant cultures, as modern cities contain many worlds, but also to designing new cities that embrace the developmental trajectory of the human system at all scales. As noted in Book 1 (Hamilton, 2008) these design approaches can also apply to designing space stations, and space colonies (such as those being considered by Musk on Mars (Titcomb, 2017). And these design elements certainly presage Book 4 in the Integral City series, with its exploration of the evolutionary eras of the human hive.

REFERENCES

Adger, N., Aggarwal, P., Argawala, S., Alcamo, J., & etal. (2007). *Climate Change 2007: Impacts, Adaptation and Vulnerability, Summary for Policy Makers.* Retrieved from http://www.ipcc.ch/

anon. (2000). Millennium Development Goals. Retrieved December 21, 2017, from UN: http://en.wikipedia.org/wiki/Millennium_Development_Goals

anon. (2011). World Health Organization Global Alert and Response (GAR). Retrieved December 21, 2017: http://www.who.int/csr/don/en/

anon. (2017a). Sustainable Development Goals. Retrieved December 11, 2017, from Wikipedia https://en.wikipedia.org/wiki/Sustainable_Development_Goals

anon. (2017b). Very impressive' marine life enters North America on debris from Japanese tsunami. Retrieved December 21, 2017, from CBC http://www.cbc.ca/news/technology/japanese-tsunami-marine-life-west-coast-1.4311877

Beck, D. (nd). Stratified Democracy. Retrieved December 20, 2017, from http://www.humanemergence.org/essays/stages_of_social_development.htm

Brown, L. (2008). *Plan B 3.0.* New York: W.W. Norton & Company.

DeKay, M. (2011). *Integral Sustainable Design: Transformative Perspectives.* London, UK: Earthscan.

Diamond, J. (2005). *Collapse: How societies choose to fail or succeed* (first ed.). New York: Penguin Group.

Eddy, B. (2003). *Sustainable Development, Spiral Dynamics, and Spatial Data: A '3i' Approach to SD*. Paper presented at the Spiral Dynamics integral, Level II, Ottawa, 2003.

Eddy, B. (2005). Place, Space and Perspective. *World Futures*, 61, 151–163.

Esbjörn-Hargens, S., & Zimmerman, M. (2009). *Integral Ecology: Uniting Multiple Perspectives on the Natural World*. Boston: Shambhala Publications Inc.

Gladwell, M. (2002). *The Tipping Point: How Little Things Can Make a Big Difference*. Back Bay Books.

Glenn, J. C., Gordon, T. J., & Florescu, E. (2011a). *State of the Future* 2011: The Millennium Project.

Glenn, J. C., Gordon, T. J., & Florescu, E. (2011b). State of the Future 2011 Electronic Research CDpp. (8000).

Greiving, S., Wanczura, S., Vossebuerger, P., Sucker, K., & Fourman, M. (2007). *Multidimensional Integrated Risk Governance: Scalable Resilience and Risk Governance Concept Including Guidelines on Stakeholder Involvement*. London, UK: UNIDO, IKU.

Gunderson, L. C., & Holling, C. S. (Eds.). (2002). *Panarchy: Understanding Transformations in Human and Natural Systems*. Washington, DC: Island Press.

Hamilton, M. (2008). *Integral City: Evolutionary Intelligences for the Human Hive*. Gabriola Island BC: New Society Publishers.

Hamilton, M. (2010). Meshworking Integral Intelligences for Resilient Environments; Enabling Order and Creativity in the Human Hive. Paper presented at the Enacting an Integral Future Conference.

Hamilton, M. (2011). Big Picture for Sustainability Leadership: Life Conditions for Leading from our Deepest & Widest Perspectives. Paper presented at the Embody Integral Leadership Conference.

Hamilton, M. (2014). Meta-Framework for Security in the Human Hive: Integrally Aligning Sustainability Responses to Trajectory of Evolutionary Threats. *Systems Research and Behavioral Science, Syst.Res.* 31, 614–626. Retrieved from doi:10.1002/sres.2310

Hamilton, M. (2017). *Integral City Inquiry and Action: Designing Impact for the Human Hive*. Phoenix, AZ: Integral Publishers.

Hamilton, M., & Sanders, B. (2013). *Integral City 2.0 Online Conference 2012 Proceedings: A Radically Optimistic Inquiry Into Operating System 2.0*. M. Hamilton (Ed.) Retrieved from http://www.scribd.com/doc/120713339/

Integral-City-2-0-Online-Conference-2012-A-Radically-Optimistic-Inquiry-into-Operating-System-2-0

Hochachka, G. (2005). *Developing Sustainability, Developing the Self: An Integral Approach to International and Community Development*. Polis Project on Ecological Governance, University of Victoria.

Hochachka, G. (2015).—Integral Transformation of Value Chains: One Sky's Integral Leadership Program in the Brazil Nut Value Chain in Peru and Bolivia. Retrieved December 22, 2017 from Integral Leadership Review http://integralleadershipreview.com/12393-115-integral-transformation-value-chains-one-skys-integral-leadership-program-brazil-nut-value-chain-peru-bolivia/

Landry, C. (2007). *The Art of City Making*. London, UK: Earthscan Comedia.

Landry, C., & Murray, C. (2017). *Psychology & the City*. Bournes Green Near Stroud, UK: Comedia.

Lifshits, Y. (2016). Neocities and Neodistricts:A Framework for Building Cities of The Future. Retrieved December 21, 2017 https://medium.com/@yurylifshits/neocity-aa102731911b

Linton, J. (2010). *What is Water? The History of a Modern Abstraction*. Vancouver, BC, Canada: UBC Press.

Lovelock, J. (2009). *The Vanishing Face of Gaia*. New York: Harmony Books.

McKibben, B. (2007). *Deep Economy: The Wealth of Communities and the Durable Future*. New York: Time Books Henry Holt and Company, LLC.

McKibben, B. (2011). 350.Org. Retrieved January 10, 2010, from 350.Org: http://www.350.org/

Meadows, D. (2008). *Thinking in Systems*. White River Junction, VT: Chelsea Green Publishing.

Monbiot, G., & Prescott, M. (2007). *Heat: How to Stop the Planet From Burning*. Toronto: Anchor Canada.

Page, A., & Johnson, R. (2011, August 13). Global Population Analysis. *National Post*.

Rees, W. E. P. D., & Wackernagel, M. (1994). *Ecological Footprints and Appropriated Carrying Capacity: Measuring the Natural Capital Requirements of the Human Economy*. Washington, DC: Island Press.

Sahtouris, E. (1999). *Earthdance: Living Systems in Evolution*. Retrieved from http://www.ratical.org/LifeWeb/

Sahtouris, E. (2010). Celebrating Crisis: Towards a Culture of Cooperation. A New Renaissance:Transforming Science, Spirit & Society. London: Floris Books.

Sahtouris, E. (2017). A Tale of Cities and Cells: Our Human Evolutionary Agenda. Retrieved December 7, 2017 https://www.ethicalmarkets.com/a-tale-of-cities-and-cells-by-elisabet-sahtouris/

Taylor, G. (2008). Evolution's Edge: The Coming Collapse and Transformation of our World. Gabriola Island, BC: New Society Publishers.

Titcomb, J. (2017). Mars City: Human missions to space colony will start in 2024, Elon Musk says. Retrieved December 22, 2017, from The Telegraph http://www.telegraph.co.uk/technology/2017/09/29/mars-city-human-missions-space-colony-will-start-2024-elon-musk/

van Schaik, P. (2016). Urban Hub 1: Smart Sustainable Thriveable Cities. UK: Integral Mentors.

van Schaik, P. (2017a). Urban Hub 2: Methodologies & Planning Thriveable Cities. UK: Integral Mentors.

van Schaik, P. (2017b). Urban Hub 3: Integral Theory Thriveable Cities. UK: Integral Mentors.

van Schaik, P. (2017c). Urban Hub 4: Integral Workbook Thriveable Cities. UK: Integral Mentors.

van Schaik, P. (2017d). Urban Hub 5: Visions and Worldviews Thriveable Cities. UK: Integral Mentors.

van Schaik, P. (2017e). Urban Hub 6: Visions and Worldviews 2 Thriveable Cities. UK: Integral Mentors.

van Schaik, P. (2017f). Urban Hub 7: Visions and Worldviews 3 Thriveable Cities. UK: Integral Mentors.

van Schaik, P. (2017g). Urban Hub 8: What We Can Do Cultivating Change Thriveable Cities. UK: Integral Mentors.

VanSusteren, A. (2007). Metropolitan World Atlas. Rotterdam: 010 Publishers.

West, G. (2011). Why Cities Keep Growing, Corporations and People Always Die, and Life Gets Faster. In J. Brockman (Ed.): Edge.org.

West, G. (2017). Scale: The Universal Laws of Growth, Innovation, Sustainability and the Pace of Life in Organisms, Cities, Economies and Companies. New York: Penguin Press.

Wilber, K. (1995). *Sex, Ecology and Spirituality: the spirit of evolution*. Boston: Shambhala Publications Inc.

Wilber, K. (1996). *A Brief History of Everything*. Boston: Shambhala Publications Inc.

Wilber, K. (2000). *A Theory of Everything*. Boston: Shambhala Publications Inc.

Wilber, K. (2006). *Integral Spirituality*. Boston: Shambhala Publications Inc.

Wilber, K. (2007). *The Integral Vision*. Boston: Shambhala Publications Inc.

Wood, P., & Landry, C. (2008). *The Intercultural City: Planning for Diversity Advantage*. London, UK: Earthscan.

Wright, R. (2004). *A Short History of Progress* (Avalon ed.). New York: Carroll & Graf Publishers.

Zimmerman, M. (2010). *Changing the Conversation: Rethinking the Climate Change Debate from an Integral Perspective*. Paper presented at the Enacting an Integral Future Conference.

Zimmerman, M. E. (2005). Integral Ecology: A perspectival, developmental, and coordinating approach to environmental problems *World Futures, Volume 61, Issue 1 & 2 January 2005, pages 50–62* (Issue 1 & 2), 50–62.

Conclusion

Chapter 16, as a **conclusion** to the book summarizes key points from the three sections **and offers a "Now What" methodology for aligning Caring, Contexting and Capacity Building.**

WAKING UP THE HUMAN HIVE: ALIGNING CARE, CONTEXT AND CAPACITY FOR GAIA'S REFLECTIVE ORGANS

CHAPTER SUMMARY

This chapter reviews key points from the three sections of the book: caring, contexting and capacity building for waking up the human hive. It rests on the aspiration that individual cities are evolving to become Gaia's Reflective Organs and together the world's cities are evolving into Gaia's Reflective Organ System. The new science that recognizes cities as complex adaptive systems is expanded to include placecaring qualities that are necessary to sustain placemaking capacities. The Integral City 4 quadrants of intentions, behaviors, cultures and infra/structures provide a framework for perspectives, worldviews and evolving capacities of the 4 Voices of the city: citizens, civic managers, civil society and business. The chapter reviews a methodology to address the VUCA (volatile, uncertain, complex, ambiguous) challenges to city sustainability and resilience and synthesizes how the Master Code of Care creates a strategy for cities to build both stakeholder and city value as they become Gaia's Reflective Organ system.

Keywords: Gaia, reflective organs, reflective organ system, science of cities, VUCA, caring, contexting, capacity building, species intelligence

CITIES ARE REFLECTIVE ORGANS OF GAIA

To the planet, cities are like organs of a living system. Traditionally cities are connected most tightly internally (like organelles in an organ)—where the city mirrors, manages and adapts to the smaller scales of human systems within it. We have learned from both Jacobs (2001) and Diamond (2005) that cities as societies are most connected with their trading partners who supply the resources which build its infrastructures, feed its energy and enable sustainability and even resilience. Traditionally those linkages came from other cities within the same nation (or a mother nation or "trade friendly nation-neighbor") but now we are in an era where cities (in democratic countries) are totally unconstrained to resource themselves from anywhere in the world—including from countries whom their own nation considers hostile.

As a result of this globalization of trade, cities have greater power than ever to undermine the stability of nations (from which cities have gained much of their cultural and systemic life conditions). However, most national governance systems have largely shortchanged the capacity of cities to govern themselves in ways that could optimize their wellbeing. The tensions between city and state are becoming intolerable—and nations are slowly but painfully waking up to the strange possibility that cities may hold the upper hand in the survival game (West, 2017).

The human species still battles within itself for ownership and control rights to resources that within the context of a living system must (if the continued life of the living system is our ultimate value) be superseded by responsibilities to life on the whole planet, which supports all life.

In an attempt to call forth such a world-centric perspective, Integral City through an emerging global constellation of communities of practice using the frameworks from Books 1 and 2 (Hamilton 2008, 2017)) has aligned the intelligences, inquiry, action and impact designs that cities need in order to live in service to global wellbeing. In this Book 3, we have explored how cities act as organs not just to a nation but act as an organ system to the whole planet. In this context, we have recognized cities as Gaia's Reflective Organ system.

THE SCIENCE OF CITIES

When we look at cities through an Integral City lens, we gain multiple perspectives. With an Integral framing (Appendix B, Map 1) we can see the city through 4 quadrants or lenses:

- human intention (UL)
- behavior (UR)
- cultures (LL)
- organizing systems and structures (LR).

These 4 quadrants provide a framework for holding not only different perspectives but also worldviews and emergent capacities. The capacities are further elucidated through the unfolding of the 8 levels of human system development that reflect the complexification of life conditions across human history.

Another way to look at this is that, the Integral City perspective reveals a lineage of human evolution and individual development, where the whole person embraces increasing circles of care and compassion, growing capacities from egocentric to ethnocentric to world centric to Kosmocentric (which we identify at the city scale as Traditional, Modern, Postmodern and Integral).

The elegance of the Integral framing of the human condition is that it is fractal and can be applied at all levels of scale from individuals, to families, teams, organizations, communities, cities, (nations) and eco-regions (see Appendix B, Map 2) (Hamilton, 2015). Because of its fractal nature, this model then offers us not only a map for humans to track their developmental capacities but also to recognize the zones of greatest probable dissonance. For it is precisely between the quadrants, circles of care and scales of human enterprise that eruptions are most likely to occur. In these zones, the multiple realities of human existence rub against each other like tectonic plates causing volcanic eruptions of angry worldviews (think of the Middle East and Catalonia), earthquakes of lost or invaded territory and despair (remember the Ukraine, Rwanda, North Korea) and tsunamis of overwhelming forces (consider colonizers of all stripes).

Science now tells us that cities outlive countries and nations—and their association as federations of concentrated urban life and resources, within nations, gives them particular power that is increasingly being tested by many stakeholders (West, 2017).

VOLATILE—UNCERTAIN—COMPLEX—AMBIGUOUS = VUCA WORLD

Cities and city stakeholders live in a "VUCA" world. Those are the conditions of human life (if not all life) at this time on the planet. Humans are not even the only cause of our "VUCA "life conditions—for we have a whole evolutionary cycle of threats that impact us.

In Chapter 6 I identified the key threats that face us—like geological strata—from our evolutionary past—and how they impact the world today. They include:

- **Psycho-Cultural-Social Threats**
- **Bio-Genetic-Ecological Threats**
- **Food Scarcity**
- **Climate Change**
- **Water Misuse**
- **Energy Transitions**

The challenges to and from each of these strata have created this whole new class of contexts—dubbed by the military as the VUCA world—one that is **Volatile, Uncertain, Complex** and **Ambiguous**. This can seem so overwhelming (and or subtly invasive) that our normal human reaction is a form of consensus trance (Patten, 2018) where we act as if we are powerless in the face of seemingly impossible situations and we act as if we are not threatened, all the while our very beings are being stressed and stretched out of alignment.

As a result of these life conditions the city stakeholders need to develop context-sensitive strategies for building integration capacities capable of:

- sensing the natural environment
- honoring spiritual and elder practices
- manifesting/ focusing/ powerful expression
- following authorized ways

- organizing for strategic results
- serving community justice and diversity
- designing systems that flex and flow
- supporting the principles of life on the planet.

INTEGRAL CITY STRATEGIES FOR GAINING ENERGY & RESOURCES

A city that is a living system must survive, connect with its environment and create conditions for sustainability and resilience (Capra, 1996).

In this book, Integral City offers 3 strategies to do so:

- **Deepen Care;**
- **Raise Contexts for resilience by responding at all scales to VUCA threats as opportunities to grow (also known as "trigger points");**
- **Widen Capacity for readiness in individuals, organizations, systems and cities.**

In Book 4 of this series we will explore how authority, power and influence evolve a fourth strategy, namely to Enable Collaboration at all scales to align dependence, independence and interdependence in a planetary system of Integral Cities.

DEEPENING CARE: START WITH THE MASTER CODE

At time of writing the most complex set of standards identified to support city wellbeing are the Sustainable Development Goals (SDB's) (anon, 2017). However, the SDG's will only be effective if leadership takes action to respond to their data-driven signals. We know from systems theory that the place that has the most leverage to change within the city system is with the city leaders and stakeholders themselves. Leaders play such a vital role, because when leaders are willing and able to change they can gain an "overview" perspective of the whole system (Meadows, 2008). Integral City has proposed that leaders do not exist in just one quadrant but co-exist and tetra-arise in all 4 quadrants (See Appendix B, Map 1). So, it is critical to create the conditions where leaders from all 4 Voices come to the table with the willingness to change. And willingness only comes when people care.

Growing Caring Grows Carrying Capacity

In our research, we discovered that the science of the 4 quadrants combined with the Master Code, works best when we bring together all the stakeholders of the city—the 4 Voices. When the 4 Voices come together, we create conditions to wake them up and grow them up, as a city that is able both to "placecare" and "placemake" (Hamilton, 2017).

Placecaring tends to arise from activating the Left Quadrants (Appendix A) to:
- Care for Self—activates Inner Growth of Individual (I)
- Care for Others—activates Inner Growth of Collective (We).

Placecaring then enables placemaking.

Placemaking arises from activating the Right Quadrants (Appendix A) to:
- Make Place for Self— activates Outer Growth of Home, Work/ Economy (It)
- Make Places for All—activates Outer Growth of Infrastructure, Systems, Development (Its).

In the modern era, cities have tended to focus primarily on placemaking, either ignoring or denying the importance of placecaring. But, it turns out that cities who develop their caring capacity are cities who develop their carrying capacity for economies, systems and infrastructures. Thus, we have learned that caring and carrying capacity need to be in balance.

When we only build value for one stakeholder or one quadrant, the city grows in an unbalanced way. While developers and business naturally focus on placemaking capacities (Right Quadrants), and citizens and civil society naturally focus on placecaring capacities (Left Quadrants), in order to flourish, cities need to bring placecaring and placemaking into an organic flow and balance.

Inner Caring Grows Outer Capacity for Building

When placecaring and placemaking are in balance, this creates energy, resources and readiness for change and resilience in the face of both good times and VUCA threats.

Together, we can even adapt placecaring and placemaking strategies in the context of different neighborhoods and different communities. One-size solutions do not have to fit all challenges (and one-size approaches will prevent the optimization of highest potentials amongst different locations, cultures and sectors.)

Cities who balance placecaring and placemaking develop the capacity to rapidly respond and evolve into new ways of being and becoming together. The 4 Voices of the City can work together at multiple scales to energize the value for all.

RAISING CONTEXT: BUILD VALUE THROUGH PLACECARING AND PLACEMAKING

When we consider the principle of balancing placecaring with placemaking, we often arrive at two questions:

1. **Does the City Build Value for the Stakeholders?** or
2. **Do Stakeholders Build Value for the City?**

The answers emerge from exploring the strategic opportunities that cities have, to create habitats that grow caring capacity, so that they create the condition to grow economic and infrastructural carrying capacity.

The 4 Voices of the city start this approach by unpacking the Master Code. They can consider to what extent they are able to:

1. **Care for Self so we regenerate;**
2. **Care with/for Others so we can support each other;**
3. **Work together in all Contexts as 4 Voices to create strategies to face VUCA threats; and**
4. **Align all the Cares above so that we can care for the Planet.**

Fundamentally, the 4 Voices of the city can co-create the conditions for deepening care, raising context and widening capacity so they can improve the effectiveness of the various functions of the city. If every voice wakes up in the city to work together we can co-generate the capacity to design cities with resilience—and the energy to develop vision, values and strategies. Collaborating in this way creates a whole new way of operating.

Ultimately the application of an Integral City approach to building stakeholder value creates a methodology of care to protect against all kinds of VUCA threats. We can see that it makes sense to:

Take Care of Yourself—to counter *Volatility*;

Take Care of Others and all Life—to co-exist despite all Life's **U**ncertainty;

Take Care of this Place—to serve it in all its *Complexity*;

Take care of this Planet—to steward it in all its diversity and **A**mbiguity.

As individual cities grow caring, contexting and capacity building, then we will cultivate value for a whole planet of cities as a living system—a whole Planet of Integral Cities.

WIDENING CAPACITY: DEVELOP A MESHWORK OF CITY ORGANIZATIONS

When cities are faced with VUCA challenges they become the flash points of anger, fear and concern within nations—and if these dissonances are not addressed—cities become the potential trigger points for inflaming the rest of the country—and its neighbors—making living conditions dysfunctional for everyone. The only hope for designing solutions that can flex and flow is to bring to the table the 4 key stakeholders who champion the qualities of the 4 quadrants within the city (Hamilton, 2017):

- **(UL) Citizens champion intentions and will;**
- **(UR) Civic Managers enact behaviors and actions;**
- **(LL) Civil Society connects cultures and relationships;**
- **(LR) Business/Developers organize infra/structures and systems.**

In the context of this VUCA world, it is a sobering realization that, at this stage of evolution it seems our city organizations are generating "heat" but neither direction nor function towards sustainable existence for the whole city. City capacities need strengthening at all scales from individual to organization. Furthermore, it is at the organizational scale that most leverage may be obtained, because organizations are not islands, but supply chains of mutually influencing capacities (Laloux, 2014).

Recognizing the power of economic and social supply chains, it is time for us to ask, how can we use our caring capacities and city intelligences (Appendix C) to generate a meshwork (see Glossary for definition) to align and implement organizational strategies in ways that support the wellbeing of the whole city and eco-region? In fact, we need to ask, how can we align systems of organizations within the city, to empower our reflective capacity at all scales on behalf of Gaia?

Varey (2010) suggested that we need "an appreciation of an 'ecology of ideas' . . . to guide the ecology of thought to enable our future and our peace". Varey's proposition, surely also applies to the dilemma we face to amplify our understanding of reflective capacity as being embedded not only in thought and idea ecologies but also in the ecologies of organizations (Laloux, 2014) that exist in the city (for more on organizations see Chapters 9 and 10).

The city as a living system is like a dojo where stakeholders can learn their way through a series of organizational practices that earn them the privilege and freedom to articulate core competencies like masters (and thereby reinvent organizations—as we propose in Chapter 11). In most cities, a whole spectrum of Level 1 to 6 organizations (as seen in Appendix B Map 4) offers a series of studios where stakeholders can learn the rudiments of reinventing themselves, their teams and organizational forms. Building on our skill sets we must recognize the spectrum (and holarchy) of Level 1 to 6 organizations that co-exists in our cities as foundational to its future growth.

All living systems must be able to survive, connect with their environment and regenerate (Capra, 1996). (These processes are axiomatic to a circular economy in a living system). If we consider organizations to be living systems, then we must recognize the necessary and inextricable connections each organization has with all the other organizations and people that exist where they do business—especially because they provide the very context of (mostly) Level 1 to 6 (and a few Level 7) capabilities.

In the current state of human affairs, our organizations appear misaligned. We act as if we are resistant to change (which includes ignoring the messages of our Diversity Generators (see Chapter 8)). As a result, we are underperforming and/or failing in most of the domains represented in the 4 quadrants of city realities (see Appendix B Map 1). Even where we demonstrate high creativity (such as the high-profile endeavors of entrepreneurs like Elon Musk, Richard Branson or the late Steve Jobs), we usually lack alignment to aliveness, Principles of Living Systems, Integral City Intelligences or the Master Code of Care.

Thus, the opportunities for the human hive to emerge an elegantly functioning and optimally creative "organ of reflection" are evolutionarily blocked because we are just starting to read feedback loops like Sustainable Development Goal measures (see Chapter 15; anon, 2017) that tell us if our circles of care are aligned for wellbeing. (Even the bees who have mastered the fine art of being Gaia's garden-generating organ, are suffering setbacks in their operations through the troubling experience of colony collapse disorder (CCD) perhaps because of the very uninformed reflective capacity of the human hive (which likely has caused or contributed to toxic pesticides, pollution, over work, reduction of genetic diversity, climate change and other CCD triggers (Benjamin & McCullum, 2009; Brackney, 2009; Gould & Gould, 1988; Hamilton, 2009; Weidenhammer, 2016; Winston, 2014).)

While there is much speculation (and no agreement) over the cause of CCD, it is a troubling warning that in order for the human hive to realize its full potential as Gaia's "reflective organ", we must cultivate our inner gardens of reflection with greater understanding, disciplinary practice, guidance and effective systems of reflection. Diamond (2005) and others have pointed out that the time is running out for us to wake up to our evolutionary calling. Lovelock (2009) has emphatically reminded us that we have an obligation to harness the creative process bestowed upon us by the evolutionary Universe and focus the capacities of our 4 Voices (Christensen 2015a, b), the output of our organizations, and the collaboration amongst cities (as the fifth voice, that we explored in Chapter 3), for the very survival if not the full formation of Gaia's reflective organ.

A "weak signal" of hope is emerging in the reports of early improvement from the Sustainable Development Goal (SDG) Livability Index (anon, 2017). This tool provides basic "course correction" data on the minimum qualities of "livability"—but it is only an entry point for the deeper qualities of aliveness and living systems that cities need to gauge their thrivability (van Schaik, 2016a, 2017a,b,c,d,e,f,g). Nevertheless, the emergence of the SDG's (and its predecessor the MDG's (anon, 2006)) hints that learning about the roots of aliveness and living systems has started and we must be encouraged to commit to continuing its expansion.

NOW WHAT? A METHODOLOGY FOR ALIGNING CARING, CONTEXTING, CAPACITY BUILDING

In order to grow relevant values, cities need a methodology for coping with VUCA threats, that integrates a whole systems, integrated approach to aligning caring, contexting and capacity building. As we have outlined in the foregoing chapters, related designs for security systems, managing diversity and developing cities, such an approach to VUCA would align the following practices.

Practice 1. Understand Contexts
1. Identify the severity of VUCA Threats.

Practice 2. Map Threat(s)
2. Name and evolutionarily map the VUCA threat(s) in the system using the evolutionary map (Appendix D) and the 5 maps (Appendix B).
3. Identify the purpose for change. Facing the VUCA threats provides the impetus or catalyst to change. Create the vision for changing the city from what to what; e.g. mitigate, adapt or eliminate threat?

Practice 3. Engage Stakeholder Care
4. Use Integral maps (Maps 1, 2, 3, 4, 5) to find the agents for city change—engage as many stakeholders in the process as possible—actively seek out diversity and make room for difference.
5. Enable leadership to emerge to address the threat(s) at the appropriate level of complexity.

Practice 4. Design Capacity Building Processes
6. Amplify the threat to the city so others can see it.

7. Integrally identify the resources needed to facilitate the change and invite and involve stakeholders to contribute to them.

Practice 5. Align Methodologies

8. Co-design Integral methodologies for city change that self-organize passion, purpose, priorities, people, and planet. Expect it to be messy. (See Book 2 (Hamilton, 2017) for meshworking designs.)

Practice 6. Track Feedback Loops

9. Create target-based feedback loops and Integral vital signs monitors so that participants can self-correct and develop operational city structures that work.

10. Make the feedback accessible to all by publication and display; e.g. community newspapers, online media, real time intelligence display systems.

11. Pay forward to other stakeholders, cities, eco-regions, the Integral learning for prevention, mitigation and/or adaptation.

SPECIES INTELLIGENCE CAN DESIGN SUSTAINABLE, RESILIENT REFLECTIVE ORGANS

Each city (as a unique human system) needs to take the responsibility to serve global sustainability and resilience.

Bees have an intimate relationship with their eco-regions that not only enables them to thrive within the hive but to create conditions in their environmental habitats that literally grows their energy supply for next year.

Bees pollinate gardens without. The amazing effectiveness of the honey bee's system for individual and hive survival (as described in Appendix E) has lessons for understanding human systems—including aligning the circles of care within Gaia's creative and "reflective organs" (Hamilton, 2008, 2017).

Laszlo (2006), reminds us that "No new chapter in human civilization will ever emerge if we just sit around with our hands in our laps waiting for a holistic convergence that will foster a new way of thinking. A critical mass of people in society must stand up to make it happen. That means you and me, and many others around the planet. And now is the time to get started." Wilber (2017) reiterates the picture painted by Clare Graves of the cataclysmic leap of meaning-making and action-taking that faces us now in a confusing "post-truth" world. Likewise, Patten (2018) paints a stark picture of the predicament the human species now faces, but invoking Ghandi, Patten calls for us to be the change we wish to see in the world, because it is not too late.

These reminders from deep time and current wisdom sound like a clarion call to mature our currently sub-functional circles of caring, so we can empower the city as the reflective organ with the capacity to collaborate with other cities. In this way we can cultivate for the human species "the gardens within" as seminal to forming a "Reflective Organ System" for Gaia. Our waking up now, will make the pivotal difference to enacting decisions for the wellbeing of the human hive, that will serve the 7th generation from now.

REFERENCES

anon. (2000). Millennium Development Goals. Retrieved December 21, 2017, from UN http://en.wikipedia.org/wiki/Millennium_Development_Goals

anon. (2017). Sustainable Development Goals. Retrieved December 11, 2017, from Wikipedia https://en.wikipedia.org/wiki/Sustainable_Development_Goals

Capra, F. (1996). The Web of Life: A New Scientific Understanding of Living Systems. New York: Anchor Books, Doubleday.

Christensen, T. (Ed.) (2015a). Innovative Development: Emerging Worldviews and Systems Change. Tucson, Arizona: Integral Publishers.

Christensen, T. (Ed.) (2015b). Developmental Innovation: Emerging Worldviews and Individual Learning. Tucson, Arizona: Integral Publishers.

Diamond, J. (2005). Collapse: How societies choose to fail or succeed (first ed.). New York: Penguin Group.

Hamilton, M. (2008). Integral City: Evolutionary Intelligences for the Human Hive. Gabriola Island BC: New Society Publishers.

Hamilton, M. (2015). SDi in the Integral City. In T. Christensen (Ed.), Innovative Development: Emerging Worldviews and Systems Change. Tucson, Arizona: Integral Publishers.

Hamilton, M. (2017). *Integral City Inquiry and Action: Designing Impact for the Human Hive*. Phoenix, AZ: Integral Publishers.

Jacobs, J. (2001). *The Nature of Economies*. New York: First Vintage Books Edition.

Laloux, F. (2014). *Reinventing Organizations*. Retrieved from http://www.reinventingorganizations.com/purchase.html

Laszlo, E. (2006c). *Science and the Reenchantment of the Cosmos: The Rise of the Integral Vision of Reality*. Rochester, VT: Inner Traditions • Bear & Company.

Lovelock, J. (2009). *The Vanishing Face of Gaia*. New York: Harmony Books.

Meadows, D. (2008). *Thinking in Systems*. White River Junction, VT: Chelsea Green Publishing.

Patten, T. (2018). *A New Republic of the Heart: An Ethos for Revolutionaries*. (*Sacred Activism*): North Atlantic Books.

van Schaik, P. (2016). *Urban Hub 1: Smart Sustainable Thriveable Cities*. UK: Integral Mentors.

van Schaik, P. (2017a). *Urban Hub 2: Methodologies & Planning Thriveable Cities*. UK: Integral Mentors.

van Schaik, P. (2017b). *Urban Hub 3: Integral Theory Thriveable Cities*. UK: Integral Mentors.

van Schaik, P. (2017c). *Urban Hub 4: Integral Workbook Thriveable Cities*. UK: Integral Mentors.

van Schaik, P. (2017d). *Urban Hub 5: Visions and Worldviews Thriveable Cities*. UK: Integral Mentors.

van Schaik, P. (2017e). *Urban Hub 6: Visions and Worldviews 2 Thriveable Cities*. UK: Integral Mentors.

van Schaik, P. (2017f). *Urban Hub 7: Visions and Worldviews 3 Thriveable Cities*. UK: Integral Mentors.

van Schaik, P. (2017g). *Urban Hub 8: What We Can Do Cultivating Change Thriveable Cities*. UK: Integral Mentors.

Varey, W. (2010). *Pscyhological Panarchy: Steps to an Echology of Thought*. Paper presented at the 54th Meeting of the International Society for the Systems Sciences, Wilfrid Laurier University, Waterloo, ON, Canada.

West, G. (2017). *Scale: The Universal Laws of Growth, Innovation, Sustainability and the Pace of Life in Organisms, Cities, Economies and Companies*. New York: Penguin Press.

Wilber, K. (2017). *Trump and the Post-Truth World*. Boston: Shambhala Publications Inc.

PROFILES: AUTHOR & CONTRIBUTOR

Author can be contacted via www.integralcity.com

AUTHOR

Dr. Marilyn Hamilton is author of the Integral City Book series, including: *Integral City: Evolutionary Intelligences for the Human Hive* and *Integral City Inquiry & Action: Designing Impact for the Human Hive.* She is Founder of Integral City Meshworks Inc. and TDG Holdings Inc. Marilyn leads a practice community using Integral City frameworks and practical tools to support multi-stake-holder groups in transforming their whole city and eco-region into habitats that are as sustainable and resilient for humans as the healthy beehive is for bees. She incubates transformation strategies for City Staff, Civic Leaders, Civil Society, Business Entrepreneurs and Community Participants that integrate their contributions with purpose, place, priorities, people and planet. As Thought Leader and Project Leader Marilyn calls herself an "AQtivator", leading teams to develop integrated resilience strategies that optimize official city plans and sustainability goals. She aligns multiple capacities with Environmental, Economic, Social and Cultural Capitals. She energizes community engagement, focuses decision making and designs dashboards for monitoring city performance and managing risk.

CONTRIBUTOR

Jordan Bruce MacLeod is co-founder and editor of InsideMoney.org. He is also co-founder of digital security company Elevator Software Corp. Jordan's current research interests include the nature of money and the evolving dynamics between economies and value systems. He lives in Charlottetown, Prince Edward Island, Canada with his wife, Lesley, and daughter, Lily.

GLOSSARY

Adaptation: How a system behaves to adapt for survival as its life conditions or context changes.

Caring Capacity: a term coined to describe the capacities of the left hand quadrants of the Integral Model related to consciousness (Upper Left) and culture (Lower Left). Caring Capacity measures the increasing circles of care embedded in the Master Code, ranging from self-centric to ethno-centric to global-centric to Kosmo-centric.

Carrying Capacity: a term coined to describe the capacities of the right hand quadrants of the Integral Model related to behaviors (Upper Right) and systems/infrastructure (Lower Right). Carrying Capacity measures the increasing levels of complexity that materialize as actions, functions, artefacts, systems and infrastructures that enable and support the expanding circles of care measured in Caring Capacity. In terms of the city carrying capacity levels are often described as pre-modern, modern, post-modern and post-post-modern (or Integral) (for example in the architecture discourse).

Community of Practice: a community of practitioners who have developed norms and/or agreements about how to replicate a practice in any human sphere—whether that is professional like accounting; commercial like insurance claims processing; artistic like stone sculpture; or agricultural like growing organic fruits.

Conformity: Homogeneity; a characteristic of a social system where patterns of behavior or consciousness are similar across the population.

Conformity Enforcer (CE): A term borrowed from Howard Bloom (Bloom, 2000) to describe the members of a population who enforce behaviors that conform to the expectations or norms defined by that population. He uses an example of the honey bee behavior to illustrate that 90% of the forager bees will follow the simple rules that reward them for collecting pollen and nectar from productive resource (flower) patches. In human terms, Conformity Enforcers represent the members of the population whose behaviors conform to the values systems shared by the majority of the population. Conformity Enforcer behavior coalesces around a values-based "Centre of Gravity".

Conformity Enforcement: The act of enforcing conformity in a system, usually through the aggregation of power to do so.

Diversity: Heterogeneity; a characteristic of a system where patterns of behavior and consciousness are different from the population norm.

Diversity Generator (DG): A term borrowed from Howard Bloom (Bloom, 2000) to describe the members of a population whose behaviors diverge from the expectations or norms practised by the majority of that population. The purpose of Diversity Generation within a population or species is to expand options as life conditions change and enable adaptation to new life conditions. For example, in honey bee populations Diversity Generators (about 5% of the hive) source different resource (flower) locations and types than CE bees. This information is generally ignored when CEs are generating sufficient resources, but is acted upon when CEs deplete sources of resources (flower patches).

Diversity Generation: The act of generating difference in a system.

Fractal: A fractal is a repeated non-linear pattern that recurs at infinite scales in nature, arising from the following of simple rules embedded in the nature of the fractal entity; examples include coastlines, cloud formations, trees, social insects (bees, ants, termites) villages, organizations, body parts, galaxies and neurons. (Hamilton, 2008a)

Holarchy: A hierarchy of hierarchies or holons; or a hierarchy of whole systems; a higher-order system that includes all the lower-order systems in its functioning.(A term originally coined by Arthur Koestler.)

Holon: A whole system made up of other whole systems. (A term coined by Arthur Koestler which Ken Wilber made central to his Integral framework.)

Homo Sapiens Sapiens: The human who is conscious of his/her consciousness. A term coined by Barbara Marx Hubbard.

Human Hive: a metaphor for the city, applying the concept of an integrated living system, to a species' collective habitat, like the beehive is to the honey bee (apis mellifera), the human hive (or city) is to humans (homo sapiens sapiens). The term was popularized and explored in Integral City: Evolutionary Intelligences for the Human Hive (Hamilton (2008a).

Hyperdiversity: Heterogeneity amplified (in oversupply); a characteristic of a system where diversity has been generated in oversupply to the proportion of normative patterns; i.e. there is more difference in the system than homogeneity.

Integral: a term describing a whole system that integrates and synthesizes multiple perspectives, levels of development, lines of development, and types of form. In this Book Series, I am using the Integral Metamap developed by Ken Wilber (Wilber, 1995, 1996a, 2000b, 2007) with major contributions from Beck and Graves (Beck, 2000b, 2001, 2002b; Beck & Cowan, 1996; Beck & Linscott, 2006; Graves, 1974, 2003, 2005) popularized as Spiral Dynamics with influences from other integralists (Gunderson & Holling, 2002; Laszlo, 2004, 2006a, 2006c, 2006d). It has four quadrants (upper left for subjective, upper right for objective, lower left for inter-subjective, lower right for interobjective) and eight + levels of development. Spiral Dynamics describes the eight levels of development in terms of emerging levels of complexity. These eight levels are often compressed into the five stages of: traditional, pre-modern, modern, post-modern and Integral.

Intelligences: capacities that enable life to adapt, survive and thrive in any given life conditions. In terms of an Integral City 12 Intelligences have been identified at the city scale (see Appendix C).

Integral City Activator: the general description for urban professionals who design and implement Integral City principles, processes and practices. Three levels of competency are described in the Book 2, Introduction as Practitioners, Catalysts and Meshworkers (Hamilton, 2017).

Integral City Assessor: a professional urban practitioner who uses the Integral City 12 Intelligences, Values and/or Voices to assess and report on the levels of evolutionary emergence, complexity of values systems and participation of the 4+1 Voices of the city.

Integral Intelligences: a cluster of intelligences that are integrated so that they work together to optimize the function of whole systems. In the Integral City they are identified as Contexting, Individual, Collective, Strategic and Evolutionary intelligences. In this Book 3 of the Integral City series, they are clustered as Caring, Contexting and Capacity Building intelligences.

Knowing Field Plus Integral Cities:

Knowing: we can come to know a city, know about it, and be guided around it.

Knowing: the city itself as an energetic entity has a knowing capacity within it.

Knowing: a way of perceiving beyond the five senses.

Cities: are the largest human systems yet created.

Cities: include all the dynamics of individual, family, organizational and community systems co-existing in rhythms, cycles, patterns and fields.

Cities: are collective expressions of the human species, like a Human Hive.

—(Douglas & Hamilton, 2013a)

Kosmic Address: a term coined by Ken Wilber (Wilber, 2006) to locate a phenomenon within the Integral map of four quadrants (perspectives) and eight levels of complexity (altitude). He further unpacks this concept, with considerable granularity (proposing a kind of calculus) to locate both the observer and the observed. For the purposes of this Integral City usage Kosmic Address = altitude + perspective.

Master Code: a core principle of the Integral City that describes the increasing circles of care that must be practised and aligned for whole city system coherence. Practicing the Master Code entails caring for Self, so that you can care for Others, so we can care for this Place (City) so we can all care for the Planet.

Meshwork: a term from the brain sciences describing how the brain develops through self-organizing connections that emerge hierarchical structures. The term is borrowed to describe how to align human systems into functions that fit and flow with natural conditions.(Beck, 2000a; De Landa, 1995). The emergence of patterns in the brain, results from the neuro-chemical connections of synapses that produce a hairnet-like mesh of axons (Bleys et al., 1996), characterized by major primary connective pathways that produce and intersect secondary, tertiary and many further levels of connectedness. It appears that the meshwork self-organizes connections and when a certain density and/or repeated use of pathways arises, a hierarchy of complexity emerges that enables the brain to replicate the patterns (and the capacities that arise from them) allowing retention of learning and efficiencies of energy use. This cycle of self-organizing and hierarchical patterning continues throughout a lifetime, allowing the brain to build up a repertoire of learned behavior while continuing its capacity for self-organizing adaptiveness to dynamic environments and never-ending stimuli. While we can map these structures through fMRI scanning, we can also assess the co-related structures of consciousness that emerge in the mind from ego, to ethno, to worldcentric (Beck, 2010b) as illustrated in Appendix B, Map 4.

Meshworks are fractal: they exist at individual; team; organization; sectoral; social/cultural; and city levels of complexity.

Meshworking Intelligence: an intelligence that creates a "meshwork" by weaving together the best of two operating systems — one that self-organizes, and one that replicates hierarchical structures. The resulting meshwork creates and aligns complex responsive (sustainable) structures and (resilient) systems that flex and flow. This occurs in both the conscious mind and physical brain on an individual basis. Collective intelligences also appear to have emerged that can be evolutionarily located in intersubjective and interobjective contexts.

Morphic Field: The concept of morphic or Akashic fields (Laszlo, 2004; Sheldrake, 1988, 1999, 2003, 2012) creates the possibility that we could harness the intelligence that is concentrated in the city to generate much greater (more complex) intelligence capacities than we have ever dreamed of. If we could truly learn how to think together, we could harness the massive leverage of parallel processing that has enabled us to design modern computers and neural networks (like the linking of personal computers for the SETI extraterrestrial life search project). If we can do this, we will see a significant phase shift in human intelligence that will give cities major new incentives to create optimal life conditions to better support human existence. By the same token, in an optimistic spirit, I anticipate that when this intelligence is harnessed we will finally have the power to add value to life on Earth that is both sustainable (not over-using resources) and emergent (always creating new capacities from existing resources) (Hamilton, 2008a, p. 73).

Norm: The behavior of a system that is demonstrated by the majority of the population.

Organelle: a part or sub-component of an organ that enables its biological functioning.

Organ: a part of a body system that contributes a key biological function; e.g. heart, lung, liver, kidney.

Panarchy: is a theory of change described in a book of the same name. The book describes multi-disciplinary research into transformations into human and natural systems (Gunderson & Holling, 2002). As a theory of change, a "Panarchy is a cross-scale, nested set of adaptive cycles, indicating the dynamic nature of structures depicted in the previous plots" (p. 74). Panarchy labels the four phases of creative destruction and renewal within a cycle as: exploitation, conservation, release and reorganization. Panarchy also describes the connections between cycles and their capacity to reallocate resources by "remembering" accumulated potentials from larger cycles that can influence earlier, (lower in the nest), faster cycles, as well as their capacity to "revolt" and spark change into larger, higher, slower cycles from smaller, faster cycles. For societies these reallocations might result in the three panarchy cycles of: allocation mechanisms, norms and myths (Westley) as cited in (Gunderson & Holling, 2002, p. 75).

Resilience: the state of a system that enables it to adapt to changing life conditions and persist in its survival despite the changes. Resilient systems appear to cycle through four distinct stages (see *Panarchy* definition above):

1. Conservation—where the system is structured into a fairly steady state, able to optimize resource access and deployment in replicatable operations

2. Breakdown—where the system tips into a state of disequilibrium unable to adapt resource access and/or deployment to changing life conditions

3. Resource Redistribution—where the system breaks apart into constituent elements that self-organize into divergent and incoherent exchanges

4. Exploitation—where the system self-organizes into convergent and coherent exchanges enabling exploitation of new structures for resource access and deployment

Resilient Environment: an environment that is a habitat or eco-system for a given species; e.g. like a beehive and the eco-region from which the bees collect energy in the form of pollen and nectar and pollinate the flowers and plants. In this book the author borrows this analogy to describe the eco-region of a city as the environment for the human hive.

Social Holon: a whole human system made up of multiple individuals. A social holon does not act as an undifferentiated homogenous mass, but is influenced by the internal consciousness and external behaviors of all the individual holons it contains. In terms of Integral City Maps (see Appendix B: Integral City Maps (1–5) social holons can be seen in the collective elements of Maps 2, 3 and 4.

Spirituality: a universal life force that cycles through existence as an involutionary and evolutionary impulse. The first stage of the cycle, called involution, originates at the non-dual "source" that lies at the center of existence where it descends from the invisible to the visible; from the immanent to that which is presenced; from the unmanifest to the manifest. The second stage of the cycle, called evolution, attracts all creation back to source so that it ascends from the manifest to the source; from the visible to the invisible; from gross physical bodies to subtle energetic bodies to causal energetic bodies to non-dual source.

Superordinate Goal: a goal that transcends and includes other goals in a way that everyone supports because they see that their own interests are addressed by pursuing it.

Sustainability: the state of a living system whereby the conditions of aliveness are enabled in a cycle of life, so that the system can sustain itself, connect to its environment and regenerate. In a meshwork, sustainability arises from the system organizing itself into natural hierarchical (holarchical) learned structures, so that it can minimize energy consumption and maximize effectiveness and efficiency. (In contrast to resilience where a system continually self-organizes for creative innovation and adaptation to dynamic life conditions.)

Theory U: a theory of learning and change discovered and first described by Senge, Scharmer, Jaworski and Flowers (Peter Senge, Scharmer, Jaworski, & Flowers, 2004) and since widely developed, popularized and applied by Scharmer (Scharmer, 2009). Theory U describes a process of change that occurs across a series of activities designed and facilitated to occur in this sequence:

Sensing: Suspending, Redirecting, Letting Go

Presencing: Letting Go, Letting Come, Crystallizing

Realizing: Crystallizing, Prototyping, Institutionalizing

The design of Part 1 and Part 2 of *Integral City Inquiry & Action: Designing Impact for the Human Hive* can be viewed as following a U pattern (down the left hand quadrants and up the right hand quadrants).

Voices: a term used in Integral City to describe 4 subpopulations internal to the city (aka Human Hive), in terms of their contribution to a complex living system: Citizens, Civil Society, Civic Managers, Business. The +1 Voice is represented by other cities (Human Hive) in the eco-region.

VUCA: mnemonic for *Volatility, Uncertainty, Complexity, Ambiguity.* This term was coined by the American military to describe the world of the 21st century.

APPENDICES

APPENDIX A: INTEGRAL QUADRANTS

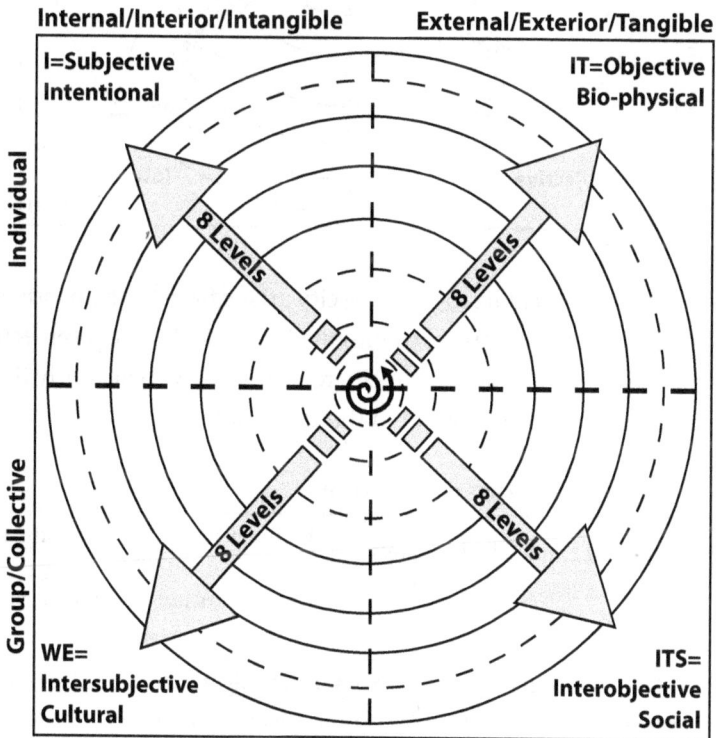

Internal/Interior/Intangible · External/Exterior/Tangible

I=Subjective Intentional · IT=Objective Bio-physical

Individual

8 Levels · 8 Levels · 8 Levels · 8 Levels

Group/Collective

WE= Intersubjective Cultural · ITS= Interobjective Social

APPENDIX B: INTEGRAL CITY MAPS (1–5)

Map 1: 4 Quadrants, 8 Levels

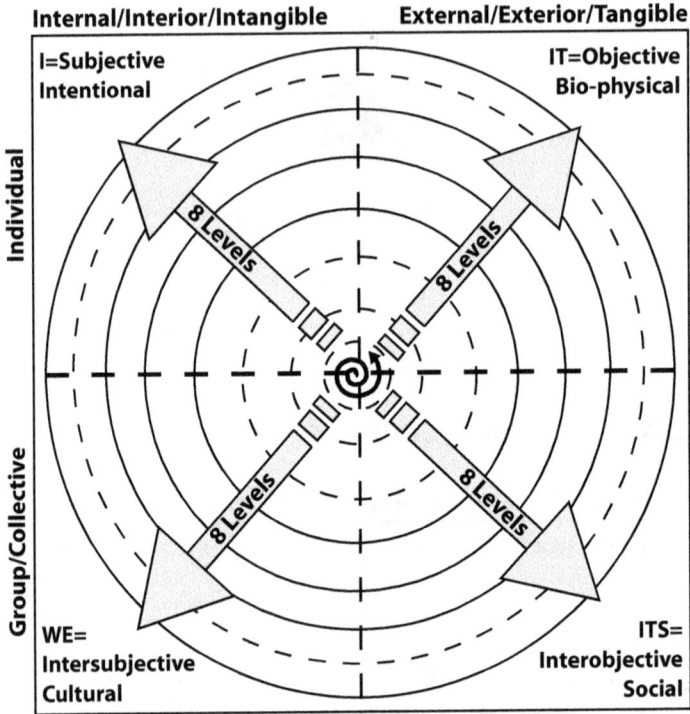

This map shows how civilization in the city arises from both an individual/ collective and interior/exterior expression (Wilber, 1995). The intersection of these two dimensions reveals four city realities that we can study through the sciences and label as set out in the table below.

Human Perspectives, Domains of Knowledge

1. Upper Left (UL): individual—beliefs interior/ internal/ subjective/intangible **Aesthetics and fine arts (I)**	3. Upper Right (UR): individual— actions exterior/ external/ objective/tangible **Life sciences (It)**
2. Lower Left (LL): collective—culture interior/internal/ intersubjective/intangible **Social sciences (We)**	4. Lower Right (LR): collective—systems exterior/ external/ interobjective/tangible **Systems sciences (Its)**

Map 1 has a series of "growth rings" that spiral out from the center along the diagonal axis of each quadrant, representing the eight stages of complexity referenced in Map 4. The outward pointing arrows on Map 1 indicate the vectors of change through these stages of complexity, expanding the four quadrants of the whole city outward from the core.

Map 1 is analogous to a "plan view" of human life and provides the perspective and altitude coordinates for what Wilber calls "Kosmic addresses" (Wilber, 2006).

Map 2: Nested Holarchy of City Systems

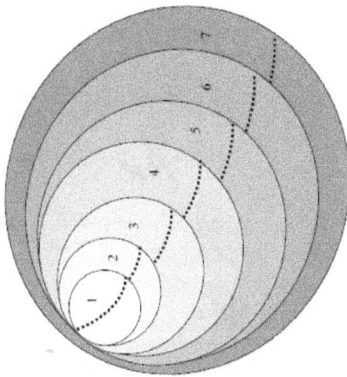

- 1 = individual
- 2 = family/clan
- 3 = group/tribe
- 4 = organizations: workplaces, education, healthcare
- 5 = community(s)
- 6 = city
- 7 = eco-region

The city as a human system is a nest of systems made up of centers (Alexander, 2004), holons (Koestler) or nested holons (Sahtouris, 1999). The systems have orders of complexity (as discussed above), so that the holons, wholes and centers are nested into holarchies (Wilber, 1996c) or panarchies (Gunderson & Holling, 2002) where levels of complexity (and scale) emerge over time.

Map 3: The Scalar Fractal Relationship of Micro, Meso and Macro Social Holons

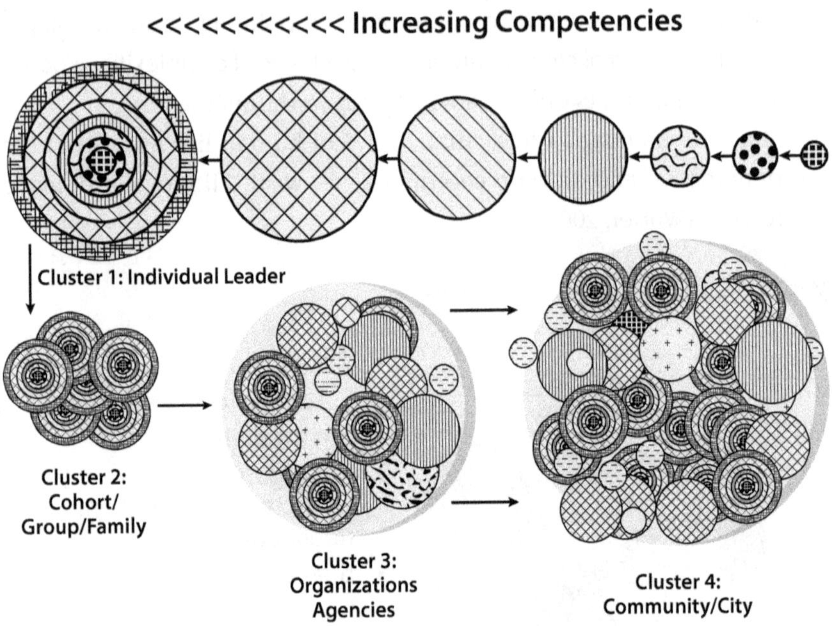

<<<<<<<<<<<< Increasing Competencies

Cluster 1: Individual Leader

Cluster 2:
Cohort/
Group/Family

Cluster 3:
Organizations
Agencies

Cluster 4:
Community/City

Map 3 shows the city as a social holon. Its qualities are not summative but dynamic capacities that come from the unique contributions of each individual holon in the social grouping. Map 3 conveys how capacity development in an individual contributes to capacity in all the social holons of Map 2, while also revealing the reality of capacity dilution and amplification in the social holons of groups, organizations and communities.

As a natural system, the dynamics of social holons are expressed by the algorithms of fractal geometry — the elegant, patterns that result from the repetition of simple rules of relationship, that apply at multiple levels of scale (like Graves' (2003, 2005) adult development patterns). West (2011, 2017) proposes that such non-linear mathematics can predict factors affecting human security like people behavior (e.g. criminal actions) and infrastructure (e.g. size of police force).

It appears that at every level of scale, fractal patterns of human systems reveal that city wellbeing (vibrant or dis-eased) is deeply intertwined in the patterns or principles that contribute to the wellbeing of individual holons and the social holons to which they belong as noted in Map 2 (Elisabet Sahtouris, 2010).

Map 4: The Complex Adaptive Structures of Change

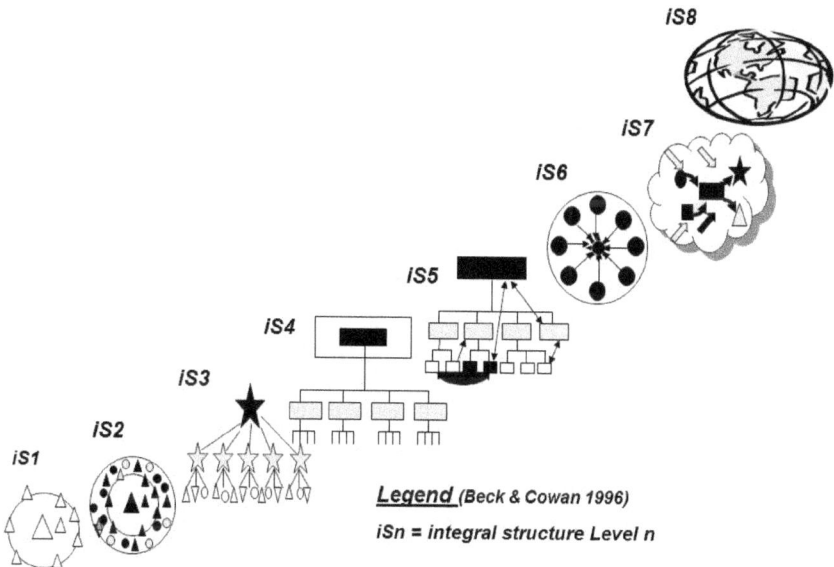

Map 4 conveys the stages of structural organizational change in the city. Living human systems in the city are constantly adapting to life conditions. Adaptations arise from both external causes (like geo-climatic incidents) and from internal causes (like bio-psycho-cultural-social triggers such as economic shifts).

Map 4 makes visible how the city's (Map 1, Lower Right) organizational structures evolve over time. (They also act as proxies for the commensurate Upper Right neural structures developing in individual brains as in Maps 1 and 3.) Map 4's trajectory of structural change, actually has no assumptions or guarantees of an ever-upward shift—the direction of change to more or less complex systems depends on the capacities of the individuals and groups (reflected in Map 3) to adapt to the challenge(s) (Beck & Cowan, 1996; Graves, 1981, 2005; Hamilton, 2008a).

Map 5: Spirituality in the Integral City

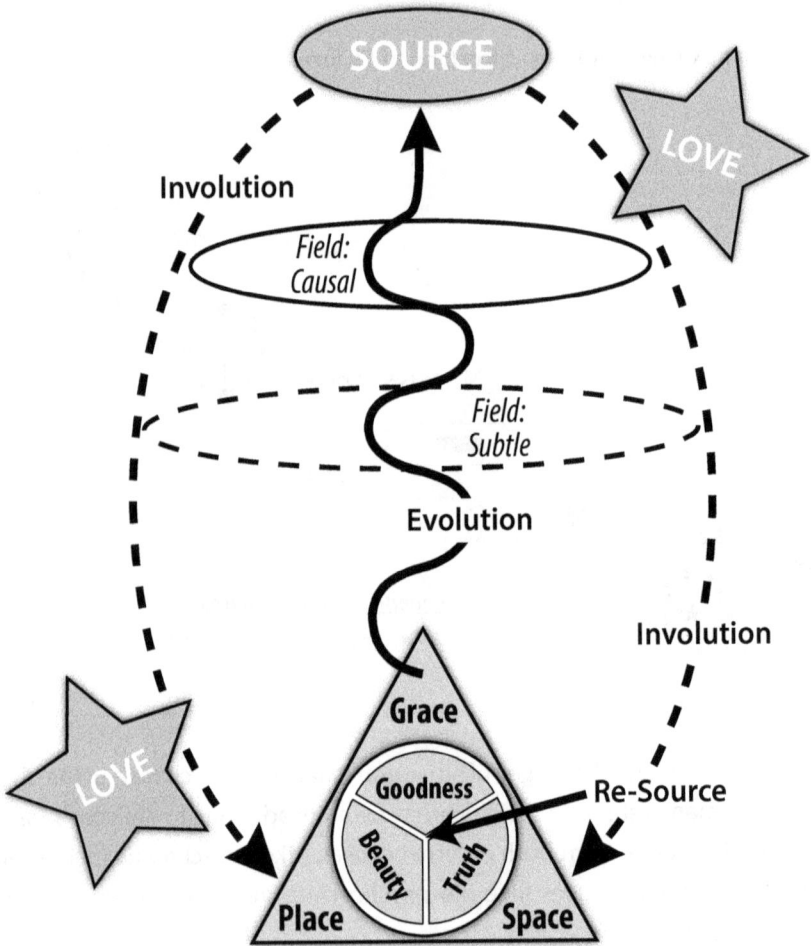

Map 5 conveys the qualities of spirituality in the city. Its zones of Grace, Space and Place reveal where the core spiritual values of Goodness, Truth and Beauty are manifested. The Kosmic addresses of these core spiritual values of the Integral City have both vertical and horizontal locations. Spirituality itself responds through these qualities and values in a holographic way as described below. (For more details see *Chapter 1: Spirituality in the Human Hive: Involutionary & Evolutionary Cycle of Love.*)

At the **Resource** level of city, spirituality emerges the manifest qualities of Beauty (UL), Truth (UR and LR) and Goodness (LL) that underpin human capacity at all scales. **Resource** holographically mirrors the core value of Beauty and the spiritual zone of Place. It is presenced through the container of the living human hive. It is accessed by Appreciation and enacted by Expression.

At the **Field** level of city, spirituality emerges the (contexting) qualities of personal and transpersonal energy that arise from subtle and causal memory patterns of evolutionary spiritual intelligence. **Field** holographically reflects the core value of Truth and the spiritual zone of Space. It is presenced by dynamic learning spiritual memory. It is accessed by Learning and enacted by Teaching.

At the **Source** level of city, spirituality exists as the Absolute, ever-present (caring) life force of spirituality that is non-dual. **Source** holographically emanates the core value of Goodness and the spiritual zone of Grace. It is presenced as the infinite ground of spiritual abundance. It is accessed by Stillness and enacted by Service.

APPENDIX C: INTEGRAL CITY 12 INTELLIGENCES

Appendix C1: Definitions of 12 Intelligences

Eco

Ecosphere intelligence is an awareness and capacity to respond to the realities of a city's climate and eco-region environment.

Emergent

Emergent intelligence looks at the city as a whole, through the lenses of, aliveness, survival, adaptiveness, regeneration, sustainability and emergence.

Integral

Integral intelligence uses four essential maps of city life to see the whole city.

Living

Living intelligence relates to the aliveness of each citizen through each of his/her lifecycle stages and the aliveness of the city through its lifecycle stages.

Inner

Inner intelligence is the 'I' space of the citizen—the seat of intentional consciousness, attention, interior experience and lines of development.

Outer

Outer intelligence is the biological 'it' space of the citizen—the space where the body acts and behaves.

Social

Social intelligence is the 'its' space of the city that gives us the capacity, to structure and systemize our environment.

Cultural

Cultural intelligence represents the 'we' life of the city—the relationships in the city which transcend boundaries that both contain and separate.

Inquiry

Inquiry intelligence asks key questions that reveal the meta-wisdom of the city.

Meshworking

Meshworking intelligence attracts the best of two operating systems—one that self-organizes, and the other that replicates hierarchal structures—to align systems that flex and flow.

Navigating

Navigating intelligence monitors and discloses the wellbeing or general condition of the city.

Evo

Evolutionary intelligence is the capacity to transcend and include the intelligences, we currently demonstrate, in order to allow new intelligences to emerge.

APPENDIX C2:

Integral City Intelligences & Principles for Wellbeing
Chapter references relate to Integral City Book 1.

Chapter 1: Ecosphere Intelligence

1. Honor the climate and geography of your city.
2. Steward the environment.
3. Add value to the earth space.

Chapter 2: Emerging Intelligence

1. Survive so holons serve each other's existence.
2. Adapt to the environment.
3. Create a self-regenerating feedback loop, by interconnecting human regeneration cycles so that they replenish the environment.

Chapter 3: Integral Intelligence

1. Map the territory integrally (horizontally through four quadrants, vertically through eight plus levels of development, diagonally through its change states, and relationally through its nested holarchies and fractals of complexity).
2. Create and sustain an Integral mapping system at the highest sustainable level of complexity, that is appropriate to the capacities of city management.
3. Learn from and update the maps annually or more often.

Chapter 4: Living Intelligence

1. Honor the dance of life cycles in the city.
2. Integrate the natural cycles of change within the city.
3. Learn how to zoom in and out at different scales to dance with the fractal patterns of the city.

Chapter 5: Inner Intelligence

1. Show up and be self-aware, present, mindful.
2. Notice the city intelligences and map them integrally.
3. Grow leadership in heart, mind, soul.

Chapter 6: Outer Intelligence
1. Manage personal energy.
2. Seek bio-physical wellbeing for self and others.
3. Nurture healthy leaders.

Chapter 7: Building (Structure-Systems) Intelligence
1. Manage life sustaining energy for all.
2. Design from the center, at all scales for all holons.
3. Build structures that integrate self-organizing creativity with hierarchies of order.

Chapter 8: Storytelling (Culture) Intelligence
1. Respect others.
2. Listen deeply.
3. Speak your story, and enable others to speak theirs, to co-create communities of Integral practice.

Chapter 9: Inquiry Intelligence
1. Ask what's working (and not) and co-generate a vision for the city's contribution to the planet.
2. Create an Integral City and community plan.
3. Implement and manage the plan appropriately at all scales in the city.

Chapter 10: Meshworking Intelligence
1. Catalyze fractal connections within the human hive.
2. Build communication bridges across silos, stovepipes and solitudes.
3. Enable meshes and hierarchies that transform, transcend and transmute capacities.

Chapter 11: Navigating Intelligence
1. Select the future destination of the city based on its vision.
2. Design and implement Integral dashboards, using Integral indicators of wellbeing for the city.
3. Notice outcomes and make course corrections to enable progress naturally.

Chapter 12: Evolving Intelligences

1. Expect the unexpected.
2. Pay attention to the rules.
3. Enable emergence and resilience by transcending and including Integral capacities at Level 8 and beyond.

Master Intelligence, Principle & Code:

Take care of yourself.

Take care of each other.

Take care of this place.

Take care of this planet.

APPENDIX C3: INTEGRAL CITY GPS LOCATOR

Homo sapiens has built several types of cities—we focus on three types of cities: the Smart City driven by technology and industry; the Resilient city driven by ecological and eco-regional interdependencies; and the Integral City driven by the Master Code.

The **Integral City GPS** tool locates these 3 city types on 3 bezels that can move both independently and in synchrony.

At the core of the Integral City GPS lies the **Evolutionary Intelligence**, which provides the energetic impulse that drives all the other intelligences. Recognizing that every city emerges along an Evolutionary trajectory is also a core distinction of an Integral City (and explains why we begin the inquiry, action, and impact cycle of Integral City Book 2 with an exploration of how to tap into the Evolutionary intelligence in the Knowing Field).

The Smart City Locator is situated on the 2nd bezel. It **uses Logic Models to track the logic** of cities—based on Strategic Rational thinking using the intelligences of Inquiry, Meshworking, and Navigating. It depends on scientific and methodical Inquiry; that is, research and development. It collects big data, maps patterns, tracks vital signs, and navigates the city's neural networks for effectiveness and efficiency. The Smart City Locator organizes the favorite functions used by Civic Managers and Citizens and asks: How are we doing in reaching targets? Do I have the basics of life? Do I have a job? Are the stores open? Do the buses run on time?

The Resilient City Locator is situated on the 3rd bezel. It is like the **Motherboard** of our intelligence system based on the natural systems we have inherited from Mother Earth. The Resilient City Locator locates our human hives in the context of their intelligences related to Ecologies and eco-regions; their Emergent responsiveness to local conditions; the basic Integral realities of bio-psycho-culture-systems; and their embedded, recurrent dynamic Lifecycles. It relates the interdependent scales of our cities in terms of their inter-city and intra-city ecologies. The Resilient City intelligences provide contexts for the Strategies of the Smart City intelligences. It is used by Civic Managers who track the external conditions of the eco-regions of our human hives—asking about climate, water, energy, population densities—to seek feedback that tells us if we are going to be successful at not just reaching our target once, but multiple years into the future. The Resilient City locator alerts Business Innovators to threats and opportunities needing remedies, adaptive strategies, innovations, and inventions. It activates a measure of large-scale systems integration. And working with these impact patterns, it leads us to the third locator.

The Integral City Locator is situated on the 1st bezel. It acts as the **core intelligence chip** that reflects the deepest intelligence of the Human Hive. It offers "Integral Intel Inside." This chip embeds the core intelligences that enable human systems to be the most advanced life systems on earth. The Integral Integrator is built on the very simple architecture of Inner and Outer, Individual and Collective Capacities. Outer Individual Intelligences include the external objective data elements tracked by the Smart City. The Outer Collective Intelligences include the external inter-objective infrastructural and systemic elements of cities mapped by the Smart and Resilient City—like the electric grid, transportation systems, and the built environment.

Inner Individual Intelligences include the internal subjective phenomena of emotions, consciousness, beliefs, mindfulness, and intentions. Inner Collective Intelligences include the internal intersubjective realities of values, worldviews, vision, and culture.

The true distinctiveness of the Integral City locator arises from the power of the Inner Capacities—Individual and Collective Intelligences—that drive city life. These Inner Intelligences in particular enable and constrain all the other intelligences because they define and delimit how we interpret big data, respond to ecological life conditions, and implement the strategies of Smart, Resilient, and Integral Cities. At their best, they add meta-capabilities to patterning, systemizing, evolving, and caring, through the means of collaborative inquiry, action, and impact.

The Integral locator points especially to the **Caring Capacities**—the ones that emerge from our attention to living the Master Code and expanding the circles of care in our lives.

As we expand our capacity to embrace greater circles of care—from self, to others, to place, to planet—we expand our capacity to develop habitats that carry and support the life conditions that we most need to be Smart, Resilient, and Integral.

Note: *Traditional Cities are not located with this GPS Locator.*

APPENDIX D: EVOLUTION OF THE WORLD

A Brief History of the World

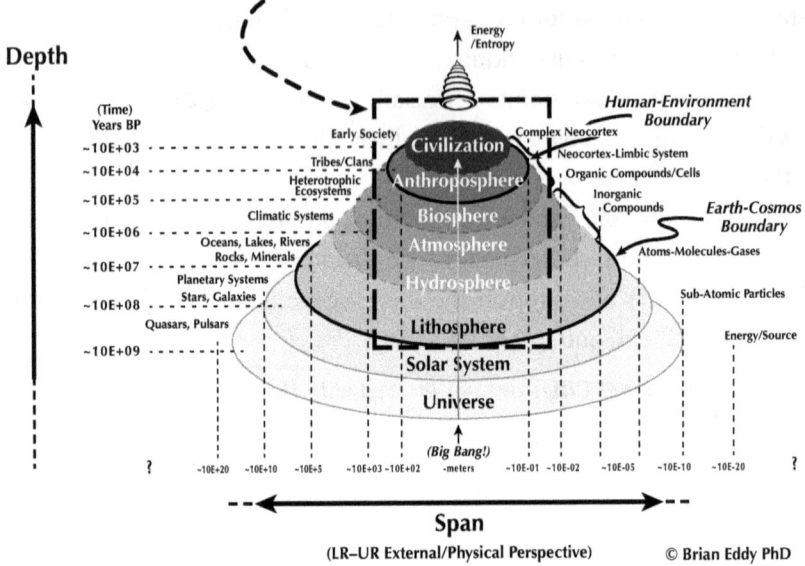

Span
(LR–UR External/Physical Perspective)   © Brian Eddy PhD

Eddy (2005) grounds the study of global environmental change within three differentiated strata: The Cosmosphere that spans the universe; the Biosphere that includes the living global environment; and the Anthroposphere that embraces the human condition. He groups the study of these into a spectrum of "pure and applied (CBA or ABC) sciences": Earth and Planetary Sciences; Life Sciences; and Social Sciences as set out in Table 11 (duplicated below for ease of access).

Eddy's evolutionary ABC framework builds on Wilber's framing of holons and holarchies (Wilber, 1995, 1996a, 2000b, 2007) and effectively integrates the human condition within global environmental change , showing the three spheres as evolving one from the other and massively entangled at all scales and times, co-creating conditions where now it is evident that the A-sphere is impacting both the B and C-spheres; for example reducing biodiversity in the B-sphere (Esbjörn-Hargens & Zimmerman, 2009) and changing the hydrological cycle in the C-sphere (Linton, 2010).

Table 11 : The ABC of Integral Geography
  (*adapted from Eddy*, 2005)

Science Cluster	Disciplines	Relevant Geographic Spheres
Earth and Planetary Sciences:	Math, Physics, Chemistry Astronomy Geology Hydrology Meteorology etc.	Cosmosphere: Universe Earth Matter
Life Sciences	Biology Microbiology Zoology Botany etc.	Biosphere: Life Living Environment
Social Sciences	Psychology Sociology Anthropology etc.	Anthroposphere: Human Individual Collective

APPENDIX E: LESSONS FROM THE HONEY BEE, APIS MELLIFERA

Adapted from (Hamilton, 2008a; Hamilton, 2012b)

Lesson 1 is based on "The Life of the Bee" Maeterlinck (1954) p. 165–6

Maeterlink says in full: *And indeed, to discover the unconquerable duty of a being is less difficult than one imagines. It is ever to be read in the distinguishing organs, whereto the others are all subordinate. And just as it is written in the tongue, the stomach, and mouth of the bee that it must make honey, so is it written in our eyes, our ears, our nerves, our marrow, in every lobe of our head, that we must make cerebral substance; nor is there need that we should divine the purpose this substance shall serve. The bees know not whether they will eat the honey they harvest, as we know not who it is shall reap the profit of the cerebral substance we shall have formed, or of the intelligent fluid that issues therefrom and spreads over the universe, perishing when our life ceases or persisting after our death. As they go from flower to flower collecting more honey than themselves and their offspring can need, let us go from reality seeking food for the incomprehensible flame, and thus, certain of having fulfilled our organic duty, preparing ourselves for whatever befall. Let us nourish this flame on our feelings and passions, on all that we see and think, that we hear and touch, on its own essence, which is the idea it derives from the discoveries, experience and observation that result from its every movement. A time then will come when all things will turn so naturally to good in a spirit that has given itself to the loyal desire of this simple human duty that the very suspicion of the possible aimlessness of its exhausting effort will only render the duty the clearer, will only add more purity, power, disinterestedness, and freedom to the ardor wherewith it still seeks.*

Lesson 2 is based on "The Global Brain" as told by Howard Bloom (2000)

A bee hive has about 50,000 bees in it—about the size of a small city. A honey beehive also has a goal. It must produce a certain amount of honey per year in order to survive—about 20 kilos per year.

Thus a beehive has a clear sustainability objective for the hive, measured in terms of energy production. Bees obtain the raw materials to produce honey by creating 5 roles within the hive—not the usual suspects most of us are familiar with like drones and queens. No, no these roles have much more purpose and innovation to them:

About 90% of the hive are **Conformity Enforcers (CE)**. Their job is to fly to flower patches and harvest as much nectar and pollen as they can. They use the "waggle dance" form of communication to let sister bees know where to find the resources. When 90% of the hive is doing the same dance—it's like a Rock & Roll rave—the energy produced attracts a lot of attention and reinforces successful finds.

About 5% of the hive are **Diversity Generators (DG)**. Their job is to fly to different flower beds than the Conformity Enforcers. As a result, their waggle dance contains different information—more like an Irish Jig than Rock & Roll? When the Conformity Enforcers are at peak performance the Diversity Generators are not noticed because their communication is drowned out by the Conformity Enforcer "rave".

However—a small per cent of the hive are **Resource Allocators (RA)**. Their job is to reward the performance of Conformity Enforcer and Diversity Generator bees. When Conformity Enforcer performance lags (after depleting the resources in one flower patch), Resource Allocator's withhold rewards until the point that Conformity Enforcer bees are not only de-energized—they become downright depressed. You can imagine them walking around completely bummed out—the party is over—btw, they can measure depression in bees by measuring their pheromones. Eventually when the Conformity Enforcer's energy is lowest, they finally take note of the Diversity Generator Irish Jig (communication) and switch their resourcing flights to new locations.

An even smaller per cent of the hive **are Inner Judges (IJ). Some say this is even a hive intelligence. The Inner Judges** work with Resource Allocators to assess and reward performance, so that the hive can achieve its sustainability goals.

The fifth role is a whole hive role—it is created through **Inter-Group Tournaments (IT)**. This role actually emerges from the competition between hives within the bee's eco-region; i.e. the territory they share with other hives competing for the same resources.

These **five roles** create a resilience strategy that depends on the performance of both CE's and DGs and innovation to support the hive and the species. But the bees have taken **their sustainability strategy beyond the hive to scale at the regional level of resilience**. Because of course as they gather resources for themselves, they pollinate their eco-region, thereby creating energy renewal for next year. This means the bees have developed a **double sustainability loop** that supports hive survival AND **regenerates** the energy resources in their eco-region. The **Inter-group tournaments operate at the level of species survival**—ensuring any hive that gets an edge in the DG innovation and evolution curve is the one most likely to survive and pass on its learning.

APPENDIX F: IMAGINE YOUR CITY

Appendix F1: Imagine the City as a Human Hive

Imagine the city as a human hive— a living "reflective" organ of Gaia whose city purpose is in service to Gaia's wellbeing and sustainability and is embraced by its citizens.

Imagine human hives who can resource their purpose with internal and external resources and funding.

Imagine the human hive as a living innovation eco-system, where we enable the connections between the 4 Voices of the city—Citizens, Civil Society, City/Institutional Managers, Business/Innovators—so they not only thrive today but create a legacy of life conditions for the next generations to evolve and thrive.

Imagine human hives who know how to connect. They can map their existing connections, align people to purpose and priorities. They can amplify what works, let go of what doesn't and continuously improve the value they contribute to Gaia.

Imagine human hives who learn from each other and develop the whole system of human hives in an evolutionary direction.

If we can imagine such a city, we can imagine creating and implementing plans for the glocal-scale challenges of climate adaptation, energy shifts, water management, food security, financial performance and cultural vibrancy. To do so, we can imagine how to release resources now trapped in city sectors, silos and stovepipes. We can imagine the frameworks, tools and processes that catalyze new conversations, build on the underlying values and recalibrate the assets, capacities and capitals into meshworks of economic, environmental, social and cultural interests. We can imagine creating the model for community engagement, city development, business strategies and communication technologies to evolve the intelligences in our cities into thriving human hives.

APPENDIX F2: IMAGINE YOUR CITY AS A THRIVING INNOVATION ECOSYSTEM

1. Imagine that Your City honors its values, history, traditions and culture so that it conserves what works well and teaches it (or shares) with others, including children, youth, seniors, business, civil society, and city hall.

2. Imagine that Your City is open to creative change so that it can replace what does not work well with what can work better, and even inspire people to want more change.

3. Imagine that Your City discovers the wisdom and resources to create itself as a valued and valuable city—for its citizens, families, organizations, communities, neighborhoods, sectors, state and country.

4. Imagine that Your City appreciates the great diversity in the city—from workers who produce value, to innovators and artists who generate diversity, to investors and resource allocators who find and manage resources for worthy projects, to integrators who see the city as alive for humans as a beehive is for bees.

5. Imagine that Your City has an innovation eco-system that provides it with a thriving economy that draws on its history of success in its early history and co-creates new opportunities through innovation laboratories at its universities and businesses.

6. Imagine that Your City's education and training sector in conjunction with business and civil society, commits to the high school graduation as a minimum target for its children; coop and intern opportunities for youth; and with governments creates the conditions for full employment for all adults.

7. Imagine that all students in Your City learn—in school—mutual trust and respect; how to dialogue with others; how to cooperate through teamwork with others; and how to coordinate projects and processes to produce life-giving results.

8. Imagine that Your City commits to balancing interests for a healthy economy and wellbeing amongst its citizens through engaging with

all the Voices of the city in making decisions, managing plans and achieving goals.

9. Imagine that Your City has an integrated sustainability plan so that it measures, tracks and exchanges sustainability data related to energy, water, food, finance, economic production and climate, that it shares internally with city stakeholders and externally with other cities in the region.

10. Imagine that Your City understands how it adds value to the economy and positions itself strategically in relation to other cities in the region, the eco-region and Your Nation.

11. Imagine that Your City has excellent information systems that inform the decisions of not only city hall, but all businesses, citizens, civil society, institutions (healthcare, education, spiritual) and other government levels (state, regional, national).

12. Imagine that the management of Your City meshworks so well by integrating stakeholders that it is a model for other cities of its size in Your Nation, Your Continent and the world.

13. Imagine that Your City's ability to respond to stresses (economic, physical, cultural, social, psychological) at all levels of scale, creates a resilient city, because all stakeholders working together (in a meshwork(1)) create the conditions for everyone in the city to communicate with each other willingly and regularly.

14. Imagine that Your City is fully wired (optically/live-WIFI/IT) so that all parts of the city could communicate internally and externally with the rest of the world.

15. Imagine that Your City practices transparent governance, accountability and accessibility to information so that people feel safe to share, care and relate to each other fairly.

16. Imagine that Your City balances efficient management with enough extra resources that the city is resilient to change.

Footnote

For definition of *Meshwork* see Glossary and Appendix C2

APPENDIX F3: EXAMPLE: TIMELINE FOR IMPLEMENTING "IMAGINE YOUR CITY"

Month 0 20xx: Connect to Your City's Center: Tour the City, Meet 4 Voices and Coalesce Authority, Power and Influence

Month 2 20xx: Imagine Your City Center

1. Imagine that Your City Center discovers its values, history, traditions and culture so that it conserves what works well and teaches it (or shares) with others, including children, youth, seniors, business, civil society, and city hall.

2. Imagine that Your City Center was open to creative change so that it could replace what does not work well with what can work better, and even inspire people to want more change.

Month 6 20xx: Your City Center Charette

3. Imagine that Your City Center discovers the wisdom and resources to re-create itself as a valued and valuable heart of the city—for its citizens, families, organizations, communities, neighborhoods, businesses sectors.

4. Imagine that Your City Center appreciates the great diversity in the city center—and how to engage the stakeholders to contribute to concept plans, designs, preparation for construction.

Month 9 20xx: Your City Center @ Neighborhood Regeneration Model

5. Imagine that Your City Center is a model for other Your City neighborhoods—so that they can learn from the model of stakeholder engagement to bring new life to other parts of the city

6. Imagine that Your City Center's education and training sector in conjunction with business and civil society, committed to the high school graduation as a minimum target for its children; coop and intern opportunities for youth; and with governments created the conditions for full employment for all adults.

7. Imagine that all students learn in school mutual trust and respect; how to dialogue with others; how to cooperate through teamwork

with others; and how to coordinate projects and processes to produce life-giving results.

Month 11 20xx

8. Imagine that City Hall commits to balancing interests for Your City
Center's healthy economy and wellbeing amongst its citizens through
engaging with all the Voices of the city in meshing functions, making
decisions, managing plans and achieving goals.

Q1 20xy

9. Imagine that Your City Center is part of Your City's integrated sustainability plan that it shares internally with city stakeholders and
externally with other cities in the region.
10. Imagine that Your City Center understands how it adds value to the
economy and positions itself strategically in relation to Your City's
other neighborhoods.
11. Imagine that Your City Center has excellent information systems
that inform the decisions of not only city hall, but all businesses,
citizens, civil society, institutions (healthcare, education, spiritual)
and other government levels (state, regional, national).
12. Imagine that the management of Your City Center is so well integrated with all stakeholders that it is a model for other city centers.

Q2 20xy

13. Imagine that Your City Center's ability to respond to stresses, contributes to Your City as a resilient city, because people practise mutual trust
and respect to communicate with each other willingly and regularly.

Q3 20xy

14. Imagine that Your City Center is fully optically/alive/IT wired so that
all parts of the city could communicate internally and externally
with the rest of the world.
15. Imagine that City Hall practices with Your City Center transparent
governance, accountability and accessibility to information so that
people feel safe to share, care and relate to each other fairly.

16. Imagine that Your City Center demonstrates the balance between efficient management and enough extra resources that the Your City Center is resilient to change.

APPENDIX G: PANARCHY CYCLE

Resilience Cycles & 4 Roles *(Panarchy, Gunderson & Holling, 2002, Hamilton, 2012*

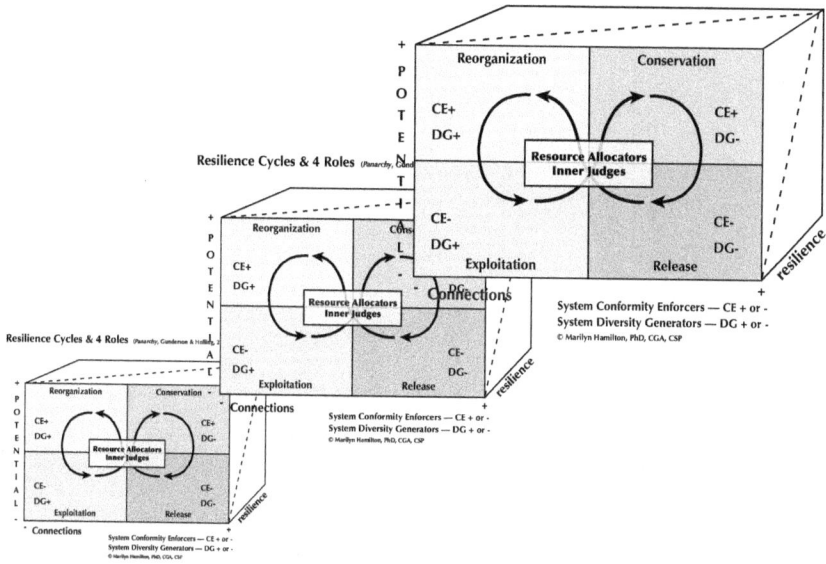

Panarchy: is a theory of change and resilience described in a book of the same name. The book describes multi-disciplinary research into transformations into human and natural systems (Gunderson & Holling, 2002). As a theory of change, a "Panarchy is a cross-scale, nested set of adaptive cycles, indicating the dynamic nature of structures depicted in the previous plots" (p. 74). Panarchy labels the four phases of creative destruction and renewal within a cycle as: exploitation, conservation, release and reorganization. Panarchy also describes the connections between cycles and their capacity to reallocate resources by "remembering" accumulated potentials from larger cycles that can influence earlier, (lower in the nest), faster cycles, as well as their capacity to "revolt" and spark change into larger, higher, slower cycles from smaller, faster cycles. For societies these reallocations might result in the three panarchy cycles of: allocation mechanisms, norms and myths (Westley) as cited in (Gunderson & Holling, 2002, p. 75).

Panarchy is discussed in several chapters of this book: 1, 2, 5, 8, 12, 13, 15.

In the image above, the Panarchy change cycle is related to the roles of Conformity Enforcers, Diversity Generators, Resource Allocators and Inner Judges described in Chapter 8 on Diversity Generation.

REFERENCES

Able, J. (2005). Wombat. Retrieved December 19, 2017, from Foundation for Global Community http://www.globalcommunity.org/flash/wombat.shtml.

Abrams, N. E., & Primack, J. R. (2006). *The View from the Centre of the Universe: Discovering our Extraordinary Place in the Cosmos.* New York: Riverhead Books, Penguin Group.

Adizes, I. (1999). *Managing Corporate Lifecycles.* Paramus, NJ: Prentice Hall Press.

Adger, N., Aggarwal, P., Argawala, S., Alcamo, J., & etal. (2007). *Climate Change 2007: Impacts, Adaptation and Vulnerability, Summary for Policy Makers.* (2). IPCC Secretariat Retrieved from http://www.ipcc.ch/

Alexander, C. (1977). A *Pattern Language.* USA: Oxford University Press.

Alexander, C. (2002). *The Phenomenon of Life.* (September 1, 2004 ed. Vol 1). Berkeley, CA: Center for Environmental Structure.

Alexander, C. (2004a). *The Luminous Ground.* (September 1, 2004 ed. Vol. 4). Berkeley, CA: Center for Environmental Structure.

Alexander, C. (2004b). *The Process of Creating Life.* (September 1, 2004 ed. Vol. 2). Berkeley, CA: Center for Environmental Structure.

Alexander, C. (2004c). A *Vision of a Living World.* (September 1, 2004 ed. Vol. 3). Berkeley, CA: Center for Environmental Structure.

Anderson, T. D. (1992). *Transforming Leadership: New Skills for an Extraordinary Future*. Amherst, Mass: HRD Press, Inc.

Anderson, T.D., Ford R., Hamilton, M. (1998). *Transforming Leadership: Equipping Yourself and Coaching Others to Build the Leadership Organization*, Second Edition. CRC Press, Taylor & Francis Group: Boca Raton, FL.

anon. Gross National Happiness Index. Retrieved May 23, 2016, from Wikipedia https://en.wikipedia.org/wiki/Gross_National_Happiness

anon. Walkerton E. coli outbreak. *Wikipedia*. Retrieved from https://en.wikipedia.org/wiki/Walkerton_E._coli_outbreak

anon. (2000a). Dignity Village. Retrieved December 19, 2017, from Wikipedia https://en.wikipedia.org/wiki/Dignity_Village

anon. (2000b). Millennium Development Goals. Retrieved December 21, 2017, from UN http://en.wikipedia.org/wiki/Millennium_Development_Goals

anon. (2004) No Fixed Address. (2004, January 24—31). *Vancouver Sun*.

anon. (2011a). Global Report on Human Settlement 2011 Hot Cites: Battle-Ground for Climate Change. Retrieved December 29, 2017, from UN Habitat http://mirror.unhabitat.org/downloads/docs/E_Hot_Cities.pdf

anon. (2011b). World Health Organization Global Alert and Response (GAR). Retrieved December 21, 2017 http://www.who.int/csr/don/en/

anon. (2014). Overview Effect. Retrieved July 7, 2014, from Wikipedia en.m.wikipedia.org/wiki/Overview_effect

anon. (2017a). The Life Cycle of the Honey Bee Family. Chatsworth, California: The Valley Hive.

anon (2017b). Budapest. Retrieved December 11, 2017 from Wikipedia https://en.wikipedia.org/wiki/Budapest#Early_history

anon. (2017c). Sustainable Development Goals. Retrieved December 11, 2017, from Wikipedia https://en.wikipedia.org/wiki/Sustainable_Development_Goals

anon. (2017d). Overview Effect. Retrieved December 13, 2017, from Wikepedia https://en.wikipedia.org/wiki/Overview_effect

anon. (2017e). https://www.economist.com/blogs/graphicdetail/2017/08/daily-chart-10. *The Economist*, (August 16, 2017). Retrieved from http://www.economist.com/node/21542773?fsrc=scn/tw/te/ar/bossesunderfire

anon. (2017f). LGBTQ Community. Retrieved December 15, 2017, from Vancouver City website http://vancouver.ca/people-programs/lgbtq-community.aspx

anon. (2017g). 2011 Vancouver Stanley Cup riot. Retrieved December 15, 2017, from Wikipedia https://en.wikipedia.org/wiki/2011_Vancouver_Stanley_Cup_riot

anon. (2017h). Very impressive' marine life enters North America on debris from Japanese tsunami. Retrieved December 21, 2017, from CBC http://www.cbc.ca/news/technology/japanese-tsunami-marine-life-west-coast-1.4311877

Anderson A., Anderson, R. (1997). Street as Metaphor in Housing for the Homeless. Journal of Social Stress and the Homeless, Vol. 6.(No. 1).

Armstrong, K. (1993). A History of God: The 4,000-Year Quest of Judaism, Christianity and Islam. New York: Ballantine Book.

Aunger, R. (2002). The Electric Meme: A New Theory of How We Think. New York, NY: The Free Press.

Barnett, T. P. M. (2005). The Pentagon's New Map: War and Peace in the Twenty-First Century (trade paperback ed.). New York: The Berkley Publishing Group.

Baron-Cohen, S. (2003). The Essential Difference: The Truth About the Male and Female Brain. New York: Basic Books.

Bateson, G. (1972). Steps to an Ecology of Mind. New York: Chandler Publishing Company, Ballantine Books, Inc.

Beck, D. (nd). Stratified Democracy. Retrieved December 20, 2017, from http://www.humanemergence.org/essays/stages_of_social_development.htm

Beck, D. (1999). The Search for Cohesion in the Age of Fragmentation: From the New World Order to the Next Global Mesh. Paper presented at the State of the World Forum, New York.

Beck, D. (2000a). MeshWORKS™: A Second Tier Perspective & Process. The Spiral Dynamics Group. Denton, TX.

Beck, D. (2000b). Stages of Social Development: The Cultural Dynamics that Spark Violence, Spread Prosperity and Shape Globalization. Paper presented at the State of the World Forum, New York.

Beck, D. (2001). Human capacities in the integral age: How value systems shape organizational productivity, national prosperity & global transformation. Paper presented at the International Productivity Conference, Singapore. http://www.integralworld.net/beck7.html

Beck, D. (2002a). The Color of Constellations: A Spiral Dynamics Perspective on Human Drama. Paper presented at the Bert Hellinger Constellation Conference, Germany.

Beck, D. (2002b). Spiral Dynamics in the Integral Age. Paper presented at the Spiral Dynamics integral, Level I, Vancouver, BC.

Beck, D. (2006). Spiral Dynamics Integral, Level I Course Manual. Denton, TX: Spiral Dynamics Group.

Beck, D. (2010). Natural Designs for Meshworking. Retrieved from Gaiaspace, Meshworking, Private.

Beck, D. (2010, May 31, 2010). [personal email communication].

Beck, D. (2012). The Integral Dance: How a Master Code Pollinates and Preserves the Culture of Bumblebees. Integral Leadership Review, (June). Retrieved from http://integralleadershipreview.com/7174-the-master-code-spiral-dynamics-integral

Beck, D. (nd). Stratified Democracy. Retrieved from http://www.humanemergence.org/essays/stages_of_social_development.htm

Beck, D., & Cowan, C. (1994, 1997). The Future of Cities. Article. The National Values Center, Inc. Denton, TX.

Beck, D., & Cowan, C. (1996). Spiral Dynamics: Mastering Values, Leadership and Change. Malden, MA: Blackwell Publishers.

Beck, D., & Linscott, G. (2006). The Crucible: Forging South Africa's Future (hardcover ed.). Columbia, MD: Cherie Beck, Coera.us, Center for Human Emergence.

Benjamin, A., & McCullum, B. (2009). A World Without Bees. London, UK: Guardian Books.

Benyus, J. M. (1997). Biomimicry: Innovation Inspired by Nature. New York: William Morrow and Company Inc.

Blackmore, S. (1999). The Meme Machine. Oxford, UK: Oxford University Press.

Bleys, R. L. A. W., Cowen, T., Groen, G. J., Hillen, B., & Ibrahim, N. B. N. (1996). Perivascular Nerves of the Human Basal Cerebral Arteries I. Topographical Distribution(16), 1034–1047. Retrieved from http://journals.sagepub.com/doi/full/10.1097/00004647-199609000-00029 doi:10.1097/00004647-199609000-00029

Bloom, H. (2000). *The Global Brain: The Evolution of Mass Mind from the Big Bang to the 21st Century*. New York: John Wiley & Son Inc.

Brackney, S. (2009). *Plan Bee: Everything You Ever Wanted to Know About the Hardest-working Creatures on the Planet*. New York, NY: Penguin Group Inc.

Brown, B. (2005a). Theory and Practice of Integral Sustainable Development—An Overview, Part 1: Quadrants and the Practitioner. AQAL Journal, 1(2).

Brown, B. (2005b). Theory and Practice of Integral Sustainable Development—An Overview, Part 2: Values, Developmental Levels and Natural Design. AQAL Journal, 1(2).

Brown, B. (2005c). Theory and Practice of Integral Sustainable Development—An Overview, Part 3: Current Initiatives and Applications. AQAL Journal, 1(2).

Brown, B. (2011). *Conscious Leadership for Sustainability: How Leaders with a Late-Stage Action Logic Design and Engage in Sustainability Initiatives*. (PhD), Fielding, Santa Barbara.

Brown, B. (2013). The Future of Leadership for Conscious Capitalism. Paper presented at the Conscious Captialism Conference 2013.

Brown, L. (2008). *Plan B 3.0*. New York: W.W. Norton & Company.

Buhaug, H., Urdal, H., & Ostby, G. (2013). Sustainable Urbanization and Human Security. In L. Sygna, K. O'Brien, & J. Wolf (Eds.), *A Changing Environment for Human Security: Transformative Approaches to Research, Policy and Action*. Abingdon, Oxon, OX: Routledge.

Buzan, T. (1988). *Make the Most of Your Mind*. London: Pan.

Buzan, T. (1989). *Use Your Head*. London: BBC Books.

Buzan, T. (2001). *Head Strong*. London: Thorsons, HarperCollins Publishers.

Cameron, J. (1992). *The Artist's Way*. New York: Jeremy P. Tarcher/Putnam Books.

Capra, F. (1996). *The Web of Life: A New Scientific Understanding of Living Systems*. New York: Anchor Books, Doubleday.

Christensen, T. (Ed.) (2015a). *Innovative Development: Emerging Worldviews and Systems Change*. Tucson, Arizona: Integral Publishers.

Christensen, T. (Ed.) (2015b). *Developmental Innovation: Emerging Worldviews and Individual Learning*. Tucson, Arizona: Integral Publishers.

Coghlan, D., & Brannick, T. (2007). *Doing Action Research in Your Own Organization* (2nd ed.). Thousand Oaks, CA: Sage Publications Ltd.

Combs, A. (2002). *The Radiance of Being: Understanding the Grand Integral Vision Living the Integral Life.* St. Paul, Minnesota: Paragon House.

Consumers of Tomorrow: Insights and Observations About Generation Z. (2011). Grail Research, A Division of Integreon.

Cook-Greuter, S. (1999). *Postautonomous ego development: its nature and measurement.* (Doctoral dissertation), UMI Dissertation Information Services UMI #9933122, Harvard Graduate School of Education, Cambridge, MA. Available from UMI Dissertation Information Services UMI #9933122 database.

Cook-Greuter, S. (2002). The development of action logics in detail. Retrieved from www.cook-greuter.com

Cruz, T., & Forman, F. (2017a). Latin America and a New Political Leadership: Experimental Acts of Co-Existence. In J. Burton, S. Jackson, & D. Wilsdon (Eds.), *Public Servants: Art and the Crisis of the Common Good* (pp. 71–90). Boston, MA: MIT Press.

Cruz, T., & Forman, F. (2017). Un-walling Citizenship. *Avery Review: Critical Essays on Architecture,* 21(Winter), 98–109

Cummins, R. A., Eckersley, R., Lo, S. K., Davern, M., Hunter, B., & Okerstrom, E. (2004). The Australian Unity Wellbeing Index: An Update. Paper presented at the Proceedings of the 5th Australian Conference on Quality of Life, Deakin University, Melbourne.

Csikszentmihalyi, M. (1993). *The Evolving Self: A Psychology for the Third Millennium.* New York: Harper Perennial, Harper Collins.

Dale, A. (2001). *At The Edge: Sustainable Development in the 21st Century.* Vancouver: UBC Press.

Dawkins, R. (1976). *The Selfish Gene.* Oxford, UK: Oxford University Press.

Dawson-Tunik, T. L., Commons, M. L., Wilson, M., & Fischer, K. W. (2005). The shape of development. *The European Journal of Developmental Psychology,* 2(2), 163–196.

DeKay, M. (2011). *Integral Sustainable Design: Transformative Perspectives.* London, UK: Earthscan.

De Landa, M. (1995). Homes: Meshwork or Hierarchy? http://www.mediamatic.net/article-200.5956.html. Special: Home issue. Retrieved December 28, 2017.

De Landa, M. (1997). A Thousand Years of Nonlinear History. New York: Zone Books.

De Landa, M. (2006). A New Philosophy of Society: Assemblage Theory and Social Complexity. London: Continuum.

Diamond, J. (1992). The Third Chimpanzee: the Evolution and Future of the Human Animal. New York: HarperCollins Publishers.

Diamond, J. (2005). Collapse: How societies choose to fail or succeed (first ed.). New York: Penguin Group.

Douglas, D. C., & Hamilton, M. (2013). Knowing Cities: The Knowing Field and the Emergence of Integral City Intelligence. The Knowing Field(22).

Dutrisac, M., Fowke, D., Koplowitz, H., & Shepard, K. (nd). Global Organization Design: a dependable path to exceptional business results based on Requisite Organization principles. Retrieved from Toronto.

Eddy, B. (2003). Sustainable Development, Spiral Dynamics, and Spatial Data: A '3i' Approach to SD. Paper presented at the Spiral Dynamics integral, Level II, Ottawa, 2003, Ottawa, ON.

Eddy, B. (2005). Place, Space and Perspective. World Futures, 61, 151–163.

Eddy, B. (2006). The Use of Maps and Map Metaphors for Integration in Geography: A Case Study of Mapping Indicators of Sustainability and Wellbeing. (PhD), Dept. of Geography and Environmental Studies, Carleton University, Ottawa.

Egan, G. (1990). The Skilled Helper. Pacific Grove, CA,: Brooks/Cole Publishing Company.

Eoyang, G. (1997). Coping With Chaos: Seven Simple Tools. Cheyenne, Wyoming: Lagumo Corp.

Eoyang, G., & Olson, E. (2001). Facilitating Organization Change: Lessons from Complexity Science. San Francisco: Jossey-Bass Pfeiffer.

Esbjörn-Hargens, S., & Zimmerman, M. (2009). Integral Ecology: Uniting Multiple Perspectives on the Natural World. Boston: Shambhala Publications Inc.

Fernandez-Armesto, F. (2001). Civilizations: Culture, Ambition and the Transformation of Nature. New York: Touchstone.

Flood, R. (1999). Rethinking the Fifth Discipline: Learning Within the Unknowable. London: Routledge.

Florida, R. (2005). Cities and the Creative Class. New York: Routledge.

Florida, R. (2008). Who's Your City: How the Creative Economy is Making Where to Live the Most Important Decision of Your Life. Toronto: Random House Canada.

Florida, R. (2017). The New Urban Crisis: How Our Cities Are Increasing Inequality, Deepening Segregation, and Failing the Middle Class—and What We Can Do About It. New York: Basic Books.

Forman, F., & Cruz, T. (2015). Changing Practice: Engaging Informal Public Demands. In H. Mooshammer, P. Mörtenböck, T. Cruz, & F. Forman (Eds.), Informal Markets Worlds—Reader: The Architecture of Economic Pressure. Rotterdam: nai010 Publishers.

Forman, F., & Cruz, T. (2017b). The Cross-Border Public. In G. Urbonas, A. Lui, & L. Freeman (Eds.), Public Space? Lost and Found (pp. 172–195). Cambridge: MIT Press.

Fowler, J. W. (1981). Stages of Faith: The Psychology of Human Development and the Quest for Meaning. San Francisco,: HarperSanFrancisco.

Francis, P. (2015). Encylical Letter Laudato Si: On Care for Our Common Home. Rome: The Holy See.

Gardner, H. (1999). Intelligence Reframed; Multiple Intelligences for the 21st Century. New York,: Basic Books, Perseus Books Group.

Gasper, D. (2010). The Idea of Human Security Climate Change, Ethics and Human Security. Cambridge, UK: Cambridge University Press.

Gauthier, A., & Fowler, M. (2008). Integrally-Informed Approaches to Transformational Leadership Development Paper presented at the Conference—Integral Theory In Action: Serving Self, Community and Kosmos. John F Kennedy University, Pleasant Hill, CA.

Gilligan, C. (1982). In a Different Voice: Psychological Theory and Women's Development. Cambridge, MA: Harvard University Press.

Gladwell, M. (2002). The Tipping Point: How Little Things Can Make a Big Difference. New York: Back Bay Books.

Glaser, I., & Bridgman, R. (1999). Braving the Street: The Anthropology of Homelessness. New York: Berghan Books.

Glenn, J. C., Gordon, T. J., & Florescu, E. (2011a). State of the Future 2011: The Millennium Project.

Glenn, J. C., Gordon, T. J., & Florescu, E. (2011b). State of the Future 2011 Electronic Research CD (pp. (8000).

Glesne, C. (1999). *Becoming Qualitative Researchers: An Introduction*. New York: Longman.

Goleman, D. (1997). *Emotional Intelligence*. New York: Bantam.

Gould, J. L., & Gould, C. G. (1988). *The Honey Bee*. New York: Scientific American Library.

Graves, C. (1971). A systems conception of personality: Levels of existence theory. Paper presented at the Washington School of Psychiatry, Washington, DC.

Graves, C. (1974). Human Nature Prepares for a Momentous Leap. *The Futurist*, 8(2), 72–78.

Graves, C. (1981). Summary statement, The emergent, cyclical, double helix model of the adult human biopsychosocial systems. (Publication no. http://www.clarewgraves.com/articles_content/1981_handout/1981_summary.pdf). Retrieved December 5, 2017.

Graves, C. (2003). Levels of Human Existence: Transcription of a Seminar at Washington School of Psychiatry, Oct. 16, 1971. Santa Barbara: Eclet Publishing.

Graves, C. (2005). *The Never Ending Quest: A Treatise on an Emergent Cyclical Conception of Adult Behavioral Systems and Their Development*. Santa Barbara, CA: ECLET Publishing.

Gray, J., Hunt, J., & McArthur, S. (Eds.). (2007). *Organization Design, Levels of Work & Human Capability: Executive Guide*. Toronto: Global Organization Design Society.

Gregory, T. A., & Raffanti, M. A. (2009). Integral Diversity Maturity: Toward a Postconventional Understanding of Diversity Dynamics. *Journal of Integral Theory and Practice*, 4(3), 41–58.

Greiving, S., Wanczura, S., Vossebuerger, P., Sucker, K., & Fourman, M. (2007). *Multidimensional Integrated Risk Governance: Scalable Resilience and Risk Governance Concept Including Guidelines on Stakeholder Involvement*. Retrieved from London, UK.

Gunderson, L. C., & Holling, C. S. (Eds.). (2002). *Panarchy: Understanding Transformations in Human and Natural Systems*. Washington, DC: Island Press.

Haidt, J. (2006). *The Happiness Hypothesis: Finding Modern Truth in Ancient Wisdom*. Cambridge, MA: Perseus Books Group.

Hamer, D. (2004). *The God Gene: How Faith is Hardwired Into Our Genes*. New York: Doubleday.

Hamilton, M. (1998). Ethnographic Codebook Developed for Doctoral Research *The Berkana Community of Conversations: A Study of Leadership Skill Development and Organizational Leadership Practices in a Self-Organizing Online Microworld* (2007 ed., Vol. I). Abbotsford, BC: TDG Holdings Inc.

Hamilton, M. (1999). *The Berkana Community of Conversations: A Study of Leadership Skill Development and Organizational Leadership Practices in a Self-Organizing Online Microworld.* (PhD dissertation), Columbia Pacific University, Novato, California.

Hamilton, M. (2000). How Building a Leadership Organization Prepares the Way for Learning. In T. Anderson (Ed.), *Every Officer is a Leader: Transforming Leadership in Police, Justice, and Public Safety.* Boca Raton: St. Lucie Press.

Hamilton, M. (2001). *Review, revise, reframe, MALT program design review: Discussion paper.* Royal Roads University. Victoria, BC.

Hamilton, M. (2006a). Integral Metamap Creates Common Language for Urban Change. *Journal of Organizational Change Management,* 19(3), 276–306.

Hamilton, M. (2006b, 7/15/2006). Sustainable Beehives: Lessons and Strategies for Sustainable Cities? *Sense in the City.* 1.8.

Hamilton, M. (2007a). Approaching Homelessness: An Integral Reframe. *World Futures: The Journal of General Evolution,* Volume 63(2), 107–126.

Hamilton, M. (2007b). Leadership to the Power of 8: Leading Integrally in the 21st Century. *Sense in the City,* July.

Hamilton, M. (2008a). *Integral City: Evolutionary Intelligences for the Human Hive.* Gabriola Island BC: New Society Publishers.

Hamilton, M. (2008b). Leadership Development: Accelerating the Development of Post-Conventional Leaders. *Sense in the City,* October.

Hamilton. M. (2008c). Integral Methods from the Margins: Finding Myself in the Research—A Retrospective of Integral Leadership Development Methods Using Online Dialogue Analysis, a Competency Development Framework and Action Research. Paper presented at the Conference—Integral Theory in Action: Serving Self, Community and Kosmos, John F. Kennedy University.

Hamilton, M. (2009). *How Much Is Enough? Evolving Lessons From the Beehive.* Paper presented at the UBC Life and Career Centre, Vancouver, BC.

Hamilton, M. (2010a). Integral City: Meshworking Evolutionary Intelligences for the Human Hive and Eco-Region Resilience. Retrieved June 30, 2018, from http://integralcity.com/

Hamilton, M. (2010b). Mapping the Values of Abbotsford and Developing a Prototype for an Integral Vital Signs Monitor of City Wellbeing. Retrieved June 30, 2017, from www.integralcity.com.

Hamilton, M. (2010c). Meshworking Integral Intelligences for Resilient Environments; Enabling Order and Creativity in the Human Hive. Paper presented at the Enacting an Integral Future Conference 2010, Pleasant Hill, CA.

Hamilton, M. (2010d). Integral Spirituality in the Human Hive: A Primer. *Trialog*, 2010(4), 10–17.

Hamilton, M. (2011a). Big Picture for Sustainability Leadership: Life Conditions for Leading from our Deepest & Widest Perspectives. Paper presented at the Embody Integral Leadership Conference, Venwoude Conference Centre, nr Utrecht, NL. Powerpoint Slides.

Hamilton, M. (2011b). Monitoring and Releasing the Creative Energy of Cities: A Practical Framework for Measuring What Really Makes the Difference. *City, Culture and Society*, 2(1), unpublished manuscript.

Hamilton, M. (2011c, April 20, 2011). Almere Principles Guide City Growth. *Integral City Blog*. Retrieved from http://marilyn.integralcity.com/2011/04/20/almere-principles-guide-city-growth/

Hamilton, M. (2012b). Meshworking Evolutionary Intelligence for the Human Hive. Paper presented at the Building Sustainable Communities 5, Kelowna, BC.

Hamilton, M. (2013). Meta Security in the Human Hive: Integrally Aligning Sustainability Responses to Trajecectory of Evolutionary Threats. Paper presented at the International Society Systems Science 2013, Haiphong, Vietnam.

Hamilton, M. (2014). Meta-Framework for Security in the Human Hive: Integrally Aligning Sustainability Responses to Trajectory of Evolutionary Threats. *Systems Research and Behavioral Science, Syst.Res.* 31, 614–626. Retrieved from doi:10.1002/sres.2310

Hamilton, M. (2015). SDi in the Integral City. In T. Christensen (Ed.), *Innovative Development: Emerging Worldviews and Systems Change*. Tucson, Arizona: Integral Publishers.

Hamilton, M. (2017a). *Integral City Inquiry and Action: Designing Impact for the Human Hive*. Phoenix, AZ: Integral Publishers.

Hamilton, M. (2017b). Integral City: Meshworking Evolutionary Intelligences for the Human Hive and Eco-Region Resilience. Retrieved from http://integralcity.com/

Hamilton, M., Douglas, D. C., Beck, C., Aurami, A., & Arnott, J. (2016). We-space, Integral City and the Knowing Field. In M. Brabant & O. Gunnlaugson (Eds.), *Cohering the We Space: Developing Theory and Practice for Engaging Collective Emergence, Wisdom and Healing in Groups* (pp. 131–154). San Francisco: Integral Publishing House.

Hamilton, M., & Sanders, B. (2013a). City-Zen-tricity: A Fractal Non-Local Leap Toward Kosmocentricity Taken With Integral Kosmopolitans on an Evolutionary Mission. *Journal of Integral Theory and Practice.* Retrieved from https://foundation.metaintegral.org/products/volume-9-number-1-june-2014

Hamilton, M., & Sanders, B. (2013b). *Integral City 2.0 Online Conference* 2012 *Proceedings: A Radically Optimistic Inquiry Into Operating System 2.0* M. Hamilton (Ed.) Retrieved from http://www.scribd.com/doc/120713339/Integral-City-2-0-Online-Conference-2012-A-Radically-Optimistic-Inquiry-into-Operating-System-2-0

Hamilton, M., & etal. (2013c). *Integral City 2.0 Online Conference* 2012 *Appendices: A Radically Optimistic Inquiry Into Operating System 2.0—36 Interviews* M. Hamilton (Ed.) Retrieved from http://www.scribd.com/doc/123005653/Integral-City-2-0-Online-Conference-2012-Appendices-A-Radically-Optimistic-Inquiry-into-Operating-System-2-0-36-Interviews

Hawken, P. (2007). *Blessed Unrest: How the Largest Social Movement in History is Restoring Grace, Justice and Beauty to the World.* New York,: Penguin Books.

Hawken, P. (2017). *Drawdown: The Most Comprehensive Plan Ever Proposed to Reverse Global Warming.* New York: Penguin Books.

Henderson, H. (1997). Looking Back From the 21st Century. *New Renaissance*, Vol. 7(No. 2). Retrieved from http://www.ru.org/backis.html

Henderson, H., Lickerman, J., & Flynn, P. (Eds.). (2000). *Calvert-Henderson Quality of Life Indicators.* Bethesda, MD: Calvert Group, Ltd.

Hochachka, G. (2005). *Developing Sustainability, Developing the Self: An Integral Approach to International and Community Development.* Polis Project on Ecological Governance, University of Victoria.

Hochachka, G. (2015).—Integral Transformation of Value Chains: One Sky's Integral Leadership Program in the Brazil Nut Value Chain in Peru and Bolivia. Retrieved December 22, 2017 from Integral Leadership Review http://integralleadershipreview.com/12393-115-integral-transformation-value-chains-one-skys-integral-leadership-program-brazil-nut-value-chain-peru-bolivia/

Henderson, H., Benyus, J. (2012). Statement on Transforming Finance Based on Ethics and Life's Principles. *New Renaissance, Vol. 7*(No. 2). Retrieved from http://www.ethicalmarkets.com/statement-on-transforming-finance-based-on-lifes-principles/

Holling, C. S. (2001). Understanding the Complexity of Economic, Ecological, and Social Systems Ecosystems. Vol. 4, pp. 390–405.

Holling, C. S. (2003). *From Complex Regions to Complex Worlds.* University of Florida.

Homer-Dixon, T. (2006). *The Upside of Down: Catastrophe, Creativity, and the Renewal of Civilization.* Toronto: Alfred A. Knopf Canada.

Howe, N., & Strauss, W. (1992). *Generations: The History of America's Future, 1584 to 2069.* New York: Harper Perennial.

Inglis, J., & M., S. (2005). Approaching the Complexity of Homelessness. *Unpublished manuscript.*

Jacobs, J. (1992). *The Death and Life of Great American Cities.* New York: Vintage Books.

Jacobs, J. (1994). *Systems of Survival.* New York: First Vintage Books Edition.

Jacobs, J. (2001). *The Nature of Economies.* New York: First Vintage Books Edition.

Jacobs, J. (2004). *Dark Age Ahead.* New York: Random House Canada.

Jaworski, J. (1996). *Synchronicity: The Inner Path of Leadership.* San Francisco: Berrett-Koehler Publishers.

Kauffman, S. A. (1993). *The Origins of Order: Self-Organization and Selection in Evolution.* New York,: Oxford Press.

Kegan, R. (1994). *In Over Our Heads: The Mental Demands of Modern Life.* Cambridge, MA: Harvard University Press.

Kegan, R., & Lahey, L. L. (2001). *How the Way We Talk Can Change the Way We Work: Seven Languages for Transformation.* San Francisco: Jossey-Bass.

Kegan, R., & Lahey, L. L. (2009). *Immunity to Change: How to Overcome It and Unlock Potential in Yourself and Your Organization.* Boston, MA: Harvard Business Press.

Koestler, A. (1976). *The Ghost in the Machine.* New York, NY: Random House.

Korten, D. (2015). *When Corporations Rule the World.* San Francisco: Berrett-Koehler Publishers.

Laloux, F. (2014). *Reinventing Organizations.* Retrieved from http://www.reinventingorganizations.com/purchase.html.

Lama, D., & Cutler, H. (1998). *The Art of Happiness: A Handbook for Living.* New York: Riverhead Books.

Landry, C. (2007). *The Art of City Making.* London, UK: Earthscan Comedia.

Landry, C., & Murray, C. (2017). *Psychology & the City.* Bournes Green Near Stroud, UK: Comedia.

Laszlo, E. (2007). *Science and the Akashic Field: An Integral Theory of Everything.* Rochester, Vermont: Inner Traditions.

Laszlo, E. (2006a). *The Chaos Point: The World at the Crossroads.* Charlottesville, VA: Hampton Roads Publishing.

Laszlo, E. (2006b). *Science and the Reenchantment of the Cosmos: The Rise of the Integral Vision of Reality.* Rochester, VT: Inner Traditions • Bear & Company.

Laszlo, E. (2006d). Ten Benchmarks of an Evolved Consciousness *The Chaos Point: The World at the Crossroads* (pp. pp. 80–81). Charlottesville, VA: Hampton Roads Publishing.

Lifshits, Y. (2016). Neocities and Neodistricts:A Framework for Building Cities of The Future. Retrieved December 21, 2017 https://medium.com/@yurylifshits/neocity-aa102731911b

Linton, J. (2010). *What is Water? The History of a Modern Abstraction.* Vancouver, BC, Canada: UBC Press.

Lipton, B. (2005). *The Biology of Belief: Unleashing the Power of Consciousness, Matter and Miracles.* Santa Rosa, CA: Mountain of Love/Elite Books.

Lovelock, J. (1972). Gaia As Seen Through the Atmosphere. *Atmospheric Environment,* (Vol. 6, p. 579).

Lovelock, J. (1991). *Healing Gaia*. New York: Harmony Books.

Lovelock, J. (2009). *The Vanishing Face of Gaia*. New York: Harmony Books.

Maeterlinck, M. (1954). *The Life of the Bee*. New York: Mentor.

Marcotullio, P., & Solecki, W. (2013). Sustainability and Cities: Meeting the Grand Challenge for the Twenty-First Century. In L. Sygna, K. O'Brien, & J. Wolf (Eds.), *A Changing Environment for Human Security: Transformative Approaches to Research, Policy and Action*. Abingdon, Oxon, OX: Routledge.

Maturana, H., & Varela, F. (1987, 1992). *The Tree of Knowledge*. Boston: Shambhala.

McDonough, W., & Braungart, M. (2002). *Cradle to Cradle: Remaking the Way We Make Things*. New York: North Point Press.

McIntosh, S. (2007). *Integral Consciousness and the Future of Evolution: How the Integral Worldview is Transforming Politics, Culture and Spirituality*. St. Paul, Minnesota: Paragon House.

McKibben, B. (2007). *Deep Economy: The Wealth of Communities and the Durable Future*. New York: Time Books Henry Holt and Company, LLC.

McKibben, B. (2011). 350.Org. Retrieved December 13, 2017, from 350.Orghttp://www.350.org/

McKnight, P. (2012). No Such Thing as a Natural Born Woman. Retrieved from http://www.vancouversun.com/health/such+thing+natural+born+woman/6649556/story.html

McQuade, A. (2005). Reviving our Interiors: Serving the Mentally Ill Living on Our Streets. AQAL, Vol. 1(No. 4).

McTaggart, L. (2001). *The Field: The Quest for the Secret Force of the Universe*. New York: Harper Perennial.

McTaggart, L. (2011). *The Bond: Connecting Through the Space Between Us*. New York: Free Press.

Meadows, D. (2008). *Thinking in Systems*. White River Junction, VT: Chelsea Green Publishing.

Midgley, G. (2000). *Systemic Intervention: Philosophy, Methodology, and Practice*. New York: Kluwer Academic/Plenum Publishers.

Midgley, G., Munlo, I., & Brown, M. (1998). The theory and practice of boundary critique: Developing housing services for older people. Journal of the Operational Research Society, 49:5, pp. 467–478. https://

ezproxy.royalroads.ca/login?url=http://links.jstor.org/sici?sici=0160–5682%28199805%2949%3A5%3C467%3ATTAPOB%3E2.0.CO%3B2-S. *Journal of the Operational Research Society*, 49:5, pp. 467–478. Retrieved from https://ezproxy.royalroads.ca/login?url=http://links.jstor.org/sici?sici=0160–5682%28199805%2949%3A5%3C467%3ATTAPOB%3E2.0.CO%3B2-S

Miller, J. G. (1978). *Living Systems*. New York: McGraw-Hill Book Company.

Mitchell, E., & Williams, D. (2001). *The Way of the Explorer: An Apollo Astronaut's Journey Through the Material and Mystical Worlds* (2nd ed.). Buenos Aires: Richter Artes Graficas.

Moir, A., & Jessel, D. (1991). *Brain Sex*. New York: Dell Publishing.

Monbiot, G., & Prescott, M. (2007). *Heat: How to Stop the Planet From Burning*. Toronto: Anchor Canada.

Montgomery, C. (2014). *Happy City: Transforming Our Lives Through Urban Design*. New York: Farrar, Straus and Giroux.

O'Fallon, T. (2010). The Collapse of the Wilber Combs Matrix: The Interpenetration of the State and Structure Stages. Paper presented at the Enacting an Integral Future Conference, John F. Kennedy University.

Oxford Online Dictionary. (2011). Retrieved December 15, 2017 http://oxford-dictionaries.com

Page, A., & Johnson, R. (2011, August 13). Global Population Analysis. *National Post*.

Patten, T. (2010). Toward the Emergence of Integral Evolutionary Spiritual Culture. Paper presented at the Enacting an Integral Future Conference, John F. Kennedy University.

Patten, T. (2018). *A New Republic of the Heart: An Ethos for Revolutionaries* (*Sacred Activism*). North Atlantic Books.

Peirce, N. (Producer). (2014, July 7, 2014). Finally, clear performance data for comparing the world's cities. [article] Retrieved from http://cityminded.org/finally-clear-performance-data-comparing-worlds-cities-1173?utm_source-ReviveOldPost

Pierce, N., Johnson, C., & Peters, F. (2008). *Century of the City*. New York: The Rockefeller Foundation.

Quilligan, J. B. (2008, Fall Winter). Global Commons and Society as Global Commons Organizations. *Kosmos*, VIII, p.26.

Quilligan, J. B. (2009a, Spring Summer). The Commons and Integral Capital. *Kosmos*, VIII, pp. 30–35.

Quilligan, J. B. (2009b, Fall Winter). People Sharing Resources: Toward a New Multilateralism of the Global Commons. *Kosmos*, IX, pp. 30–35.

Rapaille, C. (2006). *The Culture Code: An Ingenious Way to Understand Why People Around the World Live and Buy as They Do.* New York, NY: Broadway Books.

Ray, P., & Anderson, S. R. (2000). *The Cultural Creatives: How 50 Million People Are Changing the World.* New York: Harmony Books Member Crown Publishing Group, Random House Inc.

Rees, W. E. P. D., & Wackernagel, M. (1994). *Ecological Footprints and Appropriated Carrying Capacity: Measuring the Natural Capital Requirements of the Human Economy.* Washington, DC: Island Press.

Rico, G. L. (1983). *Writing the Natural Way.* Los Angeles: Jeremy P. Tarcher Inc.

Robertson, B. (Producer). (2007, June 28, 2011). Holacracy Brief Overview and Quick Reference Guide, Based on Organization at the Leading Edge: Introducing Holacracy. Retrieved from http://www.holacracy.org/?page=resources_home

Robertson, B. (2017). Holacracy How It Works. Retrieved from http://www.holacracy.org/how-it-works/

Robinson, J. (2012). Personal Communication: Tour of the UBC Centre for Interactive Research in Sustainability. In M. Hamilton (Ed.) (John's tour of CIRS building identified 7 factors of sustainability: 4 quantitative—energy, water, structural, GHG/emissions and 3 soft—health, productivity, happiness ed.). Vancouver.

Rockström, J., W. Steffen, K. Noone, Å. Persson, F. S. Chapin, III, E. Lambin, T. M. Lenton, M. Scheffer, C. Folke, H. Schellnhuber, B. Nykvist, C. A. De Wit, T. Hughes, S. van der Leeuw, H. Rodhe, S. Sörlin, P. K. Snyder, R. Costanza, U. Svedin, M. Falkenmark, L. Karlberg, R. W. Corell, V. J. Fabry, J. Hansen, B. Walker, D. Liverman, K. Richardson, P. Crutzen, and J. Foley. (2009). Planetary boundaries:exploring the safe operating space for humanity. *Ecology and Society*, 14(2), 32.

Rockström, J., Steffen, W., Noone, K., & etal. (2009). Planetary Boundaries: Exploring the Safe Operating Space for Humanity, art32. Retrieved from http://www.ecologyandsociety.org/vol14/iss2/art32

Sahtouris, E. (1999). *Earthdance: Living Systems in Evolution*. Retrieved from http://www.ratical.org/LifeWeb/

Sahtouris, E. (2010). Celebrating Crisis: Towards a Culture of Cooperation. A *New Renaissance:Transforming Science, Spirit & Society*. London: Floris Books.

Sahtouris, E. (2017). A Tale of Cities and Cells: Our Human Evolutionary Agenda. Retrieved December 7, 2017 https://www.ethicalmarkets.com/a-tale-of-cities-and-cells-by-elisabet-sahtouris/

Sandercock, L. (2000). When Strangers Become Neighbours: Managing Cities of Difference. *Planning Theory and Practice*, 1(1), 13–30.

Sandercock, L., & Lyssiotis, P. (2003). *Cosmopolis II: Mongrel Cities of the 21st Century*. London: Continuum International Publishing Group.

Sanguin, B. (2007). *Darwin, Divinity and the Dance of the Cosmos: An Ecological Christianity*. Kelowna, BC, Canada: Wood Lake Publishing Inc.

Sanguin, B. (2008). *Emerging Church: A Model for Change and A Map for Renewal*. Kelowna, BC, Canada: Wood Lake Publishing Inc.

Scharmer, C. O. (2009). *Theory U: Learning from the Future as It Emerges*. San Francisco: Berrett-Koehler Publishers.

Senge, P. M. (1994). *The Fifth Discipline: The Art and Practice of the Learning Organization*. New York,: Currency Doubleday.

Senge, P., Kleiner, A., Roberts, C., Ross, R., & Smith, B. (1994). *The Fifth Discipline Fieldbook: Strategies and Tools for Building a Learning Organization*. New York: Currency Doubleday.

Senge, P., Scharmer, C. O., Jaworski, J., & Flowers, B. S. (2004). *Presence: Exploring Profound Change in People, Organizations and Society*. New York: Currency Doubleday.

Sheldrake, R. (1988). *The Presence of the Past: Morphic Resonance and the Habits of Nature* (1995 ed.). Rochester, Vermont: Park Street Press.

Sheldrake, R. (1999). *Dogs That Know When Their Owners Are Coming Home: And Other Unexplained Powers of Animals*. New York: Three Rivers Press.

Sheldrake, R. (2003). *The Sense of Being Stared At: And Other Aspects of the Extended Mind*. New York: Three Rivers Press.

Sheldrake, R. (2012). *Science Set Free*. New York: Deepak Chopra Books, Crown Publishing Group, Division of Random House.

Simon, D., & Leck, H. (2013). Cities, Human Security and Global Environmental Change. In L. Sygna, K. O'Brien, & J. Wolf (Eds.), *A Changing Environment for Human Security: Transformative Approaches to Research, Policy and Action.* Abingdon, Oxon, OX: Routledge.

Smith, L. G. (2010). *The World in 2050: Four Forces Shaping Civilization's Northern Future.* New York: Dutton.

Sokol, D. (October 2008). Repositioning Practice: Teddy Cruz. Retrieved December 28, 2017, from Architectural Record http://archrecord.construction.com/features/humanitarianDesign/0810cruz-1.asp

Stevenson, B., & Hamilton, M. (2001). How Does Complexity Inform Community? How does Community Inform Complexity? *Emergence,* 3(No. 2), pp.57—77.

Stewart, I. (Writer) & I. Stewart (Director). (2010). "Hot Rocks" Geography [TV]. In BBC (Producer): Knowledge Network.

Strauss, W., & Howe, N. (1997). *The Fourth Turning: An American Prophecy, What the Cycles of History Tell Us About America's Next Rendezvous with Destiny.* New York: Broadway Books.

Stringer, E. T. (1996). *Action Research: A Handbook for Practitioners.* Thousand Oaks, CA: Sage Publications Inc.

Szaklarksi, C. (2012). Too soon to say if other pageants will follow Miss Universe Canada's transgender precedent: official. Retrieved from http://news.nationalpost.com/2012/05/19/too-soon-to-say-if-other-pageants-will-follow-miss-universe-canadas-transgender-preceden-official/

Taylor, G. (2008). *Evolution's Edge: The Coming Collapse and Transformation of our World.* Gabriola Island, BC: New Society Publishers.

Titcomb, J. (2017). Mars City: Human missions to space colony will start in 2024, Elon Musk says. Retrieved December 22, 2017, from The Telegraph http://www.telegraph.co.uk/technology/2017/09/29/mars-city-human-missions-space-colony-will-start-2024-elon-musk/

Thomas, R. R. (1996). *Redefining Diversity.* New York, NY: AMACOM.

Torbert, W., & Associates (Eds.). (2004). *Action Inquiry: The Secret of Timely and Transforming Leadership.* San Francisco: Berrett-Koehler Publishes Inc.

Torbert, W. R., Livne-Tarandach, R., Herdman-Barker, E., Nicolaides, A., & McCallum, D. (2008). Developmental Action Inquiry:A Distinct Integral Theory That Actually Integrates Developmental Theory, Practice, and Research. Paper presented at the Conference—Integral Theory In Action: Serving Self, Community and Kosmos, John F Kennedy University, Pleasant Hill, CA.

Turnbull, C. (1972). *The Mountain People*. New York: Touchstone Simon Schuster.

Ulrich, W. (2000). The 12 Critically Heuristic Boundary Questions. In G. Midgley (Ed.), *Systemic Intervention: Philosophy, Methodology, and Practice* (pp. 141). New York, NY: Kluwer Academic/Plenum Publishers.

United Nations Human Settlements, P. (Ed.) (2005). *The State of the World's Cities 2004/5*. London: Earthscan.

van Schaik, P. (2016). *Urban Hub 1: Smart Sustainable Thriveable Cities*. UK: Integral Mentors.

van Schaik, P. (2017a). *Urban Hub 2: Methodologies & Planning Thriveable Cities*. UK: Integral Mentors.

van Schaik, P. (2017b). *Urban Hub 3: Integral Theory Thriveable Cities*. UK: Integral Mentors.

van Schaik, P. (2017c). *Urban Hub 4: Integral Workbook Thriveable Cities*. UK: Integral Mentors.

van Schaik, P. (2017d). *Urban Hub 5: Visions and Worldviews Thriveable Cities*. UK: Integral Mentors.

van Schaik, P. (2017e). *Urban Hub 6: Visions and Worldviews 2 Thriveable Cities*. UK: Integral Mentors.

van Schaik, P. (2017f). *Urban Hub 7: Visions and Worldviews 3 Thriveable Cities*. UK: Integral Mentors.

van Schaik, P. (2017g). *Urban Hub 8: What We Can Do Cultivating Change Thriveable Cities*. UK: Integral Mentors.

VanSusteren, A. (2007). *Metropolitan World Atlas*. Rotterdam: 010 Publishers.

Varey, W. (2010). Pscyhological Panarchy: Steps to an Ecology of Thought. Paper presented at the 54th Meeting of the International Society for the Systems Sciences, Wilfrid Laurier University, Waterloo, ON, Canada.

Weaver, L. (2017). Turf, Trust, Co-Creation, and Collective Impact. Retrieved December 10, 2017, from Tamarack Institute http://www.tamarackcommunity.ca/library/turf-trust-co-creation-collective-impact

Weidenhammer, L. (2016). *Victory Gardens for Bees: A DIY Guide to Saving the Bees*. Douglas & McIntyre.

West, G. (2011). Why Cities Keep Growing, Corporations and People Always Die, and Life Gets Faster: A Conversation With Geoffrey West (5.23.11). In J. Brockman (Ed.), *Edge*: Edge.org.

West, G. (2017). *Scale: The Universal Laws of Growth, Innovation, Sustainability and the Pace of Life in Organisms, Cities, Economies and Companies*. New York: Penguin Press.

Wheatley, M. (1992). *Leadership and the New Science: Learning about Organization from an Orderly Universe*. San Francisco: Berrett-Koehler.

Wheatley, M. (2006). *Leadership and the New Science: Learning about Organization from an Orderly Universe*. San Francisco: Berrett-Koehler.

Wheatley, M., & Kellner-Rogers, M. (1996). A *Simpler Way*. San Francisco: Berrett-Koehler.

Wheatley, M. J., & Kellner-Rogers, M. (1998). *The Promise and Paradox of Community*. Jossey-Bass, Inc.

Wheatley, M. J., & Nickerson, J. E. (Aug-98). *Cape Cod Lectures*: Private Notes.

Wigglesworth, C. (Producer). (2006, December 14, 2017). Why Spiritual Intelligence Is Essential to Mature Leadership. Retrieved from http://www.godisaserialentrepreneur.com/uploads/2/8/4/4/2844368/spiritual-intelligence-n-mature-leadership.pdf

Wigglesworth, C. (Producer). (2002, December 14, 2017). Spiritual Intelligence and Why It Matters. Retrieved from http://www.godisaserialentrepreneur.com/uploads/2/8/4/4/2844368/spiritual_intelligence__emotional_intelligence_2011.pdf

Wigglesworth, C. (2006). Conscious Evolution: Where the Universe is Going and How to Join the Journey. Houston, TX: Spiralling Conscious, LLC.

Wigglesworth, C. (2011). Deep Intelligence & Spiritual Intelligence: Why is It Relevant for You? For Leaders? For the World. *Integral Leadership Collaborative*: Integral Leadership Review.

Wigglesworth, C. (2014). *SQ21: The Twenty-One Skills of Spiritual Intelligence*. New York: SelectBooks.

Wight, I. (2002). Place, Place Making and Planning. Paper presented at the ACSP, Baltimore.

Wilber, K. (1995). *Sex, Ecology and Spirituality: the spirit of evolution*. Boston: Shambhala Publications Inc.

Wilber, K. (1996). A *Brief History of Everything*. Boston: Shambhala Publications Inc.

Wilber, K. (2000a). *Integral Psychology*. Boston: Shambhala Publications Inc.

Wilber, K. (2000b). A *Theory of Everything*. Boston: Shambhala Publications Inc.

Wilber, K. (2001). *Marriage of Sense and Soul*. New York: Random House.

Wilber, K. (2002). *Boomeritis: A Novel That Will Set You Free*. Boston: Shambhala Publications Inc.

Wilber, K. (2006). *Integral Spirituality*. Boston: Shambhala Publications Inc.

Wilber, K. (2007). *The Integral Vision*. Boston: Shambhala Publications Inc.

Wilber, K. (2017). *Trump and the Post-Truth World*. Boston: Shambhala Publications Inc.

Wilber, K., Patten, T., Leonard, A., & Morelli, M. (2006). *Integral Life Practice: A 21st Century Blueprint for Physcial Health, Emotional Balance, Mental Clarity and Spiritual Awakening* (1 ed.). Boston, MA: Integral Books.

Wills, E. H., Hamilton, M., & Islam, G. (2007a). Subjective Well-being in Cities: Individual or Collective? A Cross Cultural Analysis. Paper presented at the Wellbeing in International Development Conference, University of Bath.

Wills, E. H., Hamilton, M., & Islam, G. (2007b). Subjective Wellbeing in Bogotá (B), Belo Horizonte (BH) and Toronto (T): A Subjective Indicator of Quality of Life for Cities. Retrieved from Bogotá: World Bank.

Winston, M. L. (2014). *Bee Time: Lessons from the Hive*. Boston: Harvard University Press.

Wood, P., & Landry, C. (2008). *The Intercultural City: Planning for Diversity Advantage*. London, UK: Earthscan.

Wright, R. (2004). A *Short History of Progress* (Avalon ed.). New York: Carroll & Graf Publishers.

Zimmerman, M. (2010). Changing the Conversation: Rethinking the Climate Change Debate from an Integral Perspective. Paper presented at the Enacting an Integral Future Conference, John F. Kennedy University.

Zimmerman, M. E. (2005). Integral Ecology: A perspectival, developmental, and coordinating approach to environmental problems. *World Futures*, *Volume 61, Issue 1 & 2 January 2005, pages 50—62* (Issue 1 & 2), 50—62.

INDEX

Symbols

4 Voices, xxxvii, 1, 31–32, 41, 44–45, 55–56, 59–60, 70, 79, 200, 204, 279–281, 291, 295–297, 300, 337, 340

12 Intelligences, xviii–xix, xx, xxxiv, xxxvii, 33, 55–56, 58, 64, 115, 252, 254, 259–260, 262–263, 280, 311–312, 324

A

Abbotsford, xlii, 48, 63, 143, 171, 354–356

Abrams, N. E., 29, 48, 154, 169, 345

activators, xxxvi, 16, 57, 311

Adaptive Structures of Change, xv, xix, 8, 102, 152, 321

Adger, N., 99, 108, 283, 345

Adizes, I., 191, 195, 345

Administrators, 164–165

Alexander, C., iv, xx, 6, 14, 20, 23, 36, 42, 46, 48, 101, 151, 169, 267, 319, 345

Anderson A., 347

Anderson, R., 242, 347

Anderson, T. D., 140–141, 143, 346, 354

Anthroposphere, xiv, xviii, 93, 97–100, 108, 209, 259–260, 266, 269, 270, 275, 332–333

AQAL, xxi, 16, 49, 61, 120–121, 165, 196, 244, 349, 359

Armstrong, K., 11, 23, 347

Aunger, R., 36, 48, 347

B

Barnett, T. P. M., 88, 91, 347

Baron-Cohen, S., 156, 169, 347

Bateson, G., 36, 48, 347

Beck, Don, xl, 10–13, 16, 23, 36, 38, 48, 49, 76, 87, 89, 91, 96, 100, 107–108, 120–123, 125, 128, 131, 141, 149, 153–154, 156, 160, 169, 187, 195–196, 216, 218–219, 224, 231, 236, 241–243, 250, 256, 272, 276, 283, 311–313, 321, 347–348, 356

Benjamin, A., 49, 300, 348

www.ingramcontent.com/pod-product-compliance
Lightning Source LLC
Chambersburg PA
CBHW062115040426
42336CB00041B/936